BORN TO WIN

by

Patricia V. Craige

Doral Publishing, Inc.
Wilsonville, Oregon
1997

Published by Doral Publishing.
8560 Salish Lane #300, Wilsonville OR 97070-9612.
Order through Login Publishers Consortium, Chicago IL.
Printed in the United States of America.

Consulting Editor Dr. Nina P. Ross.
Edited by Luana Luther.
Cover art by Mary Jung.
Cover design by Doug Hewitt and Graphica Pacific Design.

Library of Congress Card Number: 96-84690
ISBN: 0-944875-40-8

Craige, Patricia V.
    Born to Win / by Patricia V. Craige
                — Wilsonville, Oregon :
    Doral Pub. , 1997.

        p. ; cm
        Includes bibliographical references and
        index.
        ISBN: 0-944875-40-8
1. Dogs—Breeding.   2. Dog breeders
I. Title.

SF427.2.C   636.7'082 dc20

This book is dedicated

to the people and dogs who taught me early in life

true jewels are made of flesh, not stone.

And to my dear friend, Colleen Williams,

who continues to reenforce that lesson.

C O N T E N T S

Preface   vii
Acknowledgments   ix
Introduction   xi
Identifying the Four-Legged Players by James P. Taylor   xiii

PART I. WINNING TAKES A PLAN   1

In the Beginning 2
So You Want to be a Breeder 5
Doing Your Homework 14
Bonehead Genetics 44
Sex Chromosomes: How They Affect Your Breeding Program 53
Thinking About Your Breeding Program 55

PART II. WINNING MEANS PUTTING YOUR PLAN INTO ACTION   69

Selection 70
Role of the Judge in the Selection Process 81
Foundation Stock: The Brood Bitch 87
Some Brood Bitches to Appreciate 99
In Search of the Sire 106
A Look at Sires Who Made a Difference 116
Profiling a Pedigree 142

PART III. WINNING MEANS HARD WORK   147

Kennel Facilities and Management 148
Picking Puppies 153
Raising Puppies 165
Behavior 166
Ways to Relieve Boredom 168
Bad Habits to Select Against 168
Conditioning and Nutrition 170
Problem Solving 174
Time Management 177
Records 179

PART IV. WINNING MEANS HAVING FUN — 183

The Dog Show and Its History 184
Evaluating Master Judges.. 186
Handling.. 187
Inside the Ring and Out - Sportsman's Dog Person 190
Ways to the Winners' Circle 193
Advantages of a Do-It-Yourself Campaign 195
Friendly Rivals 197
Westminster Kennel Club - The Greatest Show on Earth 205
Spotlight on a Vintage Year - 1973 213
Awards and Records 213
The Medicis of the Dog World 219
Dealing with Stress 221
Traveling with Dogs... 224
Advertising 226
Knowing When to Say When 228

PART V. WINNING MEANS SPECIAL PEOPLE IN YOUR LIFE — 229

The Love of Dogs and Those Who Love Them 230
Who Motivates the Motivator 231
Very Special People.. 232
Foster Families 252
Sampling the Humor of Dog People 255

PART VI. WINNING MEANS FACTORING IN THE FUTURE — 259

Looking at the Future 260
Registries.. 264
Grading Systems... 265
Changes in the Breeds... 266
Today's Youth: Tomorrow's Master Breeders............................ 267
Dreaming the Dream.. 270

Bibliography — 273

Biographical Sketch of the Author by Nina P. Ross — 275

Index — 281

P R E F A C E

The nature of such a work as this precludes the possibility of doing two things the author would like to have done:

      1. Thank each person individually who has contributed to this work. Even though you may not be mentioned by name, your contribution was very much appreciated.

      2. Recognize all the great dogs out there that could have been included, especially in the sections on producing sires and dams. The animals included were a random sampling of the bloodstock and breeding methods utilized by the many *master breeders* whose contributions over the years have contributed so much to the wonderful world of dogs. Unfortunately many equally deserving animals and their *master breeders* are not included simply because of logistics.

I only wish that each and every great producer could have been appropriately recognized in an all-inclusive volume. Instead, what we have here is a representative sampling. —P.V.C.

A C K N O W L E D G M E N T S

There is no way one can show appropriate appreciation to the many people who contributed so much of their time and talents to make this work possible. My heartfelt thanks go especially to Dr. Nina P. Ross, whose considerable computer skills transformed my rough drafts into acceptable presentations to send to the publisher. Not only did Nina show the patience of Job in dealing with me, she turned work sessions into enjoyable occasions.

To Dr. Hal Engle, a member of the veterinary faculty at Oregon State University, goes my gratitude for his advice on dealing with genetics. Not only is Dr. Engle a renowned scholar in the field, he also has practical experience in his own breeding program with Brittanys and English Setters. F. S. "Wes" Cartwright and Noreen Cartwright were of great value with their contributions that served to pull things together.

Terry Stacy, my friend since childhood, helped jog my memories of yesteryear as recollections were put to paper. His feedback was much appreciated. A special acknowledgment also goes to Dr. Richard Smith, of Strathroy, Ontario, for sharing his vast knowledge, as well as his anatomical artwork. He was always there when I phoned him for advice.

A very special thank you goes out to all the people who dug through files and searched for old photographs and mementos to share. They were supportive with interviews, comments, and good humor. Of particular importance to this project was the effort put forth by Bonnie Threlfall in helping with pictures and the contributions of John Ashbey Photography.

And most of all, my sincerest appreciation to my husband of two years, Charles E. "Chuck" Trotter, without whose encouragement the book would not have happened. Not only was he indulgent of the astronomical phone bills associated with much of the research, he cheerfully accepted the demands on my time as I pecked away on my trusty typewriter—commenting more than once that it was time to invest in a computer. Furthermore, he served as constructive critic by being the first to read each draft and provide feedback. If ever I have known a man who was *Born To Win*, it is my powerful critic and best friend!

The private Chapin Horowitz Collection of Books on Dogs, housed at the College of William and Mary in Williamsburg, Virginia, was germane to this effort. Its collection of 9,000 dog books is second only to the library of the American Kennel Club. My appreciation is extended to those whose personal libraries were made available to me. My everlasting gratitude goes to those of the past and the present who served as my teachers and advisors, inspiring me to attempt such a venture.

x

I N T R O D U C T I O N

What the book is not:
...it is not a book on the reproductive system;
...it is not a book on how to handle the mating of the dog and bitch or how to whelp the bitch;
...it is not a book on how to wean your puppies or how to raise your puppies;
...it is not a book on how to train your dog for show, obedience, or field trials;
...it is not a book on how to handle your dog at a show;
...it is not a book on how to feed your dog or treat diseases.

What the book is:
It is a book about the philosophy and learned experiences of one breeder-exhibitor sharing some practical ideas based on a lifetime in dogs.

At one time or another we all have proclaimed to zealous persons whom we have known: "You should write a book!"and it is an expression we have heard others proclaim to us. Like many things in life, it is one thing to *make* the challenge and another thing to *take* the challenge.

There have been many wonderful and informative books written by numerous authors who are much more knowledgeable than I on the subject of the science of genetics and dog breeding as a specific discipline within that science. Therefore, it came as a surprise to me to find myself at a desk attempting to be creative. For certain, it gets my mind off the gap left by no longer running the drill on the campaign trail every weekend!

One of the first problems I encountered was the question of what to name the prospective book. Fellow breeders who have agonized over what to name a very promising puppy—or deciding which puppy is special enough to be granted that name you have been saving for years—will commiserate with this problem. After all, as much as we dream of the possibilities of the newborn in the nest with names running through our minds, my efforts in this case would result, hopefully, in a new kind of baby for me. Thus the name was very important.

Breed to Succeed seemed like a good name, for it is what we all hope to do; however, breeding a good animal is not enough, for the dog must be nourished properly long before the dam is ever bred, the progeny not yet a gleam in its father's eye. The litter must be brought into the absolute, ultimate environment and the resulting puppies raised, trained, and conditioned like Olympic athletes. If everything falls into place, one day the very special athlete will stand proudly on the podium, gold medal around the neck, listening as the nation's anthem is played, for all to salute. Such an Olympian exudes an air of one **BORN TO WIN.**

Do I have a magic formula I can share that will make such lofty goals simple as well as possible? No. For no one has all the answers. Do I have an easy 10-step plan you can follow for sure success? No. The truth is, in the endeavor to breed quality dogs that make it to the top, the secret is *no secret*—just hard work and plenty of it—*forever and ever.* I can sum it all up by paraphrasing my hero, Thomas Jefferson: "The harder I worked, the luckier I got."

When one looks at the growing sport of showing dogs, it is obvious that there are a lot of people out there who are dedicated to the goals of participating in the process of selecting breeding stock, whether they realize it or not. Among their numbers are many who are truly and sincerely committed to breeding the best. The more a person knows about the breed—function and essence of type—the better that person is able to use the strengths of the standard while accepting its weaknesses. No matter how hard we try and how much we think we know, there is always something to learn. If this book can offer one single suggestion, no matter how seemingly insignificant, that helps one breeder breed one dog that is a step forward for that breed, it has served its purpose.

What the reader must keep in mind is that what works for the Vin-Melca family of Norwegian Elkhounds might not work for another breed or even for another line of Norwegian Elkhounds. Yet it is hoped that this book can stimulate thought that will lead the reader on separate intellectual pursuits that, when combined with the aforementioned hard work, will bring the breeder desired results. Keep in mind that the author is *not* a geneticist *nor* a veterinarian. Therefore, suggestions in the book should be treated just as that—suggestions. When the book refers to specific Vin-Melca dogs by name, the reader may wish to refer to the following section for more information on those dogs (see Identifying the Four-legged Players by James P. Taylor).

Why, then, attempt to write such a book? Because it seemed like my dogs were not reading the books, or if they were, they were not always adept at following the book. As good as many of the books were that I used as references, it was not always possible to find solutions to my problems. Perhaps a book dealing with practical problems might be in order.

Several years ago, I attempted to play bridge even though I had little innate aptitude for playing cards. After devouring books on the subject and bypassing everything from natural disasters to man-made ones on the front pages of the newspaper, I would jump right to Goren's columns on the subject. It seemed I was always dealt hands that never appeared in the morning paper! With that memory and the encouragement of many who are dear to me, this book will represent my best effort to produce something of practical use to the breeder.

The fact is that the book shares ideas that worked for one breeder—period. What works for you is what works for you. The idea of different strokes for different folks can be applied to many things in life, including the development of a line that produces beautiful dogs that do credit to the breeder and the breed.

Breeders must be open to change at the same time doing what is best to attain their breeding goals. If your breeding program is progressing in the direction you desire, you are doing the right things.

If it is not satisfying your goals, keep in mind that if you continue to do what you have always done, you will get what you have always gotten. In living our lives, most of us do not make the same mistake once or twice. We make it over and over again. As Clarence Darrow said, "History repeats itself. That's one of the things wrong with history!"

Recognize, then, that the best use of the book is to stimulate the reader's own innovative thinking, and that nothing is written in stone. Change for the sake of change is meaningless. You may be doing the best possible job already. If it isn't broken, don't fix it.

IDENTIFYING THE FOUR-LEGGED PLAYERS
by James P. Taylor

From the very beginning I have been into the winning records of the country's top dogs. As inconceivable as it may seem, no one had ever compiled an all-breed list of the top-winning dogs and bitches in history until I did such a list in 1985.

While conducting this research I became acutely aware of the incredible contributions given to the sport of dogs by the lady of Vin-Melca, Patricia Craige (now Trotter). Her Norwegian Elkhounds have been #1 in this country continually for almost 30 years. No kennel of any breed has bred more top winners than Vin-Melca, but Pat had taken it several large steps further. She trained, conditioned and handled most of the dogs herself. At the same time, she continued her teaching career.

Not only did the numbers of champions, Top Ten finishers, specialty show and all-breed BIS winners become astronomical, the Vin-Melca animals became foundation stock for others as well. My dear friends Freeman and Betty Claus of Redhill Kennels in Southern California were among the many whose breeding programs were enhanced by incorporating the Vin-Melca dogs into their lines. Because of the numerous animals involved, it is not possible to name each of the top Elkhounds produced by this kennel.

The following dogs represent the most significant of them and appear in alphabetical order (all carry the Vin-Melca prefix):

Before Dawn. Named after the Calumet Farm Eclipse-award-winning filly; finished with a Specialty BOB from 6-9 Puppy Class then was moved up from that class to win three consecutive all-breed BISs; retired with a Group third at the 1983 Westminster show; dam of Ch. Vin-Melca's Bombardier; #2 All Time winning male in the breed; Quaker Oats winner.

Bombardier. Sired by BIS Ch. Vin-Melca's Barnstormer; winner of 39 All Breed BISs; Science Diet All Breed Top Ten twice; Quaker Oats Award winner; sire of a Quaker Oats winner; BOB at Westminster 1991, 1992, 1993.

Calista. Top Winning Norwegian Elkhound of All Time with 66 All Breed BISs; two-time Quaker Oats winner; two-time Westminster Group Winner; #2 All Breeds in 1990; #3 All Breeds in 1989; In 1989 and 1990, defeated more than 140,000 dogs with 22 BISs in '89 and 44 BISs in '90; dam of 11 champions, including a Quaker Oats winner and a two-time Westminster Group winner.

Homesteader. #11 All Breeds in 1974; Westminster Group winner in 1974; BIS in Santa Barbara; Son of Howdy Rowdy.

Howdy Rowdy. #2 Sire All Time All Breeds with 166 champion progeny as the Hound Group's Top Producing Sire; National Specialty winner; sire of National Specialty winners; Multi-all-breed BIS winner; sire of multi-all-breed winners; *Kennel Review* Top Western Hound in 1968; Hound Group third at Westminster in 1969; Century Club Sire *H.I.S. Publications* award.

Last Call. All Time Top Producing Bitch with 27 champion progeny; held All Time BIS record for bitches prior to her half-sister Calista; multi-specialty winner and dam of specialty and all-breed BIS winners; BIS Chicago International; dam of 1986 Westminster Group winner Ch. Vin-Melca's Call To Arms; BOB and Hound Group third Westminster in 1982.

Marketta. Eighth-generation All Breed and Specialty BIS winner; Quaker Oats winning daughter of both a Quaker Oats winning sire and dam; Westminster Hound Group winner in 1994 and 1995; retired, dam of her first litter in 1996.

Nimbus. All Time Winning Male in the breed with 63 All Breed BISs; ranked #2 and #3 all breeds; Quaker Oats winner; Westminster Group winner in 1977 and 1979; BIS Beverly Hills, Golden Gate (twice), Ventura, Channel Cities,; Group winner at Santa Barbara; sire of 37 champions; in 1985, his multi-BIS-winning sons Ch. Vin-Melca's The Smuggler, Ch. Vin-Melca's Buckpasser and Ch. Vin-Melca's Southern Rain ranked #1, #2 and #3, respectively, in the breed as well as scoring highly in the Hound Group ratings.

Rebel Rouser. #2 Norwegian Elkhound in the U.S. in 1962, she was the turning point in the Vin-Melca breeding program and dam of BIS Ch. Vin-Melca's Vickssen, grandam of Ch. Vin-Melca's Vagabond. Dam of the great producing bitch Ch. Vin-Melca's Rabble Rouser.

The Smuggler. #2 Hound in the U.S. in 1984; #1 Norwegian Elkhound in U.S. in 1983, 1984, 1985; winner of 25 All Breed BISs; Multiple Specialty winner; Santa Barbara Group winner; BIS Chicago International; BOB and Hound Group second at Westminster in 1985; Sire of group-winning Top Ten ranked Ch. Vin-Melca's The Smuggler.

Vagabond. Top Dog All Breeds, All Systems in 1970; first breeder-owner-handled dog ever to accomplish this in the U.S.; Quaker Oats winner; Westminster Group winner in 1970 and 1971; California Beaters Club Award; BIS Santa Barbara; first Norwegian Elkhound ever to rank in Top Ten All breeds; credited with bringing the breed into its own as an American show dog; sire of outstanding brood bitches; sire of All Breed BIS winners and National Specialty winner; turning point for the breed.

Valley Forge. #5 All Breeds in 1973; # 1 Hound in 1973; Quaker Oats winner; BIS at Kennel Club of Beverly Hills, San Fernando, Oakland; group winner at Santa Barbara and Golden Gate; #1 Norwegian Elkhound in U.S. in 1972 and 1973; sire of merit.

Vickssen. All Breed BIS winner; #1 Norwegian Elkhound in U.S. in 1966 and 1967; sire of Vagabond and two other BIS sons; National Specialty Stud Dog winner; first male to be housed at Vin-Melca.

When I interviewed Pat in 1992, she had retired Calista (Sarah) to the breeding program and was campaigning Bombardier. I asked what else the Vin-Melca breeding program could possibly produce to make history. Well, the breeding of these two Quaker Oats winners produced the first Quaker Oats winner from such a union. Their daughter, Ch. Vin-Melca's Marketta, became the only award winner in Quaker Oats history with both a sire and dam who were award winners. Marketta, like her beautiful mother before her, won two Hound Groups at the Garden proving that some are Born to Win.

James P. Taylor is well-known as the marketing director and associate director of *Show Sight Magazine* and has been associated with dogdom's premier publications since joining the staff of *Kennel Review Magazine* in the 1980s, where his expertise with statistics began. James became interested in dogs as a boy, attending his first Westminster show at the tender age of three, and has enjoyed success in the show ring with both his Maltese and Akitas. A native of Southern California, he currently calls Atlanta, Georgia, home.

A Dedicated Dog Breeder All His Life

Like many of us hooked on dogs, his love of dogs and horses started during his boyhood. It continued to be his favorite hobby throughout his life. He researched and studied his pedigrees as he worked with his dogs, always striving to improve his bloodlines. This continued effort to improve his breeding program resulted in the importation of several dogs from *The Continent*.

He regularly got up in the wee hours of the morning for an early breakfast before he, his friends, and his hounds went out in search of the fox. His love of horses was equally strong and resulted in his importing some excellent Dalmatians to complete his coaching picture.

His dogs loved him and gave him their all, both at work and at play. Some years his records indicated that he whelped as many as four large litters in a 10-week period.

Twice his breeding activities were curtailed when he went off to war, and each time he returned to find his kennels a mess and his dogs in much poorer condition than he himself kept them in. Each time he was forced to rebuild his facilities and get back in touch with his animals. This sounds familiar enough to modern dog breeders!

He had few if any equals in the sport of the chase, riding to the hounds with the expertise of the extraordinary horseman. Not only was he meticulous enough in keeping his breeding records straight—they would have satisfied the American Kennel Club (AKC)—his financial records of his dog hobby would have met with the approval of the Internal Revenue Service (IRS). Most of us would envy his documentation skills with his paperwork, a tedious task for an active man like him, just as it is for us.

His breeding program became so consistent that any Foxhound breeder in the world would appreciate it, for the dogs were of such correct pack type that you could throw the proverbial blanket over them.

Long before the AKC and the IRS, he was a leading American dog breeder and fancier. He was also "the father of his country," our first president, George Washington. You probably have his picture in your wallet.

AMERICA'S FIRST PROMINENT DOG BREEDER
(Courtesy Virginia State Library, Richmond, Virginia)

PART I

WINNING

TAKES A PLAN

In the Beginning

The history of man's relationship with his best friend dates back to antiquity. As far as we know, the dog is the only animal to domesticate itself—that is, to choose to live with man on his own volition with no coercion from man. This eventually resulted in the dog becoming man's cooperative servant and best friend.

Primitive man's artwork is clear evidence that dogs joined man in the hunt and other cooperative efforts to survive and, in time, dogs began to emerge with traits that favored success at the designated job. Natural selection had always favored the survival of animals who could adjust to the extremes of climate in their environment, thrive on the available food supply, and, in general, develop those traits that would create hardy animals in successive generations.

Nowhere is the adage, *form follows function*, applied more appropriately than in the early formative years of the species itself and the early forerunners of the breeds that were to come later. Dogs soon followed their evolution in developing characteristics that best adapted them to their environment with the development of traits that enabled them to perform certain tasks desired by their primitive masters. Sometimes the adjustment was as basic as developing a coloration that would blend in with the surroundings—a form of camouflage. Other times, the adjustment was a gradual change in the skeleton that produced a speedier, racier dog more capable of exposure to extreme heat, such as the sight hound who adapted to running down prey in the desert. The mountain version of the same animal might have heavier bone and more coat to adjust to differences in climate, terrain, the work place, and type of prey.

Exactly how any specific breed evolved from the earliest wolf or Tomarctus is not clear. Nor is it exact as to which animal first evolved into some semblance of a breed we can recognize today. Dogs of different types could have been evolving in different parts of the world at similar times in world history.

Norwegian Elkhound fanciers claim to have one of the oldest of the Arctic dogs, based on evidence of elkhound-like skeletons that date back several thousand years to the days of primitive Vikings. Yet breeders of Samoyeds and Chow Chows, for example, could also make similar historical claims and be justified.

Legitimate claims by sight hound enthusiasts to be the first could be made by those with Greyhounds, Pharaoh Hounds, Afghan Hounds and Salukis. Indeed, more than one source suggests that dogs similar to Afghans accompanied Noah on the Ark.

According to American Kennel Club (AKC) records, a pariah-type dog existed in the Americas long before the Europeans came. It is thought that the Spanish were the first to bring dogs from the Old World in the 16th Century, and the breeds were probably similar to Mastiffs and Greyhounds. Generations of elementary school children were taught erroneously that Columbus discovered the New World because that is what the record indicated. The operative word is *record*.

Because primitive Vikings kept no known written records, their explorations and settlements some five hundred years earlier in Newfoundland were not recognized until this century when archaeologists verified their presence using radiocarbon dating. Other evidence indicates the Chinese, too, may have preceded Columbus, sailing into harbors off the coast of Los Angeles long before Europeans considered the Earth might be something other than flat.

Records of dogs and their evolutionary development are rather scarce until the breeds reached western Europe where the English, in particular, started keeping pedigrees and records. Just as our own Constitution owes its birth to the Mother Country's history through English Common Law and on back to the Magna Carta in 1215, so does the AKC and our entire purebred dog population owe the inhabitants of the British Isles for their contributions to the improvements of so many breeds.

As early as the 1500s, a book written in England described several groups of dogs: sight hounds, scent hounds, spaniels, setters, terriers that went to ground and others that were bred for baiting and fighting, mastiffs, and shepherd or herding dogs. Evidently, the northern breeds had not yet reached England.

Therefore, it comes as no surprise that the British held the first dog show of record in 1859 as an endeavor to aid breeders of fine dogs to gather together their best animals in competition to select breeding stock. In October of 1874, the first American dog show was held in Mineola, New York, and the very next day the Tennessee Sportsmen's Association held a combined dog show and field trial in Memphis, Tennessee. Both of these dog shows were conducted under the rules of The Kennel Club (England). In May 1877, the Westminster Kennel Club held its first dog show, followed shortly thereafter by the formation of the AKC and, in time, the resulting and all-important stud book. No wonder Westminster is so revered by America's dog fanciers—it preceded AKC!

The original stud book published the name of every animal registered with the AKC. Later, only those animals that produced a litter that had been registered would find their way into the stud book. Thus, one could research the stud book and backtrack through previous volumes to ascertain the ancestry of any animal AKC had registered. It is important to realize that once the stud book is closed, ensuing generations of breeders have only the genes contained by the original dogs with which to work. Any new genetic material added to a breed's gene pool later is through the occurrence of mutation. (Future technology might include adding new genetic material through gene splicing.)

Whether the dog as we know it descended from the same ancestor—*canis lupis*—is of little real significance to us today. Perhaps dogs more or less occurred in different parts of the world in a random way at varying times. Perhaps Ice Age interaction or connecting continents allowed similar animals in varying forms to roam all over the world, changing those forms as they migrated to function better in their new and different environments.

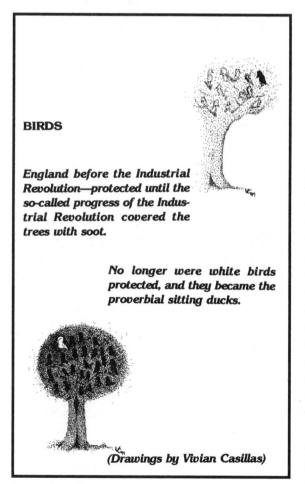

BIRDS

England before the Industrial Revolution—protected until the so-called progress of the Industrial Revolution covered the trees with soot.

No longer were white birds protected, and they became the proverbial sitting ducks.

(Drawings by Vivian Casillas)

Either way, natural selection could intervene to change the animal either slowly through evolution or rapidly and dramatically through mutation. If all dogs from the Chihuahua to the Great Dane do, in fact, trace their ancestry back to *canis familiaris* and its ancestor, *canis lupis*, does it mean that because they all have a common ancestor there is no such thing as an absolute purebred dog?

It is important to accept the fact that mutations occurred at some point as an explanation as to why primitive animals were not identical or more alike. Mutations are sudden changes in the genetic-information process caused by things only scientists understand. No matter, as we can get an appreciation of how adept Mother Nature is at the mutation game by looking at the problem facing medical technology presented by modern bacteria. Almost as rapidly as research laboratories develop new antibiotics, the bacteria adjust and develop new resistance to them. In fact, a very real concern of the scientific community as we approach the 21st Century is finding ways to stay ahead of the various germs' abilities to mutate and overcome medicines designed to prevent or destroy them. Although mutations are usually harmful, some are anything but.

Try to picture a flock of white birds whose habitat was among light-colored trees with near white bark in pre-industrial England. The flock was well hidden and protected from its predators until the so-called progress of the Industrial Revolution covered the trees with soot and filth, leaving the white birds against the black background as proverbial sitting ducks for their predators. As the flock started dwindling in numbers, previously scarce black mutants now survived to breed on and develop the flock into a color

PREDATORS AND PREY

A long-term study of the relationship between the predator and prey that gives us insight into the progenitor of dogs in their natural habitat is taking place on Isle Royale in Northern Michigan, and this relationship is the on-going interaction of two inbred species.

For almost 40 years, this study in an isolated and controlled by nature environment has tracked the relationship of the two species that inhabit the island—the wolf and its food supply, the moose—or the hunter and the hunted.

The 210-square-mile island is now a protected national park with no roads, cars or other vestiges of modern civilization. Thus, it is truly isolated from outside influences that might interfere with Mother Nature at work.

The relationship of the wolf and the moose shows that in some periods of time the population of the hunters will increase and that of the hunted decrease. Then the pendulum swings back and the situation is reversed.

During extremes of winter, moose seem to suffer the most. There are losses of the young, the old and the sickly during these starving times caused by bitter temperatures and unusually heavy snowfall that damages the food supply for these herbivores.

During such times, wolves proliferated in such numbers that it was no longer in their best interest. Then their population started to decline.

How much of this was natural selection is not known. It is thought that parvo virus might have thinned the wolf population during the '80s. In time, the numbers of wolves started increasing again.

Alas! The good times were not to last and once again wolves fell on hard times. Whether it was due to inbreeding, disease or other factors, the pack population started to decline.

Finally, scientists were forced to interfere enough to tag some of the wolves. Most of those involved in the study were concerned about the small gene pool, as they felt that the family had become victim of its own inbreeding with decreasing vitality the consequence.

When just recently it was discovered that the pack was again thriving with healthy youngsters amongst its numbers, it was thought that inbreeding, when accompanied by the unrelenting rigors of a very harsh Mother Nature, had indeed weeded the pack.

In so doing, the vitality of the pack had been infused with the blood of those inbred for hardiness and health, reaffirming that Mother Nature knows what she is doing.

that accommodated the changes to the trees. Now the flock consisted mostly of black birds that fit into the changed environment. The rigors of nature are very demanding—adapt or die.

I find the relationship of the herbivore and carnivore interesting. Female herbivores that had a delay between giving birth to their young and passing the afterbirth had a higher newborn survival rate. The delay of an hour or more gave the newborn more time to adjust to its new environment, become ambulatory, and follow its mother to safer surroundings before the passed afterbirth drew scavenger predators. These are just a couple of examples of Darwin's theory of natural selection through survival of the fittest at work. The list is unending.

What about dog breeding and the selection involved with it? What started out as natural selection all those years ago when the species was sorted out, first by nature and then by early man, evolved into a far different process. Although a number of performance dogs today are still selected through the more natural criteria, most of today's purebred dogs are chosen through artificial selection. This choice is made by the breeder to please the breeder.

Artificial selection or human control of the breeding population, based on criteria other than survival, led to the development of many different breeds of dogs bred for a specific purpose. During the development of a breed, if there were no dogs available in the breed that possessed the desired qualities, breeders used other breeds and crossbred to introduce new traits to get a better and more functional end product. This quest for specific breeds to serve a specific purpose has resulted in the development by man of more than 400 breeds of dogs, some very well-known to all of us and others known to only a few interested people in a restricted locale.

Of these 400 or more breeds, some could still survive in the wild. Most, however, could survive only in the environment man provides. Some breeds have been so man-made that they cannot reproduce without man's assistance. With this artificial selection goes a tremendous amount of responsibility for the sincere and dedicated breeder.

Breeders who breed the more natural breeds might simulate Mother Nature. In place of that demanding and harsh judge, become a breeder who expects your animal to do those things for which it was bred. Become one who simulates natural selection in an ongoing effort to create a hardy line of animals that enjoy a long and healthy life and exhibit great character as well as beauty. Breeders who concentrate on the more man-made breeds might set their own methods of working within the artificial selection process to keep their dogs as natural as possible while seeking the characteristics that set the breed apart. By combining a form of simulated natural selection with the best possible means of artificial selection, it is hoped that progress can be attained.

So You Want to be a Breeder: The ethical breeder lives for his dogs and not off his dogs

The breeding of purebred dogs is both an art and a science, thus the true breeder is a very artistic genetic engineer. The breeder plans a breeding program in much the same manner as the architect plans a building or a bridge. In examining the pedigree—or genetic blueprint—of an animal, one can determine if the engineers or breeders involved in producing this animal arrived at the end product by plan or by a series of individual matings that represented no real *grand design*.

The ethical breeder is a purist who does not expect his animals to earn their keep through stud fees and puppy sales. The ethical breeder lives *for* his dogs and not *off* his dogs. This breeder breeds for the enjoyment of the end product and the sense of accomplishment achieved by success. This success can come in the form of looking out the window in sheer pleasure as one of your dogs trots across the yard effortlessly—or it can come with accolades in the show ring.

Breeders must be constantly dedicated and rededicated to the fact that the most important thing a dog can be is man's best friend. Breeders must keep in mind that there are already too many dogs, and each breeding must be done with great care, no matter how inconvenient, or it should not be done at all. Breeders must take the long-term picture of the breed, not just the breedings they are considering now.

Breeders must continue their struggle to produce the picture of perfection for their breed. The dog in their mind's eye must be sound of mind and body as well as of correct type for its breed. The fact that dogs are big business for some people must never compromise the purist ideals of the breeder.

Breeder responsibility to other breeders is just as important as breeder responsibility to the public. One of the major by-products of DNA information is that it would be a positive step towards more openness with breeders. It is vital that breeders understand that blame is not the name of the game in dealing with accountability. A breeder who has previously unknown disease recessives surface is no more guilty than a devastated mother and father who have produced a child with Down's Syndrome. (See Florence Palmer - Progressive Retinal Atrophy[PRA])

To be a breeder is as important a responsibility as it is to be a parent, not something that should be entered into casually. Every dog a breeder brings into the world is that breeder's personal responsibility and must be located into a secure home appropriate for it.

What It Takes to be a Respected Breeder

Leonardo da Vinci would have made a good breeder—he was curious, creative, dedicated, and eternally fascinated with his work. Furthermore, his expertise at mixing paints was appreciated by fellow Renaissance artists, who respected his innovative and scientific thinking, and when something did not work, he wanted to know why. If you want to be a respected breeder, you have your work cut out for you. It is a long-term commitment not unlike taking the vows to a religious order. Discipline and work must be combined with the ongoing enthusiasm and excitement of youth if you want to do it all: Breed, Show, and Win. Do not worry about the youth bit—if the work of breeding and raising quality dogs doesn't finish you off, it will energize you and keep you young.

To be a breeder you must have general knowledge about dogs. That is, you must know what makes a good dog good—knowledge that would lead you to pick a sound dog, correctly constructed, in any breed, with possible exceptions that would prove the rule. Knowing your dog as a dog requires you to know anatomy.

Breed-specific knowledge must be added to your general knowledge of the dog. This involves much study of the history and origin of your breed as well as an understanding of the purpose for which it was bred. The next step is to study your standard as though your life depended on it. It is amazing the people who breed and show dogs who have no idea what the breed standard has to say about their breed—or worse still, have read it and just disregarded it. It is vital to have general knowledge about dogs and breed-specific knowledge about your breed. **It is absolutely mandatory to know the difference**.

BREED-SPECIFIC CONTRADICTIONS TO GENERAL DOG KNOWLEDGE

It is important for the potential breeder to realize that some of the general information about dogs may not be correct when referring to a given breed. Most breeds prefer that the dogs have angles similar to those described in the Notion of Motion section.

A notable exception to this rule of thumb is the Chow Chow, which is built significantly straighter in its angles that these other breeds. The breed standard spells out that the angle of the shoulder blade to the upper arm is 110°, rather than the 90° shoulder angle called for by most breed standards, and the standard goes on to explain that this results in less reach.

The Chow Chow standard balances this front end by calling for hindquarters with little angulation at the stifle joint, resulting in stilted action of the rear. When one sees handlers racing Chows, one has to wonder if they have a clue what the breed is all about.

Most breeds prefer the dog stand on straight front legs that are parallel when viewed from the front. The Bedlington Terrier standard calls for the forelegs to be wider apart at the chest than at the feet.

If you are going to breed Miniature Pinschers, you might want to follow the advice of the great English "Min Pin" breeder, John Stott, who says you will get lost if you demand that the Min Pin come at you exactly like every other breed, for in so doing, you may very well sacrifice the good hackney-like action with its correct lift and correct break at the wrist. Like the Tennessee Walking Horse champion I saw recently, the action may be somewhat loose coming at you but magnificent from the side view with a back that stays perfectly straight and firm while sloping toward the rear, which is well under the animal. That is to say that most of the action is in the front with the accommodating strength and drive of synchronized hocks and a strong rear. Miniature Pinscher breeders are just like breeders in any other breed, they must learn when to make allowances in their breed that would not be acceptable in another breed in order to prevent losing sight of the forest while looking at the trees. Master breeders know where their breeds may experience exceptions to the rule.

This brings the breeder to the next requirement—total objectivity. If you can take your knowledge of dogs in general and your breed in particular and synthesize it into objective decision making, you are on the road to becoming a successful breeder. You must be willing to work for what you get. The most appreciated rewards in life are those for which you work. You will not make it in "dogs"—unless you are so wealthy you can pay others to do all of your work and decision making—if you are not prepared to spend thousands of hours working at your passion to breed quality animals.

Patience is not only a virtue in the *good book*, it is also a necessity in the breeding of purebred dogs. There are no short cuts in the breeding programs of those who have made it to the top. The need for instant gratification that is so indicative of our society will not work in the world of purebred dogs—for ours is a success story based on delayed gratification. The emphasis on style, glamour and "pretty" at the expense of what is underneath all of this is a grave danger faced by the breeder. This modern phenomenon is certainly not limited to the world of purebred dogs.

Our politicians, entertainers and even our lives reflect an attitude that cares more about how things look rather than how they really are. Such thinking leads to disaster both in the world of dogs and in life itself.

Perhaps this is why the average fancier lasts five years in the world of purebred dogs. I am assuming you are not average and are willing to undertake this magnificent obsession shared by those of us who breed dogs as a lifetime commitment.

You are prepared to be the dedicated student who will learn and acquire the education necessary to be a real dog person. You must be prepared to learn the mechanics of the machinery if you are going to understand how it runs. Then you can worry about the style of what covers the machine, its color, and its attractiveness. As a breeder, you will realize that a beautiful, stylish, exotic animal that is not functional is useless. A plain, non-flashy animal made right is useful and the beautiful, exotic rare animal that is also made right is priceless. As a breeder, it will make your life worthwhile.

What Your Mother Told You is True

Beware that you do not rush into your breeding activities to select the beautiful at the expense of everything else. What your mother told you is true: "Beauty is more than skin deep," and "pretty is as pretty does." In effect, you are going to combine hard work with the knowledge of structure, type, performance and breed quality to produce the dream dog. And you will stay dedicated to this idea: "There is only one reason to breed a litter and that is to improve upon your breeding stock—not to sell puppies, not for show-and-tell, not to set records, and not to present a world full of unwanted dogs with more of the same" (courtesy of Betsy A. Leedy, Miniature Poodle breeder and judge).

As a breeder, your future success will depend on your early start, your selection of foundation stock, and mentors to help you along on the road to your destiny. It is imperative that you start with the very best stock available or you will spend years endeavoring to improve. Start off with an excellent bitch or two and do not attempt to have a stud dog on your premises.

In working with your mentor who has invested years of resources in the dogs, be willing to give something in return for what is being shared with you. The busy, longtime breeder is always grateful to the novice who comes to the place and helps bathe and groom dogs, leash-break puppies and train youngsters. The old-timer is grateful and free to do other things, as well as encouraging you, and you learn from the experience.

If you are an aspiring terrier star, you should be more than willing to help with the kennel chores to get a George Ward, Peter Green or Lydia Hutchinson to share knowledge with you. If you want to breed the perfect Poodle, a Jacky Hungerland or Anne Clark would appreciate your helping hand in return for sharing with you. If Pugs are your forte, Charlotte Patterson should find you camped on her front step.

To have a lasting influence on the breed, experienced breeders think generations ahead with both dogs and people, for they know nothing is forever. If you are sincere and dedicated, they want you in their breed for the good of its future. Such a mentor as one of these greats lives on long after individual dogs and people are gone—for theirs is a legacy of the elite of the dog world. Such a breeder is remembered by ensuing generations, long after that person is gone. If you are lucky, you will be one of those carrying on. You are, in effect, the family of the future. Good breeders have their own purposes to breed an animal that satisfies them. The ultimate dream is to breed one that satisfies the breeder and every other expert, too.

Good breeders are totally committed to their dogs. It is a way of life for them. They are prepared to make sacrifices. When friends, if they still have any non-doggy ones, ask them to parties and fun events and their best bitch is due to whelp, they stay home. Social events, sporting events, symphonies, and a million and one other things that normal people do for enjoyment are missed because their animals require care. Nonetheless, you should try to avoid reaching the point where all you do is related to dogs, or you will experience burnout.

Because good breeders are also good people who need to stay in touch with the real world, too, programming positive activities can energize their lives. Especially stimulating are artistic and intellectual activities that help keep the creative juices flowing. Good breeders avoid allowing dogs to become a fortress behind which they get so lost in the world of dogs that they are lost from the real world.

ENGLISH SPRINGER SPANIEL Ch. Chinoe's Adamant James, center, pictured taking the breed from the puppy class in 1969, handled by the author. Adamant James, two-time Westminster BIS winner was bred by Ann Roberts, sister of handler Clint Harris on the left with Ch. Canarch Inchidony Sparkle, bred by Clint's other sister Mary Lee Hendee. Mary Lee placed the good Canarch bitch Inchidony Brook with her sister, and D.J. was the result of a half-brother, half-sister mating. On the right is Ch. Canarch Yankee Patriot C.D. with handler Mike Atkins. Mentor Fred Young, who had been asked by the author to give his opinion of this exciting young Springer, watches from ringside. "He's going to be a top one," prophesied Young. In 1971, it was a privilege to be the first to congratulate Harris on D.J.'s first Best in New York, as the author was next to him in the ring. (Photo courtesy of Mary Lee Hendee)

Fred Young, mentor and friend, pictured handling Ch. Silver Son's Danny av Vel-J-Nic to a win under Gordon Parham in the early 1960s. Danny was bred and owned by Fred's mother Velma Nichols, and when asked about breeding to him, good friend Fred advised me to use his sire. The author was always close to Fred and Margaret Young, setting up with them at shows and enjoying their company whenever possible. Margaret Young Renihan recently celebrated with a party in honor of Fred's mother Mrs. Nichols on the occasion of her 90th birthday. (Bennett Associates photo)

Working with 150 fun-loving eighth graders five days a week was a wonderful way for me to keep my perspective.

Choosing a Mentor

In deciding who will be your mentors, be careful! Follow your head over your heart. Just because you really like someone does not mean that person is the best source of help for you. The last thing you need is for someone to reinforce your already incorrect concepts—if you have any. It is not the curriculum nor even the classroom that makes for successful education. It is the great teacher.

Beware of potential mentors who have a messiah-like complex but not the knowledge to back it up. Such cult-like zealots are true believers whose ignorance is masked by their convictions. Because they are so dedicated to their own thoughts and thinking, it does not occur to most people to question them. Make sure you question their competence, knowledge and influence.

Always remember that if you want to learn from someone who has spent a lifetime at it, be willing to experience those never-ending chores firsthand. These experiences will be a learning situation for you and a great deal of help to what ranks right up there with the working mother as an overworked person—the successful dog breeder!

In breeding dogs like anything else in life, never expect something for nothing. The ultimate reality is that you, the breeder, will bear the final responsibility for your choices. Use all the teachers you can find who have value, but recognize that in the final analysis you are more or less on your own. Here are guidelines to assist you in choosing mentors. You can work with an established breeder whom you trust both intellectually and morally. Established breeders have a consistency in their breeding programs, which is a testimony to their constant objectivity and clarity of thinking. Working with the established breeder is a good move, especially if that person, your expert, does not get stale before you are wise enough to recognize it, or hit dead-end streets, refuse to be objective, or become jaded. The advantage

Mentors meet at Westminster: Two of the great mentors of the 20th Century were the author's mentor, Johnny Davis, and Mrs. Lynwood (Peg) Walton of the famous Lyn-Mar Acres Basset Hound Kennels. Pictured here in 1955 when the world class judge Alva Rosenberg narrowed the breed down to two sons of Peg's famous Ch. Lyn-Mar Acres Clown, the older champion with Davis was defeated by the nine-month old youngster shown by Peg. Mrs. Walton has been a model mentor for a generation or more of Basset breeders, and her successful students include Joan Urban, Michael Sosne and Eric White, as well as many others. Mr. Rosenberg has his back to the camera. (Photo from the collection of Mrs. Walton. It was taken before Westminster became a show for champions only)

The Honorable David C. Merriam (on the left) credits his entire Bull Terrier philosophy to the late Raymond Oppenheimer of Ormandy fame. Although an ocean separated the young Merriam and his mentor, frequent correspondence and communication spiced with many trips to England over the years cultivated this life-long friendship. As the older gentleman pioneered the full-headed Bull Terrier, considered the essence of modern breed type, his younger follower was one of many who helped spread the message. From such close-working comrades, breeds receive dedicated leadership that greatly affects breed improvement. Theirs was a true mentor success story. (Photo courtesy of Mr. Merriam)

to you is that your growth is concentrated. The disadvantage is obvious—*you are putting all your eggs in one basket*. So make certain it is a strong basket!

Another option is to expose yourself to all available information, finding out as much as you can from as many different reliable sources as possible. Using human resources, books, films and videos, articles and magazines, you will collect a storehouse of materials, knowledge and information. Furthermore, this type of educational venture will enrich your experiences with seminars, specialties, hands-on work with several mentor-breeders, conversations and dialogues as you accumulate as much information as possible. There will be comfort in knowing that you are doing your best to collect the information that will allow you to make the most informed decisions.

The disadvantage is that such scattered information and differing opinions might be disjointed and contradictory, leading you to confusion. The obvious advantage is that if you are discerning and study in a rational and studious manner—not helter-skelter—you will accumulate information to assist you in making wise choices.

No matter what system you choose—the first, second or a third that falls somewhere between the two extremes—it is the people you select to work with that will help you grow in a positive way. Thus, you must be very careful of charlatans and Pied Pipers. Be advised that some of these people are very skilled at salesmanship, yet may not have the desired substance upon which you can build your education. In the words of Elizabeth Barrett Browning: "The devil's most devilish when respectable." Also to be avoided are those with negative personalities who trash everyone but themselves. Even very knowledgeable people are not worth it if they are full of hostility and negativity that will rub off on you. Seek learned people who are upbeat and personable. Remember that any relationship is somewhat like a marriage and should be carefully investigated with more than the emotion of the moment. Look before you leap.

Setting Goals

There are breeders and there are breeders. Just what is meant by this? Consider the levels of golfing. The duffers and hackers take up the sport and do one of three things: stay at their incompetent level and enjoy their occasional round; improve enough so they do not embarrass themselves and break into the 90s with their eyes on the 80s; or, if they are really goal-oriented and have the potential, they become scratch golfers and club champions.

Breeders also come at various levels. Like the duffers and hackers, the beginning breeder has modest goals. A duffer is anybody with the greens fee and a set of clubs. A beginning breeder at worst—as defined by AKC—is the owner of the bitch at the time of the mating. Some breeders are happy with just the experience of the litter itself. These are dogdom's duffers enjoying their occasional round.

Another beginning breeder might be happy with a championship, depending on the breed. In some breeds, a beginner's goals might be just to point a dog. In my own breed, almost any beginner can finish a dog if it has no major or crippling problems. This is not necessarily true in competitive breeds like Doberman Pinschers, German Shepherd Dogs or Golden Retrievers.

At the next level, is the competent breeder with goals in mind that include improving the breed in

> "If you don't know the port to which you sail, no wind is a good one."
> —Seneca, Roman philosopher/statesman

general and his own line in particular. Such a breeder wants his animals to be competitive under both breeder-judges and all-rounders. Such a breeder wants to breed quality animals—and learns the difference—that are sound in mind and body. This good breeder knows the difference in average animals, good ones or great ones. Such a breeder will contribute to the overall improvement of the breed and, perhaps, be one of its unsung heroes. These people are the nuts and bolts of the fancy. Their contributions are meaningful and permanent as they go quietly on their way, breeding quality animals over the years. They are golf's club champions who shoot par, or close to it. In golf they are known as "scratch golfers."

The Master Breeder: To master something—anything—you must first become its slave.

The *master breeder* is more than the scratch golfer. The *master breeder* is more like the experts at the top on the Professional Golfers Association tour, really influencing the future direction of this sport. The *master breeder* has a purpose that is a passion—to raise the classic dog. The *master breeder* not only produces great dogs for himself, but great dogs for others in the breed to utilize for the good of all. The *master breeder* produces the big specialty winners, dogs in the Top Ten, and those that go on to make producing records as well as show records. The *master breeder* knows which of those records is the most important. To master something—anything—you must first become its slave. And the *master breeder* does just that. The *master breeder* is an artistic genetic engineer combining the best traits of the artist and the scientist to create a magnificent end product. The *master breeder* is every bit the sportsman that the great champion golfer is, even to the extent of feeling the pressure of losing it on occasion. If that happens, the *master breeder* is well-rounded enough to make proper amends.

The *master breeder* is unique and has something special to contribute. Yet, even the *master breeder* has times when he feels unsure, when the opinions of others have him temporarily questioning his own judgment, and when he wonders if he is doing as well as he could. Because of his total commitment and objectivity that is often painful, the *master breeder* keeps on, working toward that ultimate responsibility of breeding better dogs.

Sometimes the breeder will have to grab on to those private moments of pleasure provided by the dogs, as the down times can be most lonely. That is when one must take comfort in realizing that others who share this magnificent obsession and dedicate a large portion of their waking life to dogs also experience devastating setbacks. It involves picking yourself up more than once. Like the Oriental proverb: "Fall seven times; stand up eight."

Continued rededication serves as an affidavit that the true breeder will need great vision with the desire to be creative and the willingness to be a workaholic en route to the *master breeder* goal. Some breeders are multi-talented, creative artists producing works with pen and ink or on canvas, as well as in the whelping box. The very artistic *master breeder*, Peggy Westphal of Dachshund fame, is a marvelous example of such versatility. Others, not so blessed, turn to their animals to stimulate and experience creativity.

The dedicated breeder is that architect who uses a pedigree as his blueprint. His building materials are living, breathing sires and dams rather than concrete, steel, plaster and wood. And the monument he constructs is as proud as any cathedral in the precious ability to lick his face in love.

Since these breeders have been working for years, often a lifetime, to improve a breed, beginners are wise to build on the progress made by them. Even beginning golfers buy the best clubs they can afford and do not try to design their own as starters. To launch your breeding dreams requires establishing goals.

The first goal is to select a breed, one that needs you and one that you need, for you will be dedicating yourself to its future welfare. The next goal might be to determine what would be your first measure of success—would it be to breed a homebred champion? This is an admirable goal, all the more so in breeds that are very competitive and where major points are a rare commodity.

Is your goal to breed a dog capable of winning an important specialty? A group placer? A group winner? A best-in-show winner? Reaching for the stars might mean that your grasp will go beyond your reach, but so what?

Do you wish to establish a line of quality animals or breed one big star? Do you wish to recover a gene pool or type within a breed that has been lost to the breed? Do you aspire to maintain a particular look in a breed—a look that might otherwise be lost because those who contributed it are no longer breeding? As you establish your line, remember that breeds have been saved by such visionaries. Those of us who have been in dogs for many years know such people who have fulfilled those very goals within our breeds. Sometimes these people are members of an unknown, unnamed fraternity who shared such dreams. They were the unsung heroes who left the results of their life's work in the gene pools of today's breeds to be harvested and properly perpetuated by the breeds' caretakers. Or unhappily—as the case sometimes is—to be abused and trashed in the disintegration of their beloved breed.

Purebred dogs have been improved in the 20th Century by those so dedicated. Their legacy is left for future guardians who will carry our sport into the 21st Century and beyond. Older breeders take great comfort from aspiring *master breeders*, knowing that their personal efforts will be protected, preserved and nurtured in the future.

Somewhere down the road, a great one will come along again that traces its ancestry to the work being done by today's breeders, who in turn built on the work done yesterday by yesterday's breeders.

Right: The late Florence Palmer, of Torvallen Norwegian Elkhounds, was an outstanding example of a responsible breeder. In 1960, when she learned that her excellent line of dogs was affected by PRA, this honorable master breeder brought the problem to the attention of the Norwegian Elkhound Association of America and then removed the affected dogs from her breeding program. Florence is pictured with her Best in Sweepstakes Puppy, (Ch.) Vin-Melca's Before Dawn, at the Parent Club National Speciality she judged in 1982. (Photo by Marietta Jones)

Below: Ch. Vin-Melca's Before Dawn (Ch. Vin-Melca's Namesake X Ch. Vin-Melca's Morning Star) accomplished an amazing feat in the summer of 1982 when she was "moved up" from 6-9 Puppy Class to Best of Breed Competition and scored three consecutive All Breed BISs on the competitive Montana Circuit, justifying Florence Palmer's faith in her. Owned by the author and Edward B. Jenner, Before Dawn was named after the great Calumet Farm racemare. The Westminster breed winner in 1983, she placed third in the Hound Group. She is the paternal grandam of two-time Westminster Group winner Ch. Vin-Melca's Marketta through her BIS son Ch. Vin-Melca's Bombardier. (Callea Photo)

Even though it might seem you are in the loneliest game in town, take heart in knowing your endeavors do not take place in a vacuum. They occur like so many links in an unending chain. The first link began with prehistoric dog and the final link will lead to eternity. Every breeder must strive to put the strongest links possible in that chain.

The breeder's aim could be as simple as having an occasional litter. The enjoyment of each litter will be enhanced by making it the very best litter possible. In attempting to breed the perfect one, keep in mind that it is difficult to breed the perfect dog from imperfect parents. That is why most of us have never seen the perfect dog; nevertheless, we recognize the varying degrees of imperfection.

In setting your goals, remember that to be a breeder is as important a responsibility as to be a parent, not something that should be entered into casually. Every dog the breeder brings into the world is that breeder's personal responsibility and must be put into a secure home appropriate for it. Accountability in all phases of the activity is the breeder's creed. Otherwise there is no *master breeder*.

Doing Your Homework

Summarizing the job description and goals of a potential *master breeder* brings home the message that the degree of difficulty involved in producing greatness is not a matter of random good luck. Like the graduate student, preparing diligently for his future profession in the real world, the potential *master breeder* must do his homework.

Preparation will involve the study of the physiology of the dog as an athlete, as well as the physiognomy of the dog in accordance with the standard for its breed. Having accomplished this, the potential breeder will understand the concepts of type and soundness and how they relate to each other philosophically, psychologically, and practically. It's time to hit the books!

The Notion of Motion

What could be more beautiful than a gorgeous "typey" animal in motion? This breathtaking creature personifies fluid liberty of motion, at the same time it displays energy-saving economy of movement. There is a precise balance of power and grace made possible by thoroughly clean, correct construction.

Correct motion is an amazing phenomenon that is absolute in its balance between freedom and control—a balance achieved only by those athletic enough to have great flexibility at the same time their body control utilizes total collection and stability. Such an animal is truly the living, breathing example of the magnificent description, *poetry in motion*. The gait of such an animal has a certain tempo, and like a symphony by Beethoven or a play by Shakespeare, it seems to flow.

This fluid tempo comes in all sizes, shapes, forms and styles. It can be found in the effortless working gait of a gun dog or a hound, the pendulum gait of a terrier, the rolling motion of the Pekingese, the shuffle of the Bulldog, the amble of the Old English Sheepdog, the lift of the Afghan, or a number of other breed-specific movements. No matter which breed you study, the great ones will have that rhythm and coordination. They will corner well and have a sure turn of foot. These qualities are exhibited only by those animals presenting the practical picture of what we learned in geometry—*the whole equals the sum of its parts.*

Sometimes this mathematical hypothesis is not easy to translate into an evaluation of the dog and its moving parts. For one thing, even if we are experts on the physical construction of the animal, our eye is not always able to comprehend the whole picture. Only the truly skilled have the gift to do it in a matter of moments. To really understand gait, one must spend a lot of time in various forms of study, including, but certainly not limited to, the use of slow motion films of the animal in action.

To understand the mechanics of movement, one must accept that there are a number of elements that enter into the final product: anatomy, musculature, neurological factors, biochemical (the body's fuel system), the heart and psyche, as well as intangibles, such as desire and will. In this case, the whole becomes more than the sum of its parts.

Locomotion, then, is a complex exercise involving coordinated series of activities leading to correct limb movement. The walk, trot and pace are *symmetrical* gaits in which the movements of the legs on one side are repeated by the legs on the other side half a stride later. The run and gallop are *asymmetri-*

Long-time Norwegian Elkhound breeder Jeanne Smolley described Ch. Vin-Melca's Vagabond as poetry in motion. The first Elkhound to place in the Top Ten All Breeds, he was #1 Dog All Breeds, All Systems in 1970. He covered a maximum amount of ground with a minimum of effort, held the correct profile, and handled corners with total athletic coordination. Catherine (Casey) Gardiner found his bones and angles to be in correct length and balance, producing this grace in motion. (Photo by Robert Smolley)

Ch. Vin-Melca's Calista (Sarah) at the Astrohall where she enjoyed BIS success. Sarah was in her element exhibiting great extension on the real grass brought indoors for a natural setting. Sarah was blessed with the correct sternum and length of ribcage accompanied by a short loin. With her well-angulated shoulders and powerful quarters, she was able to stride easily. (Photo by Perlmutter)

Ch. Vin-Melca's Love Call, BIS winning daughter of a BIS dam. Owned by Janet Allen and the author, "Tess" was named after the mother of actress Betty White during a Mother's Day visit in 1983. Her movement shows the correct profile in motion holding her topline while covering ground. Tess was ranked in the Top Ten in 1986. (Photo by Callea)

Ch. Vin-Melca's Howdy Rowdy, BIS sire of BIS progeny, moving in the Hound Group in the Cow Palace, San Francisco, in 1968 at the Golden Gate Kennel Club show. Howdy was the sire of 166 champions and the tail male sire of a great sire line. He was a stallion of a dog with the natural look of a sire. (Photo by Jayne Langdon)

Ch. Vin-Melca's Bombardier exhibiting front reach in the right foreleg with excellent follow through on the left foreleg showing return of upper arm at work. A dog with well-laid-back shoulders and good reach of neck, he has a well-muscled rear with good follow through of hindquarters. This moving picture was taken by Mike Work, who handled him to several of his 39 All Breed BIS victories.

cal gaits in which the legs on one side do not repeat the movements on the other side. Correct smooth strides have less jarring contact with the ground, reducing wear and tear on the animal.

Because the trot is a diagonal gait for the dog in which the left rear foot hits the ground at the same time as the right front foot for kinetic—moving—balance, it is highly synchronized and most likely to show the best and the worst in the gait. This is why the trot is the gait of choice in judging dogs. It is also why some judges like to see a dog trotted slowly, or for that matter, walked. Horsemen, too, like to see the animal walk and trot.

Both the horse breeder and the dog breeder have created a large number of breeds, most of which have little resemblance to the ancient, primitive animal. Yet each was bred for a specific purpose, and in altering the original look of the animals to meet specific needs, even early man was working in an evolutionary manner to produce animals built for a given type of work.

Thus, he was selecting for correctness that allowed efficiency and energy-conserving locomotion so that he could get the most mileage out of his animals. The luxury of easy replacements was not available in the way it is today. And that very well may have been for the good of the order.

So, no matter which breed is your choice, you must strive to breed the dog that is built to serve that function. Even if the function is to be a lap dog, the animal must have a sound body free of pain to enjoy the good life.

Anatomy

"Anatomy is the first structure of art." No less an authority than the great Renaissance artist and scientist, Leonardo da Vinci, made the aforementioned statement. When one considers that this classic artist painted *The Mona Lisa* and *The Last Supper*, as well as a host of other great works, one must realize that here is an idea to embrace.

Usually the artist is perceived as just that—artistic but hardly scientific. Yet Leonardo spent endless hours dissecting human bodies as he studied to learn everything possible about anatomy. His work on cadavers was an endless quest to ascertain what was under the exterior beauty of the human body. It was Leonardo's belief that to understand the components of the body was to improve his ability to translate his knowledge to canvas. They just don't make them like Leonardo anymore!

Just as Leonardo studied the interior design of the exterior appearance, so must you, the dog breeder, if you want to put your pretty picture into a functional form. Just as this talented genius spent hours, days, and years studying the intricate details of the interior, so must you, the potential dog genius, know the interior in hopes of producing classic artwork in the form of the dog. Just as the study of genetics and breeding require you to be both an artist and a scientist, so does the study of locomotion, according to the greatest authority of them all—Leonardo da Vinci.

It is impossible to discuss anatomy without first defining conformation. Likely definitions would include any or all of the following:

- The manner in which a thing is formed.
- The way an animal is put together.
- The make and shape of the animal.
- The form and structure.
- The way the parts are arranged.

Yet a discussion based on any one of these foregoing definitions would be incomplete without at least an elementary description of the skeleton. Quite simply stated, the skeleton is a composite of the bones of the body fitted together in their natural places.

Do you have to be an expert in anatomy to be a good breeder or a judge? It would help if you had a working knowledge of the parts, but you do not have to memorize the Latin terminology, or spell each one correctly, to become adept at understanding conformation and the relationship of the moving parts to each other. One of the greatest horsemen I have ever known was an uneducated cowboy (a spitting image of the Marlboro Man) who knew more about the legs on a young horse than did the veterinarian or the farrier.

The skeletal system is like the foundation of a house, and if you start with one that is correct, you have made the right beginning. For example, you read in many standards that the preferred shoulder angulation is 45 degrees to the horizontal and 90 degrees to the humerus.

This is the ideal slope of shoulder—also known as layback—and the closer you get to 45 degrees, the better. However, there are many useful animals with quite good gait that will measure somewhat less than the ideal in shoulder angle. The important thing to remember about the angles is that they must complement each other if the dog is to be an athlete. That is to say that the angles in a dog's body should be similar if the dog is to function properly. Poorly matched parts lead to awkward, unathletic movement. Today, some of our breeds are struggling with this conflict. They have angles of one kind in the front end and angles of another in the rear end. Golden Retrievers, Irish Setters and Cocker Spaniels come to mind because the breeders are so concerned about the problem.

Disproportionate angles tend to tire a dog because he must work hard to overcome his lack of synchronization. This, along with other factors, may explain why sometimes dogs that are straighter at each end than desired will nonetheless move acceptably. They are in balance.

So a basic requirement is that the angles of the shoulder and the angles of the hip complement each other. Equally important is for the four vital bones involved—two at each end—to be of the approximate same length and correspond to each other in a correct fit. I will be eternally grateful for the coming of Catherine "Casey" Gardiner into my life in the 1970s, for she is the lady who figured out many

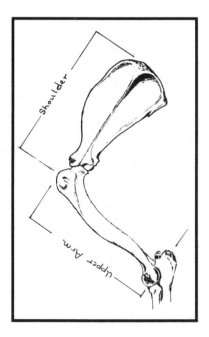

Balance in length of bones and angles. Front and rear. Norwegian Elkhound Breeder Dr. Richard Smith (Vestlykke Kennels in Canada) illustrates the balance necessary to the animal of correct conformation. The drawings show angulation, proportion and in proportion. Shoulder left and pelvis right.

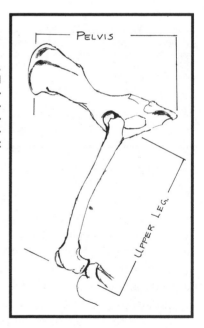

things she shared with others—things that had been previously unexplained.

The length of the scapula (shoulder blade) will correspond to the length of the pelvis (hipbone), and it will also correspond to its front-end partner in length—the humerus (upper arm). The upper arm length will not only correspond to the scapula, it will also correspond to its rear partner, the femur (upper leg bone) in length.

The laws of nature, applied to athleticism, require that these four bones be in correct balance both in length and set on (angulation) if the animal is to function properly. Casey proved that in the Norwegian Elkhound these bones would be approximately six inches in length and the angles would be in the neighborhood of 40 degrees or more.

If those four bones are correspondingly correct and the animal has a good layback of shoulder, the rest of the skeleton should fall into place even if the dog is an achondroplastic breed, such as a Basset

Hound, with great length of body and very short legs. Angulation, proportion, and *in proportion* are the basis for correctness upon which to build your dream dog. Just as you would not knowingly buy a house with poor underpinnings or an automobile with faulty wheels, you do not want to breed dogs that are not built on the correct foundation and without the right wheels.

The spine acts as the foundation does for the house. The accompanying bones of motion become the wheels of the vehicle. The spinal column is the support system for the dog, and it functions somewhat like a suspension bridge in that it connects the front to the rear in much the same way as the Golden

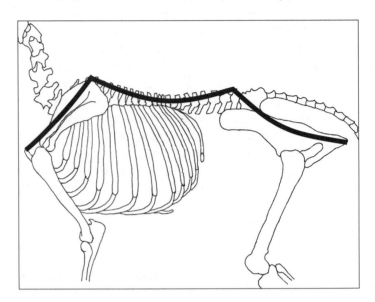

The spine is the dog's support system. It acts like a suspension bridge with the building materials of bones, ligaments and muscles performing the jobs of concrete, strings and support wires. Drawing by Dr. Richard Smith.

Gate Bridge connects San Francisco to Marin County. Because the law of gravity acts on this suspended weight, the spine has to have some curves to accommodate the force. Thus the spine has a gentle curve behind the withers—first nine thoracic vertebrae—at the mid-back area of the last four thoracic vertebrae. This is the dog's bodily divide with the center of those vertebrae carrying most of the suspended weight.

If this perfectly constructed natural bridge is flawed by a neck that is too short, a loin that is too long and too slack, or any other number of conformational faults, the dog's ability to support his weight in the most efficient manner is compromised. Any deviation from the norm changes both the center of gravity and the support system, concentrating strain, stress and concussion wrongly. Therefore, the whole dog becomes subject to breakdown. This breakdown comes both in the form of topline collapse and inability to perform his job in the easiest way for the longest amount of time. In other words, he would assuredly lack endurance among other things.

In order to picture how the dog's version of the Golden Gate works, you have to understand that the bones are comparable to the concrete part of the structure while ligaments and muscles of the back act as strings and support wires. The closer the support systems are, the less potential stress involved. This is why some of the elongated dogs, Dachshunds for example, are prone to back problems. They have a long bridge.

The question of why so many breeds ask for a straight topline—distance between withers and tail— when it is obvious that the actual spine curves is answered by the conditioning and muscling of the dog. If you have a well-conditioned animal, the muscles will fill in the crevices of the skeleton to give a smooth outward look to the back. Without the curves to absorb stress, the back would be too rigid to do its job. Greyhounds and Whippets are examples of dogs whose clearly defined curves indicate their flexibility.

In addition to the previously mentioned bones of the front assembly—scapula and humerus—a very important bone is the forearm, which provides most of the propulsion furnished by the front end.

Undoubtedly, its contribution to both speed and agility is why a breed standard such as the Saluki singles it out.

The length and angle of the pastern determine its ability to absorb shock. If it is too upright and short, it will not properly absorb concussion. If it is too long and let down, it will damage tendons and be too weak to do the job. The pastern and foot are all part of the complete front-end assembly. When that assembly is too upright, the animal suffers with cramped strides, short, nonathletic choppy gait and a general lack of elasticity.

While thinking front-end assembly, it is important to remember that the neck is vital to good balance. Not only does it bring proper coordination as the connector between the head and the body, together with the head it helps guide the body. At the gallop, the head acts as a weighted pendulum, rhythmically pulling the body forward at each stride. A short neck interferes with balance and action, and when accompanied by a poor shoulder, which it usually is, will cause short, choppy, fast-forward-type steps that are exhausting and incorrect.

The chest cavity and ribcage are of great importance, for they provide the housing and protection of the vital organs. Breed standards calling for spring of rib take that into account. But so do breed standards calling for a different configuration such as that of the sight hounds in which great barrel and spring of rib would interfere with speed. These racier animals get their volume and cubic inches from a powerful oval-shaped ribcage with great depth, giving plenty of organ capacity. The Borzoi standard calls for a rather narrow chest and slightly sprung ribs that are very deep.

The English Foxhound standard, on the other hand, calls for a hound of great girth, spelling out a 31-inch girth on a 24-inch dog for plenty of organ space. The racier American Foxhound standard states, "...narrower in proportion to depth than an English Foxhound..." and calls for a 28-inch girth.

Although a number of standards—the Beagle, for instance—call for a short back, many standards take it beyond the distance of withers to tail and describe the short-loined animal. Such short coupling allows only a small area of unsupported back. Furthermore, with the rear closer to the main body on such a dog, the propelling power is where it should be to get maximum effect.

Obviously, the back cannot be so short that the integrity of the rib cage is compromised. Such a caricature of a dog loses valuable organ space and will lack sufficient room to house all the apparatus necessary for life as well as necessary for endurance. As with everything else on the correctly structured animal, the pieces must fit and conform to each other while complementing the whole.

Since the hind legs provide most of the propelling power, it is important that they are made right. Both the hock joint and the hip joint are subject to hard work and must be right if they are to be up to the job. Correctly made legs and joints that are complementing in length of bones and angles will assure equal distribution of weight and stress.

Joints form the union between bones and are unremarkable until something goes wrong. Their job is to enable movement between the bones without friction. The hip joint is a ball and socket joint. The socket is formed by the pelvic bone and the ball is the upper end of the femur. One of life's many mysteries to me is why dogs have so much problem with this joint while horses do not.

The stifle joint can be a problem area with locking or slipping of the patella (knee cap). Although the problem can occur in well-angulated animals, it seems to be more prevalent in those with straighter stifles. Laxity of ligaments contributes to the cause. Sometimes this condition is seen in Beagles in which the stifle will lock so that the dog has no flex in it. If it is just a temporary catch, the dog will hop for a few strides until it works free and is able to stride normally once more. Cocker Spaniels and a number of toy breeds are also victims of this problem. Chows are a straight-stifled breed particularly plagued by patella problems.

Too little angle in the stifle (straight stifle) causes stress in the middle of the back. Too much angle at the hock bringing the dog's rear feet forward under his body causes the dog to be sickle hocked. This particular abnormality causes too much strain on the joint. Although some sources state that this conformation is not disastrous for draft horses the way it is for other horses, we have yet to hear an

CATHERINE (CASEY) GARDINER

CATHERINE "CASEY" GARDINER
AND THE CORRECT KERRY BLUE TERRIER IN ACTION

All her life Catherine Gardiner was a dedicated breeder of Kerry Blue Terriers, as well as a student of animal structure and its relationship to movement. She founded a school based on these ideas and formulated programs to educate enthusiastic dog fanciers in every phase of the sport. Her students included novices embarking on a vocation or avocation in dogs, as well as experienced fanciers who sought to advance their own knowledge through her energetic educational efforts. Fondly called Casey by her many friends and admirers, she became an avid artist as well as an articulate teacher. She developed methods by which animals could be measured to ascertain their performance potential and their shortcomings. In addition to the influence her work had on this author, very prominent dog people, such as Rachel Page Elliot, Lawrence "Skip" Stanbridge, Dr. Richard Smith and Betty McHugh, were greatly affected by her work. These are only a few of the many whose personal knowledge was enhanced by her having touched their lives.

Catherine Gardiner's in-depth research on the Kerry Blue Terrier resulted in a number of books and courses of study at the School of Canine Science that will serve as her permanent legacy. For years she studied motion, anatomy, paw prints and films as she collected her information. Casey worked with Dr. R.D. Whitford, Ontario Veterinary College, University of Guelph, with specimen studies and dissections. Her work led her to measure large numbers of dogs over decades and subsequently resulted in her drawings and explanations of Kerry Blue gait.

Her model was her homebred Can. and Am. Ch. Kerrycroft's Alexander, who was three years of age at the time his mistress did this work. These illustrated explanations show how a square dog, correctly made, can cover a maximum amount of ground with a minimum amount of effort. In addition to the correct structure and desired athleticism, Casey emphasized the necessity of proper temperament and its role in well-coordinated gait. She wanted her work to serve as an inspiration to breed clubs to achieve illustrated works in their quest for education. Long before it became fashionable, Casey and her outstanding peers in this Canadian vocational project were developing a prototype training program to help young people acquire appropriate dog skills before stepping into careers handling, training, and grooming dogs. All Kerry Blue Terrier drawings are courtesy of the estate of Catherine Gardiner. (Picture from *Dogs in Canada*)

STATIC OR STANDING BALANCE: Static balance appears to be achieved in the Kerry when the overall length of the Scapula, Humerus, Pelvis and Femur are all approximately the same length and at the angulation shown in the illustrations.
PERPENDICULAR LINES: In the forelimb, when standing naturally, a perpendicular line dropped from the tip of the spine of the Scapula, usually touches the back of the elbow and the Accessory Carpal bone of the Carpal joint. A slight slope to the pastern will place the line behind the paw. These reference points are clearly visible or easily felt.

THE TROT: The trot has been used for these illustrations primarily because it is considered to be the long distance mode of locomotion of the dog. It consists of diagonal striking and swinging phases, requiring the ultimate in split second timing and synchronization to allow the striking forelimb to remain on the ground the exact time as that of the DIAGONAL striking rearlimb.
Left: KINETIC OR MOVING BALANCE. Kinetic balance may be achieved in a dog with this conformation, if the temperament is such that the brain impulses will coordinate the muscle action, allowing movement with the least amount of effort.
Middle: START OF THE GAIT. As the dog starts to move, take careful note of how the head is raised. This will aid in lifting the right forelimb up and the paw back in preparation for the forward swing. It will also aid in shifting the weight onto the left striking (supporting) forelimb and back to the right striking (propelling) rearlimb, which is in readiness to propel the body forward. The left rear limb is ready to begin the swinging phase.
Right: INCREASING SPEED. The head moves down and forward and shifts the weight or mass forward, which in turn aids in forward movement. The muzzle will usually be over the paw of the swinging limb for ideal kinetic balance. If the paw is raised too high it may swing ahead, but will strike the ground under the muzzle. Check the illustrations carefully and note how the striking left forelimb and right rearlimb remain in the same place and visualize the fact that the body ONLY is being propelled over the forelimb by the rearlimb.

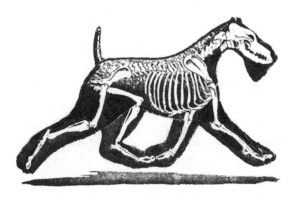

MAXIMUM SPEED: A dog with this conformation reaching maximum speed will have all four limbs off the ground in a moment of suspension (flying trot). The need for split second timing and synchronization is critical at this point. The left striking (supporting) forelimb must be lifted up, with the paw back, to enable the left swinging rearlimb to slide under and strike ahead of where the left forepaw leaves the ground. The dog is carried forward by momentum when the four feet are off the ground, therefore the distance that the striking left rearlimb strikes the ground ahead of the print of the left forepaw will be in relation to the height and the length of the dog, also the speed at which it is traveling. Side wheeling (or such an illusion) will be created, if the timing is such that the left rearpaw must strike to either side of the left forepaw print. Such reaching beyond can be achieved only by the athletic animal performing the flying trot.

Alaskan Malamute person praise it. Draft horse people say that sickle hocks, if not too extreme, allow the animal to get his legs under him and really push off.

The correct skeleton we have described can be pictured in these forms:

1. Square: Described in varying ways in the standards. Some of these dogs will measure about the same from withers to ground as from forechest to buttocks. Other standards state point of shoulder as the forward measurement. Many dogs are categorized as square in build. Some examples of the square breeds are: Norwegian Elkhound, Boxer, Doberman Pinscher, Great Dane, Keeshond, Chow, Fox Terrier, Welsh Terrier, Chinese Shar Pei, Schipperke, Afghan Hound and Affenpinscher.

2. Off Square to Slightly Rectangular: These dogs are described by their standards as off square or slightly longer than tall. Some of the standards will give exact ratios while others use in-depth explanations to describe them. Off square to somewhat rectangular dogs include the Samoyed, Siberian Husky, Akita, Great Pyrenees, Pharaoh Hound, Briard, German Wirehaired Pointer, Portuguese Water Dog, Chihuahua, Papillon, Newfoundland, German Shepherd Dog and Bichon Frise.

3. Elongated: Much longer than tall, these breeds' standards often specify ratios such as twice as long as tall or other descriptive terms for the achondroplastic. Fewer dogs fall into the elongated form of the Dachshund, Pembroke Welsh Corgi, Cardigan Welsh Corgi, Basset Hound, Skye Terrier and Dandie Dinmont Terrier.

No matter what the breed of choice, the basics are the same. Getting your generic dog information down pat will prepare you to get into the specific nuances of your breeds. Good shoulders and strong backs and loins are pretty universal. Your goal is to strive for the best possible skeleton for your breed of choice. The bones, their length, their angles, and their integrity of joints will serve as your building blocks. Once you have this excellent skeleton, you will have the perfect moving dog—or will you?

Motion: A New Twist To 'If They're Made Right'

"If they're made right, they'll move right" is what you have always heard. Did you ever wonder why some dogs must not have gotten that message? Did you ever scratch your head over a dog that looked lovely on the line and fell apart moving? Or one that did not catch your eye at all until it moved? The assumption is that if the skeletons are right, they will move right. Like the old song said, "It ain't necessarily so."

There is much more to the mechanics of motion than anatomy, even though that is the vital starting point. Some dogs outmaneuver their angles because of great athleticism and flexibility. Other dogs do not move up to their structure because they lack athleticism and flexibility.

The right muscles, ligaments and tendons are all part of the picture that is athleticism. So, the correct skeleton is the all-important required structure with musculature being the cohesive factor that starts pulling it all together.

The late Curtis Brown, an engineer of great renown and the much-loved author of *Dog Locomotion and Gait Analysis*, felt that galloping dogs such as sight hounds and Doberman Pinschers could be expected to have less angle at the point of shoulder than trotting dogs. Mr. Brown theorized that some breed standards calling for the 90-degree scapula to humerus angle—with 45 degrees angle of the scapula to the horizontal—were most unrealistic.

Sight hounds demonstrate the epitome of flexibility in the canine world. This flexibility allows them to perform the double suspension gallop in which all four legs are off the ground twice during the distance of the stride—once when they are completely tucked up and again when they are completely stretched and flattened out in full stride. Correct tuck-up and strength of loin are necessary to complete this picture of grace that would be impossible without their supple conformation.

Is it possible to have too much flexibility? Or, for that matter, too much angulation? Yes. Anything is possible. Too much flexibility can create more stride than the dog can handle or effectively control.

Too little flexibility, which is more often the case, will unduly restrict the stride. Although it is rare, too much angulation, as in the case of sickle hocks, causes wasted energy and time because so much of both is required to straighten the joint. Again, if it causes more length of stride than the animal is able to handle, excessive angulation becomes counterproductive. One does not see excess angulation nearly as often as insufficient angulation. Too little angulation causes the dog to work himself to death just doing routine exercise.

We are indebted to Patricia Gail Burnham for sharing the results of her numerous studies on the flexibility issue. This sight hound expert concluded that the ideal animal would have the perfect combination of components allowing sufficient flexibility to produce excellent freedom of stride while retaining enough inflexibility to have a strong support system and good body control.

The expression "body texture" has been used as the total composite of those things aside from bone structure that make an animal great. This ideal combination of muscles, tendons, ligaments and flesh means that the animal can store the optimum amount of energy. The more energy for its weight that the animal can store, the more endurance and class it will exhibit at work.

Johnny Davis taught me early on to appreciate body texture: "If you can breed a well-angulated, naturally hard dog, you will have something special." I treasure the now worn and dog-eared letters he wrote to me in the early 60s when I first moved to California.

Ch. Vin-Melca's The Virginian was one of my all-time favorite dogs STANDING. And, he was made right as far as skeletal structure was concerned. However correct the bones of the front end were on this dog, he was unable to cover ground at all, being "tied in" at the elbow with ligament and/or muscle inadequacy. Therefore he was unable to utilize his correct length of humerus and angle of both it and the scapula. He was a dog that contradicted the axiom, "if they're made right, they move right." Subsequently, he was removed from the breeding program, neutered and placed with the family of Don Blakeman, a fellow history teacher in Carmel. He lived as their beloved family pet until the ripe old age of 15, while his litter brother Ch. Vin-Melca's Valley Forge went on to become a Quaker Oats winner. (Photo by Lloyd Olson)

Johnny preached to me about how to avoid the more-is-better syndrome in my breeding program. The issue on that occasion was the subject of bone. I had a couple of bitches who were too fine-boned and was seeking potential sires to help remedy the problem. His studies revealed that on cross-section, the most athletic bone had proven to be oval, rather than round. Johnny explained to me that too much bone made the animal clumsy and unable to trail game without tiring. He pointed out that some breed standards calling for the roundest of bone were written by horse people dealing with animals who are naturally very fine-boned for their size, such as thoroughbreds. Subsequently, their version of *round bone* might be prone to exaggeration by modern dog breeders reading and mistakenly interpreting their written word.

Furthermore, according to Davis, the dog with sufficient bone will not only accumulate muscle around that bone, if the dog is being properly and regularly exercised, it will also lay on or build bone. Johnny was ahead of his time with some of his thinking, as recent studies on osteoporosis have supported his theory. This muscling and bone strengthening would give the illusion of rounder bone without the accompanying clumsiness caused by being *over boned*. At the same time this very wise man cautioned me to avoid over-refinement, for "the Elkhound is not a refined breed." Seeking the substantial, most functional amount of oval bone became an early priority, and it was with great pride that I took Vagabond's sire, Vickssen, to Virginia to show to Johnny in 1965. When Vickssen later produced Vagabond, it always seemed that my departed friend was looking over my shoulder, still imparting the right advice from the hereafter.

Musculature

In dealing with muscles, it is important to understand that the intrinsic muscles belong to the animal by virtue of the fact that the animal exists. The involuntary rhythm of the heart muscle is such an example. Extrinsic muscles are those that you see and are voluntary muscles. The intrinsic muscles control internal force and action, and extrinsic muscles provide range of movement and the limiting factors of their action.

Muscles acting in harmony with bone lengths and angles produce the potential of the canine machinery in motion. Natural muscle mass can do everything from working to prevent hip dysplasia to working to produce speed. When a breed standard calls for arch of neck, it is referring to the muscles that create the arch and give the neck strength. If an animal's neck is too short, the muscles are thick and stuffed, and the smoothness required of the arch is lost. Because muscles work from end to end, their length as well as their strength and efficiency develop in proportion to the leverage made available by their angulation. The muscles of the hindquarters are larger, thicker and more powerful than those of the front.

The very leverage that works for the animal in one location can work against the animal in another; for example, the 90-degree perfect scapula-humerus angle works for a long stride. Yet, too much angle in the pastern can cause excessive pressure and subsequent breakdown.

As the *master breeder* and dog person, you must look for the exactly correct skeleton for the breed of your choice. You would hope that the assembly of bones will then be accompanied by the most appropriate musculature for that specific dog. Do you now have the dog that is built right and moves right? Yes, if the rest of it is right.

Nerves

According to reports given at a symposium by the University of Pennsylvania, normal gait and locomotion are produced in cooperation with the complicated functions of the central and peripheral nervous system. Reading through some professional literature a number of years ago brought the realization that without a central nervous system delivering all the right signals, the bones and muscles could not act in the proper manner. There are some major differences involving the cerebral cortex in the central nervous system of humans when compared to that of man's best friend. Dogs have two more legs than man to coordinate into the complex weight-bearing process of movement.

This is far too complicated for me to understand, but the material was brought to my attention when one of our puppies started circling. Out came the references to see if I could figure out the problem. Although I never figured exactly what caused the puppy's problem, and unhappily he went on to develop hydrocephalous requiring euthanization, it brought home the delicate balance of the central nervous system and the absolute need for it to be in perfect working order for everything to fall into place for proper gait. The whole process of gait is just as dependent on the signal system as it is on that of the bones and the muscles.

Fuel Supply

Equally important to the resulting overall picture of gait is the fuel supply, or biochemical metabolic system. Perhaps the most in-depth studies of fuel consumption by the dog at work have been done in cooperation with participants in the famous Iditarod Race, a grueling race for man and dog over a one-thousand-mile-plus trail in Alaska, and that of racing Greyhounds. The muscle content of glycogen and triglycerides not only varies between amounts in the fast twitch muscle fiber and slow twitch fibers, it can vary from breed to breed and from individual to individual.

A large degree of input in the animal's ability to tolerate exercise will depend on the metabolic performance of the animal in relationship to energy provided by glucose and fatty acids. The best muscle is that muscle most able to oxidize these fuels. Slow walks at long distances increase endurance produced by slow twitch muscles. Interval training and sprinting practice improve fast twitch performance.

According to the work done and reported by Dr. David Kronfield (AKC *Gazette*), the animal's muscle health is a most delicate balance of aerobic and anaerobic processes, utilization of muscle fuels intra-muscularly and extra-muscularly, and correct metabolizing of carbohydrates and fat while exercising. For these processes to function perfectly, the protein buildup of muscle and red blood cells must also be in sync.

The muscle fiber type of each athlete—human or canine—will determine which job he does best. Animals that are speedsters need the burst of energy provided by fast twitch muscle fiber. Some animals are required to have both a burst of speed and endurance, and these athletes will have the required muscle fiber ration to achieve that. Sports medicine today is making rapid progress in helping us understand the various factors at play in the determination of an animal's ability to perform.

In observing dogs over the years, I've noticed that heavily muscled dogs that are over built will tire much faster than their correctly muscled competitors. Being muscle bound may be a turn on to weight lifting fans but it is not much use to the canine athlete. Lest you think it is simply lack of desire to keep on performing or lack of exercise conditioning, remember that sports medicine scientists think that the tendency is to inherit muscle fiber potential just like other characteristics. In essence, the canine athlete has to inherit all the other factors—including muscle fiber—as well as the skeleton to do it all.

Coming and Going

One of the most interesting and lively debates between world class dog experts occurred in the summer of 1976 when two celebrities engaged in a public literary debate in the *English Dog World*. Tom Horner, of Bull Terrier fame, set forth the concept that the great majority of breeds move the forelegs and hind legs parallel with the feet the same distance apart as the elbows and hocks. He was contradicting McDowell Lyon's thinking that as the speed increases, the hind legs will come toward the center line or converge for more efficient movement. Furthermore, his article in great depth challenged theories of Rachel Page Elliot and her conclusions as published in her book, *Dog Steps*, as well as on film. Horner's credentials in the terrier circles of England were impeccable and Mrs. Elliot is an internationally acclaimed expert on anatomy and dog gait. So respected is she in her own breed—the Golden Retriever—that the National Specialty was dedicated to her in 1993. As this book goes to press, the Parent Club is attempting to enlist the services of this grand lady of dogs for their educational forum to be held at its next national show in 1997.

The point that is important here is that these were world-class experts who could not agree on the coming-and-going movement as it applies to most breeds. The reason I emphasize this is because I feel breeders, exhibitors and judges do not always agree on it. Therefore, I take into account that those who want terrier-like parallel movement—I like to call it railroad track movement—are not going to be happy with a dog that converges, and *vice versa*.

In one of the best articles I have read on this subject (AKC *Gazette*—Pointer column), Wayne Cavanaugh described *soundness* as the absence of lameness, no interference of limbs, no observable abnormalities, and no wasted motion. In the most concise manner possible, Mr. Cavanaugh discussed the proper way to assess gait, in my opinion. It is cleanliness you are looking for when watching the animal come straight to you and go away. It is efficiency you are assessing from the side. The side view is the profile of type in motion.

In assessing my own dogs, I have always come up with some of the following thoughts: 1) The perfect dog will be utterly true coming and going and have a gorgeous free and easy side gait; 2) Since none of them are perfect, they must have two of these three to be excellent and more or less flawless; 3) One of the two must be the side picture to satisfy me.

In other words, I am trying to breed a high-stationed, short-coupled animal with lovely reach and drive obtained by excellent shoulder angulation and accompanied by a powerful driving rear. On a short-loined dog, this is not an easy task. A more rectangular dog can achieve this more easily. So if the dog is compensating a little at one end or the other, and does it well and athletically, he is acceptable to me. Such a dog was Smuggler. With tremendous rear drive and side gait, he would roll his front a little to get it out of the way of his powerful hind legs. He did not crab or side wind.

One summer when I had the time to work him up to it, I roadworked him up to seven miles at a steady trot. By the time he got to five miles, the roll got less and less, and at seven miles it was gone. (Why didn't I work him that far on the day of the show? Because his tongue hung out so far it took away his look and he loosened his tail too.) When he got tired, he stopped wasting motion. Probably he modified his strides by shortening them a little and no longer needed the slight roll to accommodate the longer stride.

In assessing well-angulated dogs with excellent side gait, you might have to be somewhat forgiving of coming and going. **Do not take this as a license to breed unsound dogs**. Because the well-angulated animal has so much more range of motion than his straighter-angled brethren, more potential exists for deviation and minor irregularities in coming and going, especially with square breeds.

Do not forgive straighter-angled dogs for being anything other than absolutely true on coming and going. Because of the reduced range of motion involved, the straighter-angled animal that moves poorly coming and going has more severe conformational defects than a simple deficiency of angulation.

COMING AND GOING
The Golden Retriever

Proper front, moving. The straight column of bones from point of shoulder to foot provides the most efficient transmission of power. The feet converge in order to stay near the centerline of gravity, but never interfere with each other. The faster the trot, the more the feet will tend to converge. A dog is single tracking when the feet are set down directly ahead of one another on the line of travel. This is not a fault, unless the dog is interfering. Because of the well-developed chest, a retriever should not be expected to move as smoothly in front as some other breeds; but he must move easily and efficiently. Single tracking or crossing over as a result of some structural fault is, of course, undesirable.

Good rear at the trot. As the feet converge with increased speed, the straight line from hip to foot is maintained. Convergence allows the dog to more easily keep his center of gravity over the line of travel, (i.e., over the point of support). Correct Golden Retriever "coming" and "going" courtesy of Marcia Schlehr.

Correct movement coming as exhibited by Ch. Vin-Melca's Vagabond at Lake Tahoe in 1969. Working in snow or wet sand will allow you to check your dog's tracks. This picture illustrates the front legs converging toward the centerline at a fast trot. Notice the straight column of support that stabilizes the dog's center of gravity at this gait. (Photo by Jayne Langdon)

Because a dog has lovely side gait does not mean it can resemble a mix-master coming and going. Any useful animal who does not have the side gait that I love must have totally clean front and rear coming and going or it will not get into my breeding program. Nor does being totally sound coming and going forgive a dog for not having adequate side gait. For me to want to breed to it, it has to have at least two of the three—preferably one of those is side gait. I take comfort in this quotation from the Brittany standard: "Clean movement, coming and going, is very important; but most important is side gait, which is smooth, efficient and ground covering."

Back to School

In geometry class you learned that the whole equals the sum of its parts. And in physics you learned that a vital role is played by the center of gravity when discussing motion. Now you are trying to put all of this together in your attempts to master the notion of motion, and you don't have to be Euclid to understand it.

The center of gravity is the point at which the weight is concentrated, or that point at which all weight is evenly distributed around it. Hypothetically, this is the point at which the dog would be balanced if you suspended him in the air. It is the balancing point at which all forces are equal. Gravity itself is the acceleration of the dog's body toward the core of the Earth. If you have ever taken a spill in a ring with a concrete floor, you know how strong it can be.

The center of gravity is constantly being displaced when the dog is in motion. The better the athlete the less the center is displaced. The less the variation of the center of gravity, the greater the athlete's ability. Experts say that single tracking at some gaits reduces the stress of excess displacement of the center of gravity. In most dogs the center of gravity is located near the lower front area of the chest.

Several things can change the center of gravity for a dog: 1) The longer the body, the further the center of gravity is from the front; 2) The neck is too long or too short; 3) The head is exceptionally large; 4) The front is exceptionally wide and heavy; 5) The loin is exceptionally long; 6) The legs are too long and open-angled and the animal is straight shouldered; 7) The legs are too short.

If you were breeding Bulldogs, your studies would teach you that the Bulldog's center of gravity is low and much more forward than that of almost any other breed. Remember that the origin of the dog had him hanging onto a bull, and although that sport has been outlawed for well over a century, breeders must strive to breed the dog that looks like it could do the job. A Bulldog was built heavy in the front and lighter in the rear so that his weight would be where he needed it—up close to the bull. A

Left: Ch. Vin-Melca's The Smuggler was a dog of exceptional angulation who was also high-stationed and extremely short in loin. His configuration accompanied by a marvelous temperament made him a personal favorite. Pictured here winning BIS under Judge Roland E. Adameck at Longview-Kelso Kennel Club, he was the #2 hound in the U.S. Sired by Ch. Vin-Melca's Nimbus X Ch. Vin-Melca's Victoria, Smuggler won 25 All Breed BISs, including Chicago International. (Photo by Carl Lindemaier) **Right:** Smuggler pictured at Westminster where he was second in the Hound Goup in 1985. (Photo by Callea)

lighter rear end not only made the job easier, it also put less stress on the dog's back as the bull tried to throw him off. The Bulldog's enormously heavy head and shorter neck with its well-muscled arch all contributed to a forward center of gravity enabling him to do that job.

There is a very good reason in the job description of each breed that accounts for a somewhat different location of the center of gravity in various breeds of dogs. No matter where the center of gravity is located on a given breed, remember that the great athletes in any breed are the ones with the most stable center of gravity. When the center of gravity is constantly off balance, it causes a greater expenditure of energy and less ease of movement. Athletes are adept at handling the changing center of gravity to a new base of support, whether Bulldog, German Shepherd Dog or Miniature Pinscher.

Athletic ability has a similar grace in man, dog, horse or bird. This is why your studies should include watching great athletes at work as well as watching animals from other species in motion. Athletic prowess is achieved in many sporting endeavors by the best combination of conformation, musculature, balance, coordination, conditioning, training and the will to win.

That all-important will to win gives the dog the desire and character to perform, whether it is a Bulldog, German Shepherd Dog or Miniature Pinscher. Yet the cooperation of a skilled handler is necessary to show the unique gait of each breed to its best advantage.

The capable Bulldog handler will allow his charge to roll into its unique and peculiar gait in which a loose-jointed shuffle produces the desired sidewise motion. The Shepherd handler will give his dog the freedom of movement to show his extraordinary elasticity, and the Miniature Pinscher will be encouraged to show off his high-stepping, free-reaching, hackney-like action to best advantage. These handlers understand that the correct communication through the lead signals the dog on how to use his head, and where the head goes, the body will follow. With the proper teamwork of man and dog, the absolute correct picture of proper gait for the breed is achieved. Correct gait as it appears in the ring is the culmination of selective breeding, proper conditioning and proper presentation.

The athletic dog will move with little effort and perform his job easily. His ability to do that job is dependent upon the following: 1) A skeleton that has correct relationship of bones to themselves and

LEARNING TO THINK BREED SPECIFIC

No matter which breed you select, you *must* have both general and breed specific knowledge in order to do your breed justice. Since the Bulldog is a very unique fellow, let's take a look at some specific things about the beloved "sourmug."

In viewing the sketch looking down on the breed, the reader can see that most of the dog's weight is in the front end, giving him a forward-placed center of gravity. This forward-placed center of gravity must work in concert with the longer rear legs, accounting for the unusual rear assembly that allows the hocks to turn somewhat inward and the toes to turn somewhat outward in what is usually described as cow-hocked, although this term is not included in the Bulldog standard.

We are indebted to the work of the Bulldog Club of America for attempting to clear up some of the misinterpretations about this most unique gait. Historically, British Bulldog fanciers have used the idea that the Bulldog leads with his shoulder while gaiting,

resulting in a sidewinding sort of motion along with the characteristic shuffle. The Bulldog Club of America Education Committee believes the correctly-made Bulldog can achieve the loose-jointed, shuffling, sidewise motion that gives the characteristic roll required by the standard without crabbing or sidewinding. The diagram (below) shows the straight path of the widely-set front legs and the close-moving in-and-out track of the rear legs.

This combination produces the sidewise roll of the breed, which can be verified by watching the path of the tail or the skin over the loin. This roll in the rear accommodates the forward center of gravity as well as coordinates with it. If Bulldogs are your breed, you would have to know these specific and most unusual traits of breed type in order to breed and show correct Bulldogs. And this holds true no matter what your breed of choice might be. For every breed has some nuances about it, major and/or minor, that set that breed apart and contribute to its type.

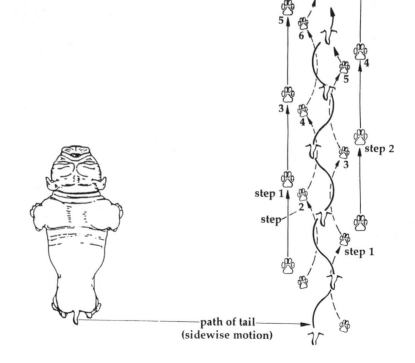

Gait. The style and carriage are peculiar, his gait being a loose-jointed, shuffling, sidewise motion, giving the characteristic "roll." The action must, however, be unrestrained, free and vigorous. NOTE: The trace of the tail, left to right to left to right, provides the sidewise motion and, with all other gait characteristics, the very desirable "roll" is obtained. (Drawing by Russ Thomas, Text by Robert Newcomb. Courtesy of the Bulldog Club of America)

path of tail (sidewise motion)

KEEP MOVING

To get into all the elements that constitute great movement, you need to do your homework. There are some wonderful books out there by the experts, such as McDowell Lyon, Curtis Brown, Rachel Page Elliot, and Casey Gardiner. It is important for you to use the experts to give you adequate knowledge to make decisions upon which your gene pool will depend.

If you have been athletic and are an involved sports fan, watch the great sporting contests on television to expand your horizons. Especially vital for your learning are events involving horses and track and field events featuring world class human athletes. Participation will enrich your knowledge even more, not to mention your physique. On your morning jogs notice how some of the runners on the track do it with effortless ease. Others exhibit wasted motion with some having such off-set knees (knock knees) they not only waste motion but suffer from a poor column of support. If you get in good enough shape to run in a regular five or 10K race, you will see fewer participants with faulty conformation and unathletic gait than you see on your morning jogs. This is because it is too demanding on them to push themselves to the next plateau.

Not all gold medal sprinters come at you the same even though there are half as many legs involved to produce variables. Some sprinters will get more knee action than others. Some will have a carriage all their own. Some will have foot placements varying slightly from the runners they are trying to beat.

But all of the sprinters will have powerful buttocks and "hams," for that is where their speed comes from. Champion sprinters like Donovan Bailey, Carl Lewis, Michael Johnson and the great "Flojo" will have shorter, thicker muscles—fast twitch—when compared to the musculature of a distance runner whose muscles tend to be longer and flatter because their activity requires the endurance of the slow-twitch muscles. Take it to the next level—that of the champion marathon runner and you will notice an even greater difference.

Dog handlers, as well as their exhibits, must be fit and athletic to give the ultimate performance. That is why some of the best performances are turned in by the pair—dog and handler—who work out together. In addition to giving the handler an appreciation of

the dog's athleticism that the brief time in the show ring may not allow, it is a bonding process that brings a better sense of togetherness to the team. If your situation does not lend itself to working out with your dog, there are other ways to stay in shape. Mary Roberts, award-winning owner/handler, jumped rope to maintain the endurance required to show her well-known German Shepherds.

The author, pictured here in 1956 participating in a track and field event, has been a runner all her life. She still runs with her dogs today and plans to continue as along as she is physically able. (Photo courtesy of College of William and Mary, Norfolk Division)

each other, including correct angles; 2) Musculature and flexibility; 3) Neurological system that sends all the right messages with appropriate reflexes; 4) Biochemical system utilizing the correct nutrition in the body's fuel system; 5) True teamwork achieved by the desire of the dog and the cooperation of the handler.

Evaluating Your Dog's Gait

Sometimes it seems gait is analyzed to the extreme. Watching some dog shows it appears that certainly there is a great deal of concentration on watching the dog go down and back. The most knowledgeable of the judges will spend more time evaluating the dog's side gait, for that is the most important view from which to judge the overall dog. It is the picture of type in motion.

This profile view allows you to see if maximum distance is being covered with the least amount of effort. Correct side gait is efficient and unlabored, elastic and free. It is important to remember that many dogs with seemingly correct footfall when viewed from the front or the rear fall apart when viewed from the side.

Your job is to be your own multipurpose person—that is, to evaluate the gait as though you were a discerning expert in your breed. Study your breed. Each breed has its own nuances that you must know in order to evaluate it in a meaningful way. Please remember that much of the material in this book is generic and it is your job to make it breed specific. Assume the roles of breeder, handler, trainer, judge and competitor when you evaluate or you will get lost. Here are some ways to study and watch your dogs:

1. Sit in your yard on the outside of the fence and wait for your dogs to lose interest in you. Then watch them move around on their own as you evaluate them for athletic ability, grace and ease of movement. Make notes on how they do it and save the notes for later references. If possible with your setup, watch them from your window as they move across and around the yard.

2. Invite a good friend with great knowledge of dogs to help you study. Be open-minded and receptive to this knowledgeable person's input and objectivity. That person is doing you a great service.

3. Have someone else move the dog for you. Study it coming and going and spend a lot of time watching it from the side.

4. Work the dog on foot, beside a bicycle, or—with great caution—beside the car. Watch and study it carefully, using a loose lead.

5. Videotape the dog under good conditions and run the video over and over in slow motion and at regular speeds. Compare your dog's gait with those on the breed video available from the AKC. Have your trusted friends help you make those comparisons.

6. And finally, ask yourself if this is the ultimate athleticism to perform the job the dog was bred to do. Would you risk your life on it? It's your call! If you have studied all of this, you might be the exact mathematical expert who now understands that the whole equals the sum of its parts and most of all, you know what these parts are.

History and Purpose of Your Breed

Understanding the historical purpose of your breed helps you develop a feel for it. An in-depth study and research of the beginnings of your breed and the purpose for which it was developed are absolutely necessary to aid you in your quest to become a *master breeder*. Many of the cosmetic window dressings that make dogs pretty in the eyes of the uneducated would not be sought by those well-meaning people if they understood the breed. It means the dog would be at a disadvantage doing his job and even might suffer from the consequences. I am grateful to Leo Tolstoy for the following observation: "It is amazing how complete is the delusion that beauty is goodness."

There is no better example of that than the coat of the Norwegian Elkhound, or any other breed whose original job involved being exposed to the extreme elements of a rugged climate. An Elkhound's coat should be harsh and weather resistant on the outside and the second coat—undercoat—should be soft and protective. An Elkhound with a beautiful but incorrect open coat would not be protected while hunting in the harsh environment of the moose in Norway—tracking through alternately freezing and thawing waters that must be repelled by the proper coat. In fact, the sameness of the open coat means that when the dog gets wet, the wet penetrates right to the skin. The harsh outercoat on the correct dog will keep the undercoat dry and warm.

In the more than 45 years that I have been involved in this breed, there have been unique stories about dogs' coats that were the result of the talkers being ignorant of the facts. One example that comes to my mind was an early Best in Show Norwegian Elkhound of the 1950s—Ch. Baard of Greenwood. Baard was bred by Linda Scott, owned by Worth and Kay Fowler, and handled by E.R. "Bob" Hastings, today a multi-group judge.

Baard had a correct, close, hard coat with a quite adequate undercoat. Because it was a flatter, shorter coat than the numerous and somewhat open-coated dogs being shown against him (and incidentally beaten by him) his competitors circulated rumors that Bob was clipping his dog's coat. It is one thing to over trim an Elkhound's underline, tail and breeches to create a synthetic sculptured look, but it would be quite another to clip it all over. For each of the guard hairs on an Elkhound has three definite segments starting with the lightest color at the hide and ending with black on the tips. To trim the dog as accused would mean to remove the black guard hair, which of course, had not been done. Because Baard was being shown against some very plush open-coated dogs, it was assumed he was wrong.

The flat desired coat is difficult to find these days but as important as ever. This is not about being the prettiest dog. It is about being the best dog. The best dog is one that satisfies the original purpose the dog was bred to perform in the historical context of the development of the breed. (See Type and Soundness.)

Many breeds are blessed with those of pure vision who have studied their breeds and have seen the light. These dedicated dog people have become missionaries and guardians whose twofold purpose is to take the message of their breed to all while serving as the protectors and caretakers of the breed's original purpose and function.

George Bell of the famous Bel S'Mbran Salukis is such a person. George videos Saluki specialties and makes the tapes available to judges and others who would learn more about his breed. He provides commentary and critiquing of dogs to such students in every setting from one-on-one to large numbers at seminars. He travels at his own expense to do whatever he can for the good of the order—spreading the word of truth about his breed.

This is no personal agenda for this man, as he and his wife, Sally, have already done it all with such great animals as Ch. Bel S'Mbran Bachrach and Ch. Bel S'Mbran Aba Fantasia. Furthermore, they have always practiced what they preached, as their coursing activities date back decades. Well over 25 years ago, they had developed films they shared at hound seminars on the double suspension gallop of the sighthound. In discussing Salukis with George, not only will one get the total feel for the breed, but one will also learn the small nuances of the Saluki that usually go overlooked. For example, the Beduoins preferred the Saluki to toe out slightly to assist it in quick and sudden turns in the desert. Although it does not appear in the breed standard, one would not want to fault a Saluki unduly for what some experts consider a desired trait, even if one did not reward it.

Marcia Schlehr is on a similar mission on behalf of her favorite breed, the Golden Retriever. Marcia is among those dedicated to preserving the qualities for which the breed was developed to work in the chilliest of waters and handling various vegetation in pursuit of the game. Recognizing the inherent dangers to any breed that has become as popular as the Golden has led Marcia to develop a very special publication affectionately called the "blue book" of Goldens (A Study of the Golden Retriever) to assist fanciers in a better appreciation of the traits that constitute excellent breed type. This work is designed to avoid the cosmetic Golden unable to withstand the rigors associated with the hunting and retrieving of upland game and waterfowl. Marcia's personal mission dates to 1967 when she began doing illustrated work for the Parent Club newsletter.

Falsely accused of a clipped coat, Ch. Baard of Greenwood was a BIS Norwegian Elkhound of 1958. Baard's correct, close coat was criticized by unknowing competitors whose own open-coated dogs led them mistakenly to think he was clipped. E.R. (Bob) Hastings handled for owners Kay and Worth Fowler. (Roberts Photo)

Mentor extraordinaire George Bell handles Saluki Ch. Bel S'Mbran Aba Fantasia to the 1982 Westminster Hound Group blue under Judge Mrs. James E. Clark. A homebred co-owned with wife Sally, "Fanny" exemplifies the breed type of this exotic Eastern breed. Today, her breeders are on a mission to take the message of retaining the purity of the breed to those who wish to learn. The famous Riverlawn Irish Wolfhound name is represented by trophy presenter Peter R. Van Brunt. (Photo courtesy of John L. Ashbey)

Jeffrey Pepper is a dual-purpose missionary whose pursuit of excellence embraces both the Golden Retriever and Petit Basset Griffon Vendeen (PBGV) in particular and a number of other breeds in general. Jeff's work, like Marcia's, has involved him in any number of seminars, breed study groups, and other educational activities. His published materials have been used by judges and breeders as references in their quest to improve their knowledge about these breeds. Furthermore, his responsibilities include involvement in volunteer work in a number of organizations dedicated to dogs and those who love them.

The PBGV breed is also fortunate to have Nick and Ellen Frost among its advocates. They are dedicated to keeping this ancient breed, new to the American dog-show scene, true to its original purpose, size and temperament, as well as its presentation in the ring. This naturally casual and tousled animal with its delightfully extroverted attitude is not just a rough-coated Basset Hound, and it is good to know that these guardians of the breed are available to guide the breed's future in the right direction.

To hear Joel Samaha, professor and teacher extraordinaire, lecture on his breed is akin to sitting at the side of Socrates as one learns applied philosophy about the Irish Wolfhound. Joel's disciples in turn help take the message to the fancy about their beloved breed, and those who enter this realm develop an enduring appreciation for the splendor that is this giant greyhound-like animal. Surrounded by a literal ton of Wolfhounds, Joel will walk and talk through them with exacting standards that create an understanding of the strength and speed that each dog possesses along with the important attribute of commanding appearance. It is a genuine learning experience.

The revered Muriel Freeman has spent a lifetime devoted to protecting her favorite breed, the Rottweiler. This elegant lady has unselfishly given hours and hours of her time and expertise to help those in her breed understand the physical attributes of the breed and its mentality. She has educated one and all on who should own this breed and how it should be nurtured, especially conscious of the perils threatening any guard dog breed of such rapidly growing popularity. This has been achieved through seminars, educational groups, lectures and writing the definitive book on the breed.

The point of all of this is that there are missionaries out there whose purpose it is to protect their chosen breeds from fad and fashion so that it represents the true traditions of its historical development and original purpose. These experts are writers, lecturers, breed mentors and friends. It is your job as a prospective *master breeder* to seek out these people and utilize them so that you, too, will become a guardian of your breed as well as a fancier. You will know you are on the road to becoming an expert in your breed when you can take the previously mentioned Tolstoy quote and turn it around so that the goodness (read correctness) of the animal is what represents beauty to you, not some pretty trapping that has nothing to do with the correctness of the breed nor its purpose.

Sometimes even Parent Clubs as influential as the Doberman Pinscher Club of America (DPCA) are unable to stop the caprices of fad and fancy. Consider the recent infatuation with the albinoid Doberman now occurring in the breed. Not only does this genetic misfit have no historical background or

Bad things happen in the best of families as proved by these snapshots of a dwarf Norwegian Elkhound puppy of Vin-Melca breeding whelped in the 1970s. Although appropriately neutered and placed in a pet home, this puppy nonetheless left a permanent message as his legacy; and that is that all breeds have the potential of mutations that take them away from their purpose. Even if such mutations should "catch on" with the consumer as a cute fad, they are wrong and must be guarded against by the responsible breeder. (Photos by Nance Richbourg)

purpose, it is a color freak of nature associated with a wide variety of health disorders. The worst nightmare scenarios of those who opposed blues and fawns being accepted 40 years ago are now coming true.

Meanwhile, the DPCA in its role as the breed's guardian is attempting to deal with this problem and not compromise the breed's gene pool. All breeds have the potential to become the victims of genetic mutation as well as genetic drift that takes the breed away from its original purpose. No matter how rare and unusual something of this nature may be, it is not necessarily desirable.

Because we live in a marketing-oriented society, any breed has the potential to be subjected to outside influences that would take it astray from its original purpose. These influences become all the more dangerous when they come from inside the fancy. If you are going to dedicate yourself to a breed and pursue a program aimed at achieving *master breeder* status, then accepting the responsibility of preserving the integrity of your breed's original purpose is a very important part of the overall picture. Anything less is a "cop out."

Knowing Your Breed Standard

"A breed standard is, by definition, the description of the ideal specimen of the breed. It is the word pattern breeders are striving to create in living flesh. It is the word pattern by which dogs are judged at shows." (AKC's *Guide for Writing Breed Standards* with permission from AKC)

One might wonder why there is such a variety in the format and definition of the breeds as far as standards go. The answer lies in antiquity and in modernity and everywhere in between. The answer lies in those who wrote a brief, to the point standard for their breed, assuming as Mr. Jefferson so succinctly stated in the Declaration of Independence that some *truths are self-evident*. It also lies with those who thought every inch of the dog and every nuance of the breed should be described in minute detail to the "nth" degree—and somewhere in between!

A brief history of breed standards is in order. Although it can hardly be termed a word picture as such, the Old Testament portion of the *Holy Bible* describes the Greyhound as "comely in going" (written by King Solomon in Proverbs 30:29-31). The first reported breed standard was written in Greek almost two thousand years ago and described a good Greyhound. The author was Arrian of Nicomedia, a Grecian historian and philosopher under the rule of the Romans, Hadrian and Marcus Aurelius. The standard appeared in a book he wrote on Greyhounds and coursing. It described, among other things, the breed as being lengthy from head to tail with light and well-articulated heads. It was a much lengthier standard than the standard by which the breed is currently judged in the show ring. Greyhound history buffs would applaud many of the descriptions of the dog, including broad loins and sweeping, firm haunches. This historical document was translated into English in the mid-19th Century.

The Stonehenge works of 1867 and thereafter carried written models for several breeds. Written by John Henry Walsh (who judged at England's first official dog show in 1859), the book divided the dogs into forerunners of what we know today as groups—divisions made according to the work of the dog: scent hounds, sight hounds, bird dogs, draft dogs, and flock dogs or keepers of livestock. Terriers were categorized appropriately with hunting dogs in those formative years.

FOUR BREEDS THAT KEPT THEIR INDIVIDUALITY*

In 1929, when the AKC published its first Complete Dog Book (the first edition was known as *Purebred Dogs*) the book carried a disclaimer stating that the AKC "assumes no responsibility for drawing up or forming these standards." Thus, those breeds submitting standards for that edition were submitting standards not officially approved by AKC. In the event that their Parent Clubs have been satisfied with those standards, choosing not to change the standard in the ensuing years, their standards were not officially approved. Ever wonder why there is no date on the standards of the Bloodhound, Greyhound, American Foxhound or Saluki in the 1992 edition (most recent) of *The Complete Dog Book*? You can look it up!

*In 1996, the American Bloodhound Club produced an updated version of the standard now approved by the AKC.

As breed-specific groups of fanciers formed, their clubs continued to perfect the breed standards to ensure that the judge and the breeder had written directions to get everybody on the same wave lengths. These standards found their way to our shores along with the quality animals that came from Europe to the United States.

Early American breed clubs called the shots on writing their breed standards, which gave them a common-law right to the breed standards. This precedent caused the AKC some problems with several of the breed clubs in the 1980s and 1990s, when the attempt was made to reformat all the breed standards to a conforming chronology, format and language. The issue resurfaced when the question arose as to whom the standards actually belonged to—AKC or to the breed clubs. Obviously, the system for achieving the right standard for each breed can only work properly when the Parent Club and the AKC work in concert for the good of the breed.

Many breed standards, such as those of Foxhounds, were created by horsemen who used terminology familiar to them. This resulted in continuing discussion about what was meant by such terms as "standing over a lot of ground," for example. The horsemen took for granted that some things are implied. Because the English Foxhound standard does not specify how Foxhounds should gait, does this mean it is of no concern to the breeder? Indeed not! It means that this long-lived (1935) standard written by horsemen assumes one can take the word picture and translate it into correct English Foxhound movement.

Just the description of shoulder and "true arm" (upper arm) tells you the animal is expected to have good reach. The hindquarters are called propellers, meaning they are expected to drive the dog. Like a good hunter's horse then, the English Foxhound should have good reach and drive if one correctly converts this word picture to movement.

Since the horseman considers sound to mean absence of lameness, no interference or wasted motion, and normal athletic useful motion, it was not deemed necessary to go into that in the standard. If you are going to breed foxhounds, you best learn when to go to the past to find the answers upon which to make breeding decisions for the future.

This is true for any breed. If you want to breed the correct animal, you must know its origin and history to understand why the given animal emerged in the correct form for its breed. A culmination of history, purpose of the breed, and the knowledge of good dogmen as to what build made the dog best to satisfy its purpose is how fanciers arrived at the breed standard. Because breed standards are not perfect—after all they are the product of human endeavor—it is important to know when and why to go beyond the standard to attain information that will make it possible for you to know your breed extensively.

A breed standard can be described as the design, or blueprint, for a particular breed of dog. It is a word picture of the prototype of that breed, the standard of perfection. It is the criterion by which every dog is measured. Just as the Constitution is a documentary blueprint for a specific government, so then is the breed standard a written plan or design for a specific breed of dog. As such, each breed standard is an important document, a document created by a committee of intellectuals with a common interest.

All important documents are used in different ways by those who refer to them. A Supreme Court justice refers to the Constitution in seeking guidance to form legal opinions, probing not just the document itself but other relevant information with an expert eye in the continuous search for the proper function and intent of the law as well as its application. Such individual expertise is based on years of schooling, study, research and experience. Furthermore, the resources involved are built upon centuries of history recorded by mankind.

A world-class dog expert uses the available guiding documents in much the same way, going beyond a studied knowledge of the breed standard to the unwritten laws that played a part in its creation. This is not to imply that the chief justice or the dog judge ever disregard the guiding document. Because of this intense research and knowledge, however, they do reach the ultimate in understanding the document and the particular reasons for certain nuances that might otherwise go unexplained.

The Border Terrier standard refers to the fact that the head resembles that of an otter in the GENERAL APPEARANCE, while the section on HEAD elaborates on the Border Terrier head. (Photo by Michael Work)

The average citizen must know something about the Constitution in order to be an informed voter and an individual who knows his own rights. So must the average dog fancier have a similar working knowledge of his favorite breed's standard to be an astute participant in the activities of that breed. And just as the citizen realizes the trials and tribulations legislation is exposed to in committees, so too must the dog person realize the breed standard is the product of man operating in committees. As such, standards are often wordy, sometimes contradictory, and seldom simple. Like legislation, standards are often subjected to amendments, compromises and adjustments to satisfy those whose opinions and support are necessary to pass them into law. Therefore, the end product may no longer satisfy the purist because to get it passed involved those compromises. Nonetheless, the process seems to work.

Dog judges and breeders have studied the blueprint and are in a position to use the document in the best interests of the breed. Knowing how to utilize what is implied as well as what is explained is part of their expertise. How to use the document of choice is of interest to all fanciers, from the world-class dog person to the eager novice with his first purebred dog.

The most important part of a well-written breed standard is the **General Appearance** that describes the breed in a word picture and is the design of the dog, especially when studied with the **Proportion** section. The **General Appearance** and **Proportion** sections combine to describe the make and shape of the breed and are absolutely necessary to comprehend the essence of breed type. Is the dog square? Off square? Rectangular? Elongated? Is the dog racy? Chunky? Curved? Angled? Built for endurance? Built for speed? A worker? A hunter? A lap dog? These are the questions that, when answered properly by the standard, give one the correct feel for the breed.

In order to know a breed, it is absolutely necessary to know what features make the breed unique. Often those features will be presented in the **General Appearance** and elaborated upon in the appropriate section of the standard. For example, the **General Appearance** for the Border Terrier refers to the fact that the head resembles that of the otter while the section on **Head** describes the head in greater detail.

One problem in studying standards occurs in the section entitled **Proportion**. Most standards calling for a square dog describe the square formed by equal distances from forechest to rump and withers or top of shoulders to ground. Other standards draw attention to the distance from withers to tail and withers to ground as equal This is a matter of semantics, as when discussing proportion with the experts in those breeds, it sounds as though the intent is about the same. The Standard Schnauzer standard calls for the height at the highest point of the withers to be equal to the length from breastbone to point of rump. The English Springer Spaniel standard, as published in AKC's 1992 edition of *The Complete Dog Book*, states that the length of topline (the distance from top of the shoulders to the root of the tail) should be approximately equal to the dog's shoulder height. Realizing that this actually described a rather long dog—not their intent at all—the Parent Club revised the standard recently even though it had been reformatted in 1989. Now it describes the length from point of shoulder to buttocks.

Another breed that acknowledged the language confusion was the English Cocker Spaniel. In 1988, the Parent Club changed its description from "length of back from withers to tail set should approximate height from ground to withers" to "...with height at withers slightly greater than the distance from withers to set-on of tail." One of the advantages in dealing with standards is that Parent Clubs have the

This AKC computer interpretation of square as described in the outdated English Cocker Spaniel standard: "...length of back from withers to tail set should approximate height from ground to withers." The literal interpretation of the standard by computer shows the dog in the upper illustration to be a very long dog indeed, certainly not the intent of the Parent Club. When measured literally, this translates to the "drag of the breed" rather than a correct English Cocker. Acknowledging that this matter of semantics was misleading, the Parent Club changed the breed standard to read as follows: "...with height at the withers slightly greater than the distance from withers to set-on of tail." Reflecting this change, the lower illustration is more what English Cocker fanciers have in mind. (Computer work courtesy of AKC)

right and responsibility to change them when change will bring a better understanding of the breed to the fancy. This is an important area to study, and if you are not sure what your standard is requiring, ask the experts in your breed to clarify the meaning.

Perhaps the Great Dane standard states proportion in the best terms: "In ratio between length and height, the Great Dane should be square." In the same vein, the Lakeland Terrier standard says: "The dog is squarely built." It is interesting that both of these standards make an allowance for the bitch. Most standards describing off-square or rectangular proportion are usually clear.

The expert's eye evaluates the **Proportion** of the animal in a heartbeat. The less-skilled eye will take longer to measure the animal's profile to determine if it meets a particular standard's requirement for square, off-square or rectangular or elongated.

In the coated breeds, the job may be more difficult and call for the hands to verify if the distance from the elbow to the ground is indeed half the height of the dog at the withers, and so on. Height can be deceiving in some of the coated breeds with the ruff giving the animal an appearance of being larger than it actually is. This is also true of dogs who carry themselves with a lot of confidence to appear taller than they measure.

Substance is usually simply stated in standards and relatively easy to interpret. The descriptions of substance are logical and in accordance with the animal's job description. To read the Borzoi description of the "bones straight and somewhat flattened like blades" gives one a serious feel for the elegance of this breed, as does the simple statement "fine bone" in the Italian Greyhound standard.

The respected Derek Rayne has long made the statement: "You should be able to tell what breed it is if all you can see is the head." This on-target quotation says it all. Does the picture created by head, ear and eye project the character of the breed? Undeniably, some breeds are more of a head breed than others, with more emphasis placed on the head by the standard. Collies and Bulldogs come to mind, as do Pekingese and Pugs.

The **Neck, Topline** and **Body**, like the **General Appearance** and **Proportion** sections, help create the picture of the breed—that is the profile or type of the dog. This picture starts with the head and follows the contours to the tail. The basic progenitor of dogs was a wolflike animal with moderate

SHOW RING EXAMINATION

"Putting your hands in all the right places" was the title for an ad in *Dog News* in 1989 using these candid shots taken during the BIS judging at Longview-Kelso Kennel Club. The ad spotlighted the top left photo with the judge checking shoulder angulation. The next photo shows the judge checking loin length and coupling. The bottom left photo shows the hindquarters being evaluated and the bottom right photo shows the Elkhound standing on her own. This was one of 66 All Breed Best in Shows won by Ch. Vin-Melca's Calista, fondly known as Sarah. It was the only BIS awarded a Vin-Melca dog by the Judge Charles E. (Chuck) Trotter, as he and the author were married in 1994. (Photos are courtesy of Callea Photos, who sent an album with the entire collection as a wedding present.)

length of neck and back—off-square to slightly rectangular. Thanks to breeding efforts over hundreds of years, many different body types have emerged as described by their breed standards.

When some breed standards seem to test nature by calling for a short body and good length of neck, these standards usually describe this picture as it is created by well-laid back shoulder blades and a short coupling. In order to judge the length of loin (coupling) on a coated breed, the judge will put hands on the area between the last rib and the hindquarters. Short-coupled animals will have the rear assembly close to the rib cage. Animals who combine a short rib cage with a long loin for an illusory look of squareness in a breed calling for a short-coupled, square dog have combined two faults. It is almost a case of *two wrongs do make a right*, only the so-called *right* in this case is not only fraudulent, it is not the correct square, and the breeder has two difficult problems to correct.

In assessing **Forequarters**, horse people place great value on correctness because that is where valuable animals *break down* under stress when they are not correctly made. Dog people must also value correct forequarters, for they play such a huge role in an animal's proficiency level in gaiting. Not only will well-laid back shoulders feel smooth to the hand, the blades will tilt toward the tail end of the dog. A number of standards describe the distance between the blades at their tip. The Brittany standard calls for them to have "perhaps two thumbs' width between" while the Samoyed standard states: "The withers separation should be approximately 1 - 1 1/2 inches."

While the front end guides the dog, the hind end propels it and most standards describe this driving power in their sections on **Hindquarters**. Several standards appropriately acknowledge that their breeds tend to come to the center line—converge—as the speed of the trot increases. Standard committees over the years have found this subject to be a controversial one in some breeds. Some of the committee members will embrace the previously mentioned Tom Horner theory while others will follow McDowell Lyon and Rachel Page Elliot in their school of thought.

When describing coat, the standard will present the function of the breed as vital because **Coat** is a lot more than cosmetic. Consider the Otterhound standard that states, "Coat texture and quality are more important than length," and then goes on to elaborate that, "A naturally stripped coat lacking length and fringes is correct for an Otterhound that is being worked." Some standards detail desired trimming and grooming to guide both exhibitors and judges, while others call for the dog to be shown in a more natural state.

In studying the standard for **Color**, standards should spell out which colors are acceptable if all colors are not permitted. A number of standards designate color deviations as disqualifications.

Not to be neglected is the very important part of the standard relating to **Temperament**. Judges, breeders and exhibitors must guard against poor temperament in all breeds, keeping in mind that each breed was developed to be its own special version of man's best friend. The historical context of the animal's disposition and character suited the animal to the task his master wished performed.

Therefore, the more one knows about the history of the breed and its purpose, as well as the function and essence of type, the better one is able to use the strengths of the standard to breed better dogs while accepting the standard's weaknesses and dealing with them accordingly.

Perhaps you breed Gordon Setters, for example, and the standard asks for an approximate 90-degree angulation of shoulder blade and upper arm, with shoulders "laying well back." The standard also calls for a straight pastern. You find it hard to get both of these in the same dog. Which would you sacrifice to get the essence of the gun dog? One would hope it would not be the shoulder!

Knowing which elements of the standard are vital to the breed and take precedence over others will determine what type of breeder you will be. The breed standard must serve as your bible, but remember, even Lucifer can justify his actions through misleading quotations taken out of context from the good book. Nonetheless, just as the *Holy Bible* is the reference for practicing Christians, so is the *standard* the reference for practicing breeders. You must give it more than lip service.

Type and Soundness, or is it Type Versus Soundness?

No subject in the world can cause more controversy when introduced into a conversation of any gathering of dog people than the issue of which is more important: type or soundness. Sometimes it comes out as type versus soundness, almost like a football game or some other competitive activity. The implication is that the two are incompatible.

Type is what differentiates one breed from another. It is the collection of all the characteristics and traits that make a given breed different from others. It is apparent in the contour, make and shape of the animal. It is the essence of the breed in looks and behavior, in ability and in function.

In the words of Golden Retriever expert Marcia R. Schlehr in *Dog News*, July 1995: "Type is far more than merely 'beauty.' Type is what makes a breed itself and not something else—and it is inescapably, though not exclusively, linked to function."

Experts may answer the question of which is more important by saying: "You can't have type without soundness." Certainly in an ideal world, no typey dogs would lack soundness. Literally speaking, the experts are right as we shall see. Perhaps the statement should be altered just a tad to become, "You shouldn't have type without soundness." Why? Because the original look and character—the make and shape—of every breed was achieved by nature in cooperation with primitive hunters who picked the better conformed dogs to do their jobs over the centuries. Even though some poorly made animals would excel from time to time because of their uncommon heart and desire, most of the time animals who best performed their jobs were those who found it easiest to perform their jobs because they were made right for that job. So the caveman was selecting for type even though he did not know it.

In essence, the performance or job description determined the contour and look of the animal. The job provided the test for soundness by demanding it for both the work of the breed and the natural evolution of the breed to take place. Call it Mother Nature at work.

Remember, in those days there were no veterinary hospitals to assist the developing process, so those that did not measure up did not continue in the gene pool.

Therefore, form and function can never be separated in reality, if you are a purist. The form (type) and the function (ability to do the job) are so interrelated that the ongoing discussion of which is more important, type or soundness, becomes an academic exercise. **A case could be made that in judging the dog what contributes to the dog doing its job is a virtue; what interferes with the dog doing its job is a fault.**

The key idea is to understand that we are discussing the original look and character of the breed, not necessarily one and the same as what we have today. In many breeds, the culmination of generations of humans working with more generations of dogs, changing the dogs to suit the man, or allowing them to change in accordance with their gene pools without the assistance of Mother Nature has created drastic changes. Translated, man has shut out natural selection to accommodate artificial (man-made) selection.

Because human beings are subject to varying tastes unlike the more consistent tests of nature, they have changed the fashions in some breeds as drastically as the generations have changed the fashions in clothing. In changing the interpretation of type by taking it to some incredible extremes, the breeders have in fact strayed from the original type to a more modernized version of it. The newer version may not require the same degree of soundness or functional expertise as the unforgiving work once demanded.

If you can avoid making the type/soundness issue a game of tough mental gymnastics, it might be simple. If a breed of dog evolved to do a specific job or jobs, it evolved in the form to do that job best. But, over the years, men decided that if substantial bone is good, more bone is better. If some coat is appropriate, more is better. If a broad head is desired, a broader one is better—and so on. Almost 100 years ago, in his book, *The Show Dog*, Huntington commented, "The specimen which is possessed of the 'essential quality' in the most abnormal degree is the winner of the blue ribbon".

The accumulative effect is that the once functional animal has been taken to such extremes in type that it becomes a caricature of what it was. If the height of a Great Dane is 32 inches, does that mean he would be better at 34 inches? And best at 36 inches or 42 inches? Quarterhorse fanciers are paying the price for their pursuit of the ultra dainty foot with short, upright pasterns. Now the breed is more prone to navicular disease because it has lost its natural shock absorber. This has resulted in a lovely horse that can be led into the show ring but can no longer tolerate the work for which it was bred. At what point does extreme become incapacitating?

The Norwegian Elkhound is used today in his native Norway to hunt bear and moose (Norwegian: elg) and for trailing and standing the moose in some parts of the U.S. Although working moose is appropriately controlled by game laws, it tests the dog's intuitive hunting powers and ability to perform the task he was bred to perform. Breeders must continue to dedicate themselves to the concept that correct type is the absolute form that serves that function. (Photo by Deidi Kramer)

This is where you, the breeder, come into the picture. For as time goes on and it is no longer necessary for purebred dogs to do the original job for which they were bred, more emphasis is placed on their doing the modern job for which they are bred—*to win dog shows.* In other words, if the new concept of winning beauty contests such as dog shows is to have any real meaning, all of us involved must work together to protect the very picture of type and traits that made that breed in the first place.

The Norwegian Elkhound was developed more than five thousand years ago to hunt bear and moose. As such, he evolved into a harsh-coated, athletic, short-loined athlete, able to perform the following tasks: 1) Follow the game through icy waters where moose browse; 2) Trail the game with great endurance over hill and dale; 3) Dodge the swipe of the bear's paw or the swing of the awesome moose's rack; 4) Eyeball the prey in an arresting manner to keep it from taking flight, much like a quarter horse works cattle.

Although a fluffy, silver-coated, all-one-color Norwegian Elkhound may be pretty, it is at a terrible disadvantage during the raw weather of Norway's hunting season without the black guard hairs that provide weather-resistant protection.

Many rectangular Norwegian Elkhounds move well and could no doubt trail the moose, but it takes the square dog, agile and able to dodge the moose, to do the job. And whereas a soft, pleading look is lovely on many breeds, a good hunting elkhound has a serious expression, created by a dark, well-set, oval-shaped eye.

It is important to distinguish changes occurring due to environmental conditions such as modern coat care and nutrition from an actual deviation or straying away from type. The American Cocker Spaniel provides an interesting study here. There are Cocker Spaniels who look typey from ringside because they look short with lots of coat and can be mistaken for good Cockers. Closer examination will show their cutesy faces with their exaggerated muzzles are too short to pick up a bird. Their apparent look of good type is falsely created by straight shoulders and short upper arm. This results in sloping toplines and cute bodies covered with cotton-textured coats. These dogs are not truly Cockers of type in spite of the fact that they fool some of those watching at ring side.

Yet, in the same show there will be sporting-type American Cockers whose headpieces could carry a bird, whose necks and shoulders, length of leg, and grace of movement could quarter properly to flush the prey and whose coats would be functional for the field if not cosmetically done by the handler. What about this excessive coat? Mercifully, the standard deals with it even if the rigors of the ring do not.

A Cocker with a correct texture would not carry excessive coat if he were a working animal doing his job in the field, for the burrs and underbrush would thin it out naturally. It is the environment of Cocker pens, snoods, oiling and protecting every hair at any price that causes this look. Put the same dog into an

Ch. Torohill Trader, Cocker Spaniel, owned by Leonard J. Buck was the sire of Ch. Nonquitt Notable, and great-grandsire of the author's first Cocker Spaniel. Bain Cobb hunted over this dog—considered a turning point in the breed. (Photo courtesy of the AKC)

Ch. Bel S'Mbran Bachrach was as accomplished as a coursing champion as he was as a top Saluki in bench show competition. Pictured here at work in a field of alfalfa, Bachrach captured the National Open Field Coursing Association's coveted Christmas Cup honors. This event, held in Merced, California, featured the 60 top coursing competitors of the year. It is vital that breeders continue to breed dogs able to function in their original job descriptions if dog shows are to have a meaningful purpose other than accumulating ribbons. (Photo courtesy of George Bell)

J.D. Bothum, Siberian Husky breeder and trainer, started his Copper Creek breeding program in the 70s as a dual-purpose kennel. Bothum's dogs enjoyed success in the show ring, including some group victories, before his interest in sled dog racing became his major pursuit. His dogs exhibit the leggy, racing-dog, athletic look of the truly functional Siberian. The author was privileged to experience a dog sled ride in the high country of the Colorado Rockies behind eight of his powerful dogs, two of which were over 10 years old. Down from some of the breed's best foundation stock, these dogs are a testimonial to the fact that many of dogdom's best are quite capable of performing the job for which they were bred. (Photo by Chuck Trotter)

Ch. Jordean All Kiddin' Aside is an excellent example of a dual-purpose Brittany. "Ollie" was in the Top 10 All Breeds in 1993 as well as #1 in his breed and group. In becoming the #1 Brittany of all time, he amassed a sensational record of 50 All Breed BISs as well as 43 Specialty Shows! Bred, owned and handled by Dr. and Mrs. Dennis Jordan, he is seen here at work in the field. Brittany breeders are dedicated to keeping their breed pure as a field dog while seeking outstanding type that can score in the conformation ring. As a result, they are firm in their stand against excess coat and cosmetic trappings. At the same time, they insist on an athletic, functional animal able to perform tasks it was bred to do. (Photo courtesy of Dr. and Mrs. Dennis Jordan)

outdoor hunting environment, and the coat would take care of itself to some extent. Treat them as normal dogs with normal grooming and there would be a world of difference.

Ch. Torohill Trader was the black Cocker many experts considered to be the turning point to achieve the modern Cocker. Bain Cobb, who piloted the dog to top honors in the show ring, also hunted the dog. Ted Young Jr.'s father once field trained some of the Cockers after their ring careers ended. He even shot over some of them. These were famous Cockers of just a few decades ago. And, yes, their coats were thinned out considerably by this activity.

Throughout our many, many breeds of dogs there are untold numbers that could still do their jobs, thanks to ongoing vigilance on the part of breeders and care-keepers of the breed. The ideal answer for any dedicated breeder is to seek the best type in the purest sense on the most functional dogs. When you have to make trade-offs, let them be cosmetic. Some things may seem cosmetic that are not. Take the clipping of a Poodle as an example. If left on their own, Poodle coats will grow quite long and cord themselves. Because these versatile animals were outstanding water dogs, circus dogs and everything in between, it was impractical to let their long cords grow. Not only did the coat interfere with normal exercise, but once the dog was in the water, it became a liability due to absorbing of water by the coat. Therefore, the dogs were originally shaved all over.

But that was not the desired answer either, for now the dog's body was exposed to the elements. His vital organs were unprotected and his joints subject to arthritis from cold waters. Thus, the trims that emerged left hair that covered those organs and protected the rib cage; anklets and bracelets at the joints, including pom-poms on the hips; and hair to protect the other two areas prone to loss of body heat—the head and the tip of the tail. Since the dogs were also pets, their faces and feet were clipped so the sturdy workers would not track mud into houses.

So what seems artificial and only cosmetic is in fact a traditional way of grooming the Poodle that dates back to water dogs of the 16th Century with similar practical clips. You probably thought the clip was just a fashion that had evolved. Well, so did I until I was doing research for this book.

Remember that just as it is possible to have sound and unsound common dogs and even mongrels, so it is possible to have unsound typey purebreds. Having read and heard over and over that you cannot have type without soundness, I ask myself once more, "Why didn't my dogs read those books?" For over the years, I have had some dogs with exquisite type that did not satisfy the soundness requirement. How many times have you seen a gorgeous dog *on the line* in a large class only to cringe in disappointment when it fell apart moving? The answer is that the dog must have the correct balance of both, as well as be in perfect balance to himself.

For although the dog may never be called upon to serve its primary purpose, it must be evaluated by both breeders and judges for the correct structural build to do that job and its athletic ability to put that structure to work, reconciling, once and for all, the issue of type and soundness. Both are absolutely imperative. A wise person once advised me, "Breed for type, cull for soundness," as selecting for the functional characteristics of the breed is *type*. This person was in touch with it all and the message is simple, "A dog should not have type without soundness."

BONEHEAD GENETICS

Trying to Understand How Genes Work (Darwin, Mendel, and Me)

Maybe a good reason to call our overview of genetics *Bonehead Genetics* is because of the legions of well-meaning breeders who sincerely attempt to pursue the study of this science and get frustrated at the language. Like a lot of other things in life, it seems too complicated to fathom. But the truth is—whether the study of genetics is comfortable for you or not—if you are breeding dogs, you are a practicing geneticist.

Sometimes it seems as if I have spent my entire life trying to understand how genes work. Because I have only scratched the surface in my attempts to learn, it is vital that you accept the fact that I am anything but an expert on the subject. Thus, the information on genetics will be simple. At the same time it may serve the purpose of helping you understand a very complex subject.

GENETIC ORDER

Genetic information comes in two forms: 1) traits that are observable at birth; 2) traits the individual is genetically programmed to have that appear later in life. This can sometimes account for so-called genetic predisposition.

Many traits are polygenic, meaning that more than one gene is involved, The more genes that are involved, the harder it is to achieve consistency.

The DNA molecule carries the basic information for each individual—DNA is the messenger service. Proteins, enzymes and amino acids all participate in the process. Dog breeders need to familiarize themselves with the process enough to have a layman's understanding of it.

Nature has an orderly way of getting the genes from each parent together. The process begins in each parent with the total chromosome count of 78 halving itself to send 39 along to participate in the next step. That step occurs with orderly rejoining of the 39 chromosomes from each parent to produce the final product with 78. Theoretically, one chromosome for a given trait from one parent matches up with its mirror image from the other parent. Whichever of the like chromosomes in the match is dominant prevails.

This exact pairing and duplication process of chromosomes during cell division is nature's way of ensuring that each new cell gets a full set. Thus the blueprint for the growth and function of the entire body is present in every cell in that body.

William Bateson, a British biologist, was the first person to call the study of hereditary factors *genetics*. There are tons of books on the subject. Excellent books that present overviews of the remarkable work done in the gene-studying field are *Blueprints* and *Joy of Breeding Your Own Show Dog*, which will expand your knowledge of the subject and is closer to home for the aspiring dog breeder.

So many of the books available on genetics are complicated and written in such a way that they are difficult for an average breeder to comprehend. It is important that you understand that you do not have to be a genetic genius to breed good dogs—if you have common sense. Some great meals are prepared by skilled people who never graduated from Le Cordon Bleu.

What you must keep in mind is the fact that the same ingredients, such as garlic, rosemary, thyme, tarragon, etc., are present in the kitchens of cooks ranging from the ordinary cook to the classic gourmet chef. The secret of true success is understanding how they work together to produce the end product and its appeal to your taste. How the gourmet chef and the *master breeder* utilize the ingredients available determines their success. Sometimes a minute quantity of a particular spice in the one case and a particular bloodline in the other will mean the difference between goodness and greatness. Expertise in using genetic ingredients available to you and knowing how they work with other genetic combinations to produce the next product in your breeding efforts is similar to the efforts of the culinary artist. The vital thing to remember is that mistakes in the kennel are not easy to dispose of the way the mistakes in the kitchen are.

Contributors from the Past: Early Bloodstock Breeders

Before we get into the scientific experts who contributed to our ever-expanding knowledge of how heredity works, we need to recognize that the work done by early bloodstock breeders of various animals throughout history developed a starting point for purebred animals long ago.

These early farmers, nobles, livestock lovers, dogmen and horsemen thought that inherited characteristics were carried by the blood, and with the ongoing unraveling of the DNA code that can be read from blood, they were not totally wrong even though the blood does not participate in procreation. The ironic thing is that any cell in your body can be used for genetic research except red blood cells, which have no nucleus. Because the terms *bloodstock* and *bloodlines* have such a proud and traditional background, lovers of purebred animals still use these terms today. And rightly so.

These early breeders of bloodstock may have lacked scientific knowledge of genes and how they worked, but they more than made up for it with common sense and good instincts in selecting the best and using the appropriate bloodlines to achieve the best. One of England's most famous pack of Foxhounds had only three masters from 1796 through 1936. The Master of Foxhounds takes all responsibility for decision making in the breeding program and selection of animals retained for the pack. With only three people involved in the process of this pack in a period of 140 years, it is no wonder the pack consistency was of such excellent quality and much envied throughout England.

Such early bloodstock experts did not know why traits could be *hidden* for generations but might appear later, until Mendel came along. They did not know why certain bloodlines combined to produce pleasantly unexpected results. They used their intuition and knowledge of the animals' performances to select their breeding stock and improve their bloodlines. They learned that dogs built in a given fashion were best for a particular job, and so their selections led to certain types of dogs evolving into the breeds that we enjoy today.

Later this selection of lovely type by dog breeders was to become an art form of its own. As scientific knowledge accumulated—as it continues to do—the result was to bring together the artist and scientist into the perfect package: the informed dog breeder.

As bloodstock activity became the mainstay of breeding animals, keeping pedigrees and records became the order of the day. Although this process began in antiquity, it became a common practice with the habit of documenting the ancestry of their well-bred horses. It was a logical extension to keep pedigrees on the dogs, too. Therefore, it was no coincidence that Foxhounds were among the first dogs to benefit from selective breeding. As their masters rode the results of their horse-breeding program to the hunt, they were following the results of their dog-breeding program in search of the fox. This served as a continuing incentive to improve both horses and dogs.

Darwin: A Demon in His Day

Although we know of early dogs from the study of archeological experts, remember that during Darwin's time it was considered blasphemy to question the origin of living, breathing creatures as anything other than the work of God's grand design for life. Inquisitive curiosity in this area was punishable by any number of responses ranging from excommunication from the church to death to the heretic. One simply did not deny the *Holy Bible*. Needless to say, Darwin was considered a demon of sorts by many in his day.

It seems that for many centuries there was a lot of confusion about what was the gospel truth, and many of Darwin's contemporaries saw him as an anti-Christ when *The Origin of Species* was published.

Darwin had decided early on that there was no such thing as a fixed species. To him, this explained why there were so many differences in a particular animal from one environment to another. He decided that what was the proper shape for that animal in one location might not be for another, so the species adapted to meet the new environment. Favorable variations of that animal tended to survive while Mother Nature took care of unfavorable ones.

This hard-working, diligent man kept transmutation notebooks in which he categorized and studied 13 different finches that he thought had descended from a common ancestor and had changed to utilize the food supply which was available to them in their locale. At casual glance, these finches looked alike, but their beaks were different.

For example, a stout-beaked finch with a large, heavy head out of proportion to its body cracked tough seeds for food and a refined finch with a long thin beak ate insects. You may wonder what, if anything, such information has to do with purebred dogs. Maybe nothing at all; but perhaps if you know more about what went on before, it will help you not only understand possibilities for the future, but to utilize the good ones.

If you ever considered any similarities of two breeds like the Brittany and the Welsh Springer, it might be advisable to study the proximity of Brittany in France and Wales in the British Isles. Then investigate what differences existed in the environments of the two regions and ask yourself if the Brittany and the Welsh Springer could have shared a common ancestor. If so, would environmental and job adjustments explain the differences in the two breeds as you know them today?

Consider the diversity of size in the Saluki. The standard says, "Dogs should average in height from 23 to 28 inches and bitches may be considerably smaller, this being typical of the breed." Now that is quite a wide range, and this is a very old standard which dates the breed to antiquity. Some of the dogs were used in the desert and others were used in the mountains—two very demanding yet different environments. And that is just part of what this standard is saying.

To understand Darwin's thinking about species being subject to change is to understand why faithful protectors of the Saluki breed do not want their standard changed. It might be said that the Saluki standard is compatible with Darwin's concepts. Furthermore, this information might be of interest to the breeders of Arctic or northern breeds. Darwin was most puzzled by the fact that animals of the Far North were similar on all continents while animals of other areas—such as the finches of the Galapagos that he studied—differed greatly even though in close proximity to one another. The famous Danish explorer, Knud Rasmussen, was interested to find that Arctic natives in Europe, Asia and America spoke similar languages and shared similar cultures even though they were far removed from one another. By the way, Darwin never said that man descended from the ape, only that they had a common ancestor.

Once, some students raised the question of whether the Chow and the bear could have had a common ancestor. On page 304 of what is considered the definitive researcher's tool, *The Hutchinson's Dog Encyclopaedia*, it is suggested that the Chow Chow may have evolved from some other ancestor than those that produced "Western dogs" and alludes to the bear. If you want to get a laugh or open up a can of worms, try that one in the company of Chow fanciers.

Anyhow, Darwin believed that different species descended from common ancestors and evolved into their own distinct forms through *natural selection*, a subject that I will get back to later. He was an important player in working to solve evolution and the mysteries of genetics with his lifelong work. Along with a myriad of others, Darwin participated in putting together the pieces of the genetic puzzle. As any puzzle lover knows, the earlier on in the puzzle-solving process, the slower the pieces fit in place.

The Monk Who Monkeyed Around With Genes

Like many of the greats from history, the Austrian monk, Gregor Johann Mendel, was not taken seriously in his own time. Not only was he not appreciated, some questioned how one who had taken vows could spend such a great deal of his time experimenting with his garden peas as a lifetime's work instead of devoting all his time and effort to his work in the church. Indeed, his lasting fame came because of the pioneer work he did with genetics as an avocation, rather than the work of his religious vocation.

Mendel's work with garden peas resulted in his development of a formula that we still rely on more than a hundred years later. The formula explains how traits can disappear in one generation and reappear in the next. This kind monk's rather simple formula is based on understanding the action of dominant and recessive genes on progeny.

In each cell of the dog's body there are 39 pairs of chromosomes that are shaped similarly to *strings of beads*. The beads on the strings are genes that contain the material that passes characteristics on to the next generation. When the beads on one string match those provided by the other parent, the resulting progeny are homozygous. Translated, this means the animal is *pure* for the traits affected by those beads. It is impossible for a homozygous (pure) dominant to produce a recessive. If the beads of the two parents do not match, it means the progeny is heterozygous, exhibiting the trait of the dominant bead or gene, while carrying the hidden recessive gene for that trait.

The most widely quoted of Mendel's efforts that led to his discovery has to do with the traits of height, color and skin of the pea. The height traits were tall and short, color traits were green and yellow and texture of skin traits were wrinkled or smooth. Unfortunately, those who breed dogs work with a lot more traits than this. Nonetheless, Mendel was able to make his breakthroughs partly because he was working with fewer traits and no doubt fewer chromosomes. Human beings have 23 pairs of chromosomes for a total of 46, horses have 32 pairs for a total of 64, and dogs have 39 pairs for a total of 78. Assuming that the more pairs of chromosomes contained by the species, the more genetic

BREEDING HYBRID DOMINANT-RECESSIVES

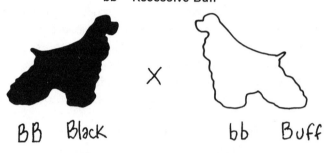

BB = Dominent Black
bb = Recessive Buff

BB Black   X   bb Buff

All puppies = Bb

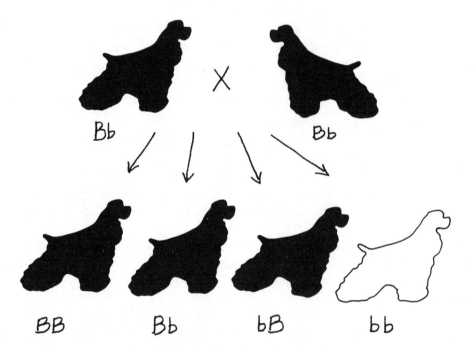

Bb   X   Bb

BB   Bb   bB   bb

If Mendel had been working with color inheritance in American Cocker Spaniels instead of with peas, this chart would illustrate his work. Like the tall pea, black is dominant. Like the short pea, buff is recessive. The top step represents the original mating of two who were homozygous (pure): one for the dominant trait and one for the recessive trait. The next step shows that all the progeny from the first generation were black, because black is dominant. Like the tall hybrid peas, they were carrying the hidden recessive (for buff). Look what happens when the hybrids are bred to each other. The genes sort themselves out in what *appears* to be a three-to-one ratio. In fact, the actual ratio is one-two-one, with one pure dominant, two expressing the dominant gene for black but carrying the hidden recessive and one pure recessive expressed as a buff. Understanding how genes behave in the simple dominant-recessive pattern is a preliminary step in breeding dogs. (Drawings courtesy of Doral Publishing)

variables are possible, it is understandable that the breeding of purebred dogs is not an easy task.

Heterozygous then means that the genetic code of the animal could go either way, passing his dominant gene for the trait, which he himself exhibits, to his offspring or his recessive gene for the trait—which he himself does not exhibit—to the offspring.

There is a 50-50 chance of the progeny inheriting either string of beads from each parent. Those dominant genes that are inherited by the progeny will be expressed or visible in their appearance. Those recessive genes that are inherited by the progeny will be hidden or masked unless the other parent contributes a matching recessive gene for the same trait. In other words, because the progeny would then have a recessive gene from each parent for the trait, it would be visible because it has no dominant for that trait to hide behind. This double recessive for the trait means the animal is homozygous for that trait—and only has one kind of gene to give for it.

How Mendel arrived at his conclusions that we acknowledge as a genetic law is of interest. In dealing with height for example, he crossed tall peas with short peas and was amazed to find all the resulting plants—progeny—were tall. His curiosity then led him to cross these resulting tall peas—

HOW MENDEL AFFECTS YOU

Pretend you are working with a head breed in which D is the dominant trait for an excellent head, correct skull and muzzle and proportion. The recessive opposite, d, of this head is cursed with insufficient width and shape of skull, poor fill under the eye and incorrect snipey muzzle.

Dd bred to Dd is the mating of two animals with good heads. Now look at what happens in the Mendelian Formula:

DD. This dog has the perfect head and will always throw it to his progeny.

Dd. This dog has a good head. Maybe it looks as good as DD, but the hidden d is poor, so some of his progeny will inherit good heads and some extremely poor heads.

dD. The same as above.

dd. This poor-headed dog has no gene except the d for a poor head to pass on.

If dd is bred to a DD, the next generation would improve, leading to the expression: "You can put heads on them in one generation." But what about the next generation? In this case, it would be better to neuter the dd animal and place him as a pet.

which unknown to him were carrying the short pea gene—and in the next generation he got both tall peas and short ones. The previous generation had all appeared tall, but they were carrying the gene for shortness.

Mendel raised more than 100,000 plants and kept detailed records before drawing any conclusions and before preparing a scientific paper on the subject. His work proved that traits do not blend. When he bred tall to short he did not get medium-size plants. When he bred yellow to green, he did not get lime.

Imagine his excitement at this discovery. Now he had some conclusions: 1) Each parent contributed one-half of the genetic material to the progeny; 2) This genetic material affected the appearance of the progeny; 3) Some of those genes were dominant over others, and when the dominant and recessive genes are in the same plant, only the dominant will show, dominant does not skip a generation; 4) If each parent contributes a recessive (short) gene to a given offspring, it is pure for short and will be short. Furthermore, it can only contribute that short gene to the next generation. If the next generation receives the dominant for tall from the other parent, the short is "hidden." Recessive can skip a generation.

If you wonder what these men from centuries past have to do with today, there is a message here that a breeder who takes an undersized bitch to an oversized dog to get the correct size will not necessarily find the correct size any easier to achieve than if he had bred a small bitch to a correct-sized dog. We are assuming that the bitch is not too small for her breed to be a viable producer.

Mendel had taken the first big step in the science of heredity. Keep in mind that it was lucky he chose peas. First of all, he could breed a lot of them in his lifetime. Since plants are not the same kind of loving, living creatures that dogs are, he probably did not get emotionally involved with them. Since all the traits he was dealing with behaved independently of the others and with a predictable simple dominant-recessive pattern, he did not have to worry about linkage, incomplete dominance, over dominance, or a number of other genetic activities, including mutations that are a lot more complex. He was able to establish that tall was dominant over short, yellow over green, and smooth skin over wrinkled—all in peas.

Furthermore, he worked out a rhythmic mathematical pattern that works itself into a consistent ratio of what looks to be three-to-one as to how the next generation appears when breeding hybrid dominant-recessives to each other, i.e., three will express the dominant look and one has the expressed recessive look.

The actual ratio is one pure dominant, two dominants carrying the recessive, and one pure recessive—in a 1-2-1 pattern out of every four offspring. If T = the tall gene and t = the short gene, here is how it looks: TT + tt = all Tt (one gene from each parent). In the next generation when Tt is mated with Tt, every four progeny sort out in this manner: TT Tt tT tt with TT being the pure dominant—has dominant appearance and only dominant genes to give.

Tt and tT look the same as TT because the dominant gene masks the recessive, but they are not pure. Both of them can throw either a dominant gene (T) or a recessive gene (t) to their progeny. The (tt) is pure recessive and can only throw that gene to its progeny.

All of us owe a great debt to the good monk for his persistent work to come up with such an equation. What happened to him when he decided to turn from peas, which he had mastered, to another plant—hawkweed—is another story. He was "blown away" by his hawkweed breeding, for this plant's producing patterns defied all the conclusions he had reached with his peas, and he readily moved on to beans. It appears that the breeding of peas is not only simpler than the breeding of dogs, it is also simpler than the breeding of hawkweed! As dog breeders, we can relate a century later to the frustrations Mendel must have felt. Furthermore, I know many equally confused dog breeders who, like Mendel, when suffering poor experiences with one breed move on to another breed.

Prepotency, the ability of a dog to pass on his characteristics to a large percentage of his progeny, is established by working within the framework of Mendel's formulas to determine which dogs are homozygous for the desired trait. These dogs cannot give their offspring anything but the desired gene for that trait because that is all they have.

Complicating the simple dominant-recessive formula is the fact that many other elements are in the genetic picture in addition to the simple dominant-recessive. For one thing, some of the traits that dog breeders desire are produced by the action of more than one gene. When genes are connected in chains, it can be very costly to get rid of an undesired gene because it takes the connected desired ones with it. For another, some genes are codominant—polygenic—meaning both are expressed. If we were referring to the color of Mendel's peas as codominant, instead of finding yellow dominant over green, Mendel would have faced a perplexing pea that was both yellow and green—not lime, mind you—but striped or parti-colored.

Partial dominance means one gene is expressed at the partial cost of another; if this were the case, the yellow of the pea would tend to modify or dilute the green. Another complicated behavior of genes is called epistasis, which is when one gene completely masks the expression of another. The gene for a completely white horse is such an example, as it is able for some reason to cover up all other color genes. Yet all white horses are heterozygous for this color, because a double white gene apparently causes the fetus to be aborted early in the pregnancy. This means that any horse with one white gene is white. Any horse with two white genes is dead.

A heterozygote produces two kinds of germ cells with respect to the gene in question. A homozygote produces only one kind of germ cell with respect to that gene. Over dominance means that the heterozygous animal is superior to either the dominant homozygous one or the recessive homozygous one. It is achieved by breeding a pure dominant to a pure recessive.

Additive gene action means that different pairs of genes attract to each other and collect to produce a more extreme phenotype or look. Perhaps this is a contributing factor in the behavior of the genes involved in the development of the Bull Terrier head in the last half century. Because breeders kept selecting for fuller heads, piling head virtue genes on more head virtue genes and never backing down on selection for head, the Bull Terrier head evolved into one of great strength, fill, power, make and shape. No other breed of dog has a head that is like it—egg-shaped and without indentations and hollows.

The confusing part of all these genetic variables that can, and do, take place is that, to date, no one knows which characteristics in each breed are affected by genes behaving in which exact manner. In some areas, we have a fairly good idea of the either/or performance of the dominant-recessive influence. In other areas the genetic picture is anything but clear.

This large number of variables is the reason why breeding is both fascinating and frustrating. It is also the reason why no one has all the answers and common sense is of such great value. What looks good on paper does not always translate to the desired result in the living, breathing picture that was promised by the paperwork. Yet without the scientific knowledge that comes to us from the past—and will continue to come to us in the future—our task would be all the more difficult.

More Ideas on the Subject

One particular scientist, Lamark, believed in some far-out idea that there was an "inheritance of acquired characteristics." Even though this idea is not scientific and may seem nutty, more than one breeder has bred to an overachiever whose main virtue is showmanship. Usually, but not always, this characteristic is acquired, not inherited. Good luck if you believed in the inheritability of acquired characteristics. If you do, then once you breed to a dog whose tail was docked, does this mean you do not have to worry about docking the tails of his progeny?

A scientist by the name of DeVries raised more than 50,000 primrose plants as he attempted to explain things Mendel had not touched. His purpose was to explain how plants could appear with traits that were not present in their parents or other ancestors. And when these plants *bred true*, DeVries knew he was working with another phenomenal concept to introduce to the scientific community. He called these results *mutations*.

The one who picked up the mutation ball and ran with it was a native son of Kentucky, T. H. Morgan, whose work was conducted in the famous "fly room" at Columbia University. Morgan became the first person to receive the Nobel Prize for his work in the field of genetics. To my knowledge, he is the only Kentuckian ever to win the Nobel Prize, which he did in 1933.

Morgan was born into a prominent Lexington family in 1866. Francis Scott Key and J. P. Morgan were among his relatives. He first tried working with mice but found them unacceptable as experimental animals for his breeding program because they were too large and took up too much room. (Wonder what his reaction would be to breeders like Lexington's own Frank and Martha Dean and their Whitehall Irish Wolfhounds?) He turned to fruit flies because he could get a new generation every two weeks. Imagine, 26 generations in one year! And, they were easy to feed as they lived on bananas.

At the time Morgan did his early work, the popular theory regarding Mendel's dominant-recessive concept included the erroneous idea that the male genetic makeup was dominant over that of the female. Here are a few of Morgan's experiments.

He bred 60 generations of fruit flies in total darkness to see if it would affect their eyesight. It did not. Those of us who breed hunting dogs who have not hunted for many generations know they do not lose their ability to hunt just because they are not using it—if we are breeding true to the breed. He examined hundreds of thousands of fruit flies' eyes under the microscope. This tedious work was mind boggling as it involved staining the minuscule eyes of tiny flies. All this exacting work resulted in his discovery of a white-eyed male mutant. Normal fruit flies have red eyes.

Morgan then bred the white-eyed male mutant to a number of normal red-eyed females which resulted in more than 1,000 red-eyed hybrids carrying the white-eyed gene. These hybrids bred to each other in the next generation produced red-eyed and white-eyed flies at a ratio approximating Mendel's work, i.e., one pure dominant red-eyed fly, two red-eyed flies expressing the dominant gene but carrying the white-eyed gene, and one pure white-eyed (recessive expressed) fly out of every four flies. However, all the white-eyed flies were males. This is the first documentation I have been able to find that reports sex-linked gene records identifying genetic activity involving sex-linked traits. This genetic mutation-information must have been carried on the Y chromosome (see Sex Chromosomes).

Morgan's prolonged studies with his flies, which were presumably from the same gene pool, led him to conclude that there was some form of mutation in about one of every 50,000 flies. This work led to the elementary mapping of genes and located specific genes—beads—on specific chromosomes—strings of beads. It led to an explanation of the *crossing-over* theory, and if mutations cross over, they are all the harder to predict.

Nobel award-winning geneticist, Barbara McClintock, later discovered that genetic elements can "jump" from one place on a chromosome to another, thus changing the activity of the genes. It is unclear to me why this happens, but it is one more cause of unpredictability with which we all must deal.

Morgan's progress, like Mendel's before him, was achieved with less complicated subjects than dogs, for fruit flies have only eight genes occurring in pairs of four. It might be said that first Mendel and then Morgan became *the father of genetics*.

Solving Mutation Puzzles

Mutations result when something happens to change the order of the DNA and the subsequent genetic instructions. Surprisingly, it is reported that mutations can even revert to their original forms. Here are some of the things that can cause mutations: A strand of DNA is not correctly copied; natural or artificial radiation stresses a cell; chemical actions cause irregular cellular behavior; a change occurs in the order of the DNA; or, any combination of these or other elements.

Once again, I am reminded of the vast differences in dealing with plants rather than animals, for plant geneticists use radiation to produce desired mutations, an option not available to the animal breeder, due to disastrous side effects. Important mutations either greatly improve the product or greatly harm it. Neutral mutations are those with minor impact on the breeding population. For example, it would depend on the desire of the first person to raise the mutation-produced achondroplastic to decide to value them or reject them. If you were a chunky monk without a horse, but with a strong desire to go on the hunt, it would be to your advantage to have an achondroplastic dog to accompany you. Thus, early Bassets became favorites of the clergy and those who walked to the hunt.

Sickle cell anemia is a hereditary disease in humans that is an example of the fragility of the DNA and its arrangement. If one particular amino acid is out of order—not missing, just out of order—the individual is genetically coded to become ill with the disease as the DNA will send out lethal instructions. The DNA is *command central*.

Interestingly enough, a mutation having to do with the susceptibility of a person to contact malaria through mosquito bites may have contributed to the incidence of sickle cell anemia. This mutation, which occurred thousands of years ago in equatorial Africa, produced the sickle cell as a protection against malaria. Individuals with the sickle cell were favored to survive malaria and reproduce at that time in man's evolution.

Now that the sickle cell is not necessary for the survival of the species, what was once a favorable mutation has become a hereditary health problem medical science must conquer, and the ancient mutation is now considered anything but helpful. Who would want to be protected from malaria if this protection became antagonistic to good health by causing a disease much worse? Gene mapping, accompanied by gene splicing, promises to conquer this disease in the 21st Century.

For years after the Three Mile Island accident in Pennsylvania, farmers in the area complained of increased incidents of abortions, birth defects, *misses*, and other assorted reproductive problems with their cows. It appears a wide variety of environmental situations can compromise the producing ability of animals as well as damaging the integrity of genetic material. Some medical experts now surmise an explanation for older parents experiencing a higher percentage of genetically defective offspring as damage caused by long-term exposure to pollution and/or radiation just in the process of living.

The theoretical genetic variations available in the DNA construction are unbelievable, numbering in the millions. The numbers of possible permutations and combinations are almost infinite, which is why breeders need to utilize available information to reduce the numbers of possible combinations. And, all of these numbers are affected by the behavior of the genes whether it be dominant, recessive, or any of the other possible variables that are out there.

The good news in dealing with dominant genes is that if an animal is pure dominant for the desired trait—DD—he will always throw it. The bad news is that you have no way of knowing if the animal is DD without a test because Dd has the same appearance. More bad news means the dominant-appearing animal could be carrying the recessive for the undesirable trait and not be pure dominant at all. In this case, what you see is not always what you get.

The good news in dealing with the recessive gene for the desirable trait is that if the animal exhibits that trait, the only genes carried for it are the recessive genes, dd. So, if you find another animal with that trait you will *fix* the trait each time you make such a breeding. The bad news is that you can easily lose the good recessive trait in one generation if you breed to a dog that does not have it. What you see is what you get only if both are recessive.

Some of this information makes it seem as if the breeding of animals is not all that complicated. And maybe it would not be if all you had to deal with was one trait. The problem is that we are dealing with so many traits, and most animals are carrying mixed genes. Ours is not an easy task. As we have said before, there is no perfect dog and no perfect bitch; therefore, there are no perfect breedings. In trying to breed perfect dogs from imperfect parents, we represent the saying: "The saints are the sinners who keep on trying!"

Sex Chromosomes: How they affect your breeding program

One of the 39 pairs of the dog's chromosomes are known as sex chromosomes because that pair determines the sex of the individual. The female possesses two X chromosomes in her body cells while the male possesses one X chromosome and one Y chromosome.

When the male cell divides to form sperm, one sperm gets its X and one sperm gets its Y. When the female cell divides, each egg gets an X. Therefore, when the sperm and egg get together, whichever of the male's two sperms fertilizes the egg first determines the sex of the progeny. If the X sperm gets there first to combine with the X of the egg, the result is XX = female. If the Y sperm gets there first to combine with the X of the egg, the result is XY = male.

In humans, more than 50 characteristics are known to be associated with the X chromosome. Because the X chromosome is considerably longer than the Y chromosome, it carries most of the genetic information. Thoroughbred breeders feel the X chromosome influences character and strength of heart. The X chromosome is especially targeted as the culprit carrier of the most information for genetic disorders. A faulty X gene that is a disease message—or mutant—can occur in the female with a healthy X gene to mask it, and the individual will be healthy at the same time she is a carrier for the disease. If she has two diseased or faulty X genes for the disease, she herself will have the disease. It is reported that more females die *in utero* than males. Perhaps this is due to the fact that they suffered from a double dose of a lethal gene associated with genetic "trash" on both X chromosomes.

Because the male can only carry one X gene, if he inherits the mutant X gene he has no healthy X gene to mask it. Therefore, he is affected. The classic textbook case for such genetic behavior explains why non-color-blind mothers can produce sons who suffer from color-blindness. Hemophilia is another such sex-linked disease. The affected male's sons will not inherit the faulty X gene, but his daughters will. They in turn can give it to their sons in a continuing zigzagging pattern.

The only X chromosome, then, that can be passed by a sire is the one he received from his dam. *Therefore, pedigrees can be structured in pursuit of excellent brood bitches by using only sires with outstanding dams.* Every daughter of a given sire receives the same X chromosome from him, for that is the only one he has to give. This is why, when one is dealing with sex-linked inheritance, the female offspring seem more like their sires and the males are more like their dams.

Y Chromosome: Evidently, there is very little genetic information carried by the Y chromosome. Nonetheless, what information that is carried by it can create a dominant sire line. A rather large portion of the X chromosome has no counterpart in the Y chromosome, and that is why a recessive X gene carried

HOW SEX CHROMOSOMES AFFECT YOUR BREEDING PROGRAM

This pedigree is an example of how breeders can structure the pedigree in order to increase the odds of getting a particularly strong female from the past into the pedigree of the present. In this case, the bitch whose "blood" was sought was Ch. Vin-Melca's Vikina, dam of the half-brothers Howdy Rowdy and Vagabond. Howdy Rowdy became the premier sire in the breed, siring both famous sons and daughters. Vagabond's contribution was as the sire of exceptional brood bitches. The only X chromosome either had to pass on to his daughters was that of their dam Vikina. Howdy Rowdy's daughter Happy Hour was in possession of one X chromosome from Vikina that she received from her sire. Her other X chromosome came from her dam Vika, another influential brood bitch in the breed. There is a 50-50 chance that Happy Hour would pass the X chromosome of Vikina to her daughter Nightcap. Since Nightcap received the X chromosome of Vikina from her sire Vagabond, it is possible she would be in possession of a double dose of the X chromosome material handed down from Vikina.

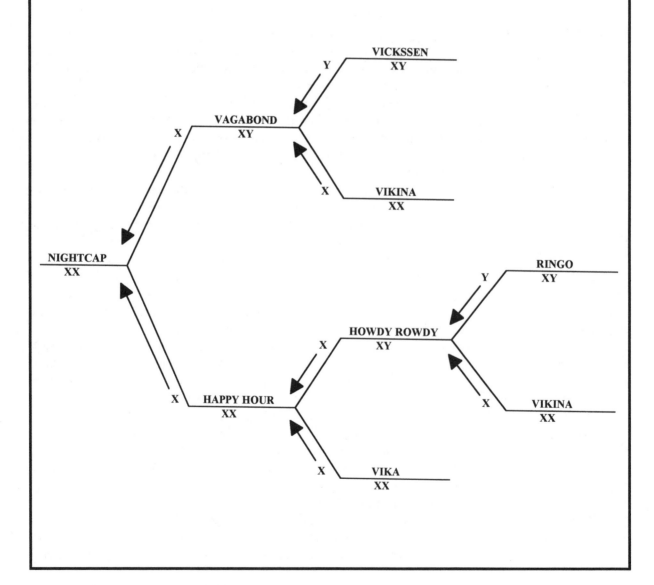

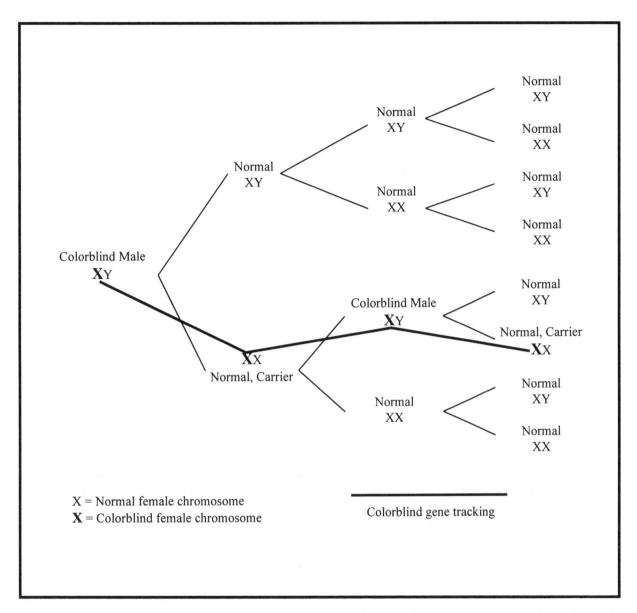

Normal
XY

Normal
XY

Normal
XX

Normal
XY

Normal
XX

Normal
XY

Normal
XX

Normal
XY

Colorblind Male
XY

Normal
XY

Colorblind Male
XY

Normal, Carrier
XX

Normal
XX

XX
Normal, Carrier

Normal
XY

Normal
XX

X = Normal female chromosome
X = Colorblind female chromosome

Colorblind gene tracking

there will express itself. One theory suggests that more males than females are conceived because the Y chromosome is smaller and, perhaps being a faster swimmer, gets to more eggs than the X chromosome.

A smaller portion of the Y chromosome has no counterpart in the X chromosome. Subsequently, Y chromosome information would be transmitted from the father to the son, which may be why some sires are prepotent only in the tail male line descending from them. They are unable to transmit the genes for some traits to their daughters who inherit no Y chromosome. Sometimes it may very well make a difference which parent contributes the gene for given traits to the progeny.

Thinking About Your Breeding Program

If you have assimilated all the reasons not to breed and still want to go ahead with it, good for you! At this point, you need to examine the acknowledged breeding theories, principles and practices that have come from the past.

Early on in my voracious readings and studies, the works of Sir Francis Galton and Bruce Lowe were brought to my attention. Galton's Law could not be considered written in stone due to some minor mathematical problems. Nonetheless, his work with color inheritance in Basset Hounds is of great significance. He decided that the resulting progeny of a given breeding received one-half of its genetic material from its parents; one-fourth from the grandparents; one-eighth from great-grandparents; one-sixteenth from great-great-grandparents, and so on. In essence, the mathematical theory is: 50 percent; 25 percent; 12.5 percent; 6.25 percent; 3.12 percent.

Although the computer could have straightened him out on the mathematics of the matter, my arguments with him would be minor because I never could balance a check book. For sure he was on target with his basic theory of the declining influence of ancestors as they moved farther back in the pedigree. And Galton gets a lot of credit because he picked one of the simpler genetic traits to track—coat color— in his experiments. Although Galton did a lot of other good work too, these color experiments were his best known contribution.

Bruce Lowe based his system of breeding on the tail female line, which I will cover in depth in the section on dams and brood bitches. Lowe studied female lines of thoroughbred mares deciding which taproot mares had the greatest influence on the classic races on British tracks. Lowe, an Australian whose studies took place at the end of the 19th Century, identified female lines according to his interpretation of their aptitudes. He then numbered these famous matriarchal families according to his estimation of the value of their contributions to the thoroughbred as a breed. Nonetheless, many bloodstock experts questioned the very method he used to rank the families, proving that horsemen like dogmen have differing opinions.

However one might question any given theory, the importance of these pioneers is that they were doing something and creating food for thought for others to make the next step. Even though there is no clear-cut magic formula yet that can guarantee foolproof results every time in the breeding of purebred animals, such efforts spawn growth in the field of breeding bloodstock.

In my early years of teaching, there was a wonderful Southern lady who was a fellow teacher and educational mentor by the name of Miss Willie Bell Mason. Miss Willie Bell kept a large banner across her classroom that stated:

> *Inch by inch, life is a cinch.*
> *Yard by yard, life is hard.*

Miss Willie Bell's words of wisdom not only encouraged who knows how many seventh- and eighth-grade math students over the years, they were etched forever in the mind of this breeder anxious to get on with it as she introduced me to patience.

And so it is with the breeding process. Progress and improvement are not overnight occurrences. If you need to have a great one now, go out and buy it. It will be less expensive in the long run to pay a fair price for a great one than to try to breed it. If you are one of those who wants to do it yourself, remember that patience is more than a virtue—it is a downright necessity in the breeding of dogs.

If taking another look at Galton's Law, recognize that the prepotency of an animal could skew or distort his mathematical general formula. For instance, a very prepotent grandsire who imprinted his genes on the next generation might through his son have almost as much influence as the resulting progeny's dam. Now theoretically, the dam should contribute half of the 50 percent allotted to the parents and the paternal grandsire should contribute one-fourth of the 25 percent allotted to the grandparents. However, suppose that this particular dam came from a weak gene pool and the paternal grandsire's very prepotent genes are heavily expressed through his similarly genetically coded son— would the theory hold up? Probably not. In this instance, the paternal grandsire would have more than his share of the 25 percent impact on his progeny, especially his sons, and the actual dam would have less than her share of the 50 percent in the overall picture. Nonetheless, as a rule of thumb, stick with such theories as Galton's unless you have reason to believe otherwise.

Although it is true that a given dog draws an equal number of chromosomes from each of his parents, it is not necessarily true that each parent contributes 50 percent to the end product genetically. If one of the parents is prepotent with a large number of dominant genes to pass on, the resulting progeny may in fact be more influenced by that parent.

Consequently, it might not read this way in the books as something you can be exact about, but sometimes a prepotent grandsire (or grandam) might be contributing more than his (or her) allotted

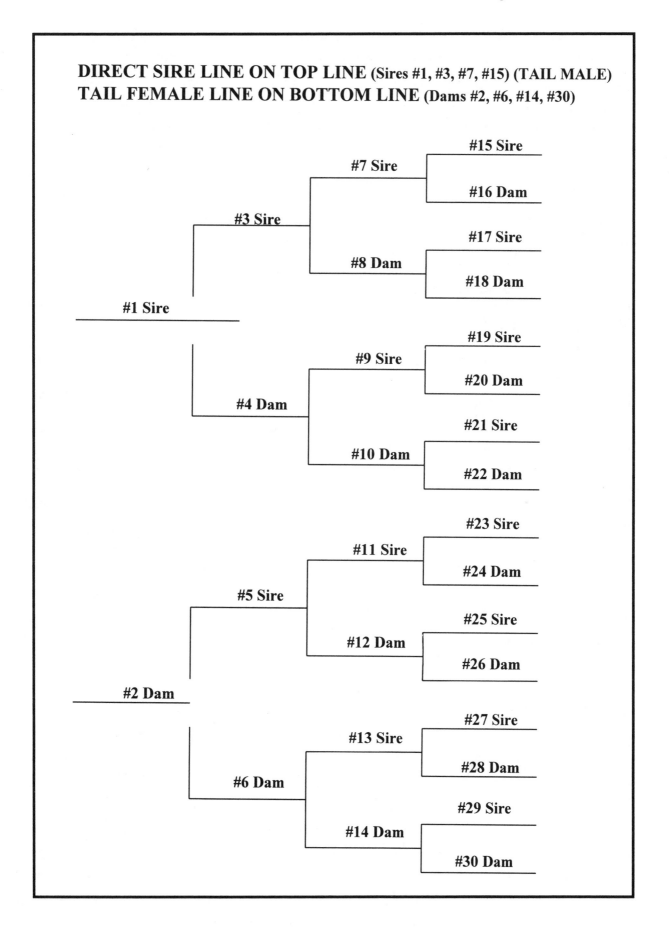

DIRECT SIRE LINE ON TOP LINE (Sires #1, #3, #7, #15) (TAIL MALE)
TAIL FEMALE LINE ON BOTTOM LINE (Dams #2, #6, #14, #30)

#15 Sire

#16 Dam

#7 Sire

#17 Sire

#18 Dam

#3 Sire

#8 Dam

#19 Sire

#20 Dam

#9 Sire

#21 Sire

#22 Dam

#1 Sire

#4 Dam

#10 Dam

#23 Sire

#24 Dam

#11 Sire

#25 Sire

#26 Dam

#5 Sire

#12 Dam

#27 Sire

#28 Dam

#13 Sire

#29 Sire

#30 Dam

#2 Dam

#6 Dam

#14 Dam

percentage share of the end product. There is no way to prove this, but my instincts tell me it's true. Please consider it as anything but scientific. The dam will always provide more influence (not genetic) on the progeny than the sire because of the environment and role modeling she provides from the time of conception to weaning.

But always remember that the prepotent animal will stamp its likeness on its offspring into the second and third generation, exerting much more than its allotted influence on subsequent generations. Usually an animal whose genes are desirable and prepotent will be inbred or linebred as breeders strive for prepotency.

Linebreeding, Inbreeding and Closebreeding

Linebreeding, inbreeding, and a favorite term that seems to cover both—closebreeding—are breeding systems that involve the matings of animals within the same family. The usual definition of inbreeding is brother-sister, father-daughter, or mother-son. The purest inbreeding is brother-sister.

The accepted definition of linebreeding is breeding within a family of dogs that involves grandfather-granddaughter, grandmother-grandson, uncle-niece, aunt-nephew; cousin-cousin; half-brother-half-sister. It might be said that linebreeding is a conservative safer form of inbreeding. Linebreeding means using relatives other than the individual parents or siblings to concentrate genes. A line represents the breeder's interpretation of type.

Other examples would be breeding the son of a great dog to the same dog's granddaughter, or the daughter to a grandson. Linebreeding concentrates similar ancestors from a line in the progeny. Or it can concentrate on one prepotent ancestor by getting him or her in the pedigree multiple times through various descendants. **A true linebreeding will return these prepotent ancestors to the progeny through both the sire and dam**.

In a sense, all purebreds could be considered somewhat linebred or inbred. Certainly this would be true in the early formation of the breed, as well as when compared to the human population. It is

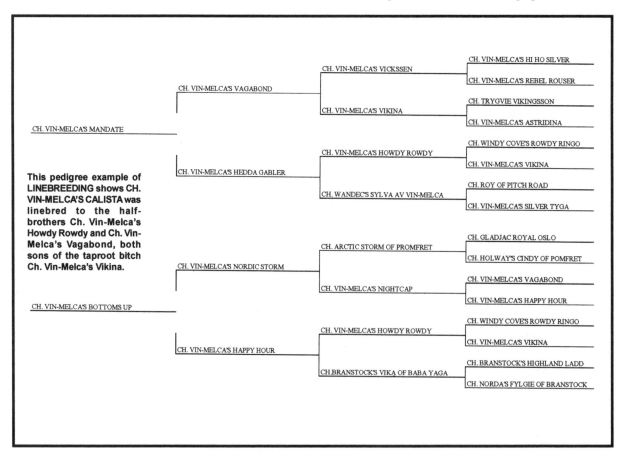

This pedigree example of LINEBREEDING shows CH. VIN-MELCA'S CALISTA was linebred to the half-brothers Ch. Vin-Melca's Howdy Rowdy and Ch. Vin-Melca's Vagabond, both sons of the taproot bitch Ch. Vin-Melca's Vikina.

CH. VIN-MELCA'S MANDATE

CH. VIN-MELCA'S BOTTOMS UP

CH. VIN-MELCA'S VAGABOND

CH. VIN-MELCA'S HEDDA GABLER

CH. VIN-MELCA'S NORDIC STORM

CH. VIN-MELCA'S HAPPY HOUR

CH. VIN-MELCA'S VICKSSEN

CH. VIN-MELCA'S VIKINA

CH. VIN-MELCA'S HOWDY ROWDY

CH. WANDEC'S SYLVA AV VIN-MELCA

CH. ARCTIC STORM OF PROMFRET

CH. VIN-MELCA'S NIGHTCAP

CH. VIN-MELCA'S HOWDY ROWDY

CH. BRANSTOCK'S VIKA OF BABA YAGA

CH. VIN-MELCA'S HI HO SILVER

CH. VIN-MELCA'S REBEL ROUSER

CH. TRYGVIE VIKINGSSON

CH. VIN-MELCA'S ASTRIDINA

CH. WINDY COVE'S ROWDY RINGO

CH. VIN-MELCA'S VIKINA

CH. ROY OF PITCH ROAD

CH. VIN-MELCA'S SILVER TYGA

CH. GLADJAC ROYAL OSLO

CH. HOLWAY'S CINDY OF POMFRET

CH. VIN-MELCA'S VAGABOND

CH. VIN-MELCA'S HAPPY HOUR

CH. WINDY COVE'S ROWDY RINGO

CH. VIN-MELCA'S VIKINA

CH. BRANSTOCK'S HIGHLAND LADD

CH. NORDA'S FYLGIE OF BRANSTOCK

important to recognize that once the stud book is closed, there is no way to bring in new traits except through accidental mutation. Therefore, the breeder must seek the best combinations of existing traits.

No doubt if you could trace the pedigree of any puppy mill puppy and the National Specialty winner in a given breed back far enough, you would find some common ancestors. Since there are 1,048,576 ancestors in 20 generations, it would almost have to be that way. How many breeds would have more than a million different dogs in the stud book 60 years ago? (This assumes that a generation is about three years.) To put the whole thing in perspective, a dog has 32 ancestors in his first five generations; 64 in six generations; 1,024 in 10 generations; 32,768 in 15 generations; 65,536 in 16 generations; 131,072 in 17 generations; 262,144 in 18 generations; 524,288 in 19 generations; 1, 048,576 in 20 generations.

Horse breeders and dog breeders don't always have the same interpretation of inbreeding and linebreeding. Horse breeders consider an animal inbred if it has the same ancestor more than once in a four-generation pedigree, while dog breeders consider that linebreeding. Others tell me they consider it linebreeding if there are one or more common ancestors in a three-generation pedigree.

Because intensive linebreeding mimics inbreeding, I like to use the term *closebreeding*. Although I have never done one of the aforementioned three inbreedings, the Vin-Melca breeding program has been a very intense form of linebreeding that, in essence, becomes its own form of *inbreeding*—thus, to avoid confusion, let's use the term *closebreeding*. It is far stronger than the normal linebreeding, but not as concentrated as true inbreeding. For the most part, it is an amalgamation of inbreeding and linebreeding. No matter whether you use inbreeding, linebreeding, closebreeding or the amalgamation of

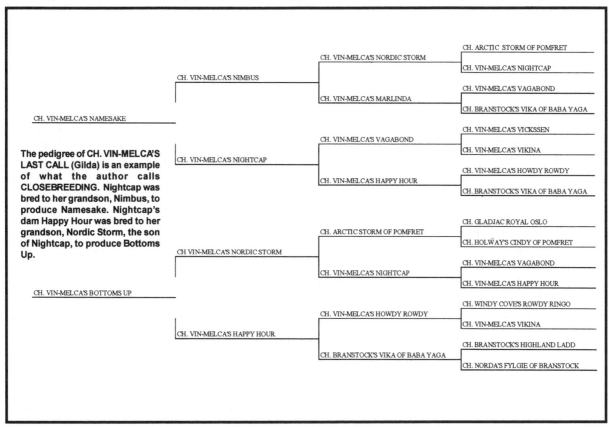

the three, it will be of no merit to your program unless the selection of the animals whose blood you seek to concentrate is based on valid premises and wise judgment.

It is unfortunate that all too often the instant expert takes great pride in linebreeding to some famous dog of the past without a clue as to what strengths and weaknesses the animal possessed, and even more importantly, those strengths and weaknesses the animal passed on to succeeding generations. This well-meaning novice apparently feels that the very presence of the famous dog's name several places in the pedigree assures greatness.

Such foolish blind faith can be costly. Not only does the breeder not know what to avoid, he may not know what to seek and select. It could be possible that *Champion Good Boy Won A Lot* should not be bred to at all, much less be the main player in a linebred pedigree. To do any form of closebreeding with success, the breeder must know the dog or dogs involved in order to know **what to seek out and what to avoid.**

Inbreeding is a lot like sin—you don't know how bad or how good it is until you get involved with it. Inbreeding does not create either good genes or bad genes—it simply concentrates them. Therefore, its effect will be in accordance with the kinds of genes that originally existed in single doses. All animals have in their gene pools the genetic material that when combined with similar undesirable genetic material from a mate can produce undesired or even lethal results. Such results can even occur from the mating of totally unrelated parents if both happen to carry bad genetic recessives—it would be a matter of coincidence. Inbreeding reduces the odds of such coincidences on the one hand and increases them on the other.

In Ancient Egypt during the Ptolemic Dynasty, the royal family kept its purity by requiring brother-sister marriages. Cleopatra was said to have been from several generations of brother-sister couplings. Until she got involved with the Romans, Julius Caesar and Mark Anthony, Cleopatra was married to her own brother.

The family of Johann Sebastian Bach intermarried for several generations with wonderful results. Johann was immortal, but not the only Bach with musical genius. In addition to him, there were several dozen other Bachs who were accomplished musicians, with 29 of them quite celebrated in their own right.

Thanks to Queen Isabella and King Ferdinand of Spain, Columbus came to the New World by accident while searching for the East. But when some kissing cousins that were descended from the royal pair later got married, the result was the madman, Don Carlos. It is important to remember that in man and dogs there are undesirable genes lurking in the background waiting to get together with more of the same to create disaster. Your job as a breeder is to prevent that from happening.

A few more human disasters that prove just how bad inbreeding can be have been documented. College students get exposed to the tragedy of the Jukes and Kallikaks in psychology classes. The name Jukes was chosen as a pseudonym for the real name of a family that the Prison Association of New York investigated in 1874. The Jukes were descended from a backwoodsman whose two sons married two Jukes sisters. Of the 709 descendants that were accounted for, 280 received public support as paupers, 140 were alleged criminals, and a large proportion suffered mental or nervous disease.

In the same manner, H. H. Goddard chose the fictitious name of Kallikak for a two-branch family that he investigated dating from Revolutionary War days. The Kallikaks were descended from an apparently normal father and a feebleminded mother. Of the 480 descendants, all were below normal in intelligence and 282 were defective either mentally, morally or physically.

These unfortunate families living in remote rural areas of the Appalachians became the victims of their own *inbreeding*. Their feeblemindedness became fixed in their genes, affecting generation after generation.

In the broadest sense, inbreeding is the mating of close relatives. However, as previously stated, all dogs in a given breed are somewhat related. During the developmental stages of any breed, inbreeding and linebreeding are unavoidable because the number of animals having the desired traits is small and they are usually related. This small gene pool in the beginning of the breed means that there is much duplication of ancestors in the background of any purebred dog.

Can inbreeding cause lessened size and loss of vigor, decreased fertility, and increases in hereditary problems and abnormalities? Yes, it can, if you are inadvertently inbreeding on such problems. However, when accompanied by rigid selection, it is the most effective way to produce uniformity of type, prepotency, and cleansing of undesirable traits from the gene pool to better the future of the breed.

Inbreeding is the most severe and demanding test of the genetic integrity of the animal. It does not create or eliminate anything. It just intensifies it. To the breeder goes the final determination of the effectiveness of inbreeding, for he is the one who eliminates the undesirable that has been intensified by inbreeding by removing it from the breeding population. Careful pruning by the gardener leaves a tree with less foliage but more quality, better able to bear fruit. *Inbreeding works only when the breeder weeds the genetic garden and continues to do so.*

The problem areas of inbreeding that result in genetic trash in the line are caused by the inbred individual having inherited a double dose of genes that were present in single doses in the ancestors and were masked by the normal genes. Genetic trash then surfaces when there is a double dose or overload of the genes. It seems that most genetic abnormalities are recessives, which is bad news when you double up but good news if you are trying to breed it out. A number of years ago, I accidentally discovered that my dogs were affected by Fanconi's Syndrome, also called renal glycosuria, that is the spilling of sugar in the urine. I stumbled onto this knowledge because the sire of Nimbus became sterile

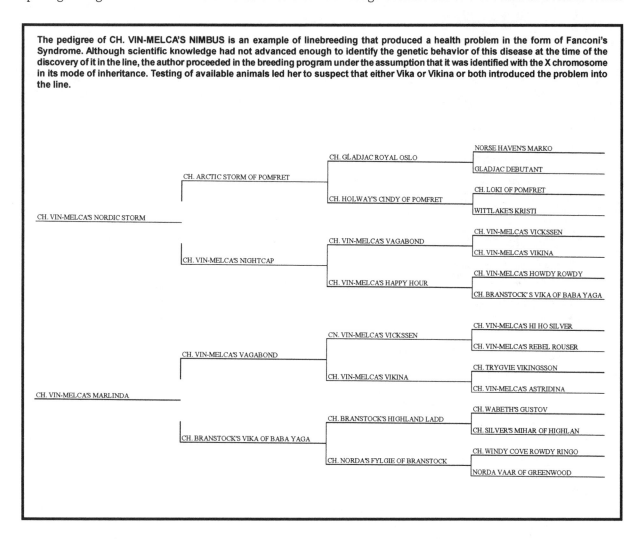

The pedigree of CH. VIN-MELCA'S NIMBUS is an example of linebreeding that produced a health problem in the form of Fanconi's Syndrome. Although scientific knowledge had not advanced enough to identify the genetic behavior of this disease at the time of the discovery of it in the line, the author proceeded in the breeding program under the assumption that it was identified with the X chromosome in its mode of inheritance. Testing of available animals led her to suspect that either Vika or Vikina or both introduced the problem into the line.

and I took the dog to the University of California Veterinary School at Davis. By the way, the temporary sterility was not caused by Fanconi's.

This problem is created by the inability of the kidneys to perform all of their filtering tasks properly—it is a tubular problem. It was a devastating blow to find out that the great Nimbus was affected, that is, had a double dose of the recessive gene for this disorder.

Before explaining how I handled the problem, it is important to realize that such diseases as Fanconi's Syndrome sometimes behave differently in various breeds. The breed that seems to suffer the most from this disease is the Basenji. To make matters worse, it sometimes does not show up until the Basenjis are four to five years of age.

This meant that every single offspring of Nimbus would be a carrier for the defective gene. If he was bred to a dam who was already a carrier, the offspring would have a higher likelihood of being affected (about 75 percent).

Facing this dilemma was difficult—but not impossible. Many animals affected by Fanconi's Syndrome spill lots of other nutrients, including but not limited to, amino acids, proteins, and potassium: 1) The good news for the Vin-Melca line was that the dogs were spilling only sugar, not other nutrients. 2) Unlike some breeds in which the problem does not surface until the dogs get older, test tapes and test sticks could be used while the dogs were puppies to determine if they were affected. 3) Unlike other breeds, the dogs did not seem to suffer any from the problem, living out their expected life span in good health. (Some packs of Arctic wolves also have this abnormality, so it may be more widely spread than previously thought.) Under normal conditions they did not seem any more prone to kidney infection or kidney failure than any other dog. 4) By becoming alert to the problem and removing affected dogs from subsequent generations and the breeding program, it was possible in time to control the problem. 5) Constant diligence must be ongoing forever, until future research can determine which animals carry the recessive *before* using them in a breeding program—and forever more each puppy born must be tested for the problem.

Ch. Vin-Melca's Nimbus in the Breed Ring at Westminster en route to Group !st. Terry Stacy (left) handled Vin-Melca's Chinook to BOW that day with owner Betty Ricks at ringside (holding catalog). (Photo by Martin Booth)

The purpose of inbreeding is to fix genes for favorable traits carried by the close relatives but it will also fix genes for unfavorable traits. Inbreeding is a useful tool in the hands of expert breeders with absolute objectivity, but they must be willing to face problems that arise with candor and accountability. It is their moral obligation to face these issues. Knowing when to say when is vital.

Without monitoring one's breeding program, lines will not flourish. World class breeders make it a point to learn how much inbreeding and linebreeding their lines will tolerate. They act accordingly in their efforts to produce exquisite type while retaining good temperament, soundness, health, and vitality. **Strict adherence to inbreeding has been responsible for the downfall of more than one great breeding program.**

Careful inbreeding and linebreeding cause a higher percentage of genes to be homozygous, reducing the numbers of variables in the offspring. Successful breeders learn to select against hereditary predisposition for disease, continuing a program of line or inbreeding, when appropriate, while selecting carefully. When closebreeding is carried on long enough in a given line, it becomes its own form of inbreeding. If you are going to inbreed heavily, you must be sure the line can stand it.

In pursuing excellent breeding methods, there is a degree of attainment and achievement that will be long-term limited by the laws of nature—that is, you can only get a dog so short backed before it becomes deformed. Take performance itself, for example. During the 19th Century, dramatic improvement in the breeding of thoroughbreds in England took place, times got faster over a 75-year period as bloodstock expertise came of age. By the turn of the century, dramatic increases were no longer happening.

Some improvement was attributed to better feeding programs and training regimens. When a horse like Secretariat comes along, it is possible that the outer limits of performance and class for that breed have been reached, i.e., it would be next to impossible for Secretariat to sire a better animal than himself (see Sire section). The same is true in dogs.

In dealing with the class of the dam, perhaps the best dams will have good show records, and a small, select few have great show records. If the pursuit of the show record gets too intense, the law of dimin-

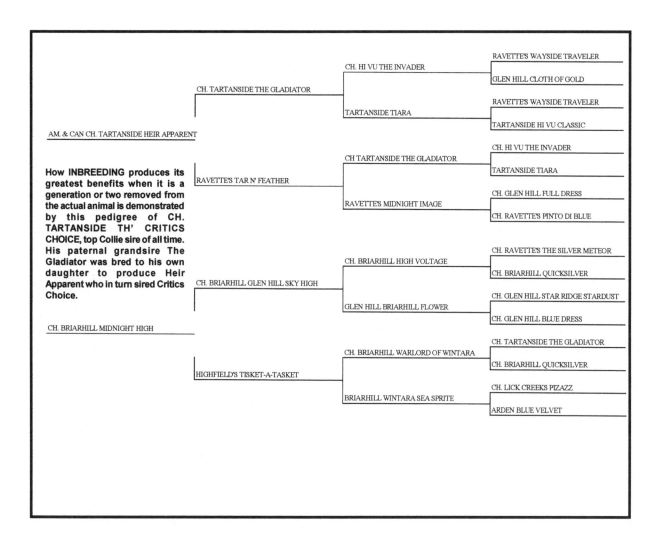

The pedigree chart shows:

AM. & CAN CH. TARTANSIDE HEIR APPARENT
- CH. TARTANSIDE THE GLADIATOR
  - CH. HI VU THE INVADER
    - RAVETTE'S WAYSIDE TRAVELER
    - GLEN HILL CLOTH OF GOLD
  - TARTANSIDE TIARA
    - RAVETTE'S WAYSIDE TRAVELER
    - TARTANSIDE HI VU CLASSIC
- RAVETTE'S TAR N' FEATHER
  - CH TARTANSIDE THE GLADIATOR
    - CH. HI VU THE INVADER
    - TARTANSIDE TIARA
  - RAVETTE'S MIDNIGHT IMAGE
    - CH. GLEN HILL FULL DRESS
    - CH. RAVETTE'S PINTO DI BLUE

How INBREEDING produces its greatest benefits when it is a generation or two removed from the actual animal is demonstrated by this pedigree of CH. TARTANSIDE TH' CRITICS CHOICE, top Collie sire of all time. His paternal grandsire The Gladiator was bred to his own daughter to produce Heir Apparent who in turn sired Critics Choice.

CH. BRIARHILL MIDNIGHT HIGH
- CH. BRIARHILL GLEN HILL SKY HIGH
  - CH. BRIARHILL HIGH VOLTAGE
    - CH. RAVETTE'S THE SILVER METEOR
    - CH. BRIARHILL QUICKSILVER
  - GLEN HILL BRIARHILL FLOWER
    - CH. GLEN HILL STAR RIDGE STARDUST
    - CH. GLEN HILL BLUE DRESS
- HIGHFIELD'S TISKET-A-TASKET
  - CH. BRIARHILL WARLORD OF WINTARA
    - CH. TARTANSIDE THE GLADIATOR
    - CH. BRIARHILL QUICKSILVER
  - BRIARHILL WINTARA SEA SPRITE
    - CH. LICK CREEKS PIZAZZ
    - ARDEN BLUE VELVET

ishing returns goes into effect and the producing record of the bitch is compromised (see Brood Bitch section).

Intense inbreeding of animals up close in a pedigree is very different from intense inbreeding a few generations back. The greater benefits seem to be achieved when the inbreeding itself is a generation or two removed than when it is the actual inbred animal itself. If the inbreeding gets more than two or three generations removed, its beneficial results are weakened if not lost altogether.

Consider a mating of father and daughter. The daughter already has 50 percent of the father's genes, meaning she will pass on to her progeny sired by her father about 25 percent of his genes. If she is bred to her own sire he will pass along 50 percent of his genes to the puppy giving the puppy about 75 percent of his sire's genetic material. If you wanted to be absolutely accurate, you could say the resulting puppy would carry 50 to 75 percent of its sire's genes. Such a breeding produced Ch. Tartanside Heir Apparent, sire of Ch. Tartanside Th' Critics Choice, top Collie sire of all time.

I have never understood why some bitches only produce great sons and some sires only produce great daughters. Is this just a coincidence? I investigated these issues in the sex chromosome, brood bitch, and stud dog sections but still do not know the answers for sure. The message of all linebreeding, inbreeding, and closebreeding is that the family is greater than the individual.

A sire that appears twice in the pedigree as both grandsires has about the same influence as if he were the actual sire. A double great grandsire would have about the same influence as if he were the grandsire. That is why linebreeding makes it possible to concentrate the greats. Linebreeding is probably the only way to hope to recover some of the genetic formula that was present in the great sire or the key bitch.

Any form of closebreeding works in concert with the strictest of selection criteria; therefore, when you study the pedigrees of great dogs, you will see evidence that intelligent linebreeding, inbreeding and closebreeding, coupled with expert selection, have their place in the breeding program.

Outcrossing is the breeding of unrelated animals within a breed. Some dog authorities consider a dog with no common ancestors in a five-generation pedigree to be *outcrossed*. Thoroughbred experts define an outcross as an animal with no common ancestors in a four-generation pedigree. But is an animal totally outcrossed if the pedigree has the name of full brothers in it? Therefore, the generation one step farther back would then have common names, but they would be "out of the pedigree" on a five-generation document.

Because outcrossing is a safer form of breeding, it has taken a bum rap. Some breeders feel it is associated with less progress and more mediocrity. It is my understanding that a number of very successful breeding programs in Europe follow the outcrossing method of breeding. Rhys Llewellyn, a great bloodstock breeder, was a proponent of outcrossing because he thought it could contribute new gene combinations to the breed. If superior selection followed such outcrossings, the breed would benefit.

Outcrossing is most dangerous when it is a series of random matings within a given breed, introducing untold numbers of unknown genes. Unfortunately, you are not playing with a child's tinker toy set when you breed quality animals. You may go to an outcrossed dog in search of some particular trait, only to find it does not appear in the resulting progeny. This is because the genes are *reassembling* themselves. You will not know until the following generation if the outcross was a success in that case.

If your outcross produces the quality you sought in the first generation, it is because the animal you used was prepotent for this trait. If the resulting dog is in turn prepotent, you could have a great one! Usually, the animals of the outcross will lack this genetic prepotency.

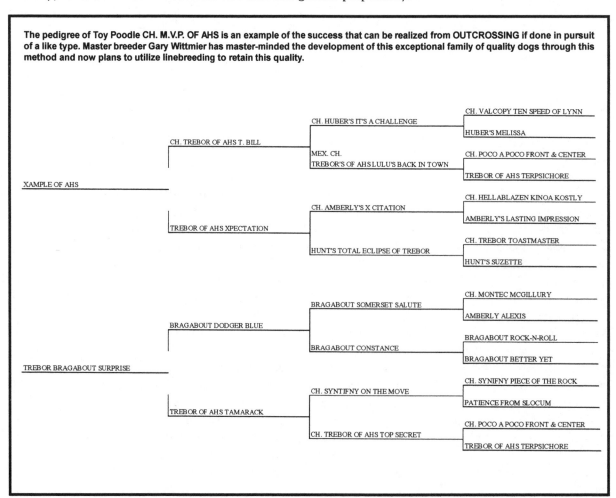

The pedigree of Toy Poodle CH. M.V.P. OF AHS is an example of the success that can be realized from OUTCROSSING if done in pursuit of a like type. Master breeder Gary Wittmier has master-minded the development of this exceptional family of quality dogs through this method and now plans to utilize linebreeding to retain this quality.

Ch. M.V.P. of Ahs, the fabulous Toy Poodle bitch who was both a Westminster group winner and Quaker Oats winner is pictured here winning one of her many groups and BISs. This magnificent little bitch is the ultimate tribute to outcrossing as a breeding method. When one has the selection talents of Master Breeder Gary Wittmier, outcrossing can be a powerful tool. Gary's key to success is the consistency of his selection process. She is pictured here with Judge Vernelle Kendrick. (Photo by Rodwell)

The best form of outcrossing involves the bringing together of two closely bred lines that are unrelated to each other. The desired result is *hybrid vigor*, which means progeny that are supposedly healthier and more vigorous.

Certainly this pursuit should be considered by any breeder who is having health problems in the line determined to be of genetic origin. Hybrid corn is perhaps the all-time success story of outcrossing two inbred lines to get the best. Not only were the yields one-third higher than other strains of corn, but the best in kernel alignment and other corn characteristics was achieved.

Dr. Braxton B. Sawyer (Kentucky Lake American Foxhounds) thought you could practice what he termed a "form of linebreeding even while outcrossing" if you selected consistently for the same traits. Some very superior lines have utilized this form of breeding. It seems to be most productive when associated with a breed that has a relatively small gene pool.

Gary Wittmier, one of the greatest breeders of Toy Poodles in history, has followed these principles with his superb animals. Gary told me that due to the closeness and limits of his breed's gene pool, it is somewhat difficult to have a breeding program that is totally outcrossed. This outcross success is possible only when one has the excellent eye of this *master breeder*. When outcrossing, the breeder is selecting for the same traits, so that similar genes are being collected within the same pedigree even if not from the same source. Gary now plans to utilize some linebreedings.

In discussing outcrossing with another *master breeder*, Connie Gerstner of Malagold Golden Retriever fame, the flip side of the coin was pointed out to me. And that is, in breeds with exceptionally large gene pools such as the Golden, an outcross can be almost as dramatic as breeding two different breeds! Therefore, the only way an outcross can be effective is when the two mates are of "like type."

You are probably doing a kind of off-the-record linebreeding if your outcrosses are always with animals of the same type, make and shape, anatomical construction, and temperament—assuming you can find them. This is not possible in some breeds.

This concept of outcrossing in search of a few traits might result in some rapid progress that will then reach a plateau as the favorable arrangement of genes occurs. Therefore, the wise breeder will then linebreed to keep the genes in that arrangement. Breeds can reach a degree of progress through one form or another of breeding, a peak if you will. Then they plateau and decline. To avoid this regression a change of breeding methods might help, then return to your original method when the time is right. Breeding of purebred animals, when it reaches a certain level, involves running hard to stay in place.

The ultimate success will be achieved by those who practice balanced breeding. Balanced breeding utilizes the very best of inbreeding, linebreeding, closebreeding and outcrossing in the most productive combinations. In utilizing the balanced breeding concept, the astute breeder immediately recognizes when the line is drifting toward an overload of one kind or another and responds accordingly.

Conclusion: It is important to recognize the vast difference between a few sprinkled great ones in a breed and the quality of the breed in general. Some ponder if the free flow of animals nationally and internationally, aided by the use of frozen and fresh-chilled semen, will produce a more uniform breed in the future.

Others worry that the breed will become so closely related due to such international exchange that there will be nowhere to go to infuse *new blood*. How would this affect the once possible isolated and thus segregated gene pools that matured to perfection to become part of the hybrid vigor equation?

The use of sperm banks is just a scratch on the surface of technology. Genetic mapping to identify undesirable genes and deal with them in the responsible and appropriate manner will open new frontiers in the breeders' quest of perfection.

Yet this quest is nothing new as it took place long before Mendel, Morgan or other experts gave the aid of their scientific knowledge to breeders. Those early breeders used common sense in selecting appropriate mates for their animals in place of high-tech assistance. Never underestimate common sense as your most valuable tool in breeding dogs. *It very well may be that a Ph.D. in genetics can tell you how to breed great dogs, but the knowing breeder can show you how.*

Nicks

Nicks are lucky combinations of genes that produce animals superior to both parents. Each parent seems to contribute all its desirable genes, thus the parents are reinforcing each other's good genes while canceling out the bad. It is a powerful stride forward to find a *nick* you can count on.

Positive nicks offer a real reason to repeat a breeding, thus making more animals of this genetic phenomena available to the gene pool. In the sixties it became obvious in his first litters that the young sire, Ch. Vin-Melca's Howdy Rowdy, produced superior progeny with daughters and granddaughters of Ch. Wabeth's Gustav. Because of this superior quality, the maiden bitch, Ch. Branstock's Vika of Baba Yaga, was added to my breeding program. Not only was she a granddaughter of Ch. Wabeth's Gustav, she was also a granddaughter of Howdy Rowdy's sire, Ch. Windy Cove's Rowdy Ringo. The mating of Howdy Rowdy to Vika produced some of the best Elkhounds of their day—including National Specialty winners and all-breed winners.

Howdy Rowdy and Gustav were definitely a truly great nick. Once you benefit from a nick, where do you go from there? Maybe you will be lucky enough to find some other quality animals from the same nick another generation or two removed that will blend in well with what you have.

Just as a positive nick can be a boon to your breeding program, so can a negative

Cartoon by Jose Prieto.

one be a bust! A negative nick occurs when two superior animals are bred to each other and the resulting progeny is inferior to both parents as well as the lines. What happened? Both the sire and the dam were high-class animals and had produced well when bred in other directions. But their resulting progeny are uniformly disappointing and lack the merits of the parents. It is also a negative nick when the offspring from one great line do not go well with the offspring of another great line.

Before you dismiss the idea altogether, examine what other similarly bred animals have produced when brought together. Try to learn from it, even if you never do understand it. Think of it simply as incompatibility of traits and gene pools.

Vin-Melca experienced two such negative nicks that come to mind. In each instance, the sire used was an outcross. Furthermore, they were sires of the highest quality who threw some very good dogs out of other lines. And what is more important, the problems that resulted in using them did not appear when these sires were used on other bitches; nor did the resulting problems appear from the Vin-Melca bitches bred within the line.

This, then, is no indictment because all of the animals involved produced very good progeny in other instances. It might be said that these two marriages were *not* made in heaven.

The first *negative nick* occurred in the late sixties when a lovely Norwegian import was bred to a couple of Vin-Melca bitches. Only one champion of good quality resulted, and that animal contributed nothing to the future of the breed's gene pool. This dog's lineage was not unknown to me, as he had both a litter brother and litter sister in California who had produced a number of good offspring for me to study. However, when used on Vin-Melca bitches, he was most prepotent in throwing his faults and not prepotent at all for his virtues. His progeny from my bitches, with the one exception, had the *worst* of both parents. Although I had to write this dog off, he went to another breeder whose bitches he did nick with and produced some quality animals. It was like the old saying: "One man's meat is another's poison." With my line it was a negative nick, with the other line it was not.

In the eighties, I outcrossed to an American line of dogs I very much admired. Although both the sire and dam had acceptable hips, the puppies had an unusually large incidence of hip dysplasia. What's worse, some that seemed acceptable to breed also threw a large incidence of hip dysplasia.

In effect, the resulting offspring seemed cursed by a higher incidence of hip dysplasia than either line had experienced before, due to a *negative nick*. One of the encouraging aspects of the futuristic field of molecular genetics is the prevention of such disasters before they happen. Whereas one does repeat the positive nick, the message of the negative nick is—don't do that again!

Summary: "Breed the best to the best and hope for the best" is an oft-repeated phrase heard wherever one ventures in the world of breeding purebred animals. Unhappily, not many people realize what it means. What it does not mean is breeding the top-winning dog to the top-winning bitch. This is the popular misinterpretation of the idea. What it really means is to breed the top-producing dog to the best-producing bitches.

No matter what method the breeder uses, the measure of success will depend on the ability of the breeder to select. *Selection* is the key to all successful breeding programs. No breeding program will survive without utilizing skilled selection that is both knowledgeable and objective. So important is selection to your success, there is a complete section on it.

In utilizing the methods of breeding to achieve your goals in breeding, it is important to remember that a breed or a given breeding program in the breed can attain wonderful heights in skillful hands. Sometimes when these degrees of excellence are reached, the program will level off and the quality of dogs will not improve much. You could compare it to a diet that is successful until you hit a plateau.

Although it is difficult to ascertain why this happens, here are a couple of probable reasons: 1) Rapid improvement resulted in superior animals until there was nowhere else to go, so things leveled off. 2) The breedings were being made one generation at a time. That is to say that the breedings were made with the idea of achieving the desired results from each mating, not to participate as a stepping stone to the future or even to the next generation.

When all the breedings are being made just one generation ahead, instead of in the overall picture of the specific breeding program, as well as that of the entire breed, progress will slow down or perhaps come to a halt. That is why it is so very important for breeders to be visionaries. Be careful of letting the mating itself be the end in itself, for it will delay the fixing of genetic superiority, causing at best a plateau, at worst a decline.

Breeders of great vision, able to get past the concept of breeding today's top winners in pursuit of one great litter, are those who can see—or feel—the potential of some animals others would miss. They seem to sense a breeding that will bring the best of the sire and the dam to the progeny not only for the next generation, but for generations to come. These people will experience waves in their breeding programs that will eventually bring them momentum in the climb to the top. They recognize the importance of "going with the flow" as Mother Nature herself would do. These breeders know their roles in the grand scheme of things.

Because of such discipline, these breeding programs will then enjoy a sudden spurt in which top-quality animals will emerge from their line. Some would consider this sudden success from an unexpected source, but usually close investigation will show this was no accident.

There is a certain rhythm of replacement in great lines. They can fall into decline for lack of a star producer even though their gene pool is good and solid. The star comes along, and the line is revitalized and greatness is reestablished.

Sometimes your dogs are losing but your breeding program is sound and solid. Don't fret, things will sort themselves out in time. Your timing could be off because a few stars and flyers are out there. If you take stock and honestly realize your dogs are being presented properly in great condition, your turn will come.

Sometimes your dogs are winning and your breeding program is not on firm ground but is in a state of chaos. If your dogs are winning it is because they are the best of a bad lot. You need to realize why things are happening the way they are and consequently improve upon the gene pool. To be satisfied with the *status quo* in a troubled breeding program, even though winning at the shows, is most naive.

Remember that a line cannot be expected to perpetuate and rejuvenate itself forever without some wise decision-making by those working with the line. Usually, it will involve the infusion of new blood either from an outcross to another well-bred line, or some family members somewhat removed from the line but still in concert with it. This is how breeders avoid *genetic drift*.

PART II

W I N N I N G

MEANS PUTTING YOUR PLAN
INTO ACTION

Selection | *What it is*: Selection as it relates to biology is defined by Mr. Webster as "any process, whether natural or artificial, by which certain organisms or characteristics are permitted or favored to survive and reproduce in preference to others." Select means singled out, chosen for excellence, or some special quality: To select is to pick out.

Select goods are choice goods—outstanding. And a select person is one who is careful in choosing, even *fastidious*, according to Mr. Webster. Negative selection is called *culling*. Culling does not mean killing. It simply means to sort out, select, or separate from a mass as inferior. To me culling simply means to remove from the breeding program. Over the years, I have been hung out to dry by more than one person who assumed culling meant much worse. In answer to their criticism, when I use the word it simply means to remove from the breeding population. Culls are simply animals that are not up to the standard to retain for the breeding program.

What it is not: Selection is not biased in action. Selection is not kennel blindness at work nor is it tunnel vision. If your selections inadvertently fall into these patterns, you are no longer being selective. You are simply picking those your emotions prejudice you to favor and doing what is pleasant and convenient. If you are not totally objective, you will continue to develop an eye that is comfortable with mediocrity and never progress beyond that. Many people spend a lifetime at this level and are satisfied with minor wins for their animals. They do not aspire to *master breeder* status.

Selection is something you do all your life—a very special form of decision making. When you go to a gourmet restaurant and several items sound delicious, you must select one for that occasion. You select your career, your spouse, your friends, your home, your clothes and your hobbies. Everything you do in life involves selection, yet for some reason many people are stopped cold by the reality of the selection process as it relates to their dogs. These loving dog fanciers are not unlike loving parents. Yet indulging in the love-is-blind theory can be traumatic with youngsters just as it can devastate your breeding program.

In 34 years of teaching eighth-graders, it was not all that unusual to meet loving but biased parents who could not cope with their children's problems. They would come to school to meet with the teachers, stating: "There is no reason in the world why Johnny should not get straight "As." Often, this

---

SELECTION: CULLING

Culling is a subject people prefer not to discuss because it has a negative connotation. Yet, Webster uses "select" as one of the words to describe cull. It also means to pick out something as inferior.

Culling to a dog breeder should mean one thing—to remove from the breeding population. To spay is to cull as a breeding animal. In fact, we can thank Mr. Webster for going so far as to say: "Poor fruit, stale vegetables and animals that are not up to standard are called culls."

In essence, culling is a form of negative selection. In its most extreme form it means the euthanization of deformed or diseased puppies. At the better end of the scale, it means selecting those dogs lacking in breeding potential and making sure they are neutered. If you are doing your job as a breeder, some very good dogs indeed will be chosen for neutering, while those that are even better will be retained for breeding. The best breeders have a number of animals that stay out of the gene pool simply because they have adequate breeding stock, and people wanting pets often prefer a neutered animal. (No doubt neutered stock of the best breeders is far superior to much of the stock being used by others.)

Until such time as those other breeders are willing to turn to the *master breeder*, it is unfortunate that lesser bitches will stay in the gene pool while better ones are spayed! It behooves all breeders to work in the best interest of the breed as they cooperate to utilize only the best. Objectivity and not subjectivity will get the job done.

was true. But in one case, Johnny was doing everything he could to maintain a B average, given his particular reading and comprehension skills. He was a B student, a darn good B student, but nonetheless a B student. His parents were "in denial." Both of these brilliant people could not accept their sunny-natured, wonderful kid for what he was—a great youngster who just might not be a world class scholar. Unfortunately, such well-meaning, yet demanding, parents who think their sons and daughters are more gifted than the facts indicate sometimes pressure their kids to a point where they become statistics. But parental pressure is not what this is about.

Selection is what this is about. And selection can be the single biggest obstacle standing between you and success in your breeding efforts. Stated more specifically: Lack of knowledgeable objectivity in your selection process can wreck your dreams. Assuming that you know dogs in general and your breed in particular, inability to look at your dogs objectively will derail all of your hard work if you do not get past it.

The purpose of this section is to help you develop your skills in the difficult process of selection. If you learn only one thing from this section it would be perfecting your selection skills. For **without** expert selection, it will not matter what sort of breeding program or methods you are using. And **with** selective expertise, it still will not matter what kind of breeding methods you use, for any of them will work due to your selection skills.

Selection is the key to breeding success no matter whether you inbreed, linebreed, closebreed, or outcross—or mix them up.

For selection to work it must be done by a person with great knowledge of the breed. This person will know the breed's history and development as well as its hereditary behavior patterns. This breeder and selector will be totally objective in applying that knowledge to the selection process—picking for traits that contribute to the type best suited to the purpose for which the breed was bred. This person will understand the advice: "Pick for type. Cull for soundness." (A gentle reminder: Cull means to select and remove from consideration, so help me Hannah! If you don't agree, check with Mr. Webster.) Selection of any kind is a positive term—one with which you will learn to be comfortable.

When you remember that all life emanated from primitive cellular material and that all dogs from a common ancestor, it is a powerful reminder that some form of selection has made all change possible. Consider that all breeds, all of the varying lines and strains within those breeds and all the individuals within those families descended from a common ancestor. How did this happen? How do we have the differences we see today? The answer is selection of one kind or another. Perhaps it was natural selection, or man-made selection or combinations. Regardless of which, it was selection of one kind or another that led to the differing breeds within the given species.

George Louis Leclerc (Comte de Buffon) recognized that pigeon breeders were changing their charges from those in the wild long before Darwin did his work. By utilizing the selection process, they were breeding better pigeons than existed in the wild, according to him, and they bred true. Selection then, is where it's *at* for the dog breeder as well as the pigeon breeder.

Natural Selection

"Life is a struggle. Only the fittest survive." Thomas Malthus, the 18th Century English clergyman who was also an early social scientist, gave us these words. Malthus had a good handle on natural selection. He believed that life and living things multiplied faster than the food supply to sustain that life. Consequently, there was a constant struggle for food and survival, with nature taking its inevitable toll.

It might not have earned him praise from church leaders, who thought he should stick closer to the scriptures, but Malthus got into the history books and biology books because of his understanding of the forces at play that constitute natural selection. Because he was educated as a mathematician, Malthus presented his formula in his own language: Populations tend to increase geometrically while food supplies tend to increase arithmetically. The resulting dilemma is a chronic oversupply of eaters constantly threatened by a chronic undersupply of available food.

Malthus presented his hypothesis to the public in his "Essay on the Principles of Population," the pioneer document that modern theorists base the *zero-population-growth* concept on to this day. The idea caught on among his contemporaries. No doubt the experiences of early dog breeders, with the weak whelp unable to push its way in to nurse or whose mother pushed it away, caused them to agree with him. Malthus was ahead of his time, but with Earth's population rapidly approaching six billion people, maybe his time has come.

Darwin was the next to wrestle with the selection process and came to the understanding that the weak or deformed did not survive. Predators constantly killed the unfit, leaving the better-formed animals to survive to beget the next generation.

If there were variations from the norm, they would survive only if the variations were favorable. Darwin was on to something. Although it is not clear if he knew those variations would be called *mutations*, he was the first to use the term *natural selection*. And certainly he was correct in recognizing that the more abundant unfavorable mutations—or variations—usually did not survive.

In the early development of all species, natural selection was at its best. As dogs evolved from *canis lupis*, the wolf, and then from *canis familiaris*, the dog, they began to assume physical differences that best suited them to their surroundings. As dogs were domesticated, their cooperative living arrangements with their new friend—man—required these changes to continue to prepare them better for their new work.

Different kinds of dogs developed according to the area, the terrain, the climate and the job description. Early on, these changes were based on natural selection, and even when man got into the act, the selections were in accordance with nature, for they were based on ability to do things that contributed to the survival of the primitive man and beast.

Natural selection could change the development of the animals in one of two ways: slowly through evolution, which is the probable result of additive gene action influenced by undramatic mutations; or, rapidly through very dramatic mutations. Mutations appear to be the explanation as to why primitive animals were not identical within a species, such as the dog, or at least why they were not more alike. Another way to think of it is as nature making *jumps*.

Mutations were previously described as sudden changes in the genetic information process caused by things only scientists understand. Sometimes, the changes will be very minor in outward appearance, but as these small changes accumulate over time, noticeable change becomes apparent.

This is natural selection as seen by Darwin. Species change to stay in tune with their environment, and this survival scheme improves the animal, whereas the selection process, as we know it, may not, due to its artificial criteria. In nature, the inferior would be eliminated in every generation by nature's demands, leaving only the strong, healthy and fit to reproduce. This is not always true in an unnatural selection system contrived by man.

Natural selection in the wild is one thing, and artificial selection by man is another. Probably, the species were healthier before man got into the act because Mother Nature is so very demanding.

Artificial Selection

Artificial selection is human control of the breeding population based on criteria different from survival. It is culling by man for the purpose of improving stock or eliminating undesirable characteristics. This elimination simply means that those animals that do not meet breeders' expectations are removed from the breeding programs and sold or used in other roles. These animals are then neutered.

Wild dogs were accustomed to roaming free, but nonetheless lived in social wolflike packs. Primitive man may have provided early domesticated dogs with the social environment as well as simulated leadership such as that provided by the pack's alpha male.

Man and dog provided for each other. Drawings on the walls of caves and in other archaeological locations are proof that ancient sight hounds and other dogs have been around for a long time. In all probability, early man picked agreeable animals that brought comfort to him, as well as being able to do their jobs.

Exactly what criteria, other than his ability to hunt, were used by early man to select dogs is unknown. But early man was not much more forgiving than Mother Nature as witnessed by this test used for selecting horses.

Several horses were locked in primitive pens and water was withheld from them for several days. When the herd was released to run for the water hole, those that arrived first were the ones that were kept. Another variation of the horse test was to withhold water again, but then to simulate battle sounds as the horses of war were released. Those who responded to the cries for war over their need for water were deemed brave enough to do battle and retained for the breeding program.

These tests seem cruel, but in those days civility and kindness were not major concerns. As man began to develop and select types of dogs to do specific jobs, he was developing functional breeds. Some breeds have remained relatively the same as their ancient ancestors to this day.

It is important to realize that every breed went through some dramatic stages during its developmental periods. Because most breeds had only a few foundation animals—especially the sires who have so much more numerical influence—some undesirable as well as desirable traits were *fixed* in that breed's gene pool. Perhaps a given prepotent sire that was a turning point in his breed was widely used by the breeders because of his excellent head, temperament and look. Unfortunately, he also sired very poor shoulders along with those virtues. A beautiful breed has been produced, but it is a breed riddled with shoulder problems. The heads are a fixed desired trait and the shoulders a fixed undesired one that fanciers come to accept as identified with that breed.

Selection Criteria

The most important thing about selection criteria is to be consistent with whatever criteria priorities that you set. A common mistake beginning breeders make is unknowingly changing their selection criteria from breeding to breeding, thus complicating their chances for improvement.

Successful breeders who produce quality dogs year after year are consistent with their selection process. They maintain a picture of the type they are trying to produce and know the ingredients that make up that type as well as those that make the type functional and sound.

General criteria for the breeder include non-breed specific characteristics, such as good health and temperament, fertility, soundness, adaptability and trainability. Breed-specific selection criteria will depend on the breed. If the breed is a head breed, such as the Collie or the Bulldog, ranking priorities would place "head" near the top of the list. In breeds such as the Kerry Blue Terrier or the Yorkshire Terrier, color would be high on the priority list, yet a number of breeds—Greyhound and Lhasa Apsos, for example—consider color to be immaterial. Your selection ability will depend on in-depth knowledge for its success—both general dog knowledge and breed-specific knowledge.

Pedigree, Conformation and Performance: These three criteria will be the basis for developing your selection skills. Ideally, it would be difficult to separate pedigree and conformation when they are both of excellent quality. You would like to believe that a dog with a good pedigree and good conformation would produce only progeny with good conformation. The sad fact is that the desired combination sometimes produces unwanted results. *The pedigree profile* investigates this dilemma.

Thirteen-year old Pat Vincent with Ch. Ulf's Madam Helga C.D., her first Norwegian Elkhound and the beginning of Vin-Melca. Every single dog to carry the Vin-Melca name traces in ancestry to this bitch with her long, swayed back and other conformation faults. *Breeding-up* with the tail female line down from this bitch was a slow process unnecessary to future *master breeders* wise enough to start with a better quallity bitch. (House Photo)

Suffice it to say if you are selecting dogs from plebeian pedigrees, it could be a long time before any progress is noted in your "breeding-up" ambition. Breeding up is very time-consuming and costly. It was lucky that I had plenty of time when pursuing this method at the age of 13 with Ch. Ulf's Madam Helga C.D., my first Norwegian Elkhound bitch. It took a lot of years to get beyond her as every single Vin-Melca animal goes back to her—sometimes I think the farther the better! She came from a pair of tough hunting dogs used in the Dismal Swamp on brown bears. Although she was bred by C.W. Turner, her parents were from the Joyce Creek hunting kennels and carried the Lindvangen and Vindsval foundation lines. Her maternal grandsire was culled from the breeding program while still a young dog when he got in too close to a brown bear. The good news was that the animals were hardy, harsh coated, and athletic. The bad news was that they lacked superior type and, unknown to me for more than 20 years, they carried the recessive red gene.

Ch. Vin-Melca's Rebel Rouser was the turning point in the Vin-Melca breeding program after her purchase as a college graduation present in 1958. She is pictured here in 1962 when she became the #2 Norwegian Elkhound in the U.S. Rebel Rouser was to become the second foundation bitch upon which the tail female line was established. Many of today's Norwegian Elkhounds feature more than 20 crosses to her in an extended pedigree. (House Photo)

Breeding-up was a slow process, and it was not until my parents bought me a puppy bitch, who was to become Ch. Vin-Melca's Rebel Rouser, as my college graduation gift in 1958, that my breeding program took a significant positive turn. Since youngsters have time to waste a number of years and Elkhounds were very scarce in those days, it was not a devastating loss of time for a teenager. But let it be an example for those of you just starting to breed. Because you love your first bitch does not mean she has to be in your gene pool.

Breeding-up is based on starting with a favorite bitch one loves too much to spay, and hoping to get a better daughter from her first litter. Then that daughter will be bred up, and so on, to the next generation and succeeding ones. Although this can be done if you have the time and other requirements necessary, improvement in your breeding program will be much more rapid if you start with a better quality animal early on.

Discarding your beloved pet bitch from the plebeian pedigree and starting your breeding program with a bitch of a patrician pedigree will provide you with a *jump start* toward success. Such a selection of a family classic to the breed will provide you with more consistent animals from which to pick.

Performance selection is practiced by more breeders than even they realize. When you breed to dogs on the basis of winning records in the show ring, you are practicing performance selection. You are basing the mating on the animal's accomplishments. In some areas, this may not be all bad, as certainly it is an indication that the animal has been tested. How it has been tested is another matter.

Performance criteria are broken down into two major categories: *subjective* performance testing and *objective* performance testing. Subjective performance records are based on the collective opinions of a number of judges. Judges can be enamored by showiness, soundness, personal favorites, and a wide range of other influences that have little to do with the genetic potential of the dog. Sometimes the judge's opinion on a rather ordinary specimen just means that the dog beat others of even lesser quality.

Records are compiled that sound impressive in print but may not be so impressive once they are analyzed. A dog that won 10 Bests in Show (BIS) in a total of 50 shows may very well be better than the dog who won 20 BIS out of 300 competitions. Or he may not. If the dog that went to 300 shows in three years was shown across the board in the stiffest competition, including circuits deep in great group dogs, his may be the more valid record. If the dog shown at 50 shows went to small out-of-the-way shows, often single shows that did not draw the top dogs, and showed to the same judges over and over, his record may be less impressive than it appears.

Some dogs are campaigned in a protective manner to keep them from ever meeting another good dog in their breed. Such records are questionable to me, for dogs that are not capable of meeting other good ones in their own breed on equal terms may be generic dogs that have little to offer your breeding program in breed-specific qualities.

Another thing to consider in evaluating show performance records in your selection criteria is the quality of the dogs being shown at the same time the one you are considering for your breeding program was campaigned. For example, there are years in which a given breed has a number of stars in it—absolutely outstanding ones that knock heads with each other often enough that they cost each other more notches on the gun. They were from a wonderful crop! Like exceptional wines, it was a vintage year. To be number three or number four in those years might be a more meaningful record than to be number one in lesser years when the superior ones were not out there—either for lack of quality animals or for lack of opportunity for the quality animals that existed. (For a close look at a truly vintage year, refer to Spotlight on 1973, Part IV.)

Opportunity is an important word in this context. For sometimes there will be superior dogs in a breed that just do not have the opportunity to acquire impressive records while lesser dogs are out there in the winners' circle. As "The Great Compromiser," Henry Clay, said: "Statistics are no substitute for judgment." If your selection criteria are on target, the show record in these cases will be put in its proper perspective.

Performance records based on objectivity are another matter indeed. Field trials of all kinds are usually objective and have great value in evaluation records for selection. This would include, but not be limited to, bird dog trials, retriever trials, flushing trials, fox hunts and other sporting contests in which the best hunters of one breeder take on the best hunters of other breeders. Hunting dog breeds are selected for nose, voice, birdiness, softness of mouth, durability, weather proofing, tractability and willingness, as well as a number of other traits that make the best hunting dogs. The same principle is true for herding dog enthusiasts. A good cattle dog is like a good cow pony. He gets in the head of the animal he is working. Not only is he athletic and able, he has *cow sense*. The job of the herding dog includes ability to cut animals for branding and shearing as well as to herd them, move them and protect them. The handling of sheep takes a special mentality on the part of the dog. He must be protective and assertive with his flock. At the same time, he must avoid frightening or abusing them.

The world's all-time performance record has to go to the Manchester Terrier known as "Billy," in the days when the killing of rats in pit-fights was a favorite sport of the working classes. Considered by experts to be the oldest of the terrier breeds and known as the black and tan terrier for many years, the Manchester was highly prized along the British waterfront for his toughness in dealing with rodents, and it seemed natural to wager on his prowess in the pits. It has been widely reported that Billy set the all-time record by killing 100 rats in 12 minutes. Now, there's a performance record to sink one's teeth in!

The dedicated obedience fancier is also in an objective arena where trainability, dependability, reliance and steadiness are necessary requirements. Furthermore, just as all the other performance animals, the dog must be sound, athletic and willing. Trainability is a high priority.

Important criteria when selecting for performance are to know if the records you are evaluating are produced by consistent or erratic performances. A good steady contender who performs day in and day out might be a better choice than a brilliant flash in the pan that has one day in the sun—the Andy Warhol 15 minutes of fame thing—and never comes close to it again.

Skilled selection is based on a long-term goal of selecting *for* and *fixing* a certain type. Even though the breeder knows this may take any number of generations and the quest is ongoing, each generation is selected with its role in the overall picture of the resulting product. It could be said that at the same time the breeder is selecting one generation at the time, it is part of a long-term selection process consisting of infinite numbers of generations.

Therefore, the breeder must select for compatibility of traits and be consistently true to that pattern, or get lost. Compatibility of traits means the animals are of a like type, have many similar virtues, and fit into their role in the breeding program. Each mating is made with animals who do not have the same weaknesses. In other words, it is breeding within a picture using animals with only slight variables. The idea is to remedy those variables. Like begets like.

Sometimes the production of traits antagonistic to soundness is the goal. Incompatibility of traits could be considered a negative genetic association. It is important to realize when you are selecting for traits that are *not compatible*. If you do not know when traits are incompatible or when traits simply cannot be fixed in their genetic makeup because they are not uniform or predictable, not only will you spin your wheels trying to get them, you will damage your gene pool losing good traits that are selection-responsive.

Such a trait in my breed is the super small ear. Although I have always admired small ears on an Elkhound, these are the head characteristics that come first with me: 1) Correct wedge-shaped formation of the entire head with emphasis on a relatively flat skull; 2) Small, correctly shaped, dark eye and good expression; 3) Fill under the eye and parallel planes with correct stop; 4) Small ears.

In my breed, the historical dogs and foundation stock for the breed did not have small ears. Breeders need to concentrate on correct head-type when selecting for small ears because most of the dogs with small ears have paid a terrible price for them: 1) Incorrect domed skulls; 2) Popping, protruding eyes with totally incorrect expression; 3) Too much stop resulting in a head that is very un-Elkhound-like. On the rare occasions when I used good-headed dogs with very small ears, they seemed to throw straight-shoulders. So I keep searching for the good-headed dog with small ears and a beautiful shoulder while aware that perhaps some things are not compatible. Alas! Lest you think otherwise, sadly some of the largest-eared dogs have dreadful shoulders too, producing a look that has huge ears nestled practically on their shoulder blades.

The author's interpretation of the correct Norwegian Elkhound head as viewed in these two pictures. The head has the desired wedge shape with emphasis on a relatively flat skull. The oval-shaped eye exhibits the right expression with sufficient fill under it. The head is broad at the ears which are firm and correctly made. The proper stop separates the head in exact proportions with the length of the muzzle approximately the same as the length of the skull and lying in parallel planes with it. (Jayne Langdon Photographs)

Experienced breeders can assist you in ascertaining qualities that are difficult to achieve at best, incompatible at worst, in your breed. You will be most fortunate if you are in a breed in which desired traits do not occur that are incompatible. So many of the qualities we seek in our dogs are multifactorial because they are the result of many traits occurring in the desired combinations. These qualities range from head, ear, eye, running gear, and coat to learning ability, temperament, and health factors.

In some breeds, it is extremely difficult to get a well-laid-back shoulder and a short, straight pastern. In others, it is hard to get a desired lean head and still satisfy the standards requirement for substantial bone. It is your task as a breeder to learn and deal with the specific difficulties in your breed. Every breed has some combinations of desired traits that are hard to achieve. Such complexities are what make the breeding of excellent dogs a super challenge. Nobody said it would be easy!

The more you understand about what your breed is about, what can and cannot be done, the more you will be able to take advantage of skilled selection for breed improvement.

Selecting for Traits: Making Tradeoffs

Successful breeders are consistent with their selection process over the years, maintaining a picture of the type they wish to produce and knowing the proper traits that make up that picture. They are consistent in their priorities, recognizing that changing the traits in the selection process will make progress all the more difficult.

It is important to recognize that the desired traits will vary from breed to breed to some extent. Size is an important selection priority in some breeds, and not so important in others. It would be counterproductive to breed the ultimate in a Pekingese if it were to grow into a 15-pound dog. It would be counterproductive to breed the best Beagle if it measured 16 inches, unless of course you lived in Australia or England.

The important thing is that the breeder have a list of preferred traits that are consistently selected for in order to show improvement in the breeding program. Such traits could include, but are not limited to, the following:

- Temperament and intelligence
- Health, longevity, soundness and hardiness
- Size and proportion
- Head, eye and expression
- Color, coat texture and coat quality
- Tail set and carriage
- Legs and feet, fronts and rears
- Reproductive ability

These are not in any particular order. However, temperament and health should be high priorities on every breeder's list. The breeder must also think ahead in considering that some genetically coded traits will be accentuated with age.

In prioritizing your traits, make sure you achieve them in the correct combination. For example, if you are seeking a higher-stationed animal with more length of leg, you also need to concentrate on keeping front-end angulation with well-laid-back shoulders so your *legginess* does not end up being the result of opening up the angles on your shoulder blades while jacking up the height of the dog. What you want to seek is the actual lengthening of the bones while retaining correct angles.

Develop your own list of traits that are important for your breed to assist you in selecting your breeding stock. Then prioritize them. Here are some traits that are high on my priority list in selecting Norwegian Elkhounds:

- Temperament and hardiness. They must be bold and energetic, outgoing with fun-loving intelligence.

- High-stationed, short-loined, and athletic. They must be well up on leg with good shoulders, short-coupling, free-moving, graceful, and athletic. Good, strong, propelling quarters.

- Good head, eye, and tail: Although head and tail are not related, I give them about equal consideration because they are such a vital part of breed character.

- Correct coat texture: The Norwegian Elkhound is used on moose in weather that alternately freezes and thaws. With the dog tracking the moose through water, a soft open coat is deadly. A hard, weather-resistant coat is a must with me.

Because no dog is perfect, the breeder must decide where compromises can be made. Tradeoffs have to be things that you and the breed can live with, and probably it is best if they are cosmetic. Remember that your tradeoffs will be just as breed specific as your positive priorities.

An example might be a very attractive, small foot with straight, short pasterns. In some breeds, this foot is desired even when accompanied by rather straight shoulders, which it sometimes is. Personally, I am not offended by a larger foot—think of it as a practical foot—as long as the pads are thick and hard, the toes are close with good integrity to the knuckles, and there is no hint of thin or flat feet.

The exaggerated, small foot is of little benefit to a working Elkhound who must follow a moose not only through icy waters but over varied terrain littered with rocks, trees and brush. A foot that is functional is an absolute necessity! A foot that is extra pretty is not. Maybe cat feet belong on cats.

When an Elkhound appears with compact feet, strong knuckles, thick hard pads and a strong pastern who also has magnificent shoulders with exceptional lay back and great upper arm, here is an animal, when properly used, who can help front assembly for generations. Here is one that can be a turning point in a breeding program.

Sometimes breeders miss an animal like this because it has an objectionable fault. Let us say this one is somewhat high in the rear and runs a little downhill. Why does it run downhill? Is it because it has that much-desired front angulation and for some reason its rear angulation is straighter? To eliminate this animal from a judicious breeding program might be a grievous mistake if other pieces of the animal are also correct. This indeed is a tradeoff. Yet, this refutes the concept of balance that might mean this dog would fit itself better if it were somewhat straight at both ends. And it would fit *itself* better. But would it fit your breeding program better?

Experienced breeders deal with such difficult decisions and seem to possess the right instincts in making their choices. If they are breeding Bassets, for example, they do *not* forgive animals that make a habit of stumbling, for they lack the athleticism to be a good rabbit dog.

Take the subject of conditioning and skin as it relates to your selection traits. A dog that is naturally hard and tight skinned with excellent angles covered by that skin is of great value in your breeding program, unless loose skin is a desired characteristic of your breed. If I am forced to accept a dog that is somewhat wetter—looser—skinned than I like, it absolutely *must* be well angulated. A loose-skinned animal that is straight angled is worthless to my breeding program, while a tight-skinned animal that is well angulated is priceless.

Every breed has its tradeoffs, and it is up to you to find which ones have to be made in your breed or your line to continue to make breed progress. If you breed Boxers, you might have to accept a little less neck than you would like to get the perfect Boxer head and the short-loined square profile. If you breed Fox Terriers, it might be especially difficult to keep the short body while seeking the great length of head and neck desired by the standard. If Irish Setters are your breed of choice, as you seek the refined elegant head you may have to sacrifice a little on bone, or conversely, if you want substantial bone on your males, you may have to accept a little more skull than you would prefer. All breeders must deal with these decisions in handling their selections of prioritized traits. Most of all, they must be consistent in their selection process.

Selection Methods

Your selection methods will determine whether you make overall but slower progress or whether you make rapid progress in one area at the expense of others. It is vital that you keep in mind that the more traits you are considering in your selection process, the less improvement you can make for each trait. Furthermore, as the number of traits for which you select increases, the less overall improvement will appear in the progeny.

A most important factor in the progress rate for any particular trait is the degree of difficulty involved in achieving it. If it is a trait determined by many genes or by complicated behavior of genes, progress will be difficult—especially if in areas that are not well documented. On the other hand, if you were selecting for color traits, progress would be made easier, thanks to all the research that has been done in color genetics. You could seek out this well-documented information, lay it out and make plans, then select accordingly. Color genetics in dogs is probably the best researched area of all.

It is imperative that you understand this thing about the degree of difficulty in dealing with different traits. Those that are very difficult to perfect can drive you crazy unless you put them in proper perspective. Consider them like the children's game of *Giant Steps*. Sometimes you take one step forward, then two back. Other times, you take two steps forward and one back. Finally, you might make a step forward and get to stay there until the next step.

Tandem

In this method of selection the breeder selects one particular trait and attempts to perfect it. Once that trait is fixed in the line, the breeder then attempts to fix a second trait and so on. The bad news is that progress is made for only one trait at a time. Therefore, you might run out of time before you run out of traits! Meanwhile, there is a wasting away of other good traits that might be possessed by the animal discarded because it lacked the number one trait. Because many of the animals that lacked that particular trait might very well have other quite good traits, this does not seem to be a good method unless used as a starting point to get a necessary breed-specific trait fixed before you move on to another method.

Yorkshire Terriers and Golden Retrievers are examples of breeds in which desired color would be a high priority. If you are in a breed with color disqualifications, you must select accordingly.

If you are going to use the tandem method of selection concentrating on one trait at a time, be sure that the trait is a very important one and do not allow yourself the luxury of making it a subjective personal preference item. In such a case, even if you succeed in fixing the trait it might be relatively unimportant.

If the trait you prioritize is positively connected with another, you will be doing your breeding program a favor. If it is negatively connected you will be establishing impossible goals for yourself.

The Point System

A selection method used with success by a number of breeders is the point system. The point system is modeled after that used by a number of breed standards; and, if you happen to be in one of those breeds you will be fortunate in that you already have a scale available. If you are not in a breed that uses a point system in its breed standard, you might want to study one that does to help you establish your own breed-specific scale of points for your selection process. A number of breed standards with emphatic differences that use point scales for you to study are Beagles, Greyhounds, Alaskan Malamutes, Airedales, Border Terriers, Brussels Griffons, Boston Terriers and Dalmatians. For the most detailed point scale of all, study the Bulldog breed standard.

After studying these various breed standards, you should be able to move to the next step—establishing a scale of points for your own selection process. You will be able to rank your priorities, awarding highest point value to the most important traits and lesser values to the minor traits. In evaluating your breeding stock, your selection method will determine your dogs' scores and you can decide which dogs are of the most value to your breeding program.

Maybe 10 to 12 traits would be a good starting point and allow adequate latitude for temperament, health and fertility to be included. If you know that a particular trait desired is relatively heritable, give it a valid point count because it is achievable. If the trait is very difficult to achieve, do not over value it on your point scale. Be careful not to overemphasize a particular characteristic at the expense of the whole or to de-emphasize a particular characteristic at the expense of the whole.

Do not be discouraged if you experience some setbacks if you are experiencing great improvement for some most desirable traits. It is not possible to make only improvements without anything else happening, and this is where your common sense will serve you well. One good thing about the point system is that if you have an extraordinary litter, such a grading will produce scores that tell you to keep more than one puppy. By the same token, if you have a disappointing litter when you were expecting great things, your scores will indicate to you that you do not need to keep any of these puppies.

The point system makes it clear why the third or fourth choice puppy from an excellent litter is far more desirable than the pick of a lesser litter.

Minimum Culling Method

As your breeding program progresses and quality animals become the norm, it is a good idea to consider a minimum standard of culling. This means you will not forgive some very *unacceptable characteristics*. Any dog that does not meet the minimum requirements—or points if using a scale—would be removed from the breeding program. This is a good time to utilize personal well-conceived theories that experience will confirm as right for your breeding program and your breed.

One vow I have kept is to be harsher on very closely bred dogs than on any others. Since my personal belief is the closer the breeding, the more dangerous the product, the puppies from such matings that do not measure up go immediately to pet homes to be neutered. This is one way to protect your breed. In fact, most puppies of close breedings go to pet homes. A rule of thumb might be that the closer-bred, mediocre animal is much more dangerous to the breed's gene pool than a mediocre animal that is outcrossed. For one thing, it gives posterity a false sense of security to see extremely well-bred animals in the background. For another, when that pedigree's *picture of perfection* produces a mediocre dog that is not so good, it means that the animal represents a concentration of undesirable genetic traits—the opposite of what the breeder had in mind.

Minimum culling levels, just like optimum selection systems, have to be well thought out and objectively implemented. Otherwise the concept has little merit. If you can figure out what is called the

DRAG OF THE BREED

Correct balanced square Chow Chow pictured above. The drag of the breed—unbalanced and short-legged— is demonstrated in the drawing below.

Courtesy of Dr. Samuel B. Draper. Artwork by June Goldsborough

drag of the breed for your breed, then no animal that has that shortcoming would be retained for breeding. Thanks to Mrs. James Edward Clark for this term, for it says it all. In any breed described in its standard as square, the drag of the breed would be a low, long, rectangular animal. If you breed a square breed, that would serve as a minimum culling level. Here are a few criteria for a minimum standard for one Norwegian Elkhound breeder:

- Must be athletic, well-made and flexible.
- Must have correct length of leg as it relates to body.
- Must have correctly made dark eyes and a flat skull.

This system works best when the overall quality of the kennel is established because there will not be all that much variation in the animals. If you have too many minimum culling criteria, no dog would ever measure up. If you have too many traits on your list of things to improve, few animals would ever measure up.

Your entire selection process is aimed at selecting the very best of each new generation while taking the lesser ones out of the gene pool. Do not encourage people to show dogs of yours that do not measure up. A breeding program is better when a few really good dogs represent it in the ring and stay in the gene pool than when it is represented by a wide array of dogs—many of them mediocre—with all of them in the gene pool. Your goal is not how many but how good!

Role of the Judge in the Selection Process

Judging dogs from the safety of ringside is one thing. Judging them from inside the ring is another, involving a rapid, mental prioritizing of breed type and virtues. At the same time, the judge is making allowances for faults in order to sort the dogs in the most expert manner and timely fashion. Due to the time and circumstances involved and the mercurial elements entering into the **on-the-day** decision, there is room for a greater margin of error in judging decisions than in breeding decisions. When a judge makes a selection in the ring, the judge lives with each decision on a short-term basis. When a breeder makes a decision, the breeder and all of the rest of us live with that decision forever! All of these factors should be considered in determining what role judges should play in your selection process.

> **"It is easy to be brave from a safe distance."**
> **—Aesop**

In a way, a dog show is a kind of performing art at the same time it is a sporting competition. The judge is the powerful critic. Just as the opinion of a *New York Times'* well-respected drama critic can make or break a Broadway show, so can the collective opinions of the judges make or break a dog's show record. They make not an iota of difference in the dog's genetic potential. Notice I did not say producing record, for that record will be predicated upon what bitches—quality and quantity—are brought to him. Nonetheless, the all-important gene pool is unaffected.

Never before in my experiences as a dog fancier have the American Kennel Club judges been more exposed to continued education and accountability. And this is as it should be. For never before has the dog fancy been so widespread and diversified. It is appropriate for the governing body, as well as various judges' organizations, to do all that is possible to improve judging. The major complaint that one hears from the judges is: "Yes, we are being educated. But we can only judge what is brought before us." This is a valid concern.

No matter which came first—the chicken or the egg—the important question is: "What comes next?" A rededication and commitment from all are in order. Judges and breeders alike must work in a continuing fashion to learn more about the breeds for the good of the order. Some judges and breeders are born with that mythical *eye for a dog* while others have to work at it. Two dear, departed ladies come to mind who were both great judges. Beatrice Godsol must have been born with that *eye for a dog*. It came so naturally to her, and she was very much at ease and at home in the ring. Ramona Van Court was a true student who worked hard to have the expertise she developed with the Norwegian Elkhound. She was years ahead of her time in attending the National Specialty judged by the great breeder from Norway, Herr Olav Campbell, av Tallo Kennels, in 1968, as her chosen requirement to learn about the breed. Until then, she had preferred incorrect, open-coated, short-legged dogs.

After studying Mr. Campbell's placements, talking to him and other experts, including Catherine Peck, to allow for any and all biases, Mrs. Van Court totally changed her judging and became a prominent judge of the breed. The message here is that although things came naturally for the very talented Mrs. Godsol, Mrs. Van Court became just as skilled in judging the breed through intense study and hard work. She had been open-minded and willing to learn. If only more of these late greats were with us today.

Unless you are a puppy mill breeder—which you are not or you would not bother with this book—you know that breeding dogs is a labor of love. Well, so is judging dogs a labor of love. Not only is it a heavy responsibility, it truly is hard work. Most people who go into judging do so from either the background of the professional handler with experience in many breeds or that of the dedicated breeder with more concentrated expertise in one breed.

The breeder is judging dogs every time he selects a stud dog or grades a litter. The judge, in effect, is breeding dogs every time he makes a selection, as long as we are all still dedicated to the premise that the purpose of a dog show is to select breeding stock. Nonetheless, when you judge a dog you must judge the entire dog, whereas there are times in breeding when you seek certain *pieces* of a dog. In this case, you might not pick the same dog to breed to that you would select if you were judging because the particular needs of this bitch are different from those of the breed in general.

Again, I am indebted to Mrs. Clark for pointing out to me in my early and continuing struggles that judging is a whole new world. You think you have some ability to judge dogs for you have been doing it all your life, but there is a difference between judging from outside the ring and inside the ring. To paraphrase the Spanish proverb: "Talking about bulls is not the same thing as being in the bull ring."

Just as the breeder becomes more skilled at selection skills and learns from mistakes, so too does the judge. It is in the best interest of the dogs if both stay open-minded and receptive to learning as long as they are in dogs. Perhaps part of the fascination of judging is the continued learning process that keeps us all on our toes and open-minded. It is a lasting commitment to intellectual growth.

As judges become more skilled in their abilities, their opinions should weigh heavier with you, particularly if you know them to be competent dog people. It is important for you to distinguish the differences in judges' opinions. You must learn to appreciate judges' opinions for just that—opinions. Whereas some wins will be sought for the record, the opinions of the best judges should be what you seek. These are the ones that should weigh heaviest in your breeding program.

An important impact on your breeding decision making can be forthcoming from both multi-breed judges—all rounders—and breeder judges. When I was young and showing a lot of Cockers, I used to think in terms of the breeder-judges being very exact in their expectations for head, elegant type, and good neck and shoulders. The all-rounders expected soundness and performance. Maybe you should think of the multi-breed judge as keeping you honest with your feet on the ground while shooting for the stars pursuing the type to please the expert breeder-judge. Keep in mind that many former handlers who now judge put up dogs they could have won with, not necessarily dogs of excellent type. These judges have a positive role to play in your selection process as long as you understand why they like your dog.

A flashing caution light you need to pay attention to is the mediocre dog that fits into everybody's comfort zone—this is the dog that has no outstanding dog faults but lacks good breed type. This is

Below: Ch. Vin-Melca's Howdy Rowdy winning the National in 1968 under Norway's Olav Campbell, who also that day awarded his baby half-brother Vagabond RWD at 14 months of age. Herr Campbell lectured to eager listeners, including Ramona Van Court, in a pioneer version of what we now call Judge's Study Groups associated with National Specialities. In those days, the Parent Club held its National every three years, and to this day holds its National biannually because of details involved in securing Norwegian experts. Howdy was handled here by Bill Liles, and the trophy presenter is Susan B. Phillips. (Photo by Evelyn Shafer)

Above: Mrs. Beatrice Godsol selecting Ch. Vin-Melca's Vagabond BIS at the San Mateo Kennel Club in 1969. Only a few are blessed with the elusive "eye for a dog" that came so naturally to Mrs. Godsol. Her excellence as a judge was instinctive and her opinions were highly esteemed by breeders, fanciers and other judges. She served as mentor to such giants in dogs as Derek Rayne and Frank Sabella. (Photograph by Bill Francis)

Left: Ramona Van Court created her own form of a Judge's Study Group long before the procedure became routine. She is shown here with a leggier, harsher-coated bitch than she had preferred previously. Ch. Vin-Melca's Nightcap was a correct hunting-type bitch—short-loined and well-stationed. Pictured here going BOS and handled by Dr. John Craige. During the taking of this picture Ramona remarked that there had been a time when she might not have appreciated this bitch, "faulting her large ears too much and not appreciating the rest of her enough." Mrs. Van Court became an outstanding judge of Norwegian Elkhounds, as well as other breeds, through her pursuit of excellence and pride in her work. (Photo by Ludwig)

Multi-group judge Mrs. L.W. Bonney, breeder-owner of the famous Tally Ho Kennels, pictured with her BIS selection of the red and white Cocker Spaniel Ch. Dau-Han's Dan Morgan at the inaugural show of the Upper Marlboro Kennel Club in 1960. Dan Morgan's breeder-owner Muriel R. Laubach (See Part V) was extremely proud of this particular win because of her respect for Mrs. Bonney, who was a dual-purpose dog person much admired for her abilities both as a judge and a successful breeder. The author is handling . (Henry Ellison Photo)

the dog that personifies the warning: "Absence of faults is no guarantee of presence of virtues." This dog is dangerous to breeders and judges. He is especially dangerous to a rather inexperienced breeder if he does a lot of winning simply because there are few dogs of better type to catch the judge's eye. The problem is that this mediocre animal becomes the owner's prototype of what a good dog is, and that person never gets past that dog. The dog has won far beyond its potential due to a number of factors, none of which have much to do with improving the gene pool.

Judges and breeders alike can fall into the trap of supporting this mediocre dog that is relatively fault free—as a dog, but not as a member of his breed—because the dog is a good mover that comes and goes, shows well and the rest of the competition is worse. The dog wins far beyond his potential, is a textbook overachiever and the hooked owner spends the rest of his doggy days trying to recreate that dog. Such a goal is detrimental to the breed and the breeder.

This breeder may be cursed forever to breed the generic dog—*unidog*. Unidog could be any breed of dog given the head, coat, and trappings of that breed. People in this predicament have not learned that the absence of faults is no guarantee of the presence of virtues.

In my breed, I have seen this happen more times than I care to admit over a period rapidly approaching the half-century mark. A rectangular dog that does not meet my breed's requirements for the short-coupled, square dog is a good mover and show dog. Well-meaning judges are comfortable putting this animal over leggier, shorter-loined, more correct type

Breeder-judges have valuable contributions to breeding decision making, especially those who have done it themselves, such as Cocker Spaniel expert Byron Covey. Together with his wife, Cameron, and son, Bob, Byron bred some of California's most outstanding Cockers for many years using the prefix Camby, which combines his and his wife's names. In 1995, son Bob campaigned the #1 All Time Sporting Dog, Ch. La Shay's Bart Simpson, black-and-tan Cocker Spaniel, to more than 100 BISs. The author is handling Ch. BeauMonde War Paint to the variety under Mr. Covey in this 1962 picture. (Ludwig Photograph)

Ch. Charmaron's Cheddar of Toy is the #1 Toy Manchester Sire of All Time with 36 champion progeny. He was bred and owned by Marie E. (Mari-Beth) O'Neill and Florence Sgrignuoli, and is pictured here with Frank Sabella judging and Mari-Beth handling at the 1983 National en route to the Variety from Veterans. Not only was his maternal grandam Ch. Renreh Lorelei of Charmaron a multi-BIS winner, she was the only Toy Manchester ever to win the group at Westminster. This BIS linebreeding went on to another generation when Cheddar's son, Ch. Pamelot's Believe It Or Not, became the all-time top winning male toy with 5 All Breeds and more than 40 Group firsts to his credit. More importantly, "Ripley" has already produced 22 champions with more on the way. (John Ashbey Photo)

dogs because he moves well and does not offend them. They are, in fact, rewarding a dog for the biggest fault of all—lack of true breed type—simply because he moves well. Time out for a trip back to McDowell Lyon. To quote from page 34 of *The Dog in Action*: "You can take any given dog, shorten its legs one inch and it will cover more ground than before the operation."

This is where you have to make some basic decisions: Do you breed dogs to please a large number of judges who do not know your breed all that well; or, do you breed dogs to meet the standard and prepare to take your losses until a greater understanding of breed type is established and your dogs start getting their just rewards? Most importantly, do you know the difference? If not, let the judges make your calls for you, for they will be right more often than not. If you do not know when the judges are making breed-specific errors, maybe you should not be breeding dogs—or else make it your business to find out.

Good judges should and do have a positive impact on your breeding program. They will see things you might miss—they see the forest while you are busy looking at the trees. Their opinions have much merit in contributing to your decision making. The following story is one such success story of a judge's positive impact.

Frank Sabella, judging the American Manchester Terrier National Specialty in 1983, demonstrated just how important the role of a talented judge can be in the selection process of a breeding program. While taking pictures of the winners of the toy variety, Frank pointed to his toy winner (from the Veterans Class), Ch. Charmaron's Cheddar of Toy, and

Ch. Salutaire Word to the Wise, standard Manchester Terrier, is the All Time Top Sire in the breed with 53 champions to date. His best progeny resulted from linebreeding on his dam's side. Accordingly, his daughters were better than his sons. He is pictured here winning a regional specialty under Dr. William Houpt, handler Myrtle Klensch. (Lindemaier Photo)

Some wins are special and meaningful, especially when they come in excellent competition under judges you really respect. Frank Sabella was not only a very gifted handler who did it all, he has become one of dogdom's most respected judges. This occasion was his first BIS assignment, which he awarded to Ch. Vin-Melca's Nimbus in 1978. Dr. Hugh Jordan presents the trophy on behalf of the Rio Hondo Kennel Club. (Ludwig Photo)

advised the lady who had the Winners Bitch to breed to this dog as he "has exactly what your bitch needs." Frank was so enthused about the idea that his optimism was contagious, and in time the bitch was sent to the dog. The resulting nine puppies from two litters all finished their championships, making their dam the top all-time producing Toy Manchester bitch. In seeing that this dog and bitch complemented each other, Frank Sabella became a vital part of the breeding program.

Ch. Charmaron's Cheddar of Toy became the all-time top-producing Toy Manchester sire, with the aforementioned nine of his 36 champion progeny from this one combination. In essence, Frank was the living embodiment of my earlier statement that the judge is breeding dogs every time he or she makes a selection. This proves that there are many people still dedicated to this premise: The purpose of dog shows is to select those dogs from which the breed should be bred.

To compound his successes that day, Frank chose Ch. Salutaire Word To The Wise as his standard variety winner and on to Best of Breed. This Standard Manchester is now the number one Sire All Time in the breed with 53 champion progeny. These are impressive numbers for small dogs to achieve.

What happens if you believe in a dog and the judges do not like him? Here is where your confidence and knowledge will join to help you through a disappointing experience. For the fact is, some excellent dogs just do not catch on. This Indian proverb might comfort you: "If you sell diamonds, you cannot expect to have many customers. But a diamond is a diamond even if there are no customers."

When Nimbus retired with 63 BISs in 1979, I brought out a son of his I thought a better specimen. With a few notable exceptions, I could not get Ch. Vin-Melca's Namesake off the ground. It floored me as he was superior to Nimbus in almost every way except charisma. After he got kicked all over the ballpark, I took him home and just used him on my own bitches. This was not by choice as I cannot remember anyone else ever asking to use him. He sired three BIS winners in his first two litters, including the exceptional bitch, Ch. Vin-Melca's Last Call—Gilda—top producing bitch in the breed and number two hound in the country the year the great Afghan Hound, Ch. Kabik's The Challenger (see color section) was Top Dog All Breeds.

The moral of the story is that you are the breeder and the ultimate responsibility is on your shoulders. The judges can help you, but they cannot do it all. When they fail to see what you see in a dog,

PRODUCER OR *REPRODUCER?*

The great producer is the one we all seek to become the *true foundation bitch* in our breeding program and for the breed. All too often, we neglect a very important part of the whole—the "reproducer." We are so into the producer bit, that we will do anything to provide the *R* and the *E* necessary for the *RE*producer.

Perhaps sophisticated veterinary techniques are a mixed blessing when considering the long-term welfare of a breeding program. This is particularly true if the results of veterinary efforts to get given bitches to reproduce are not appropriately considered in evaluating the overall picture.

Free whelping or lack of same in our more natural breeds is an area to consider. We are not talking about the exaggerated man-made breeds here. Nor are we talking about toys. Nor are we talking about occasional lifesaving situations in which modern veterinary medicine is indeed a marvelous blessing.

We are talking about animals that should be able to whelp on their own and over many generations do not, or animals that cannot participate in the reproduction process naturally.

In time, the animals in the line and perhaps in the breed itself are no longer able to breed freely without medical assistance.

Maybe Ch. Good Girl Won A Lot had only one living daughter after several futile attempts to get another litter from her. That one puppy had been delivered by cesarean section. Now she is mature and ready to breed. She, too, is difficult to get in whelp and finally has a couple of daughters by section, who then later deliver only by section.

If this is a sporting, hound or other breed expected to be natural, is the breeder fixing a line of "bad-doing" bitches who are copying the original bitch in their inability to become natural mothers?

Is there another way to get the results naturally instead of counting on the veterinarians to do it for you? This might be a good time for a breeder to get involved in holistic approaches based on ultimate nutrition and conditioning.

There is a wealth of information available on these subjects. No breeder wants to be part of the enabling process that causes the dogs to suffer such vital losses. No breeder wants to encourage problems that cost the breed its hardy strength and vitality.

Holistic alternatives are far better than medical band-aids. Then your animals will be both producers and *RE*producers!

---

trust yourself if you have the know how. For one thing, they have about two minutes to evaluate your dog. You have all the time in the world to do it and should use it. It is time well spent if it helps you avoid a breeding mistake, and all the more so if it helps you achieve a breeding success!

If you have done your homework, have a knowledgeable eye, and are objective, trust yourself. As an educator of 34 years, I spent a great deal of time outside the classroom in parent conferences that were team efforts to get these high-spirited 13-year-olds to perform. One point that was a continuing theme to the parent: You are your child's best teacher. And, this is true if the parent is objective, capable and knowledgeable. If you will be the same, you will be your dog's best judge. Then you seek the opinions of judges you respect to verify your own.

Foundation Stock: The Brood Bitch

Putting selection to work will receive its earliest test in your choice of your foundation stock. The selection of the brood bitch in particular is where it's at—especially for the small discerning breeder. Pious Arabs followed the teaching of the *Koran* in respecting horses, especially their mares. They rode their stallions into battle so as not to endanger the precious mares where "treasures grow in the wombs."

If you are just looking for a dog to show, you will be money ahead—not to mention time and effort—to locate a top breeder and buy your show dog. When retirement time comes for that dog, return and buy another. The do-it-yourself method is the most expensive way to go; nonetheless, it is also the most rewarding. With that in mind, try to keep the odds in your favor.

> "It's a funny thing about life; if you refuse to accept anything but the best, you often get it."
> —William Somerset Maugham

You do not need a kennel full of male dogs. Unless a male is a potentially great one, you do not need him at all. The very best males in the breed are available to everybody. For the most part, the great dogs in a breed are sought after and used by all the breeders. The thing that separates the great breeders from the rest is the selection of their brood bitches and the development of a tail female line. As in a lot of other things in life, it might be said that it's the bottom line that counts. The tail female line with strength goes in a direct line to a great foundation bitch.

The use of the term *foundation bitch* is often misunderstood and inadvertently taken in vain. Your first bitch may be your personal idea of a foundation bitch, and for you she is. The true foundation bitch is a foundation bitch for the breed. The *true foundation bitch* (TFB) is scarce, and sometimes she is not recognized as one until after she is gone, a phenomenon not unlike that of the great artist who is discovered after death.

Such a key bitch does not come along all the time. You might be very fortunate and buy or breed one, developing a true foundation bitch of your own. Sometimes you can get a daughter from such a bitch and carry it (the TFB) right on to the next generation.

Ch. Vin-Melca's Vikina, whelped in the early sixties, became a true foundation bitch. Sired by the

Ramona Van Court with Ch. Vin-Melca's Vikina who was a *true foundation bitch*—the dam of both Ch. Vin-Melca's Howdy Rowdy and Ch. Vin-Melca's Vagabond. (Shown at Del Monte Kennel Club in 1963 handled by the author.) Already a respected hound judge at the time of this photograph, Mrs. Van Court pursued excellence in her adjudicating by attending the 1968 National Specialty under Norway's famous hunter-judge Olav Campbell to improve her understanding of the breed. (Ludwig Photograph)

great producer, Ch. Trygvie Vikingsson, who was bred and owned by Glenna Crafts, out of Ch. Vin-Melca's Astridina, Vikina was only bred a couple of times due to the personal circumstances of a young teacher at that time. From a total of eight live puppies, five of them finished with another one lost tragically just short of his title. The other two were never shown.

From the five champions, two were multi-BIS dogs that went on to have an impact on the breed in a most positive way. The first was Ch. Vin-Melca's Howdy Rowdy, Kennel Review Hall of Fame sire with 166 champion offspring and a dog credited with bringing the Elkhound into its own. (See Sire Section) The second was Ch. Vin-Melca's Vagabond (see color section), Top Dog All Breeds All Systems in 1970 and twice winner of the Hound Group at Westminster.

Vikina son, Ch. Vin-Melca's Howdy Rowdy, sire of 166 champions, winning BOB en route to Group 3rd at the 1969 Westminster Kennel Club under Judge Robert Waters. Multi-BIS winner, National Specialty winner and Kennel Review Hall of Famer, Howdy was the progenitor of a strong tail male line of descent. Handled by the author with Bill Liles looking on. (Evelyn Shafer Photo)

Vikina son Ch. Vin-Melca's Vagabond, Top Dog All Breeds 1970, and two-time Westminster group winner, did not become a sire of sires as did his half-brother Howdy. Due to the strong genetic influence he inherited from the female side of his family, he became a marvelous brood bitch sire whose daughters went on to produce such exceptional dogs as Nimbus and Nordic Storm. (Jayne Langdon Photograph)

Ch. Vin-Melca's Saga of Redhill became the *true foundation bitch* for Freeman and Betty Claus and their Redhill Kennels. Saga produced Specialty winners and group winners, stamping her excellent leg length, good color and correct coats as well as proper hunting type on her progeny. From a family of TFBs, Saga was the sister of a number of outstanding producers and inherited one X chromosome from her sire Howdy Rowdy, that of the key bitch Ch. Vin-Melca's Vikina, his dam. (Ludwig Photo)

Not only was Vikina herself a key bitch, but her descendants went on to become true foundation bitches. Ch. Vin-Melca's Saga av Redhill became the true foundation bitch for Freeman and Betty Claus' Redhill line of Elkhounds. Her sister, Ch. Vin-Melca's Harlo, did the same thing for Bob and Grace Maddox's Rebel Ridge Kennels in Texas. Harlo's litter sister, Ch. Vin-Melca's Hanky Panky, produced BIS Ch. Vin-Melca's Valley Forge, Quaker Oats winner and number five all breeds in 1973. Another sister, Ch. Vin-Melca's Happy Hour, produced the true foundation bitch, Ch. Vin-Melca's Bottoms Up. Ch. Wabeth's Erika B. Rowdy became the true foundation bitch for Grenville and Virginia Sawyer's excellent line of Norgren Norwegian Elkhounds, and they are still producing superior specimens down from her 25 years later. These five bitches were Vikina granddaughters through their sire, Howdy Rowdy. Although they did not trace on the tail female side in this case, it is important to remember that the only X chromosome they could have inherited from Howdy was the one he got from his dam. Fifty percent of their XX was Vikina!

Ch. Vin-Melca's Just Plain Jane became the true foundation bitch for Lee and Diana Korneliusen's Sirdal Kennels in Bothell, Washington. Her pedigree boasted four strong crosses to Vikina, as well as two other key bitches. These are just a few examples of the many Vikina descendants who became outstanding brood bitches.

These breeders were aided by the true foundation bitch who saved them lost time and effort. For our purposes, let me identify what our expectations would be from a true foundation or key bitch:

- A bitch who produces mostly championship quality;
- A bitch who produces a large percentage of champions able to win breeds and group placements;
- A bitch with some progeny able to win specialties, groups and BISs;
- A bitch producing one or two classic winners able to compete at the top for such honors as Quaker Oats, BISs at classic shows and national specialties;
- A bitch whose descendants breed on!

The "breeding-on" part of the equation is the most important one, for show records are achievements of the moment while producing input affects the breed permanently.

Nothing in the world is as important to the breeding program as the selection of the brood bitch.

For every sire registered by the stud book, there are about 30 dams recorded. Therefore, each dam has that many more times the opportunity to become weaker links than do the fewer—and one would hope—more select sires. In dealing with a female line that is very strong and filled with great names, you are maximizing your chances of improving the breed.

Because of the sheer numbers produced by famous sires, people tend to overlook the contributions of the great dams and may think of them as less important than those of the great sires. This is a mistake, for when you check the pedigrees of those great sires you will usually find the names of the true foundation bitches—and often more than one.

This is why successful breeders are more concerned with the distaff side of the family. They recognize that in their own quiet way, the great brood bitches in history will predominate, often becoming the matriarchs of dynasties. Seek out your breed's great matriarchs and try to collect them in your foundation pedigrees.

The family man favors the family over the individual in seeking out his key bitch. Such a breeder knows he is better off with a well-bred bitch from a great family that was unshown or had a modest show record than a great winner with fewer genetic credentials—all the better if you can get it all in that one brood bitch prospect. You may very well be on the road to your own blue hen, taproot bitch who is the ultimate true foundation bitch.

Such a prospective brood bitch will have the following: good conformation and breed type; soundness of both mind and body; free from genetic disease and in excellent physical condition; representative of a quality gene pool.

Ch. Vin-Melca's Harlo pictured winning Best Opposite Sex at Westminster Kennel Club under Judge Charles Kellog in 1970 to the Hound Group winner Vagabond. Foundation bitch for the Rebel Ridge Kennels of Bob and Grace Maddox, Harlo was handled by Adelene Pardo to #2 in the breed in 1970. She went on to produce 20 champions for Rebel Ridge and lived to the ripe old age of 17. (Gilbert Photograph)

Ch. Vin-Melca's Happy Hour became the first bitch to win the Parent Club National Specialty in 1974, judged by Herr Olav Roig, president of the Norske Kennel Club. The trophy presenter is A. Wells Peck. This outstanding daughter of Howdy Rowdy produced another key bitch in Ch. Vin-Melca's Bottoms Up when bred to her own grandson, Ch. Vin-Melca's Nordic Storm. (Photo by Robert Smolley)

Ch. Vin-Melca's Hanky Panky with owner John Whitemarsh. Hanky was the #2 Norwegian Elkhound in the U.S. in 1971 and BOS at the National Specialty to half-brother (Ch.) Vin-Melca's Huck Finn. More important than her successes in the ring were her contributions as a brood bitch. From only two litters she produced BIS Ch. Vin-Melca's Valley Forge, Quaker Oats Winner and #5 All Breeds in 1973 and a number of other winners. (Photo by Jayne Langdon)

Ch. Vin-Melca's Bottoms Up—*true foundation bitch*—pictured winning the Hound Group under Gordon Parham handled by co-owner Dody Froehlich. At this point in her producing career, she was already the dam of two All Breed BIS winners and produced the breed's all-time winner (Calista) in her last litter. (Hansen Photography)

Always keep in mind the hundreds of thousands of possible genetic combinations so that you are aware of the gambles in breeding even with the good bitch—this is why you must start with the best. Even the animals from the classic pedigrees will produce some offspring that do not measure up, making it absolutely necessary for you to guard against the decline in the quality of her progeny. Breed her wisely.

The accompanying chart shows how this decline occurs. It is estimated that the line will regress at about 20 percent per generation so that the bitch with the *excellent* pedigree has about 80 percent of the potential of the key bitch with the *classic* pedigree for producing a great one. The bitch with the nice pedigree will produce about 80 percent as well as the excellent one and approximately 60 percent as well as the classic one, and so on. No wonder the breeder is in a constant struggle to avoid decline even when blessed with a great one—a true foundation bitch.

Considering the risks involved with the watering down of great genes in each generation, it is obvious that breeding just acceptable animals is ill-advised. Even though you own the bitch or someone gives her to you and also gives you a free breeding, it will not be a cheap enterprise. There is no such thing as an inexpensive breeding just because of the cost involved in raising the puppies correctly. If you are going to put your money into dogs, put it into the best ones possible.

Nothing is more painful than to see some of those lesser animals from the key bitch become part of the declining process. Their well-meaning breeders sell them as show prospects to well-meaning buyers who are equally inexperienced at recognizing that these puppies did not grow up to their pedigree's promise. They rationalize that if she cannot win, at least we can breed her—*if she is not good enough to show, she is probably not good enough to breed.* Love them, yes. Breed them, no.

The quality potential true foundation bitch is out there. All you have to do is educate yourself so that you will recognize her when you see her, and then seek her out. Take advantage of stock reductions of kennels of well-bred animals. Be willing to work with old-time breeders to get these bitches. There are those in your breed who have these bitches. Why should you breed anything else?

Therefore, for the optimum opportunity, go with the bitch from the classic or excellent pedigree. Avoid breeding a mediocre bitch because she is there and it is convenient. It will end up being the most expensive convenience in your breeding career. To improve the breed, only the best should be bred, and the rest should be neutered. It is imperative that breeders accept that not all of their dogs should procreate. Such discriminating criteria will keep your kennel small and manageable at the same time allowing you more interaction with your dogs.

In your formative years as a breeder, do not attempt to house your own studs. Some great breeders never house studs. The first male I kept after being in the breed for 16 years was Ch. Vin-Melca's Vickssen, a BIS winner whelped in 1964 and destined to become the sire of Vagabond.

The longer you wait to succumb to the idea of using your own sires, the better your choices will be when you get there. To continue to try to improve your brood-bitch quality is to continue to improve

Ch. Vin-Melca's Vickssen was the first male dog kept by the author after 16 years "in dogs." Her first BIS Elkhound, this dog was whelped in 1963 and was the #1 Norwegian Elkhound in the U.S. in 1966 and 1967. He sired three All Breed BIS winners: Ch. Vin-Melca's Vagabond, Ch. Vin-Melca's Valley Forge and Ch. Vin-Melca's Viscount. (Ludwig Photograph)

THE DECLINING INFLUENCE OF THE TRUE FOUNDATION BITCH

Classic Pedigree
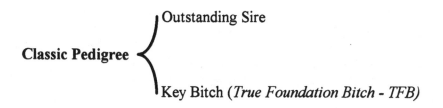
Outstanding Sire

Key Bitch (*True Foundation Bitch - TFB)*

Excellent Pedigree

Outstanding Sire

Excellent Bitch
Outstanding Sire

Key Bitch (*TFB*)

Nice Pedigree

Outstanding Sire

Nice Bitch
Outstanding Sire

Excellent Bitch
Outstanding Sire

Key Bitch (*TFB*)

Acceptable Pedigree

Outstanding Sire

Nice Bitch
Outstanding Sire

Excellent Bitch
Outstanding Sire

Key Bitch (*TFB*)

Even when using all outstanding sires in each generation, there is a gradual "watering down" of the genetic influence of the true foundation bitch (TFB) along the way. That is why master breeders strive to recreate the original TFB genetic behavior in succeeding generations by using strong brood bitch sires—sires whose dams have a pertinent contribution to make.

your breeding program. It is extremely difficult, if not impossible, to attain excellence up to the standards of the best if you do not get out of your own backyard.

In fact, the backbone of any breed is the small breeder who has concentrated on producing outstanding bitches for a number of generations. Such female families are of great value to the breed, all the more so when they start to experience an upward swing in quality. For when a potential sire comes along from that line, he could be destined to be a great one! When this happens, it is often because both the sire and the dam are from the same excellent female family.

At a recent seminar, I was asked to describe the *look* of the ideal brood bitch. What a task, for good brood bitches vary. Some athletic bitches who are nonetheless feminine have become extraordinary brood bitches. So, too, have some rather doggy bitches that were a bit rougher all over. The look of a brood bitch will vary according to the breed, and this is one of those times when doing your homework will pay off.

In evaluating a potential brood bitch you might say to yourself, "Even though this one is too big and doggy for me, her sister was typier and more refined," or some other such compromise. Good brood bitches do come in different packages and do not all fit into the same mold. Furthermore, the better the bitch the more agonizing the decision in selecting a mate for her.

When asked at that same seminar, did I think it was best to use inbred bitches with outcrossed sires, I responded, "It depends on what they're inbred to." It takes a truly expert breeder to know when it is acceptable to use an animal not in balance in conformation or in pedigree. Mrs. Browning of Tokalon Collie fame, sometimes retained Roman-nosed bitches in her breeding program to get "fill under the eye" to achieve the correct Collie head. In the breeding of dogs, nothing is written in stone.

The relative merit of the contributions made by the sire and dam is of interest. Their genetic contribution is equal. But the bitch probably contributes much more to the progeny than the sire. Consider that first of all she houses and nourishes them in a secure and warm embryonic environment for nine weeks. It is thought that even *in utero*, the fetus is influenced by a bitch's well-adjusted temperament. Then she imprints them from birth with her warmth and confidence, becoming the role model for their puppyhood. Remember that the phenotype that you see is the sum of the genotype and the environmental influences. Since the bitch provides all of the early environment until the puppies leave her nest, she obviously exerts more influence on them than the sire. It is vital that she be well-adjusted and loving as well as properly nourished and healthy.

The good brood bitch will have wonderful maternal instincts that are both nurturing and bonding. It is said that a bitch licks the newborn as a response to the taste and nutritional value of the amniotic fluid. Later, of course, the licking is a cleaning procedure. There is little doubt that the process helps the whelp obtain a sense of security.

Occasionally a bitch will not accept her puppies and has to be encouraged to bond and work with them. Since the puppies need the colostrum, it is advisable to get them suckling and nursing as soon as possible. If a first-time mother has to be delivered through a cesarean section, she should be monitored carefully until all is well, for she could wake up to find these strange, unknown creatures and react negatively. In her post-surgery state of recovery, she needs time to adjust. Once she settles down she will accept her puppies. It is the natural thing for her to do.

It is important to simulate nature as closely as possible in all phases of the breeding situation. In nature, the reproductive cycle follows a seasonal pattern aimed at producing the young at the most advantageous time of the year—that is the time best suited for their survival.

Dogs have become so domesticated that they are no longer governed by the strictest laws of nature. Nonetheless, the estrus cycle of the bitch is still somewhat triggered by the relationship of daylight to darkness as evidenced by the fact that the bitches start coming into season, one by one, as the days start getting longer in the early spring. Basenjis still cycle annually as did their pariah ancestors in Africa.

Stressful situations can interrupt this cycle or even interrupt ovulation once the bitch is in season. This might include the stress of campaigning a bitch.

Campaign Stress

It is a sad fact that many of our greatest winning bitches never reproduce at all, or do not have a production record comparable to their win record. What are the possible reasons for this? Does the stress of the campaign physically exhaust their systems? What effect does the use of hormones to prevent estrus and/or steroids to treat coat and skin problems have on the bitch's future producing career? Is it possible to campaign a bitch hard and still have her become a top producer? It must be remembered that a great bitch is effectively culled from the breeding program if she does not reproduce. Campaigning the life out of your best bitch is like eating your seed grain.

This terrible possibility is something we as breeders must avoid at all costs. We must continue to rededicate ourselves to the premise that the purpose of the dog show is to gather the good ones in a conscientious, ongoing effort to select breeding stock. This means selecting not only for beautiful animals of correct type and conformation, but hardy ones that are strong enough to stand the test.

In selecting for physical and emotional strength in our animals, we are doing artificially what would be done naturally in the wild. It is our way of working with nature to simulate the natural selection process.

Keep in mind that in nature the animal is not subjected to the same stresses abundant in the life of a show dog. Therefore, we make an effort to strengthen the bitch's reserves by proper conditioning and nutrition. The bitch will let you know when all is not well by not cycling on schedule. It is interesting to note that female marathon runners are subject to irregular cycling and even total cessation of menstrual cycles as bodies struggle to accommodate demands such exercise places upon them.

Among other things that can create reproduction problems are toxic exposures such as radon gas, chemical disinfectants, heartworm medications, changes in food and/or water, and/or change of environment. Any number of elements can cause stress to the bitch's nervous system and interfere with her body's well being.

When your bitch is not having normal seasons, it is a good bet that something is stressing her. Knowing the normal cycle pattern of her dam and sisters will help you decide if her cycle is normal for her, as some bitches follow the book at six-month intervals, others at eight months, and so on. The Vin-Melca bitches have always mimicked others in their family in this regard.

Maintaining the body's well being clearly is the most important facet of handling the show career of the future brood bitch. The bitch must be nourished by the best foods and supplemented with appropriate vitamins and minerals. As previously stated I am not a veterinarian nor a nutritionist, so in sharing the following keep in mind it is just what worked for me. What worked for my Norwegian Elkhounds might not be of much help in other breeds, or for that matter, in other families of Norwegian Elkhounds.

I have found the B-complex to be of particular importance in combating the stresses of a strenuous campaign. Vitamins A, C and E are important in fighting the effects of toxic exposures and strengthening the immune system.

Over the years, I have encouraged my dogs to eat bananas for their B-6 and potassium, as well as the soothing effect they have on the intestinal tract. Keeping the intestinal tract healthy is vital, and it can be helped by using bottled water on the road and feeding yogurt with active cultures and acidophilus capsules.

Regular, controlled exercise not only benefits the bitch in the show ring, it also adds to her proficiency in delivering puppies. A fit bitch will experience less difficulty during the entire reproduction process. Furthermore, regular exercise gives the bitch more self-confidence and is good for her psyche, turning her into a more poised animal in the show ring when she takes on the males.

The more strength of character the bitch achieves as a show animal, the more sense of self-esteem she will pass on to her puppies as their role model. Puppies are very much affected by the behavior of their dam in the early weeks, and a confident bitch will likely raise the most well-adjusted puppies.

To Breed or Not To Breed

The question of whether to breed a bitch before she is campaigned or to wait until her show career is completed depends not only on the breed, but also on the kind of animal she is within that breed. Also important are the various human factors, such as timing and the owner's choices. Breeds that are smooth-coated and emphasize tuck-up and underline do not always recover their smoothness after whelping, unless the bitch is naturally tight and wiry. Bitches who tend to be at all soft or sloppy will only get worse after a litter.

Some bitches are enhanced by motherhood and really blossom into mature show animals following the experience. This is especially true of coated bitches, who will come into a splendid coat following the postpartum shed. Usually the bitch will be ready to return to the ring at about the same time her puppies come of age for the 6- to 9-month puppy class. It seems that leggier, harder bitches benefit most from a pre-campaign litter.

Pre-Campaign Pregnancy

A major advantage to breeding the bitch prior to campaigning her in specials is that she is proven, her reproductive system has been opened up, and the breeder can campaign her longer with less fear that time will run out on her biological clock. Furthermore, her puppies will be growing up while she is being campaigned, providing the breeder the opportunity to study their strengths and weaknesses. This leads to more informed choices in selecting future sires for this particular bitch.

In 1980, a decision had to be made to campaign or breed the yearling bitch, Ch. Vin-Melca's Last Call (Gilda), who had just finished her title with a Best of Breed from the classes over the national weekend. On the one hand was the desire to special this bitch, on the other the wish to breed her to Ch. Vin-Melca's Vagabond—then nearly 14—which was even stronger. With the assistance of the veterinarian, she was bred.

In the following year, Gilda became one of the nation's top hounds and her puppies started finishing their championships. After a two-year campaign that resulted in her becoming the top-winning Elkhound bitch in the history of the breed, she went back to the whelping box and became the top-producing bitch in the breed as the dam of 27 champions. Her early litter by Vagabond influenced the choice of subsequent sires, so that none of her puppies was wasted.

In 1990, Gilda's baby sister, Ch. Vin-Melca's Calista (Sarah), not only broke her record but also became the breed's all-time top winner with 66 all-breed BISs in two years of campaigning. Unlike her sister Gilda, Sarah was not bred prior to her campaign. In November 1990, Sarah was bred and finished her '90 campaign in whelp, winning 12 groups and seven Bests in Show while carrying a litter of eight. The puppies were born on Desert Storm Day in January 1991. This athletic and fit bitch whelped the litter in less than 90 minutes. At the time of this writing, she is the dam of 11 champions, including the multi-BIS and two-time Westminster Hound Group winner, Ch. Vin-Melca's Marketta (see color section).

In addition to her regular exercise routine and a well-supplemented feeding program, Sarah's care included close monitoring of all discharges. Thus, a slight bacterial infection—possibly picked up in a public exercise pen at a show—was treated immediately with antibiotics and quickly eliminated. Slight spotting a few weeks into the pregnancy resulted in immediate increases in folic acid, which evidently helps the uterus maintain a healthy relationship with the placenta and prevents fetal loss.

Appreciating Vitality

An interesting sidelight on these two bitches is that Gilda was from the first litter of Ch. Vin-Melca's Bottoms Up and Sarah was from her third and last litter, whelped when she was almost 10. Furthermore, Sarah's sire, Ch. Vin-Melca's Mandate, a Vagabond son, was more than 10 years of age at the time of the mating. These dogs were with Fred and Dody Froehlich in Alaska, reflecting their good care as well as hardy, outdoor living in a natural environment.

Dogs that can breed into their later years should be highly valued in a breeding program, for it is proof of the line's vitality. Expectations as to how long dogs can reproduce vary according to the breed.

Left: Ch. Vin-Melca's Last Call, known as Gilda, pictured winning Best of Breed while still in puppy coat at Santa Barbara under Mrs. Thelma Brown. (Henry Schley Photo) **Right:** Gilda winning one of her 10 SBISs (in her summer coat after whelping her 1st litter) under breeder-judge Robert Caricofe.

Sarah pictured with her litter of 8 born on Desert Storm Day in 1991. (Photo by Deidi Kramer)

Ch. Vin-Melca's Calista (Sarah) winning her second Westminster Hound Group in February 1990. She was bred in November 1990 for the first time and whelped her first litter in January 1991. (*New York Times* photograph)

Even though most of my bitches have had only three litters, the litters were spaced over a period of years, giving ample time to study the progeny before selecting the next sire, and I hope, improving the odds of breeding better dogs. In a breeding program, one must keep reminding oneself that quality, not quantity, is what is important.

In considering the use of the bitch who does not make it in the show ring as a breeding prospect, there are several factors involved. If the bitch is simply not competitive because of poor quality, she should not be bred. If dogs are not good enough to show, they are not good enough to breed. If extenuating circumstances, such as a disfigurement caused by an accident or some other similar problem, exist, that is a different matter. In such cases, breeders must make decisions according to individual situations.

In assessing the breeding potential of a bitch, the class of the bitch as well as the background enter into all decision making. The health and temperament of the bitch are also part of the formula. Some very nice but not great bitches who carry superior genes, such as those carried by the key bitch, will out produce those able to beat them in the ring but carrying lesser genes.

I am personally a little more flexible in accepting minor defects in bitches than in dogs. Because you don't always know the long-term genetic behavior of these defects until you have put them into your gene pool, it seems advisable to put them into it through the bitches with their fewer numbers. This allows you latitude to study the long-term effects on subsequent generations before putting them into the gene pool through the males and their considerably larger numbers of progeny with their increased potential to damage the breed.

Once again in looking at the bottom line, it is your selection objectivity and decision-making skills that will determine the progress in your breeding program. Just the economics of breeding should prevent foolish choices on your part. It is one more of the many elements that impel you to make the wisest possible choice.

Ranking the Producers

In 1956, Irene Castle Phillips originated the first point system to rank American show dogs. Known as the Phillips System, it credited a dog winning at the all-breed level with a point for each dog defeated in group and best in show competition and was first published in *Popular Dogs Magazine*. In the beginning, the system acknowledged only the Top Ten All Breeds. Later, it expanded to include the Top Ten in each group and went on to include breed rankings too. Today, there are many different systems that give a wide number of specials being campaigned a ranking of some kind, and it's hard to keep up with them all.

In those early days, Irene did all of her painstaking "computing" without the aid of computers, going through the show records as published by the American Kennel Club and diligently recording the numbers. Because she always thought as a breeder, in 1965 Irene started another system even closer to her heart, that of tabulating sires and dams by their champion progeny as reported in the *American Kennel Gazette* and honoring them accordingly.

The ultimate achievement in her new system was the Century Club award that went to sires with 100 champions and dams with 25 champions with a special allowance for toys (due to small litters) of 17 champions. When Irene married Harold "Butch" Schlintz and developed *H.I.S. Publications*, the honorees received certificates from *H.I.S.* at the silver, gold and diamond levels as well as at the top level. Today, Irene's work is carried on by her daughter, Jacqueline Root, of Fair Oaks, California, who is working to update all the records. Although all the records for all the breeds were not completed at press time, all of the dogs profiled have at least the numbers of champions for which they have been credited. In the preface of this book, I explained that the sires and dams recognized represent a random sampling; it does not include many others who have achieved as much or more. This was not intended to be a slight to any dog or any breed but is simply due to lack of available resources and space. For example, the All Time Producing Pointer sire Ch. Marjetta National Acclaim (sire of 112 champions) is not profiled in the Sire Section, while his All Time Producing Dam Ch. Truewithem A Taste of Triumph is included in the Brood Bitch section.

Irene Castle Phillips Khatoonian Schlintz in 1955, the year before she originated her ranking systems for American show dogs. (Photo courtesy of Jackie Root)

Irene was well aware that her work was a statistical evaluation that recognized numbers put on the board by energetic breeder-owners who got caught up in the competition. She and I joked about the fact that some of the Ch. Vin-Melca's Howdy Rowdy progeny were not exactly my personal "cup of tea" even as their championships were pursued. This can happen to breeders and owners and isn't harmful as long as you know which animals to retain in the breeding program—for records and numbers have absolutely no impact on the gene pool. In my own case, the Howdy Rowdy progeny with open coats were not used in the breeding program.

In researching sires and dams to include in this book, a wide variety of breeders reported that many of their breed's great ones were considered to have contributed as many negative traits into the breed's gene pool as positive. And that is the nature of the beast, for there is no such thing as a "free" mating—one that can be totally counted upon never to affect the breed in other than a positive way. Until future science allows us to remove genetic trash from the gene pools, breeders will always be in the position of having to take the bad with the good.

Thus, in assessing animals who have had a tremendous impact on their breed's gene pool, do not make the mistake of thinking there were never negative influences. In each breed there are animals whose genetic qualities must be carefully analyzed to determine if the good involved is worth the bad. It is the responsibility of each breeder to do the homework involved in making informed judgment calls to determine those answers.

Consider producing records in much the same way as show records in your analysis. Recognize that they are much more difficult to achieve because there are so many more variables. Some stars achieve their lofty status because they are in popular hands at the perfect time, others because of hard work of all the players.

In conducting research for this book, I heard the same message over and over from *master breeders* who feel their responsibilities in all phases of breeder accountability. One strong concern is that the more marketable a breed is, the more protection it needs. More and more breeders than ever before are realizing it's not how many but how good that counts. At the same time, it is appropriate to accept that records are made to be broken even as we spotlight some of the brood bitches and sires who made them.

Some Brood Bitches to Appreciate

Top Producing Bitch All Time, All Breeds: Ch. Rich-Lin's Molly of Arcadia - Bearded Collie - Dam of 33 champions

The Ch. Rich-Lin's Molly of Arcadia success story is a textbook case of how a well-planned breeding program can come to fruition. For James and Diann Shannon had done their homework when they got into the Bearded Collie breed in the 1970s.

Their breeding expertise began in the very exacting world of the German Shepherd Dog with the work of Lloyd Brackett contributing much of their background education. The Shannons knew the quality of their original Beardie Rich-Lin's Rising Son even though he was purchased as a pet while the breed was still in the Miscellaneous Class.

It didn't take long for this exceptional animal, who dominated Miscellaneous Classes, to sell them on the breed and the conscious decision to make a plan to breed Beardies soon followed. Their research led them to the English dog many consider the greatest Beardie that ever lived, Eng. Ch. Edenborough Blue Bracken, the grandsire of their new dog. Eventually, Bracken's litter sister, Edenborough Full O' Life came to America and, much to their delight, was bred to Rising Son.

Molly was a stud fee puppy from this litter, and her acquisition helped comfort them at the premature loss of Rising Son. Like her father before her, Molly excelled in side movement because of her excellent well-angled shoulder and strong rear. A rather small bitch herself, Molly threw very feminine daughters while still producing masculine sons, a characteristic highly valued by breed authorities. Furthermore, she put the correct coat texture on her progeny, a trait not to be confused with excessive coat.

The small Arcadia breeding program has produced more than 200 champions in a 30-year period, and Molly contributed 33 of them. A true foundation bitch, Molly stamped ensuing generations with her all-over look and style. The Shannons currently have a great granddaughter that looks just like her.

Her first litter was sired by her half-brother, Ch. Rich-Lin's Whiskers of Arcadia, also a Rising Son offspring. The Shannons went back to the source for her second litter, this time taking her to another import from the same bloodline, Ch. Edenborough Happy Go Lucky, a well-bred Blue Bracken son. When bred to Lucky's son, Ch. Arcadia's Bluegrass Music, the resulting Ch. Arcadia's Cotton-Eyed Joe became a BIS winner the first time owner-handler, Teri Stepankow, a partner to the Shannons, took him into the ring. Moreover, he exhibited desired herding instincts when used on sheep.

The amazing thing about the Molly progeny was the way they all bred on, achieving awesome producing records of their own. Any number of ROMX (Register of Merit Excellent) and ROM sires and dams trace to Molly. She met all the tests of a true foundation bitch in all areas, with offspring able to win in all facets of the demanding show world. Her progeny and their progeny accounted for National Specialties, all breed BISs, herding contest honors and producing honors. Furthermore, it didn't seem to matter whom she was bred to as she clicked with each sire.

Ch. Rich-Lin's Molly of Arcadia, the #1 All Time Producing Bitch All Breeds with 33 champion offspring. (Photo courtesy of Diann Shannon)

This type of breeding, based on correct selection in the very beginning and staying within an excellent line such as the Edenborough line, shows how breeders can achieve success without using trial-and-error methods. In essence, every breeding counts and all of the puppies are appropriately utilized. This is what master breeding is all about—a small but *select* endeavor as practiced by the Shannons.

BROOD BITCH EXTRAORDINAIRE: CH. DASA'S EBONY QUEEN - ITALIAN GREYHOUND - DAM OF 30 CHAMPIONS

Good things really do come in small packages as in the case of Ch. Dasa's Ebony Queen, Italian Greyhound owned by Patricia and Richard Sapp, my neighbors in Antioch, Tennessee. It could be argued that she is the number one producer as the dam of 30 champions, a phenomenal number when adjustments for small litters of toys are factored into the equation. Certainly, I have equal respect for all of these brood bitches.

Ebony Queen was a stud fee puppy sired by the Sapp's Ch. Dasu's Blu Falcon, who was also the sire of Ebony Queen's greatest mate, Ch. Dasu's King Of The Mountain. This half-brother, half-sister breeding produced over half of the Queen's 30 champions. She was an exceptionally strong bitch, and stamped her puppies with extraordinary soundness and excellent movement both front and rear. She was a very prepotent bitch for beautiful heads and necks, throwing uniformity in her puppies.

It has been 20 years since this excellent producer rewrote the records for toys, yet in the summer of 1996, the Sapps were carefully watching a blue and white hopeful down from Ebony Queen as he nears the age to show. The continuing influence of a great brood bitch is a quality sought by all breeders.

Italian Greyhound Ch. Dasa's Ebony Queen pictured with Richard Sapp was the gorgeous #2 All Time Producing Bitch All Breeds. (Photo by Clark)

So consistent and flashy were her progeny that Pat Sapp had difficulty deciding which puppies to keep. Her daughter Ch. Dasu's Maid Marion was a multi-group and multi-specialty winner. Ch. Dasu's Ziegfield was another favorite of the Sapps.

Ebony Queen was in good company, for her favorite mate, King Of The Mountain, sired 78 champions for the breed's siring record and his son, Ch. Mira Hill N' Dale D'Dasu, sired 46 champions. If ever a producing line was a testimony to the idea of the family importance in the breeding of outstanding animals, it is this exceptional line of Italian Greyhounds.

CH. BROUGHT-MAR JELIBEAN DE CAMPO - BRITTANY - DAM OF 32 CHAMPIONS
Ch. Brought-Mar Jelibean De Campo played a vital role in two ways in the life of Dennis and Andrea Jordan's Jordean Kennels. First of all, in her own way she brought the two of them together. For Andrea was having trouble winning with her bitch, so Dennis entered the picture and put points on Jelibean.

His family raised Irish Setters and ran the boarding-grooming facility where Andrea met him when she took Jelibean for grooming.

Later, when Andrea was a bridesmaid in the wedding of Dennis' good friend, the two were thrown together again and ended up married to each other. And Jelibean was a big part of their start in Brittanys. A very sound and solid bitch of good field and show stock, she was prepotent in producing her own strength of character and stability. Her progeny had good running gear and solid toplines. And most importantly, Jelibean and her offspring served as an "exceptional educational tool" for the newlyweds, according to Andrea.

They realized they were serious about breeding good dogs and began to seek out typey dogs to use on their solid bitch to improve her weaknesses. The next generation produced more honest bitches with slightly more type, and served to open doors for the Jordans as more established breeders of Brittanys began to take them seriously and work with them to improve the breed. The good dogs they were getting from these early efforts served to inspire them to shoot for higher goals and exceptional dogs.

Jelibean was bred by Wayne and Tula Fessenden and purchased by Andrea from Coral Appleton, who owned her sire, Dual Ch. Brought-Mar Jiver De Campo. Ch. Four-Tee Desiderata was her dam.

Twelve of her 32 champions were sired by Ch. Bent Oak's Just Because JH, with all seven in one litter finishing and attaining Orthopedic Foundation of America (OFA) numbers. Two of her granddaughters are currently in residence at Jordean to add the hard-knocking hunting traits and solidness to future Brittanys.

The unique element of the Jelibean story is that her producing record provided solid hunting dogs that were finishable to two young aspiring *master breeders*, who benefited from her contributions by becoming more and more involved, studying and using such mentors as Beverly Millette of California to expand their horizons. Today, the Jordean dogs are foremost among Brittany breeding programs, thanks to the start they got with Jelibean.

Ch. Amberac's Asterling Aruba - Golden Retriever - Dam of 32 Champions

Ch. Amberac's Asterling Aruba became the foundation bitch for Mary Burke's Asterling line, the most famous of which is Ch. Asterling's Wild Blue Yonder, all-time winner in the breed with 51 BISs to his credit. He is currently the sire of 70 champion get.

Aruba was consistent in always producing excellent temperament and dogs with a sense of self. In spite of the fact that her own dam was oversized, her progeny were of correct size and famous for their flashy look and appointments. Her owner reports that no matter how she was bred she produced luxurious coats with lots of undercoat. One of her grandsons, Ch. Sassafras Batteries Not Included, accomplished the incredible feat of winning the National Specialty four times, a breed record. Her sire, Ch. Gold Coast Here Comes The Sun C.D., was the grandson of Ch. Misty Morn's Sunset CD, TD, WC, All Time Top Sire in the breed.

Aruba produced a total of 38 puppies with 32 of them finishing their championships. Four of them were BIS winners including the exciting bitch, Ch. Asterling's Tahiti Sweeti, sired by Ch. Gold Rush Judgment Day and from Aruba's first litter. Her son, Ch. Asterling's Go Get 'M Gangbuster, is approaching the magic 100 mark in the numbers of champions he has sired.

Ch. Amberac's Asterling Aruba is the dam of the all time breed record holder, Ch. Asterling's Wild Blue Yonder, as well as 31 other titleholders. (Photo courtesy of Jackie Root)

The amazing Aruba won the Brood Bitch Class at the National five times. Breeders consider her a turning point in the breed's evolution, giving a stylish show-dog persona that had not always been present in the breed. Certainly for Mary she was a once in a lifetime bitch.

Ch. Truewithem a Taste of Triumph - Pointer- Dam of 29 Champions

Ch. Truewithem A Taste of Triumph and her 29 champion offspring are a testimony to a success story of an objective breeder. Marjorie Martorella had been in Pointers for a while, but decided to regroup as she had not been happy with the results from her first breedings. Her new start was with what was to become the breed's Top Producing Bitch All Time in A Taste of Triumph, fondly known as "Donna."

This bitch was to become the true foundation bitch for the famed Marjetta line of Pointers that has contributed any number of BIS winners to dogdom including the 1986 Westminster BIS winner, Ch. Marjetta National Acclaim, also known as "Deputy." In addition to Deputy, Donna was also the dam of three other BIS winners.

Donna was blessed with a marvelous front assembly, a quality hard to find in Pointers just as in any other breed. She could be counted upon to put excellent shoulders on her progeny and these fronts were accented by very open gait with lots of reach and drive. She was sired by a personal favorite of mine, Ch. Counterpoint's Lord Ashley, the 1970 Westminster group winner. Her pedigree was line-bred on the sound breeding of the Bryant bloodlines, and these traits came down through the generations.

Her first litter was sired by her half-brother, Ch. Waldoschloss Thunderbolt, himself a son of Lord Ashley. All eight of the resulting puppies finished their titles with Ch. Marjetta Lord Carlton becoming a BIS winner as well as a top producer. *Master breeder* Martorella was very objective in assessing her litters, and tried to improve such characteristics as feet that were too big as well as striving for better heads and tails with subsequent breedings. Perhaps her typiest litter from Donna came from the outcrossed sire, Ch. Rossenarra Amontillado of Crookrise and featured the BIS winners Ch. Marjetta Lady Vanessa and Ch. Marjetta Milestone. Martorella's constant search to improve with each mating

Ch. Karolaska Honey's Abby, HOF, is the choice of Judge George Nichols in this winner's circle picture. She went on to become her breed's foremost producing bitch with 24 champion get. (Hansen Photo)

Ch. Truewithem A Taste of Triumph and *Master Breeder* Marjorie Martorella. "Donna" is the Top Producing Pointer bitch of all time with 29 champion offspring. Her son, Ch. Marjetta National Acclaim was BIS at Westminster in 1986. (Photo by John Ashbey)

Ch. Treyacres Apple Squiz is the dam of 10 champions and #2 Brussels Griffon brood bitch. Pictured with Jacque Jones, handling her to a win under E.W. Tipton of Rebel Roc Miniature Pinscher fame. For many years, his "Little Daddy" held all the records for toys and probably still would today if he had been campaigned at a time when so many dog shows were available to the stars at the top. (Alverson Photo)

Ch. Treyacres-Katy-Did-Did-It, dam of 11 champions, pictured here as a leggy 7-month old at her first show handled by her breeder Jacque Jones. "Katy" is the breed's All Time Top Producing bitch. Homestead Kennels were the proud owners. (Photo by Klein)

Ch. Honey Creek Vivacious exuded star quality in the ring and in the whelping box. Pictured winning the group under Beatrice Godsol, Vivacious was the first great winning particolored Cocker Spaniel bitch in the history of the breed. She was handled by the expert Norman Austin and owned and bred by Bea Weguson. (Photo by Norton of Kent, courtesy of Jeanne Austin)

led her to breed Donna to her nephew, Ch. Firesign's Smackwater Jack, and this litter produced Deputy. Marjorie used Jack to put more strength of character into the progeny and Deputy was proof it worked.

Although Deputy went on to become the breed's All Time Sire with 112 champions, Marjorie only used him once, as she felt her bitches already had his qualities and she needed to use other sires who could furnish traits her line needed. In effect, this very objective and practical breeder made the decision to go away from her own homebred great sire to get what her bitches needed while recognizing that the bitches of others needed what Deputy had to offer. Such analytical thinking is what creates *master breeders* and adds varied resources to the improved gene pools of the breed. That's self-discipline!

For the animals of the next generations continued to show the solid soundness that Donna had contributed to the breed while exhibiting improved essence of type. This example was exemplified by the great bitches, Ch. Luftnase Albelarm Bee's Knees, number one Dog All Breeds in 1989, and Ch. Marjetta Dark Side of the Moon. Both are destined to be seen in the pedigrees of the quality Pointers of the future.

CH. REGALIA'S GOODY GOODY OUR GANG - TIBETAN TERRIER - DAM OF 26 CHAMPIONS

Ch. Regalia's Goody Goody Our Gang was an elegant beauty of a Tibetan Terrier with lots of flair in spite of the fact that she was rather plainly marked as a black with a white chest. So sound and honest was this lively bitch that she became the dam of 26 champions with three of her progeny gaining utility degrees in obedience competition.

Out of the totally black bitch Regalia's Demon Seed, Goody was the first bitch owner Jeanette Chaix deemed good enough to breed. Because the gene pool was small in the early days of the breed and some of the dogs were plagued with problems of unsoundness, Jeanette and her partner, Robert Carder, concentrated on breeding for honest dogs with good mouths, as well as type. They searched for all-round dogs with excellent temperaments and were proud of the animals' abilities in obedience.

Goody herself was prepotent for correct tail sets and strong rears, and she produced good hips at a time when hip dysplasia was a problem in the breed. Her owners were very careful in the selection of mates. Both Goody and the runner-up to her as a producer, John and Angelee Fargo's Charisma's Passionella (dam of 20 champions) were sired by the strong Ch. Marimark's Patches of Ti Song. Because the entries were few in number in those days, the Fargos and Carder and Chaix cooperated and worked together, showing each other's dogs and enjoying dog shows as a recreational activity at the same time they worked diligently to improve the breed.

At a time when the Non-Sporting Group in California was dominated by Poodles and Bichon Frises, one of Goody's sons, Heartbreak Valentino, won five groups. But for the most part, the team concentrated on the line and did little campaigning at the specials level.

When one of Goody's descendants won the group at the recent World Show, Jeanette took as much pleasure that day in the Junior Showmanship victory of the 11-year-old English girl who borrowed another Goody descendent to win juniors. Because of the quarantine rules, the child had been unable to participate with her own dog.

The partnership of Carder and Chaix had an interesting beginning as he came as a teenager to stay with Jeanette's family. He was still there 20 years later. He was like Jeanette's son, and the two soul mates approached their breeding program with common goals. "We knew what was wrong and what we had to fix," she says. There is no doubt about it. Jeanette Chaix and the late Carder did their own thing, and, thanks to Ch. Regalia's Goody Goody Our Gang, it worked big time.

CH. KAROLASKA HONEY'S ABBY, HOF - GREAT PYRENEES - DAM OF 24 CHAMPIONS

It comes as no surprise to find a Karolaska Pyrenees at the top of the breed's list of all time producers, for this kennel has produced more than 200 champions in its years in dogs, with more than 100 of them being bred in Alaska before their relocation to Gig Harbor, Washington.

Foremost amongst the breed's brood bitches is Ch. Karolaska Honey's Abby HOF with 24 champions of record. Abby's genetic input to her puppies was typical of her line, as her offspring were structurally sound and stable. And, although she wasn't crazy about dog shows, her sons and daughters were both willing and able.

Bred by Carol Kentopp, who co-owned with her daughter Kimmy, Abby was notable for her great head and substance, qualities she passed on to the next generations. Her favorite mate was the top producing Ch. Karolaska Klumbo HOF, the sire of 11 of her champions and himself the number two All Time Sire in the breed. A solid line of bear-like dogs with great breed character emerged from Abby and her relatives. Her Hall of Fame producing designation is in honor of the award introduced by Mary Crane through the Great Pyrenees Club of America.

Although the Kentopps have not been as active in recent years as they once were, I understand that their interest is being rekindled. Perhaps the fancy can anticipate more of these wonderful dogs down from Abby and her descendants.

CH. TREYACRES KATY-DID-DID-IT AND CH. TREYACRES APPLE SQUIZ - BRUSSELS GRIFFON BROOD BITCHES OF NOTE

Master breeder Jacque Jones, of Treyacres Brussels Griffons, is an excellent example of success achieved by concentrating on the tail female line. For 35 years, Jacque and her late husband, Ray, emphasized well-bred brood bitches on the strong "bottom line" of their pedigrees. Because their choices of outside sires were always dogs of the same type, it might be said they were practicing a form of "linebreeding to a look" even when outcrossing.

The Treyacres brood bitches all must have soundness of both body and mind even though some do not consider dog shows to be fun and games. A bitch of excellent quality but not interested in showing might just stay home and attend to matronly duties, thus some of the kennel's best brood bitches were not finished. Such a bitch was the solid key bitch, Treyacres Truffles, a smooth who became the dam of the breed's Top Producing Bitch, Ch. Treyacres Katy-Did-Did-It, and maternal great-grandam of Ch. Homestead Sir With Love, bred by good friends Evelyn and John Hole. The Treyacres-Homestead cooperative effort has been of great benefit to the Griffon gene pool.

Jones looks for different things in the dogs and bitches in her breeding program. She will be more forgiving of a bitch in the areas of fanciness, headpiece, and star quality, and less forgiving of a bitch when it comes to the basics, such as soundness, body and topline. She values the smooths in her pedigrees because sometimes they help the integrity of coat quality, and correct coat is a priority with the breed.

Katy-Did-Did-It and Ch. Treyacres Apple Squiz have combined efforts to produce more than 20 champions and are the breed's top producing bitches. Squiz's grandson, Ch. Treyacres Zorro, is rewriting the records for Griffon sires with more than 60 champions to his credit as we go to print. The significant thing about these key bitches in this family of outstanding brood matrons is that their descendants are able to dominate the breed at both the all-breed level and specialty shows.

In addition to her extended family relationship with Homestead, Jones shares her endeavors with her daughter, Dayne, and son-in-law, Jeff Thomas, as well as their daughter, Tiffany. That the Treyacres influence will be felt well into the 21st Century seems assured by both the breeding program and the dedication of the people involved in it.

CH. HONEY CREEK VIVACIOUS - COCKER SPANIEL, PARTI-COLOR - DAM OF 14 CHAMPIONS

Ch. Honey Creek Vivacious and her Honey Creek kennelmates owned and bred by the incredible Bea Wegusen were the turning point for the parti-colored Cocker Spaniel. Whelped in the late 1940s, Vivacious was a star in the show ring as well as in the whelping box. Her incredible four wins of the variety at the American Spaniel Club was a one-of-a kind accomplishment, yet she lives on forever as a brood bitch for all time.

The 14 champions she produced were in a day and age when shows were fewer and the chase for records much less important. This gorgeous red-and-white bitch so influenced the breed that in 1952, 21 of the parti-colors entered at the Spaniel Club were either her children or grandchildren. She carried the day for still another Spaniel Club Variety victory over all of them.

With the help of her talented handler, Norman Austin, whose breeding intuition is legendary, Bea and her Honey Creek Cockers changed the parti-colored variety forever—putting into it the qualities that made it possible to compete with the blacks and ASCOBs. Few breeds can point to a brood bitch with more influence than that of Vivacious.

Thoughts on Brood Bitches

- Great foundation (key) bitches are usually in possession of two powerful X chromosomes.

- At the time of the mating the female's eggs all carry one X chromosome. Approximately one-half of the sire's sperm will carry the Y chromosome, and the other half will carry the X.

- Unlike other genetic information the passage of the X chromosome from the sire can be determined by whether the resulting puppy is a dog or bitch, thus allowing breeders to structure pedigrees in pursuit of excellent brood bitches.

- Every daughter of an outstanding brood bitch sire receives the same X chromosome from her sire. This is the only one he has to give. If the X his daughters receive from their dam is as good as that from the outstanding brood bitch sire, there is a strong likelihood she will become a good producer.

- In a tail female line the sires have the opportunity to strengthen the line if they had excellent dams, or to weaken it if they did not.

- Because so much genetic information is carried on the X chromosome, the dam of the sire you plan to use should be as important to you as the bitch you plan to breed to him. This is all the more meaningful to a small breeding program built on quality, not quantity.

- Keep in mind that the sire of the brood bitch gave her his dam's X chromosome. From her own dam she either received the X chromosome of her maternal grandsire's dam or that of her dam's dam.

- The brood bitch puts her characteristics back to good use and widespread use through her sons.

- The outstanding sire of brood bitches will have daughters whose sons excel at stud.

In my own breeding program, Howdy Rowdy was the great sire and bred on through both his sons and his daughters because he had strong Y and X chromosomes. His half-brother Vagabond apparently did not inherit a strong Y chromosome and did not sire strong sons. He was a superlative brood bitch sire because he had inherited a strong X from his and Howdy's dam Vikina. Two of his daughters' sons became outstanding sires even though used on a limited basis.

In Search of the Sire

The evolution of a breed takes place through a small number of sires. Historically, populations have expressed themselves in the most magnificent forms of progress in the earlier stages of their development. Some examples might be Ancient Egypt, as well as the early Greeks and Romans.

At no time in American history did our society produce the giants that lived during the American Revolution. Would that we knew where to find a George Washington, Benjamin Franklin, Thomas Jefferson, John Adams, Sam Adams, James Madison, or Patrick Henry today. Yet, all these greats were on our soil at the same time. And those were just a few of the emerging nation's movers and shakers.

Since it appears that the most improvement is made early in any breeding population, the more revered sires in a breed might very well be those who got in on the ground floor in the early development of the breed. This is as it should be, for the smaller the population, the larger the influence of a strong individual. In a population of 100, a strong individual would make a noticeable difference. Yet the difference he would make in a population of 1,000 or 100,000 or one million might be insignificant. In fact, the case could be made that as a breed progresses, it becomes more difficult to identify the great sires.

The Stud Dog

There have been times in the history of the world, as we know it, when the concept in the following quotation was no doubt functional. During antiquity when natural selection controlled the breeding population and vast areas of open land were available for dogs to roam, genes from the *alpha* male would indeed become widespread in the existing gene pool.

> "Keep on sowing your seed, for you never know which will grow—Perhaps it all will."
> —Ecclesiastics

Today, this biblical message is no longer a viable option for breeders to follow by playing the numbers game in hopes that the law of averages will turn out some winners. Such a pursuit is not only counterproductive, it is very expensive unless one is a commercial breeder.

We live in a world in which available land and resources are shrinking. Dog breeders and purebred dog fanciers are being lumped into a catchall category by a public unhappy with the overpopulation of pets. With animal rights groups aiming their formidable weapons at the cessation of breeding purebred dogs, each breeder must make sure that every breeding counts. Each mating must be part of a dedicated effort to produce the best dogs, with the least breedings, in a concerned attempt to improve the ratio of quality per puppy.

Whether you own a stud dog or seek the services of one, you owe it to man's best friend and those who love him to conduct the procedure with the utmost care. Even a bitch bred every season by the unethical puppy mill operations can never live long enough to produce the numbers that her male counterpart can. It is through the sires with their power to reproduce in large numbers that the gene pool expands so rapidly, for better or for worse. Therefore, the breeder must make the choice of the stud dog a wise one, taking every precaution to reduce the margin of error.

Breeding is considered the science of combining bloodlines. And science could be considered the combining of elements—yet the properties of elements are known and unchanging while the properties of bloodlines are not so precise.

However, what we do know is that great sires tend to be from great sire lines. In assessing these sires, appropriate consideration should be given to those whose sires were also great sires. Furthermore, it will not be surprising if their grandsire or both grandsires were also outstanding sires. When you are dealing with such a sire line, it is known as the *direct tail male line*. Keep in mind when studying this tail male line of descent that the sire always gives a copy of his Y chromosome to his sons, for it is what determines their sex.

One of the most dangerous scenarios in any breed is when large percentages of mediocre animals are used as sires and become widespread in the gene pool. As a very good friend of mine always says: "Only the best among the males in a breed should be used at stud."

Great dogs should be able to dominate the competition of their generation. They should be able to win in all circumstances and against all comers. Therefore, they should be the ones getting into the gene pools as sires. Such sires can create successful breeders from those who are wise enough to use them. Without such dogs being available to them, these same breeders might not have enjoyed more than modest success and could have been lost to the breed. **When great sires are available and breeders don't use them, these breeders will be beaten by those who do.**

When you remember how many more progeny a sire can produce than can a brood bitch, it becomes obvious that those who use the great sires will experience more progress in their breeding programs. The great sire is prepotent for virtuous characteristics and will do well with all kinds of bitches. His gene pool cooperates with a variety of pedigrees that are brought to him. In other words, not only will the best sires perpetuate their own personal virtues, they will blend harmoniously with other strains in successive generations.

SECRETARIAT: A BREED APART

Secretariat was a wonder horse who represented one of the best direct tail male lines of descent known to breeders of purebred animals. Here is his male line:

PHALARIS

PHAROS

NEARCO

NASRULLAH

BOLD RULER

As any student of thoroughbreds knows, Secretariat was not the only great horse to come down through this gene pool through this direct sire line. Of the several Kentucky Derby winners from this sire line, Northern Dancer became the best sire. Since Secretariat himself achieved the ultimate of what it

is possible for a horse to do, it comes as no surprise that he has not sired a horse of his own caliber, much less one that is better. That is not to say the pride of Virginia, where he was foaled, has not sired some excellent animals and useful ones at that, as some of them have bred on with very good results.

Thoroughbred breeders are finding Secretariat to be a better sire in the second and third generations than in the first. Furthermore, he blends harmoniously with a number of other influential sires making him a valuable component of a pedigree. However, this amazing sire from the most brilliant of sire lines has "bred on" best through his daughters, ranking high on the broodmare sire list for years. Interestingly enough, his outstanding grandson Storm Cat (out of the Secretariat mare Terlingua) is one of the great sires and is DIRECT TAIL MALE to Nearco, being by Storm Bird, by Northern Dancer, by Nearctic, by Nearco. Therefore, Storm Cat carries the Nearco blood through both sides of his pedigree!

In order for one like Secretariat to sire a horse better than himself, the progeny would have to be some kind of bionic animal as anyone who watched him demolish the field at the 1973 Belmont Stakes would agree. It might be said that a horse, or a dog, of such quality as Secretariat is almost a freak of nature—**a breed apart**.

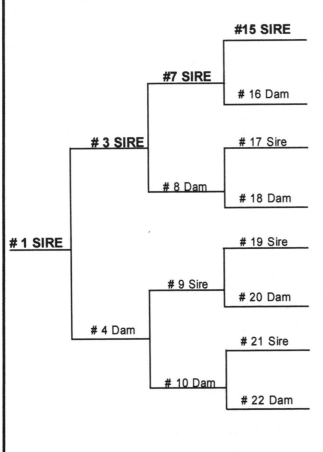

#15 SIRE

#7 SIRE

16 Dam

17 Sire

8 Dam

18 Dam

3 SIRE

19 Sire

9 Sire

20 Dam

21 Sire

10 Dam

22 Dam

4 Dam

1 SIRE

TAIL MALE LINE
Sires # 1, 3, 7, 15

The look of a sire is one of great strength for that breed, with a certain electricity of his own. He is a textbook dog who is a good-looking individual with an impeccable pedigree—sound in body and in mind. Such a sire produces no genetic disease genes and always improves on the bitches brought to him. He has strength of character and determination with a sense of self. This worthy animal becomes the basis for a program of linebreeding.

The fascinating thing about the breeding of dogs is that there is often an exception to the rule. That can be the case when a rather ordinary dog from an outstanding line of excellent animals becomes a good sire, siring animals far superior to himself. He must be a one-generation *set back* for the line caused by good genes being masked by undesired ones on this particular dog. His personal unfavorable genetic combination exhibited by his phenotype seems to have some mysterious mode of sorting the genes out in the next generation which is greatly improved. Because this animal has true depth of quality in his background, he is a better sire prospect than a casual observation might indicate. However, for the most part, he still remains an exception to the rule.

Since a sire's worth is measured by his progeny, one of the things that separates great breeders from their contemporaries is a sixth sense concerning which young males will develop into the best sires. Within my family of Norwegian Elkhounds, I have found that my fast-developing young dogs often make the best sires, and their best sons seem to inherit this characteristic behavior. Our slower-developing males have usually been good sires of brood bitches. I have no explanation—scientific or otherwise—for this peculiarity. Usually, great sires will fall into one of two categories, the more masculine dog somewhat heavy boned for his breed with the look of a stallion, or the more elegant animal for its breed with exquisite type. In my line, the former is often a faster developer siring stronger sons, while the latter will usually be a sire of late maturers who breed on best through their daughters. When you get all this in one dog, you are looking at a potentially *superb sire*. Seldom does a nice mediocre male become a great sire. It is most unfortunate that they often seem to be the very ones most often used. The truly great sires will breed on equally well through both their sons and their daughters.

If a rapid-developer-type sire's progeny do not live up to their early promise, it is wise to reconsider if he is indeed a worthwhile sire. Some of the great breeders whose theories I have studied feel that the most beneficial sire is the one whose sire and dam belong to the same female family.

Ability to sense the worth of an animal with prepotent siring potential is a talent and gift on a par with the vision of a genius and the instincts of the true psychic. Perhaps the most gifted person I have ever known in this area is Ric Chashoudian. Ric's well-deserved reputation as a judge, handler and artist is known to everyone in dogs, but it is less widely known that he is a first-rate breeder whose knowledge has contributed untold amounts of good to the gene pool of any number of terrier breeds.

Ch. Ttarb The Brat, the Smooth Fox Terrier owned by Ed Dalton and Dr. J. Van Zandt, became the top terrier sire of all time with 137 champions to his credit, and is just one of Ric's many success stories. Ric saw this dog while a puppy at a California show and immediately decided he was destined for greatness, got him on his string, and the rest is history.

Since the dog had been whelped in Tasmania, it is not as if his credentials were something Ric had been exposed to every weekend. Because Ric was able to *feel* what was possible with this dog that was bred by Mr. and Mrs. D. G. Bratt, Smooth Fox Terriers took a giant leap forward.

But The Brat was no onetime thing for Ric, as he also secured the services of the Wire Fox Terrier Ch. Sylair Special Edition and developed his siring potential so that this great sire's numbers approach the magic 100 mark, and he is now the top all-time wire sire. Ch. Jo-Ni's Red Baron of Crofton, the legendary Lakeland that Ric piloted to Best in Show at Westminster in 1976, was not only a member of a fabulous tail male sire line that Ric believed in, he became the regenerating factor for Lakeland Terriers that is behind most of the great ones in the breed today.

Whenever you see a red one, the chances are that he is behind it. While on the subject of *chances are*, Ric handled my all-time favorite terrier, the stunning Kerry Blue, Ch. Melbee's Chances Are, for Bea and Mel Schlesinger of Kansas City. If you research the pedigrees of the best of the modern Kerry Blues, no doubt Chances Are or his son, Ch. Trucote's Captain William, will be among the ancestors. And the list goes on.

TWO SMOOTHS: SADDLER AND THE BRAT

The Smooth Fox Terrier has historically been considered a classic breed. A dog with no frills and no coat to camouflage faults, the Smooth competes in the Terrier Group against many dogs dressed in a full coat.

Although the first four Westminster Best In Shows were won by Smooths (three of them by Ch. Warren Remedy), the two definitive Smooth Fox Terriers of the 20th Century are considered to be Ch. Nornay's Saddler and Ch. Ttarb The Brat. (Note: Westminster started selecting Best In Show winners in 1907.) Described as the model of his breed by the experts of the 1930s, Saddler captured the imagination of the American dog public upon his arrival in the United States and never let go. His head and shoulder were admired and publicized, as was his short, well-muscled body.

There will always be disagreements about who were the greatest dogs, especially when they come from such different eras. Nearly half a century later, the most significant Smooth Fox Terrier of them all brought a new refinement,

more length of head, and a redefinition of the essence of the breed type and character to the world of purebred dogs in Ch. Ttarb The Brat. In keeping with the modernization of the Fox Terrier, Brat was a leggier, more elegant animal than Saddler in the eyes of expert terrier people.

Regardless of which dog you prefer, there is no denying the contribution each of these dogs made in Fox Terrier folk lore. Certainly, The Brat's production record as the All Time Top Producing Terrier Sire with 137 champion progeny designates him as the one with the most impact of them all.

Pictured here on the left is Ch. Nornay Saddler in 1940, a photograph of an oil on canvas painting by Edwin Megargee from the American Kennel Club Collection, courtesy of the AKC. Above is Ch. Ttarb The Brat in a photo by Joan Ludwig.

THE SAGA OF TRUE GRIT

The story surrounding the Airedale Terrier Ch. Bravo True Grit is one of the more bizarre occurrences that come to mind in the world of purebred dogs. His sire Bengal Turith Comet had been eagerly sought by American Airedale fanciers for some time, so his arrival was greeted with great anticipation, especially on the part of the agent who had procured him, Ric Chashoudian. Ric had another reason for his excitement, as the bitch Ch. Bravo Bonanza Belle De AAA was ready to breed. The mating took place as soon as the excellent specimen from England's world-renowned Bengal Kennels arrived at Ric's place.

The next day the dog was found dead, and the autopsy was inconclusive. All concerned were broken-hearted, for many felt that Comet could have been the Airedale to revitalize the breed in America.

Their hopes for a litter from the one mating were quite guarded to say the least. But fortune smiled and the resulting Belle litter was a bonanza, producing several champions including the outstanding True Grit and his brother Ch. Bravo Star Buck.

True Grit (Toby) was a dog of great breed character with balance and type to burn. His excellent coat was the perfect finish to an outstanding example of the breed.

Furthermore, as terrier people like to say: "He was a good walker." So, Comet's loss was somewhat eased by such a son—for this dog had it all.

In 1982, while Ric was on suspension, 14-year-old Phillip "Fitz" Fitzpatrick handled Toby to Best in Show at Montgomery County under terrier expert Barbara Keenan(picture below). This was a dog who rose above all circumstances, including those of his "iffy" beginning. Not only was he a dream dog himself, he went on to face the ultimate test of a great dog—that of a producer.

The Airedale record for All Time Producing Sire stands at 76 champion progeny, a record shared by True Grit and his son Ch. Finlair Tiger of Stone Ridge, fondly called "Gator" and handled by Bob LaRouech.

In addition to making Gator the all-time breed record holder for BISs, Bob also successfully campaigned the sister Ch. Finlair Isis. For father and son to have tied the record is incredible, and terrier expert and publisher Dan Kiedrowski tells me this Airedale record is one producing record that he thinks will stand for awhile.

A further update from Dan verifies that Ch.Serendipity's Eagle's Wings, handled by Andrew Green for Joe Vaudo and his breeder Barbara Schneider, has broken the BIS record. His dam, Ch. Serendipity 's Hosanna is from the True Grit line.

So what began in a dark cloud of tragic circumstances that produced True Grit has evolved into a dominant quality Airedale line that is currently strong and vital, promising to take the King of Terriers into its rightful position in the next century.

Great kennels have been based on outstanding sires such as those Ric was able to identify. These superior sires, known in the livestock world as *herd sires*, can cause a meteoric rise in the quality of a given breeding program and in the breed itself. Sometimes it only takes one sire to create a dynasty.

Should the influence of the sire or sires begin to wane, these lines can decline with him. Therefore, it is vital that the intuitive breeder have both the talent to identify the potential of a sire and to recognize when that blood has run its course, or is in decline.

Think of it like playing the stock market. As important as it is to know when to get involved, it is just as important to know when to get out! It was best said in the following words of a very successful Hereford breeder: *A good bull is half of the herd and a bad bull is all of it.* Indeed, the sins of the father then become those of the sons.

If a line gets dependent on one sire or sires and through attrition those good sires are no longer available, people turn to sons and grandsons in an effort to get back to the original sires. Sometimes this results in a breeding program that will recover its former strength if another great sire emerges. Unfortunately, a breeding program can also go the other way while these continued recovery efforts fail, causing the entire line to sink into decline. If such a breeder continues to use *home* sires while the quality of the line is in decline, the result will be disaster unless outside blood is sought.

Ch. Sylair Special Edition, Wire Fox Terrier, is one of the great terrier sires discovered by Ric Chashoudian, and is close to having sired 100 champions. He is the top Wire Sire in the history of the breed. Pictured here winning BIS under Charles E. Trotter, judging his first "best" in 1986, and handled by Clay Coady for owners Jean Heath and William H. Cosby. (Photo by Vicki Cook)

In evaluating potential sires, remember that well-known big-name sires get superior bitches bred to them, so their success is not unexpected. When sires are making a valuable contribution to the breed with little opportunity at stud, take a good look at them. They may be prepotent. Remember Mendel and his peas and do not expect a sire who is too large to correct size on a small bitch. This is true with other breeding traits too. If you take your poor-fronted bitch with a good rear to a sire with a good front and poor rear, you might get puppies with bad fronts and bad rears. In other words, the mating of opposite faults and opposite virtues does not result in some magical average of the two. And even if you should get something that appears in the middle, it will not breed true because it carries the opposite extremes. Look for sires that are of similar type to your bitch. If you are not happy with the type of the bitch, maybe she should not be bred at all.

Perhaps these references to livestock breeding other than dogs seem unrelated to the issue. You limit yourself if you only look at what dog people do, as there is a lot to be learned out there from breeders who have little subjectivity in their methods. These objective breeders have the marketplace, race track, and other exacting measurements to guide them in their selection of sires. Furthermore, their registries often give such advice as the following notation in the American Breeders Service publication describing Holstein bulls a few years ago. The bull was of the Ivanhoe bloodline and, after listing the good traits that he sired, the fact sheet stated: "Use on animals with above average disposition." If the aforementioned bull were a stud dog, you certainly would not want to bring a sharp bitch to him.

Since owners of potential brood bitches for your sire will judge him by his early progeny, the wise stud owners will make sure that a young dog gets only the best bitches and will become adept at learning which bitches should go to the dog. They know the tendency is to blame the sire for the bad as well as credit him for the good.

A National Specialty is a good place to search for a potential sire for your good bitch. Throughout the years, some great sires have emerged from well-judged competitive Nationals. That is because a classic dog wins a classic show under a classic judge and is sought out as a sire. If he is as good as circumstances would dictate, it will be a giant step forward for the breed. If not, it will be anything but. National Specialty winners should be more than winners, they should be absolutely positive breeding influences on their breed. A sire who is especially virtuous where the breed is weak can be a real find. For example, in a breed riddled with poor neck and shoulders, a dog with an exceptionally good front assembly can effect dramatic improvement in that breed. Always ask yourself where the stud is likely to help both the bitch and the breed.

The potential great sire can be loaded with substance and masculinity, but there has to be an air of quality about him too. Some sires have a lot of class and put lovely type on their progeny, but for some reason sire no soundness factor. Go carefully when considering these sires, for they might not be worth it in the long run. Use them sparingly. Other dogs have value for their honest, sound progeny. Although these sires lack classic type, their role in the overall breeding picture should not be dismissed as their character and trueness are contributions. No wonder all breeders treasure a sire who can contribute classic type as well as soundness and integrity.

Timing can be the determining factor in a good sire becoming very influential in a given breed because he lacks the blood of a previously popular sire or has only a small concentration of it. Therefore, he may become a predominant and forceful sire in his own right, thanks to the prior sire, because he can be used extensively on dams coming down from the other. In essence, because of the timing of the individual, he is able to benefit from the siring opportunity presented by the circumstances that might not have been available at any other time in the evolution of a given breed.

To assess properly the merit of a siring record requires knowing what quality of bitches were bred to him. To be more exact would require knowing what those same bitches produced

IRISH LEADER
—ALIAS ULSTER EMPEROR

Decades ago, a dog's name could be changed when he was imported from Europe, so he could be registered under one name in his country of origin and under another in the AKC stud book. Fortunately, most importers proudly used the exact same name as the dog had been registered under in his native country. One notable exception was reported concerning an Irish Terrier who was shown and used at stud in Ireland under the name *Ulster Emperor*.

Upon coming to the U.S., the dog was registered as *Irish Leader*. Communication was not the same in those days as it is now, and Mr. Bell's invention—especially when used for purposes of long distance—was considered an extravagance rather than a necessity. Subsequently, granddaughters and even daughters of Emperor were imported to the U.S. and bred to Leader. People were inbreeding to this dog without even realizing it!

Now, although it was reported that this dog did not have the harshest of coats, American breeders went to him for his wonderful Irishman's head and look. Alas! The bad news was that his temperament was weak and—you guessed it—in the rush to get the look of Leader, as they piled up his genes for head, ears, neck and shoulders, they also piled them up for a temperament and coat that were the exact opposite of what was desired in an Irish Terrier.

Since the dog appeared in their pedigrees under two different names, many breeders did not find out for a long time just how much this dog was actually in the gene pool. Fortunately for the good of the breed, many breeders had not followed the crowd, and because of this Irish Terriers soon returned to their usual terrier demeanor.

when bred to other sires. These kinds of records are not easy to obtain and will require some leg work. If it helps you find the right sire for your bitch, or avoid the wrong one, the time will have been well spent.

It is important to understand that not all good sires in a breed will have the same, exact look. Since different strengths are needed by different bitches, that may be for the good of the order—or the dogs might become boringly alike! This sounds like a contradiction since I have stated that the breeder needs to stay with a type in a breeding program or the breeder will *get lost*. The breeder develops a feel that seeks a definite type and is true to that type, while accepting that no two are exactly alike. As breeder-judge Frank Grover succinctly stated in the *American Kennel Gazette* (December 1985) Doberman Pinscher column: "Not all Dobermans that are good ones look alike. To impose a singular 'style' is as partial an approach as to pick only dogs with excellent rears or heads, ignoring the whole dog."

Some dogs considered top winners might well have been second rate had they been out at a different time under different circumstances. When a dog becomes number one, it simply means he is the best of his generation or crop. Furthermore, it might simply mean that he was campaigned the most expertly to achieve the best results possible for that animal. It does not mean he will be the right sire to use for your bitch. Or, for that matter, with any bitch.

Since family is the most important thing in breeding, you would be better advised to breed to the number 10 dog with the right family and features than to the number one dog who is the only top show winner in his family—a kind of Lone Ranger—unlike his own relatives.

There are times when a breed is strong and a number of dogs with great strengths are available. During these times, the breed will prosper. At other times, there is little or no progress in a breed due to the lack of a great sire in the breed. The breed in general will go into decline for a while until another great sire comes along to revitalize the breed. Such a sire will be prepotent and stamp his characteristics on his progeny, again bringing the breed to high quality. Usually, such an animal will be linebred and of great value if he is from a strong female family that relates to his sire's dam.

How does one explain the emergence of a fabulous sire? In the section on linebreeding and other forms of closebreeding, I discussed how a good sire can come from a well-bred, inbred or linebred dam or grandam. This is sometimes the case when an animal is one or two generations down from an inbreeding.

However, another theory is that the great sire is an unusual form of *mutant* in that he is different from any of his contemporaries. The great English thoroughbred sire of the 19th Century, St. Simon, was three inches taller at the withers than he was in length of body. The rest of his family members were built like most good thoroughbreds with the height at the withers about equal to the length of body from forechest to rump. This horse's place in the classic pedigrees of thoroughbreds well into this century is nothing short of phenomenal.

For an animal to become a great sire, everything has to be right. First of all, the dog himself has to have all the right genetic ingredients that give him the ability to sire dogs of both sound mind and body. These dogs will be healthy in all ways with excellent conformation. Usually, the great sire will have some special virtues he is remarkable in producing with the utmost consistency.

This dog will have no genetic trash. That is to say, he will not be carrying recessives for any number of genetic disorders or abnormalities.

The timing must be absolutely right for him in two ways: 1) What he excels in producing is exactly what the breed needs at that time; and 2) Some good sires have come before him to produce daughters and other female descendants that are right for this potentially great sire at this period of time for breed progress.

Also vital to the success of the potentially great sire are those persons of wisdom to handle his career. These people will be selective in making sure the right bitches get to him. They will manage his career with great expertise and deal fairly and appropriately with the owners of the bitches, making every effort to handle all matters surrounding the matings with professionalism and integrity. They will see to it the sire is kept in optimum health and vitality.

And finally, for the true worth of the great sire to be known, his progeny must get opportunities to make their presence felt. This will necessitate that they be brought along with proper training, conditioning and presentation so they can, accordingly, be competitive in the ring.

If only there were a way to develop a master list of these perfect sires for each breed, showing what qualities each could be counted upon to reproduce. Such a dream situation would classify sires by pedigree for their characteristics, and breeders would be able to seek dogs for the correct head, front, classic type, movement or heart. Such futuristic concepts, as discussed in Part VI, show promise of computerizing the sum of all knowledge available from the past. This would explain and profile present animals that have resulted, and such information would then lead to better decision making in the future pursuit of better dogs.

Just as your breeding efforts should take you in the direction of the outstanding or great sires, so must you accumulate knowledge for avoiding sires who will not help you progress in your breeding program. This is especially important in your formative years when owners of males they personally consider "good sires" will court inexperienced breeders in hopes of attracting bitches to their studs. Some of these people are well-intentioned breeders of some renown with many years of experience in their breed. This is when you must remember that not everyone with 20 years of experience carries 20 years of learning with them. Some are truly wise and competent breeders, while others have just experienced their first year's learning 20 more times. In other words, they may have become arrested early on in their development.

Since your choice of sires will play such an important role in your future success, here are some sires to avoid in your breeding program—or at least scrutinize before using:

The Ultimate Over-Achiever

This animal is a fabulous show dog, and he is reasonably well bred. He is always *on* in the show ring, wagging his tail while baiting, willingly flying around the group and BIS ring. He is well owned, well handled, and well promoted. So what if the eye is light, the front too straight, the neck too short, and the loin too long. First of all, this dog is in a breed in which he should not be able to unfurl his supposedly tightly-curled tail to wave like a flag. Sometimes a tail fault can help cover another weakness, as in the case of a terrier-tailed Cocker Spaniel whose incorrect tail provides an optical illusion that helps cover his excessive length of body. Furthermore, the overachiever's lovely open-coat that always looks in full bloom is terribly incorrect for his breed that is supposed to have a weather-resistant coat. This dog is deadly to a breed. In a few generations, the breed will be riddled with open-coated, long-loined, straight-fronted, and short-necked dogs with bad tails and light eyes—all linebred to Mr. Wonderful. And they don't all have his showmanship and pizzazz. Now what?

The New 'In Sire'

Breeding to him is the thing to do. Everyone is doing it. Ever since this great one arrived on our shores, they have been standing in line to get to this dog. And it could end up that he deserves his popularity. But since everyone else is breeding to him, stand back and see how good his progeny is out of their bitches. Pay special attention to the progeny of bitches similar to yours in looks and breeding. Your good sense will tell you when it is time to jump on the bandwagon or to let it go by.

The Local-Boy-Makes-Good Sire

He is there, he is convenient, and he sired the winners bitch at the National Specialty. However, it was from a bitch totally unlike your bitch and from a very different gene pool. Furthermore, this year's National was poorly judged and lacked greatness in the classes anyhow. This dog is not for you. Put yourself out a little and go to the one that is.

Your Best Friend's Champion

This dog has been promoted to you beyond belief—and certainly beyond his ability to help your bitch. Your dear friend is bemoaning the fact that nobody is using her splendid creature, or worse still everybody else has bred to him. Why haven't you? Do not let a guilt trip be hung on you. With friends like this, who needs enemies?

Your Bitch's Spooky First Cousin

Yes, he is a gorgeous dog and the pedigree fits. But are you willing to accept that he got so frightened by those firecrackers on the Fourth of July that he could not finish his championship? Do you believe that normal dogs do not recover from one bad experience and go from there? Do you want to chase your puppies with a butterfly net when you accidentally set off the burglar alarm? Avoid dogs who lack strength of character in your breeding program.

The Last Gasp, Line-on-the-Decline Sire

Just because this dog's grandsire was a good champion and the grandsire's sire was the top sire all time is no reason to use this dog, for he is part of a downward trend in this line and there are lots of unknown reasons for this. Do not try to become the savior of this declining line unless you really know what you are doing.

A Look at Sires Who Made a Difference: Siring Greatness—The Proof of the Pudding

Now that I have profiled what to seek in a sire and even advised what to avoid, it is time to look at some sires who have made significant contributions to their breed's gene pool. These sires have been recognized because of their widespread influence on their breed. In some cases, they have originated a sire line that has proliferated through any number of generations of great sires that have followed them. The greatest of them bred on through both sons and daughters, became integral parts of pedigrees in harmony with other lines already existing and sometimes became part of a pattern of nicks that brought heightened quality to their breed.

> **"Few sons attain the praise of their great sires....."**
> —*Odyssey,* Book ii

Available information indicates most of our profiled sires have not been aided by the banking of frozen semen, as many of them predated widespread use of this process. Some of our younger sires will no doubt benefit from this modern technological procedure, perhaps leading to computerized record keeping that will adjust statistical use of pertinent data weighted to include this information.

All of them left their mark on their breed and leave a legacy for the sires of tomorrow to emulate and perpetuate. When there are great sires in a breed, the breed will prosper. Just take a look at the incredible records of English Springer Spaniels that trace to our first sire for an everlasting impression of the impact that can be made by the great sire.

CH. SALILYN'S ARISTOCRAT - ENGLISH SPRINGER SPANIEL - NUMBER ONE SIRE ALL TIME, ALL BREEDS WITH 188 CHAMPIONS

If ever there was a dog entitled to be named the mythical ***Dog of the Century,*** his name would be Ch. Salilyn's Aristocrat, fondly called Risto.

This marvelous liver-and-white English Springer Spaniel owned and bred by Julia Gasow is the Top Producing Sire All Time All Breeds with 188 champion progeny. Yet, that is just part of his contribution to the concept that the dog show is the showcase for the continued rededication to the selection of breeding stock. Consider the fact that his grandson, Ch. Salilyn's Private Stock, and his great grandson, Ch. Salilyn's Classic, each also sired more than a hundred champions!

His son, Ch. Chinoe's Adamant James, was the last dog of any breed to win back-to-back Westminster Bests in Show, accomplishing this show feat in 1971 and 1972. His great grandson, Ch. Salilyn's Condor (see color section), was Best in Show at the 1993 Westminster Kennel Club.

Aristocrat was Top Dog All Breeds in 1967, an accomplishment repeated by son Adamant James in 1971 and great grandson Condor in 1992. Aristocrat was also a Sporting Group winner at Westminster and all of them were Quaker Oats Winners.

The author's choice as DOG OF THE CENTURY, Ch. Salilyn's Aristocrat, pictured here winning the Sporting Group at Westminster. He is handled by Dick Cooper and the judge is Gordon Parham. "Risto" was owned and bred by Julia Gasow and is the all-time Top Producing Sire All Breeds with 188 champion progeny. His son, Ch. Chinoe's Adamant James was the last two-time Westminster BIS winner (1971 and 1972) and his great-grandson, Ch. Salilyn's Condor was BIS at Westminster in 1993. (Photo by Evelyn Shafer)

Ch. Salilyn's Citation II handled by Dick Cooper in 1960 under Judge Harry Meyer. Ch. Salilyn's Aristocrat was produced by Citation's son, Ch. Inchidony Prince Charming, from the Citation granddaughter, Ch. Salilyn's Lily of the Valley. (Frasie Photograph)

Julia Gasow handling her personal favorite Ch. King Peter of Salilyn, the dog she credited with bringing elegance to her line. (Photo by Raymond)

Ch. Salilyn's Aristocrat, on the right with Dick Cooper, and his dam Ch. Salilyn's Lily of the Valley, on the left with Ruth Cooper, winning Best in Speciality Show and Best Opposite Sex under Judge Mrs. James Warwick in 1967. "Risto" was able to put greatness into his daughters by passing on the X chromosome information he received from his dam. The Top Producing Sire All Time All Breeds bred on equally well through his sons and daughters. (E.H. Frank Photo)

When Risto became Top Dog All Breeds in 1967, he set what was then an all-time record for one year of 45 Bests in Show at a time when dogs seldom made more than 80 shows in a year. His total of 63 All Breed Bests in Show stood as a breed record until Condor set the new one with more than 100 top honors in all breed competition.

His pedigree exemplified balanced line breeding, putting the brothers, Ch. King Peter and Ch. King William (of Salilyn), in the same slot—one on the top side and one on the bottom side—in the third

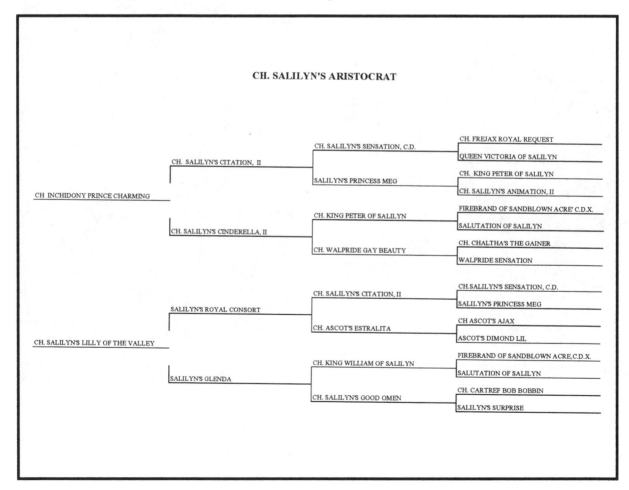

CH. SALILYN'S ARISTOCRAT

CH INCHIDONY PRINCE CHARMING

  CH. SALILYN'S CITATION, II

    CH. SALILYN'S SENSATION, C.D.
      CH. FREJAX ROYAL REQUEST
      QUEEN VICTORIA OF SALILYN

    SALILYN'S PRINCESS MEG
      CH. KING PETER OF SALILYN
      CH. SALILYN'S ANIMATION, II

  CH. SALILYN'S CINDERELLA, II

    CH. KING PETER OF SALILYN
      FIREBRAND OF SANDBLOWN ACRE' C.D.X.
      SALUTATION OF SALILYN

    CH. WALPRIDE GAY BEAUTY
      CH. CHALTHA'S THE GAINER
      WALPRIDE SENSATION

CH. SALILYN'S LILLY OF THE VALLEY

  SALILYN'S ROYAL CONSORT

    CH. SALILYN'S CITATION, II
      CH.SALILYN'S SENSATION, C.D.
      SALILYN'S PRINCESS MEG

    CH. ASCOT'S ESTRALITA
      CH ASCOT'S AJAX
      ASCOT'S DIMOND LIL

  SALILYN'S GLENDA

    CH. KING WILLIAM OF SALILYN
      FIREBRAND OF SANDBLOWN ACRE,C.D.X.
      SALUTATION OF SALILYN

    CH. SALILYN'S GOOD OMEN
      CH. CARTREF BOB BOBBIN
      SALILYN'S SURPRISE

generation. King Peter is the dog credited with putting elegant leg length and exotic type into the Salilyn breeding program. At the same time, King Peter's grandson, Ch. Salilyn's Citation II, was the dog that brought substance and solidness to the line and also appears on both sides of the pedigree. *Master breeder* Julie Gasow certainly had something in mind when she took her lovely bitch, Ch. Salilyn's Lily of the Valley, to Ch. Inchidony Prince Charming, and the results of this breeding will be felt in Springer history forever.

Another Risto son, Ch. Telltale Author, was also a prepotent sire with 84 champions of record. This amazing direct tail male sire line that produced Westminster winner Condor went from Risto to Ch. Telltale Author to Ch. Salilyn's Dynasty to Condor. Yet this line was more than a line of marvelous sires, for some of the best of the progeny were great winning and producing bitches such as Ch. Salilyn's Sophistication and Ch. Salilyn's Welcome Edition, affirming the statement that the best of sires breed on equally well through both their sons and their daughters. As outstanding producers should do, they produced well outside the line just as within it. Ch. Welcome Great Day and Ch. Chinoe's Adamant James combined to produce over 50 champions and the bitches, Ch. First Impression of Silverbow and Ch. Loresta's Fallen Angel, also were top producers.

In looking for the classic sire one could find no better example than this great liver and white. He satisfied all the criteria. He dominated the competition of his day at both the all breed and specialty level, winning the Nationals in the best competition that his breed had to offer as well as his splendid all-breed record. He bred on through both his sons and his daughters and was a *sire of sires*. Furthermore, his blood is still treasured more than three decades later by those who value Springer quality. His producing record was achieved without stored semen or artificial enhancement. Ch. Salilyn's Aristocrat stands for all time as the glorious example of the contribution a *master breeder* can make to a breed's gene pool through the classic animal. That is why, in my opinion, he is the **Dog of the Century**.

CH. VIN-MELCA'S HOWDY ROWDY - NORWEGIAN ELKHOUND - NUMBER TWO ALL TIME SIRE ALL BREEDS - 166 CHAMPIONS

When Ch. Vin-Melca's Vikina whelped her 1965 litter by Ch. Windy Cove's Rowdy Ringo, I was disappointed because the litter consisted of three male puppies. Since this mating had been designed to produce a bitch to breed to young Ch. Vin-Melca's Vickssen (the first male to become a permanent resident at Vin-Melca), plans were made to sell the three males into appropriate homes.

The robust, larger male in the litter refused to allow this to happen, as he wormed his way into the hearts of my friends, Gladys Tangen and Dr. John Craige (my former husband). The two of them combined forces to convince me this puppy must stay "at least for a while." A young teacher friend, Jean White, always greeted everyone in the mornings with "Howdy! Rowdy!" and that's what the puppy was named. Jean is married to the mayor of Carmel, California (no, not *that* mayor), Ken White, who is also a retired educator. She took great pride in the accumulation of nice wins by the puppy she had named, and he finished his championship easily.

Although Howdy went on to become the number one Norwegian Elkhound in the United States in 1968 and was *Kennel Review's* Best Western Hound that year, it is his siring record that brought him lasting fame. With 166 champion offspring and many National Specialty winners, as well as all breed Best in Show winners, he is the premier sire in the breed for all time.

There was nothing in the pedigree of Howdy Rowdy to suggest he would become such an influential sire even though his maternal grandsire, Ch. Trygvie Vikingsson, had amassed an enviable siring record. For Howdy was the product of an outcross, and the only reason for the breeding to begin with was because the paternal grandsire of Vickssen was a full brother to Rowdy Ringo, Howdy's sire. Remember, I was trying to get a Vikina daughter to take to Vickssen. (See Tesio)

Although Howdy's sire, Rowdy Ringo, had sired some very nice dogs that were doing well at the shows, he had not sired anything at all like Howdy. So when a young girl from San Jose came to me with her daughter of Ch. Wabeth's Gustav, I made the breeding with high hopes even though I had

Lana Hall and five-month old Rikkana's Outa Sight are pictured going Best in Match in 1970. When Lana's Ch. Wabeth's Gustav daughter produced several outstanding champions from breeding with Howdy Rowdy, it was a signal that something special was happening in this combination of blood lines. The Rikkana Kennels contributed outstanding animals to the breed's gene pool. Progeny down from these lines are still winning in American rings today. (Poyner Photo)

Ch. Tyken's Hustler was the best producing son of Ch. Vin-Melca's Howdy Rowdy with 37 champion progeny. Hustler was another testimonial to the famous Howdy Rowdy-Gustav nick, as his dam was a "Gus" granddaughter. He was bred by Loucille Waterman and owned by Beverly Brown of Tyken Kennels who managed his stud career. (Langdon Photo)

Can. & Am. Ch. Wabeth's Gustav, a top Norwegian Elkhound of the 1960s, was handled by Canadian Pat Tripp for breeder-owners Walt and Betty Moore of Gardiner, Washington. He put a look of absolutely correct type on his progeny and his daughters and granddaughters were superior brood bitches. (Roberts Photo)

Ch. Vin-Melca's Howdy Rowdy, sire of 166 champions. According to statistics published by the Northern California Elkhounders in "A Tribute to Howdy Rowdy," the champion get were from 55 bitches and averaged 3 champions per bitch. Four of the 5 top producers in what was called "Howdy's Harem" were daughters or granddaughters of Ch. Wabeth's Gustav. (Langdon Photo)

Left: Bev (Ricci) Brown pictured here with her first home-bred champion, Tyken's Howdi Pardner, more than a quarter of a century ago under Judge Major Godsol. Pardner was out of a Ch. Wabeth's Gustav daughter from Bev's first litter sired by Howdy Rowdy. Tyken Kennels has produced more than 40 champions and was the home of Ch. Tyken's Hustler. (Joan Ludwig Photo)

nothing on the ground to justify such optimism. When Bev (Ricci) Brown showed me her litter of magnificent-headed puppies with excellent bone and substance on a square frame, I was quite impressed. For her Tyken Kennels, it was the first homebred champion.

Another young breeder who enjoyed great success with a daughter of Ch. Wabeth's Gustav bred to Howdy was Lana Hall, of Flint, Michigan, with her Rikkana dogs. When pictures of her puppies from the breeding arrived, I became even more convinced that something special was taking place in this combination of bloodlines.

Before long, a granddaughter of Gustav's was bred to Howdy Rowdy with similar results, and it became obvious that here was a positive *nick*. I purchased another granddaughter (Ch. Branstock's Vika av Baba Yaga) who was from a Gustav son and Rowdy Ringo daughter, and a giant step forward was made in my breeding program.

Ch. Wabeth's Gustav had been a favorite of mine right from the start. He was up on leg, short in both the back and coupling and possessed of excellent breed type. This stylish dog had tremendous charisma in the ring, and handler Pat Tripp brought out that certain something in him. When Alva Rosenberg talked to me about him, I listened! Furthermore, he was sired by Ch. Viking, Ch. Tortasen's Bjonn II's full brother, out of Walt and Betty Moore's lovely foundation bitch, Ch. Sonja of Greenwood. His puppies had a compact and typey look that he stamped on them.

Mrs. Peck had brought Ch. Tortasen's Bjonn II to America from Norway, and Rowdy Ringo was his grandson. A few years later Mrs. Holver Hauff had brought younger brother Viking from her native Norway to her home in Washington state and Gustav was his son.

Without realizing it, these two ladies on opposite sides of our continent had put together the elements that resulted in the creation of the Howdy Rowdy dynasty. For any number of years over half of the Elkhounds in the Top Ten were Howdy Rowdy progeny, and for decades the same has been true for his descendants in Top Ten Competition. He was so appreciated by California breeders that, after his death, they published a special book in his memory, featuring his children, grandchildren and his impact on the breed.

Howdy Rowdy was a super sire who always improved on his bitches. Although he produced well with daughters of Vickssen, Vagabond and others, his major successes came with Gustav descendants. It was an incredible learning experience and proved that one sire's success can be dependent on another sire. It was good fortune that Gustav came along five years before Howdy. As Howdy came into his own, the daughters and granddaughters of Gus were of breeding age and available. It might be said that because of Ch. Wabeth's Gustav, Howdy Rowdy was able to become the all time Top Sire in the Breed with 166 Champion get, dozens of group winning, specialty winning, and all breed descendants with scores of his immediate and later descendants in the Top Ten for the breed. It was a classic case of one sire building upon the genetic groundwork of another. Without exact timing and opportunity, such successes are not likely to happen.

Ch. Colsidex Standing Ovation - Weimaraner - Number Three All Time Sire All Breeds - 147 Champions

Ch. Colsidex Standing Ovation, Weimaraner, sire of 147 champions, is the number three All Time Producing Sire All Breeds. Owned and bred by Judy Colan, "Joga" was the son of her Ch. Colsidex Dauntless Applause.

Standing Ovation first came to my attention when my friend Babbie Tongren, well-known judge and mistress of BenGhazi Afghan hounds, remarked that she could always "recognize his progeny by the look, style and type" he stamped on them. In addition, his offspring had great reach and drive. He usually gave good length of upper arm to his sons and daughters, a quality treasured by breeders of most breeds.

His dam was the product of a half-brother, half-sister breeding, both of which were sired by Ch. Shadowmar Barthaus Dorilis. Her sire Ch. Doug's Dauntless Von Dor was noted for producing outstanding brood bitches. To have his daughter in your breeding program was reported to be a big step in the direction of breed improvement.

Ch. Colsidex Standing Ovation winning BIS All Breeds under Judge Robert Tongren. He was bred, owned and handled by Judy Colan. Note the lovely forechest and return of upper arm on this dog. (Photo by Charles Tatham)

It comes as no surprise to learn that Standing Ovation is often in the pedigree several times of today's top-winning Weimaraners. For he was a multi-BIS winner and number one in his breed in 1977. Moreover, he achieved the amazing feat of twice winning the National Specialty from the Veterans Class. He was a dog with wonderful presence and sense of self, all of which he passed on to succeeding generations. Two of his sons are also top producers, Ch. Greywinds Jack Frost with 59 champions and Ch. Colsidex Nani Reprint with 51 champions.

When one attends a Weimaraner Specialty, one can still see his influence being felt in the breed. And since his owner was wise enough to utilize the frozen semen program in its infancy, his presence will be with us up close into the 21st Century.

CH. RINKY DINK'S SIR LANCELOT - BLACK COCKER SPANIEL - SIRE OF 135 CHAMPIONS

Ch. Rinky Dink's Sir Lancelot, the all-time top-producing Cocker Spaniel with 135 champion get, is a testimony to the achievements possible in a small breeding program. His owner-breeder Jean Peterson kept only a handful of dogs in her operation and was disappointed when five male puppies resulted from the mating of Ch. Rinky Dink's Robin to Ch. Hardy's High Spirit, a familiar story because the breeding was made to get a bitch.

In spite of this, good friends Les and Liz Clark along with Norman Austin, who had encouraged Jean to make this mating, insisted she keep this promising youngster who turned out to be a super sire. His pedigree was linebred to the Clark's great black Ch. Clarkdale's Capitol Stock.

Charlotte and Terry Stacy managed both his show career and a large part of his successful stud career. Jean credits their faith in Lance as an important factor in getting the right bitches bred to him. Lance was consistent in throwing his own nice black-and-tan markings to his progeny and like clockwork, no matter what bitches were bred to him, produced offspring that resembled him. In addition to the black and tans he sired, Lance also sired some lovely blacks with pretty heads that looked like him.

Ch. Rinky Dink's Sir Lancelot, black-and-tan Cocker Spaniel, is the leader with 135 champions in a breed blessed with outstanding producers. Jean Peterson credits outstanding stud management by his handlers Charlotte and Terry Stacy as an important factor in his siring success, as they selected the bitches that were right for him. Such an accomplishment as Lance's from a small breeding program is proof that the small breeder can achieve high honors when working with skilled and knowledgeable advisors. (Photo courtesy of Jean Peterson)

Furthermore, this prepotent sire also sired progeny with his own great reach and drive complemented by his strength of character and personality. His most well-known sons were the black-and-tan Ch. Harrison's Peeping Tom and the black Ch. Rinky Dink's Socko. Peeping Tom soared to the Top Ten All Breeds and number one Sporting Dog in the United States in 1981 under the expert guidance of his handler, Ted Young Jr. Socko was also a multi-BIS winner and number eight in the Sporting Group in 1980.

Although the freezing of semen had come of age by the time Lance was making his sensational records, Jean did not choose to utilize the process because she felt it might not be in the natural order of things. Furthermore, she was reluctant for Lance to leave home to visit the collection clinic, as in the early days those services were not so available as they are today. So Lance's record will stand at 135 champions, a marvelous number for other Cocker Spaniel greats to shoot at in the future. In a breed blessed with great producers, his record will most likely be challenged by one of his own descendents, Ch. Empire's Brooklyn Dodger, the sire of the '90s.

CH. STARBUCK'S HANG 'EM HIGH - 15-INCH BEAGLE - SIRE OF 128 CHAMPIONS

Ch. Starbuck's Hang 'Em High was whelped in 1974 and his 128th champion recently finished, with more to come! And that is because breeder David Hiltz had the foresight to bank semen on this exceptional hound in the days when the program was in its infancy. Although Hiltz had only a small number of *straws* of semen banked, he has used it discerningly and selectively with excellent results over the years.

Because international rules do not permit David to take the semen to Australia where he now lives, these banked treasures will be used on American bitches. After falling in love with the respected dogwoman, Lesley Funnell, David married her in 1989, and they are now living in her native land. Nonetheless, Americans can look forward to seeing them from time to time, as Lesley's recent adjudication of the Parent Club National Specialty proved.

Hang 'Em High was out of the good producing line of Elsy bitches through his dam, Ch. Elsy's Shooting Star. Breeder Hiltz took Shooting Star to Ch. The Whim's Buckeye in pursuit of the qualities associated with dogs bred by Dr. and Mrs. A.C. Musladin and Carroll Gordon Diaz, who co-owned Buckeye's sire, Ch. Wandering Wind, himself a top producer in the breed. Buckeye was the previous All Time Top Producing Sire in the breed with 97 champions prior to his son, Hang 'Em High.

Buckeye was a 13-inch Beagle whose maternal grandsire, Ch. Page Mill Trademark, is the only Beagle I know to win All Breed BISs in both varieties. This special hound is buried next to his old friend, Ch. Vin-Melca's Howdy Rowdy, on Vin-Melca's boot hill in Carmel.

"Prune" was the nickname David gave the newborn when Hang 'Em High was whelped because he was "one big wrinkle." He was to go on to spectacular success at stud. He could be counted on to correct toplines and rears, giving his progeny extraordinary overall balance and a good hound look. He produced any number of litters in which every puppy in the litter finished. And his correct Beagle headpiece with the desired pleading expression endured for generations.

He was the Top Sire All Breeds one year and three different mates of his also ended up in the rankings with him. Ch. Plain and Fancy's Delilah produced 23 champions, all of them sired by Hang 'Em High.

Prune was the collective result of the work of great Beagle breeders on both sides of his pedigree. The Musladins, Diaz, the Jack Abrahamsons, Margaret White on his sire's side, and Stan Elsey, on his dam's side, and, most of all, *master breeder* David Hiltz, who had the good sense to put together the results of the work of previous *master breeders* into one extraordinary pedigree destined to influence generations of Beagles. Who knows how far into the future this positive impact will be appreciated by the *master breeders* of tomorrow?

CH. DUNELM GALAXY - ENGLISH COCKER SPANIEL - PATRIARCH OF A SIRE LINE

Ch. Dunelm Galaxy (George) was described by his handler, Richard Bauer, as being like "the post office...he stamped them." No doubt about it, this gorgeous blue-roan English Cocker Spaniel owned by Ruth Cooper was a turning point in his breed. Accordingly, the Parent Club has selected him as the breed's most influential individual in history. Not only did George put his absolutely beautiful head and type on his progeny, he gave them a look so very classic for the breed and a new attitude to go with it.

The remarkable thing about a sire like Galaxy is that no matter what kind of bitch the breeders took to him, he improved on those bitches with the progeny. Not only did the puppies look like him, they were also very intelligent, as was their father. Several prominent judges remarked to Ruthie that they could "recognize a George puppy when it walked into the ring." His classic refinement and fabulous face held up with age, as witnessed by the fact that he won the breed at the American Spaniel Club at the age of 10½, a feat to be repeated later by his grandson Capricorn.

The breeding of the red-and-white bitch, Ch. Cygnet's Raspberry, to Galaxy was to have special significance on the breed for the Kenobo Kennels of Helga Tustin. Two dogs—Rabbit and Oliver Luv— from this litter were to affect the breed in a most positive way. When Oliver's daughter, Silver Charm, was bred to her Uncle Rabbit, the resulting Ch. Kenobo's Capricorn would go on to break his grandsire's siring record of 93 champions for the breed with 121 of his own. This grandsire/grandson combination sired more than 200 champions.

Goat, as he was fondly called, was the number one English Cocker in 1974 and 1975, but for all his brilliance in the ring it was as a sire that he was to gain lasting fame. A stallion of a dog, Goat won his last National at the age of 10, and it is fitting that any number of specialty winners are down from him. His all-purpose progeny not only excel in bench shows, obedience and field titles, there are 15 of them listed in the Parent Club Hall of Fame as top producers.

Although I usually think of showmanship as being acquired more than inherited, there are notable exceptions to every rule in the breeding of dogs. Am. and Can. Ch. Ranzfel Newsflash T.D. is not only a dog who threw his lovely silhouette to his progeny but seemed to stamp them with his own flair for showmanship as well. This goes in a direct tail male line to Galaxy; for Newsflash is sired by Capricorn, who is sired by Rabbit, who is sired by Galaxy.

When respected Canadian dogwoman, Virginia Lyne, took her very short-backed "cockery" bitch, Ch. Ranzfel Blue Roxanne, to Capricorn, she was seeking a dog that would allow her to retain the qualities she valued in this bitch and add a dash of elegance and style. Both Newsflash and his brother, Ch. Ranzfel Nightcap of Harwen, became multi-BIS winners, and Newsflash went on to become the sire of 32 American champions, even though he stood his entire stud career in Canada. He was one more step in this producing sire line and transmitted his delightful energy to his progeny. Such wonderful examples of tail male dominance offer breeders the opportunity to combine desired traits by using the sons of one great sire on the daughters of another in what bridge players might call a *cross-ruff* pattern.

Patterns based on superior producing sires are the building blocks of greatness in a breed. Sometimes the sons of these great sires will not accumulate the impressive statistical show or siring records as

This head study of Ch. Dunelm's Galaxy is the essence of what this prepotent sire was able to pass on to his progeny. Chosen by the Parent Club as the most influential English Cocker of them all, Galaxy is responsible for one of dogdom's most prepotent sire lines. In addition to stamping his descendents with the classic head you see here, Galaxy and his sons and grandsons bred on with their exquisite type and confidence. Such dogs create the destiny of a breed. He was owned by Ruth Cooper and his career was managed by Richard Bauer. Here is this direct tail male line:

—Galaxy
—Rabbit
—Capricorn
—Newsflash

(Photo courtesy of Bonnie Threlfall)

Ch. Kenobo Capricorn pictured at 12 years of age. Linebred to another great sire Ch. Dunelm Galaxy, "Goat" became the #1 Sire in the history of English Cocker Spaniels with 121 champion progeny. Bred by Helga Tustin and co-owned with Bonnie Threlfall, this dog was the epitome of exceptional linebreeding as the result of an uncle-to-niece breeding. He served as an incomparable connecting link in a pedigree in addition to his incredible ability to produce his extraordinary quality in the immediate generations. (Ashbey Photo)

Ch. Kenobo Rabbit of Nadou, magnificent English Cocker sire, was a vital ingredient in this incredible direct tail male line. He was the #1 English Cocker in 1972 and 1973, BIS winner and Westminster winner, sire of BIS winners and #5 All Time Sire in the breed with 55 champion progeny, including 8 top producers and 2 National winners. Again, we see the classic look of Galaxy in his son who in turn passed it on to his own son, Capricorn. Born in 1969, Rabbit lived to the ripe old age of 14, verifying the longevity of the line with himself and his offspring. He was bred by Helga Tustin who owned him with Bonnie Threlfall. (Tauskey Photograph)

Am. Can. Ch. Ranzfel Newsflash returned the Colinwood blood of the United Kingdom to his pedigree through both his sire and his dam. The ultimate winner of the coveted "Show of Shows" in Ottawa in 1980, Newsflash was owned and bred by Virginia Lyne. The following January, he was the breed winner at the American Spaniel Club. At 7 years of age he was trained to his tracking degree by Kathy Whitby. This picture is a sentimental favorite of the author for it was taken by Carmel neighbor and friend Jeradine Lamb.

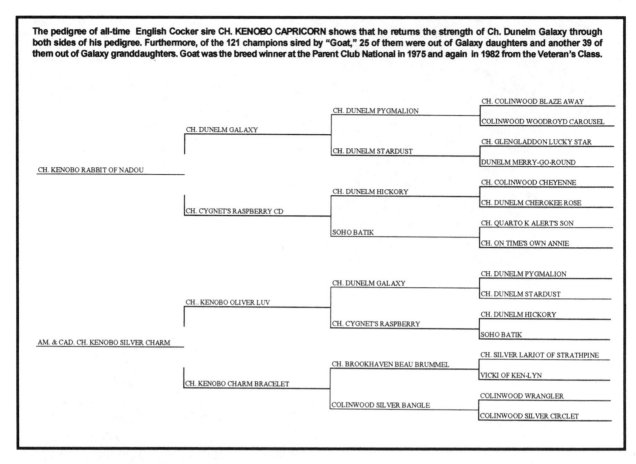

The pedigree of all-time English Cocker sire CH. KENOBO CAPRICORN shows that he returns the strength of Ch. Dunelm Galaxy through both sides of his pedigree. Furthermore, of the 121 champions sired by "Goat," 25 of them were out of Galaxy daughters and another 39 of them out of Galaxy granddaughters. Goat was the breed winner at the Parent Club National in 1975 and again in 1982 from the Veteran's Class.

lesser dogs have of other eras. That is because they are all out and competing against each other at the same time. Although this results in lesser records for each of these quality dogs, it produces better gene pools for the breed. When such sires predominate over a long period of time in a breed, it is because they have continued to add high quality to the breed, such as those descendants of Galaxy, Rabbit, Capricorn and Newsflash are still doing.

Breeders in breeds blessed with such sire lines are in a position to maintain high quality in their breed indefinitely, because their reassembling of the genes is working for the benefit of all. Such positive progress is possible when these excellent sires and their progeny are monitored closely to ensure freedom of unfavorable genetic combinations in regard to health, temperament and conformation. Because of ethical guardianship of the breed by these breeders, the breed is saved from declining genetic activity.

CH. TARTANSIDE TH' CRITICS CHOICE - ROUGH COLLIE

Ch. Tartanside Th' Critics Choice is a living tribute to a planned breeding program. The number one Collie sire of all time with 72 champions and more to come, he is a healthy 14 years of age and still holding court at Tartanside.

John Buddie, *master breeder*, is responsible for the line that produced this super-sire. An educator by profession, John worked his breeding concepts into a taxonomy that begins at the first level with knowledge and expands in continued growth with *master breeder* synthesis embracing the total concept at the highest level.

Critics Choice was sired by Can. and Am. Ch. Tartanside Heir Apparent, an inbred son of Ch. Tartanside The Gladiator bred to his own daughter. Critics Choice also has Gladiator blood through his dam, Ch. Briarhill Midnight High, proudly owned by Teri Pattison, who is the breeder of record of this top sire. (The complete pedigree of Critic's Choice appears in Part I.).

The Gladiator had been Tartanside's top producer with 49 champions prior to the ascendancy of

Ch. Tartanside Th' Critics Choice, #1 Collie Sire of All Time. He was bred by Teri Pattison and owned by John Buddie. He is a worthy successor to his top-producing grandsire Ch. Tartanside The Gladiator. Note the lovely combination of masculinity and refinement along with sweetness of expression and correct Collie ear on his wonderful head. His pedigree appears in Part I. (Photo by Krook)

his grandson. He was heavily linebred to Bellbrooke's Master Pilot, the result of a Ch. Silver Ho Parader son mated to a Parader granddaughter. Gladiator's pedigree is an excellent example of a well-balanced patterned pedigree. He has only five great grandparents because three of his grandparents each appear twice in an orderly manner, matching the topside of the pedigree with the bottomside. When one studies this pedigree, it is obvious that the architect of it had something in mind.

And that something was to build upon the solid foundation provided by the excellent blood of the Glen Hill Collies and of Stephen J. Field's great Ch. Silver Ho Parader. Parader was whelped in 1943 and became a turning point in the breed following World War II.

This foremost sire was the focal point of a direct tail male line that had a great impact on the breed. His son, Ch. Parader's Golden Image, who appears twice in Gladiator's pedigree, became a Top Sire as did Image's son, Ch. Parader's Bold Venture. This father-son-grandson trio sired 100 champions in the days of fewer dog shows and much less traveling. More important, they became an integral part of productive lines still flourishing 50 years later!

The pedigree of CH. TARTANSIDE THE GLADIATOR is an excellent example of a well-balanced patterned pedigree, containing only 5 names in the 8 positions of great-grandparents. His grandson went on to become the Top Sire in the Breed, justifying the linebreeding to Ch. Silver Ho Parader that would appear in an extended pedigree.

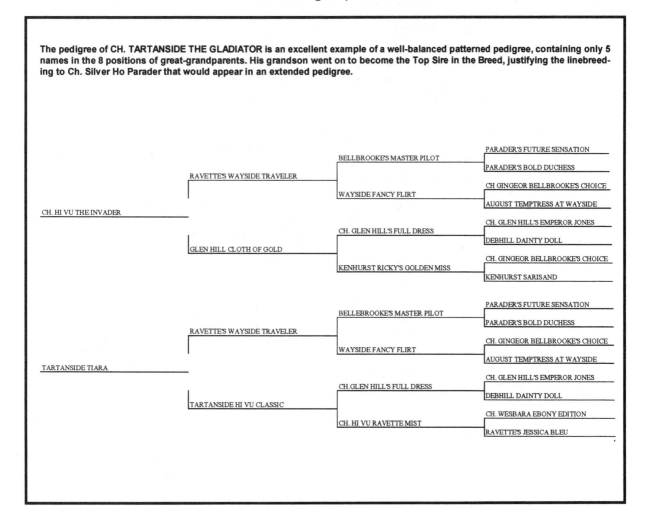

Taxonomy of Master Breeder Thinking

Category	Definition	Trigger Words And Products
Synthesis	Re-form individual parts to make a new whole.	**Compose** a new plan of attack when a breeding defect arises. **Rearrange** breeding plans when an outcross seems necessary. **Forecast** the outcomes of close inbreedings, total outcrosses. **Imagine** the qualities necessary of the forthcoming popular stud dog.
Evaluation	Judge value of something vis-à-vis criteria. Support judgment.	**Judge** a class of superior individuals and place them according to standards. **Evaluate** a series of outcross sires and select the one that best fits your needs. **Give an opinion** of why a particular breeding failed. **Prioritize** faults and virtues as deemed necessary (recommend, critique, viewpoint).
Analysis	Understand how parts relate to a whole. Understand structure, movement, and motive. Note fallacies.	**Investigate** several kennels to see how their breeding plans operate. **Classify** breeders into good, better, best. **Classify** a litter of puppies by quality. **Compare** one line of Collies to another by faults and virtues. **Solve** a breeding dilemma by working out a plan to eradicate a problem.
Application	Transfer the knowledge learned in one situation to another.	**Demonstrate** the correct way to examine a correct head. **Build** a beginning program using individuals you have. **Map out** a plan for a breeding program. **Demonstrate** your abilities in handling. **Guide** other newcomers in correct brushing techniques.
Comprehension	Demonstrate the basic understanding of concepts and curriculum. Translate into other words.	**Give examples** of dogs with faults. **Explain** the basis of inbreeding, line breeding and outcrossing. **Restate** the Collie Standard in your own words. **Explain** the importance of good grooming.
Knowledge	Ability to remember previously learned information.	**Recite** the Collie Standard. **List** the major faults. **Memorize** the first 3 generations in a pedigree. **Locate** the shoulder blade. **List** the important grooming tools.

By John Buddie, Tartanside Collies
Breeder & Educator

These pedigrees of Gladiator and his closely bred grandson, Critics Choice (See Inbreeding, PartI), indicate what discerning breeders can achieve working together and planning accordingly. Such an intense concentration of the best genes available in the breed should serve Collies well into the 21st Century.

Ch. Fezziwig's Ceiling Zero - Old English Sheepdog - An Outstanding Sire Line

Ch. Fezziwig's Ceiling Zero was the siring hero of the famous Old English Sheepdog kennels of Mr. and Mrs. Hendrick Van Rensselaer. Along with a number of other well-known Fezziwig dogs, Ceiling Zero was responsible for large numbers of champions in the rings of Eastern shows during the 1960s. He and his kennel mates did fabulous winning in the days when the Old English Sheepdog was competing in the very competitive working group. Under the skillful handling of Robert S. Forsyth, these dogs amassed incredible records at the group and BIS level as well as in specialty shows.

Ceiling Zero was a flashy and stylish dog—characteristics he passed on to his progeny. When Barry Goodman bred his gorgeous Ch. Baroness of Duroya to him, the entire litter finished. A personal favorite of mine from the breeding was Barry's outstanding Ch. Rivermist Hollyhock.

Mr. & Mrs. Hendrick Van Rensselaer's Ch. Fezziwig Ceiling Zero with his handler Robert S. Forsyth. Ceiling Zero was a remarkable sire. At the 1969 Old English Sheepdog of America's Eastern Specialty, 102 of the 135 Sheepdogs competing were his descendents. He stamped his get with his flashiness, style and elegance. (Jack Ritter Photograph)

With so much of the Ceiling Zero blood in the Eastern animals, Barry decided to go in search of a stud dog for his own bitches and brought back from Europe the well-known Swedish, Norwegian, English and Finnish Ch. Unnesta Pim. Barry describes Pim as "a Percheron stallion of a dog" and certainly when one investigated him closely, he was awesome. Some might have missed this well-built dog, for he was not marked with the popular large white shawl. But Barry appreciated his square body with a good front and outstanding hindquarters. That was where Pim excelled. He was absolutely true and very wide, a trait he passed to his progeny.

This was a classic case of a new sire representing new bloodlines emerging to capitalize on the good daughters of another sire by bringing to the gene pool those traits that were complementary. Although Pim only sired about a dozen litters in the United States, his percentage rate was incredible, leading to a total of 45 champions. Furthermore, he became an integral part of the gene pool for the breed and an important stepping stone to the next generations. Pim was an outstanding example that a plain-looking sire can have a lot to offer, and breeders need to judge a book by more than its cover. For he was able to give his progeny marvelous qualities of soundness, strength, character and constitution.

Barry Goodman phased out of sheepdogs and started breeding Gordon Setters. Once again, his breeding expertise was enjoyed by a breed, this time resulting in the good sire, Ch. Rivermist King James.

When in the summer of 1995, Joy Meyer Kelley's Int. Ch. To-Jo's Nice N' Easy broke the siring record for Old English Sheepdogs, it was a fitting tribute to his ancestry. For in the fifth generation of this outstanding sire's pedigree were a number of crosses to the Rivermist dogs, bringing both Ceiling Zero and Pim into the 1990s quite strongly for the breed. Furthermore, the intensified linebreeding to the greats of the English Kennel, Prospect, through Caj Haakonson's Bahlamb's line of quality dogs, brings a classic collection of greats to the pedigree of Nice N' Easy.

Left: Ch. To-Jo's Nice N' Easy, Old English Sheepdog, is the all-time Top Sire in the Breed with 68 champions and counting. Four of his progeny are All Breed BIS winners, as was he himself. A number of his progeny are in the Top Ten and in 1993 and 1994, he sired the #1 O.E.S. in the U.S. Pictured here winning the group at the Louisville Cluster Shows in 1988, he was owner-handled by Joy Kelley and bred by Margilee Smalley. He carries both of the great old timers—Ceiling Zero and Pim—in his pedigree. He is still active as a sire at 10 years of age as we go to press. (Booth Photo)

Below: "A Percheron stallion of a dog" was the way *master breeder* Barry Goodman described Old English Sheepdog (Int. & Am) Ch. Unnesta Pim when he imported him to the U.S. to stand at stud at his Rivermist Kennels. A square dog of extraordinary build and strength of hindquarters, Pim brought great solidity to the breed. Ability to look beneath the cosmetic trappings of a dog to appreciate its essential breed character and correct structure puts great virtues into the gene pool of a breed, as evidenced by outstanding modern producers who carry Pim's genes on to future generations. (Photograph courtesy of John Mandeville)

No wonder Jere Marder selected the then-unknown young sire as a mate for the lovely Ch. Rholenwood's Taylor Maid. The resulting three champions were all of excellent quality, with the outstanding bitch, Ch. Lambluv's Winning Maid Easy, becoming a multi-BIS winner.

In 1989, Nice N' Easy had won the breed at Westminster under Judge Robert Forsyth, former professional handler and the pilot of Ceiling Zero. This win was much treasured by Joy, who candidly confides that this nice dog was sound with good quality but "nothing fantastic" to foretell the greatness to come in his progeny. *Master breeders*, such as Joy, share this rare ability of introspection as well as forthrightness, making their contributions to the breed all the more valuable.

No matter what bitches came to him, Nice N' Easy put breed type and compact, thick dogs on the ground. And the puppies were well-angled with plenty of neck and excellent side gait. He is a five-time winner of the Ceiling Zero Award as top producing sire and currently has 69 champions with more to come. Two of his offspring, Ch. Raffles Chelsey Buns and Ch. Wullyweather's Effurtless, are National Specialty winners. Joy has been his owner and handler throughout his career. To Margilee Smalley goes the honor of having bred him.

CH. INNISFREE'S SIERRA CINNAR - SIBERIAN HUSKY - SIRE OF 112 CHAMPIONS

Kathleen Kanzler is a premier breeder whose Innisfree Siberian Huskies have helped put Siberians on the map—just as Lorna Demidoff's had done before her. Kathleen considers Lorna the breeder who most influenced the breed and talks fondly of the days when Lorna "ran them in the winter and showed them in the summer." Prior to Lorna, Siberians enjoyed an association with a real character—the one of a kind, Short Seely.

When Ch. Innisfree's Sierra Cinnar won BIS at Westminster Kennel Club in 1980 under the respected E. Irving "Ted" Eldredge, many were surprised that the highest honor in dogdom had been won by a dog who had lost part of his ear in a fight. This flawlessly moving dog could conjure up visions of a Siberian team racing across the snow-covered Arctic on some important mission of mercy. Such a scar was a badge of honor, for you could imagine him fighting wolves to protect his master and his property in some remote part of the North Country. Yet, when you saw the love and teamwork he and his lovely young handler, Trish, enjoyed, you knew that no matter how primitive the breed could be, it could still participate in this touching picture of a girl and her dog (in this case her mother's).

Ch. Innisfree's Sierra Cinnar winning BIS at the 1980 Westminster Kennel Club Show with owner Kathleen Kanzler's daughter Trish handling. Judge E. Irving Eldredge is assisted by trophy presenters Chester F. Collier (left) and William Rockefeller. (Photo courtesy of John Ashbey)

Sired by Ch. Innisfree's Sierra Beau Jack out of Innisfree's Royal Kate, Cinnar's breeders of record were Michael and Karen Burnside, and he represented more than six generations of selective Innisfree breeding. Kathleen's background in animal husbandry served her well as she watched this dog and her daughter in the Winners Circle at the Garden—a lifetime of her hard work represented in the girl and in the dog, a team on top and a job well done!

CH. SALUTAIRE WORD TO THE WISE - MANCHESTER TERRIER - SIRE OF 53 CHAMPIONS

Ch. Salutaire Word To The Wise, Standard Manchester Terrier, was the first male in his breed (toy included) ever to win the coveted red, white and blue BIS rosette (See picture in section Role of the Judge). This magnificent standard is the number one Sire All Times in the breed with 53 champions to his credit. His talented breeder, Myrtle Klensch, was seeking good shoulders when she sought the services of Ch. Brandyman's Little Tempo for her bitch, Ch. Salutaire The Real Dilly, a granddaughter of Ch. Canyon Crest Mo.

Myrtle's breeding program was based on the structural soundness of Mrs. Bagshaw's Canyon Crest dogs combined with the heads and refinement of the East Coast dogs that she introduced into her lines. The resulting Word to the Wise dog became a solid sire upon which she could linebreed with confidence, for he could be counted on to throw his refinement of type and head along with his good movement. This top sire is credited with being the dog that put the look of Salutaire into the breed. Since he was not closely bred, he was one of those rare dominant sires created by a fortunate assortment of genes. The linebreeding that resulted from him created a foundation strain that future breeders can utilize.

An interesting side light about this kennel's activity resulted from an accidental breeding of the toy, Ch. Salutaire Punchline, to the standard bitch, Ch. Salutaire Say No More C.D.

Ch. Salutaire Surely You Jest C.D. received her name because of Myrtle's embarrassment by this event. The much-loved Langdon Skarda once joked to Myrtle that he would be happy to "have one of your accidents." Taking after her sire's toy side of the family, "Jessie" became the breed's all time record holder with 100 group firsts and 22 BIS victories to her credit. In addition, she won 10 Specialty bests and a High Scoring Dog in Trial honor. Her co-owners shared the pleasure of handling her. Myrtle and Peter Rank are a true testimonial to the brotherhood of dedicated dog people, as their co-ownership relationship dates back to 1955. This little bitch took on all comers in the strongest of California competition to become the first Manchester ever to land in the Top Ten All Breeds. Her dam, Say No More, was a daughter of Word to the Wise.

Ch. Jo-Ni's Red Baron of Crofton - Lakeland Terrier - Super Sire of a Super Line

The saga of the red Lakeland Terrier in North America started with the importation of the mighty grizzled dog Ch. Stingray of Derryabah from England. This outstanding dog had already won BIS at Crufts and went on to become the only dog ever to accomplish the astounding feat of winning BIS at both Crufts and Westminster Kennel Club. That dual accomplishment earned him permanent fame, but even more important was his legacy as the patriarch of the most powerful sire line known to Lakeland Terriers in the United States.

In those days, the red Lakeland was considered an outcast by English breeders who preferred the grizzled or black and tan animals. Because historically, Foxhound packs were accompanied by terriers to unearth the fox when it went to ground, red terriers were avoided so that inexperienced hunters would not confuse them with the fox. They were discarded as pet stock and seldom used in the breeding program. Stingray's dam had been a wheaten bitch and perhaps not appropriately valued by some of the breeders. It is my understanding that other terrier breeds have evolved in certain colors for similar practical reasons, such as the West Highland White Terrier.

An exquisite square dog of beautiful type, Stingray brought the correct station and look to a breed that tended to be low on leg. This virtue was to endure through generations of Stingray descendants. His son Ch. Special Edition was of similar type with the desired oval rib cage to accompany his correct length of leg.

Upon the recommendation of Ric Chashoudian, the good producing bitch, Ch. Jorl's Jo-Ni of Sherwood, was sent to Special Edition. When the breeders expressed disappointment in the litter compared to her previous litter by Stingray, Chashoudian backed up his opinion by purchasing the puppy known as Red Baron. And the rest is history.

With Virginia Dickson as owner and Chashoudian as handler, Red Baron was to soar to Top Dog All Breeds in 1975 and capped his career by repeating his famous grandsire's win of BIS at Westminster in 1976. By this time, his impact on the breed as a sire was already being appreciated by Lakeland breeders, and this fabulous little dog was retired to devote his full attention to bettering Lakeland Terriers at stud.

And breed on he did! Californians were treated to a wide array of Baron youngsters in the ring vying for honors and defeating each other in a splendid ongoing example of what dog shows are meant to be—the very best of the breeding stock shown in the very best of condition by the very best of handlers under the very best of judges.

Their numbers included a very young Clay Coady with an early competitor of the Jean Heath-Bill Cosby joint venture—Ch. Schlosshaus's Jo Jo The Red—a dog who was to become the key sire in the Black Watch breeding program. Eddie Boyes was piloting the streamlined Ch. Lyvewyre Bold Ruler and Pat Peters was handling her own Ch. Whycroft Gypsy Baron. The fourth Red Baron descendant knocking heads with these males was my personal favorite, his delightful daughter, Ch. Terra Copper Chuca, handled by Bob Jordan. At the same time Peter Green was handling Ch. Baron's Carbon Copy for the Farrells in the East. Everywhere one went in the United States in the late 70s and early 80s, first-generation Baron offspring were there to bid for honors at all levels right on through to BIS.

And these outstanding progeny bred on to produce great ones in the next generation, and in successive generations to follow. Consider the phenomenal success of the Heath-Cosby dogs resulting in generation after generation of BIS animals and Quaker Oats winners, all with any number of crosses to Red Baron. Their current star, Ch. Revelry's Awesome Blossom (see color section), was bred by Dawn Markham from a Black Watch sire and dam.

Red Baron was a dog of exceptional cleanness, a dog of exacting squareness and detailing of headpiece. He brought a style and look to his breed that will never be forgotten as long as red Lakelands

James and Emilie Farrell are all smiles as they join handler Peter Green in celebrating the Westminster BIS victory of Eng. and Am. Ch. Stingray of Derryabah. With this win, the Lakeland legend became the only dog in history to score BIS honors at both Crufts and Westminster. Stingray was the founding father of an incredible line of American Lakelands. This commemorative candid was taken after the official show photo with Judge Major Godsol and Westminster officials. (Photo by Shafer)

Ch. Special Edition, the BIS son of Stingray, retired with 34 BISs to his credit for breeder Joyce (Peanuts) McComiskey and owners Mr. & Mrs. James Farrell Jr., and then went on to become the top Lakeland sire, a feat later to be equaled with new records by his son, Red Baron. He was handled by Peter Green. The respected Melbourne Downing was one of many judges who selected him for Group and BIS honors. (Photo by William P. Gilbert)

An absolutely incredible lineup of Lakeland Terrier brilliance occurred at the Great Western Terrier Speciality in Los Angeles in 1975. Four generations of BIS winners are pictured with Judge Grace Brewin. Ch. Special Edition (with handler Peter Green); his son Ch. Jo-Ni's Red Baron of Crofton (with handler Ric Chashoudian); his son Ch. Baron's Carbon Copy (with handler David Schaff); and, Baron's daughter Ch. Terra Copper Chuca (with handler Bob Jordon). This monumental testimony to the influence of the head of this sire line—Ch. Stingray of Derryabah—stands as an eternal tribute to a great sire line. (Missy Yuhl photo from the collection of Peter Green)

CH. AWESOME BLOSSOM: A LEGACY OF THE RED BARON

The 1996 model of the Red Baron line is on course to break all existing show records for Lakeland Terriers, and she is only three years old. Ch. Revelry's Awesome Blossom is the current Black Watch star of the cooperative Jean Heath-Bill Cosby breeding program that has enjoyed huge success in this breed for a quarter of a century.

Captain Jean Heath (Ret.), then a young lieutenant in the medical branch of the U.S. Navy, met the affable Cosby while he was recovering from shoulder surgery in 1959. As a physical therapy technician in the Navy, Bill was soon working in Jean's department. Although the two lost contact with each other for many years, a meeting in Las Vegas provided the setting for their date with destiny— and the rest, as they say, is history.

Jean had been co-breeding dogs with the respected Joan Huber of Blythewood Miniature Schnauzers, and a couple of the early Lakelands carry the Blythewood prefix. It was a natural for Heath and Cosby to share dogs along with their other common interests. In addition to their medical backgrounds, both are accomplished athletes, sports fans and music lovers, as well as best of friends. Bill takes an active interest in Lakeland activities even though he is often unable to attend many shows due to his busy television and entertainment schedule.

Blossom herself is the perfect performer for this show business super star, as she is a lively animal who really enjoys being "onstage" even at home and around the kennel. When the longtime handler of the Black Watch team, Clay Coady, does his morning workouts, Blossom participates with verve. She plays a game of furiously egging him on when

he does push-ups by running back and forth under him as he goes up. Her energy level is everything a terrier's should be and she is always fun to watch.

One of her many fans commented that she is "made the way a Lakeland should be." It is said that if a Lakeland can get his head and front legs through a hole or crevice, the body should be able to follow."That's Blossom!"

Dan Kiedrowski, *Terrier Type Magazine*, did an extended pedigree search for me, and was utterly amazed at the number of crosses to Red Baron, his sire Ch. Special Edition and his famous grandsire Ch. Stingray of Derryabah carried in her pedigree. There were 24 crosses to Red Baron himself with 35 crosses to Special Edition and 50 to Stingray! The latter two were introduced into the family tree of Blossom through other progeny in addition to Red Baron.

This incredible assortment and reassembling of the genes is an affirmation that here is a line that can tolerate such intensity of breeding because it contains no genetic trash. Blossom is the 10th consecutive-generation progeny of this line to become a BIS winner.

With such a classic pedigree there is little doubt that when her performing days are done she will take her rightful place in the annals of Lakeland Terrier history by producing a new generation of great, red Lakelands to carry on the tradition that began in America with the grizzled son of a wheaten bitch: the legendary Ch. Stingray of Derryabah, the only dog in history to win BIS at both Crufts and Westminster. The legacy continues!

assert themselves in both breed and all breed competition. It might be said that he took a color that had been considered undesirable and transformed it into something fashionable. By virtue of his own greatness, he took the Lakeland beyond the colorblindness of the fancy to make people truly "see red."

Ch. St. Aubrey Laparata Dragon - Pekingese - Sire of Distinction

Ch. St. Aubrey Laparata Dragon was a tremendous sire in a diminutive package for generations of Pekingese. His dynamic producing ability can best be appreciated by the two Westminster BISs won by his descendents, Ch. St. Aubrey Dragonora of Elsdon and Ch. Wendessa Crown Prince. (Photo by R. Burtis)

A forceful dominant sire stamps his get well into the third and fourth generations and beyond. That is exactly what Ch. St. Aubrey Laparata Dragon did in regard to toplines and tailsets. He was a lasting influence for generations of Pekingese to come. At first a rather reluctant showdog until he became part of the energy that is Luc Boileau, this gorgeous little dog came along at the right time, for the breed was having trouble with tailsets and Dragon was able to correct them no matter what was behind the bitch.

The mark of an outstanding sire is that he can be used on a wide assortment of bitches with success. Dragon was not only a correcting force when used on linebred bitches, he also had this remarkable ability to click with outcrossed bitches as well. He was truly prepotent and never failed to improve upon a bitch.

In addition to siring the 1982 Westminster BIS winner,

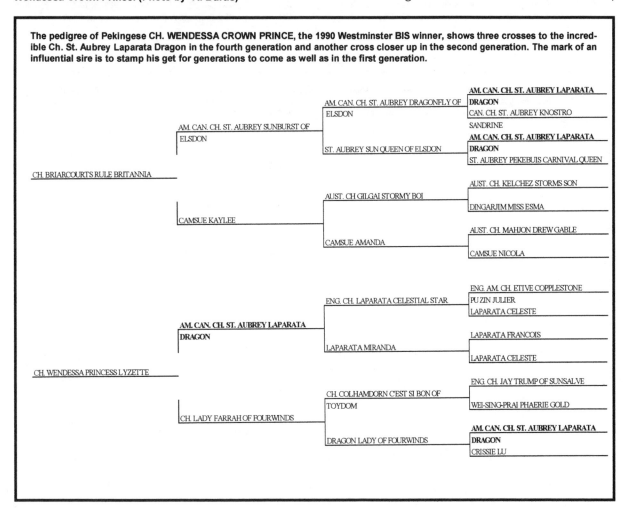

The pedigree of Pekingese CH. WENDESSA CROWN PRINCE, the 1990 Westminster BIS winner, shows three crosses to the incredible Ch. St. Aubrey Laparata Dragon in the fourth generation and another cross closer up in the second generation. The mark of an influential sire is to stamp his get for generations to come as well as in the first generation.

Ch. Electra's The Wind Walker winning a SBIS under Judge Robert Moore, handled by his breeder-owner Judy Bingham. He has great influence on the breed by siring all-breed and specialty winners. (Rinehart Photo)

Ch. Gra-Lemor Demetrius v.d. Victor with Judge Peter Knoop and handler Mike Shea. Before turning to judging, Knoop handled Ch. Rancho Dobe's Storm to back-to-back BIS wins at Westminster. (Henry Schley photo)

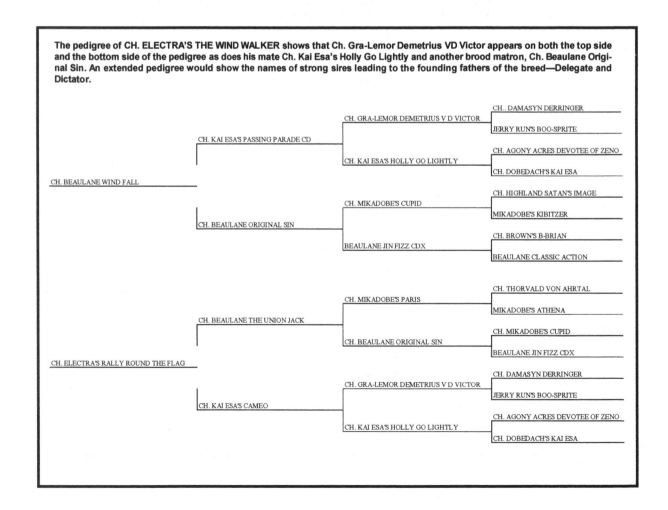

The pedigree of CH. ELECTRA'S THE WIND WALKER shows that Ch. Gra-Lemor Demetrius VD Victor appears on both the top side and the bottom side of the pedigree as does his mate Ch. Kai Esa's Holly Go Lightly and another brood matron, Ch. Beaulane Original Sin. An extended pedigree would show the names of strong sires leading to the founding fathers of the breed—Delegate and Dictator.

CH. BEAULANE WIND FALL

 CH. KAI ESA'S PASSING PARADE CD

  CH. GRA-LEMOR DEMETRIUS V D VICTOR

   CH.. DAMASYN DERRINGER

   JERRY RUN'S BOO-SPRITE

  CH. KAI ESA'S HOLLY GO LIGHTLY

   CH. AGONY ACRES DEVOTEE OF ZENO

   CH. DOBEDACH'S KAI ESA

 CH. BEAULANE ORIGINAL SIN

  CH. MIKADOBE'S CUPID

   CH. HIGHLAND SATAN'S IMAGE

   MIKADOBE'S KIBITZER

  BEAULANE JIN FIZZ CDX

   CH. BROWN'S B-BRIAN

   BEAULANE CLASSIC ACTION

CH. ELECTRA'S RALLY ROUND THE FLAG

 CH. BEAULANE THE UNION JACK

  CH. MIKADOBE'S PARIS

   CH. THORVALD VON AHRTAL

   MIKADOBE'S ATHENA

  CH. BEAULANE ORIGINAL SIN

   CH. MIKADOBE'S CUPID

   BEAULANE JIN FIZZ CDX

 CH. KAI ESA'S CAMEO

  CH. GRA-LEMOR DEMETRIUS V D VICTOR

   CH. DAMASYN DERRINGER

   JERRY RUN'S BOO-SPRITE

  CH. KAI ESA'S HOLLY GO LIGHTLY

   CH. AGONY ACRES DEVOTEE OF ZENO

   CH. DOBEDACH'S KAI ESA

Ch. St. Aubrey Dragonora of Elsdon, he sired any number of BIS winners including a most correct Ch. St. Aubrey Bees Wing of Elsdon that captured California hearts over the Santa Barbara weekend of his Quaker Oats winning year. Furthermore, the 1990 Westminster BIS winner, Ch. Wendessa's Crown Prince, boasts four crosses to him in a four-generation pedigree!

With more than 100 champions to his credit, this influential sire proved good things really do come in small packages. He was bred by the team of Nigel Aubrey-Jones and Bill Taylor, two gentlemen whose partnership has enhanced the North American dog scene for decades. Ed Jenner was his proud owner.

CH. ELECTRA'S THE WIND WALKER - DOBERMAN PINSCHER-RECORD-BREAKING SIRE

The first time I laid eyes on Ch. Electra's The Wind Walker, he was being handled by Corky Vroom as a young special. After inquiring about the handsome red-and-rust Doberman Pinscher, I remarked to Corky, "If he were an Elkhound, I would breed to him in a heartbeat." The youngster just exuded the "look of a sire."

In time, Wind Walker proved his breeder Judy Bingham had done her homework in assembling the genes that produced this exceptional sire, as his 94 champion progeny broke the breed's previous siring record that had stood for decades—that of Hans Schmidt's legendary Ch. Delegate v.d. Elbe. I remember a special dinner party that I attended, during my youth in Virginia, at the home of dear friends Carl and Pepper Barron. Schmidt and my mentor, Johnny Davis, engaged in a fascinating Doberman dialogue on breeding that I listened to avidly. Schmidt's heavy accent required intense listening and concentration to appreciate his words of wisdom so generously shared.

Delegate was tightly linebred to the great German import Ch. Jessy v.d. Sonnenhoche, whose handler Harold Correll once told me, "No one ever counted her teeth, as we were all afraid to open her mouth." Jessy had been moved from one place to another by "hooking her collar," and her kennel area was off limits to his children, including son Terry who later became a professional handler. Jessy won Germany's Grand Sieger title and went on to win the Doberman Pinscher Club of America National Specialty as well as numerous All Breed BISs.

Bingham's foundation bitch, Ch. Kai Esa's Cameo, was the daughter of Ch. Gra-Lemor Demetrius v.d. Victor and Ch. Kai Esa's Holly Go Lightly. This breeding combined the blood of Delegate's top-producing grandsons—the beautiful-headed Ch. Steb's Top Skipper and the solid Ch. Singenwald's Prince Kuhio. Skipper had been handled by Davis during my formative years of working for him.

The mating of Cameo to Ch. Beaulaine Union Jack, son of Ch. Beaulaine Original Sin, produced Ch. Electra's Rally Round The Flag, who was destined to become the dam of Wind Walker. Cameo's full brother, Ch. Kai Esa's Passing Parade C.D., had been bred to Original Sin to produce Ch. Beaulaine Wind Fall, the sire of Wind Walker. The resulting pedigree that produced Wind Walker is an excellent example of the "patterned pedigree" so admired by me and shows intense concentration of the blood of Delegate, as well as nine crosses to Ch. Dictator Von Glenhugel through his great-grandsons, Top Skipper and the lovely-headed, red Ch. Damasyn Derringer. Because Wind Walker had fewer crosses to Dictator than many of the other ranking sires of his day, he was able to be used on their daughters with great success. Dictator ranked right up there with Delegate as a "founding father" of the modern Doberman.

In an article Bingham wrote for the Fall 1995 issue of *The Doberman Quarterly*, she attributed Wind Walker's success as a sire to the wisdom of Hans Schmidt, "who banked these valuable genes." Bingham was not referring to modern banking of frozen semen. Instead, she was acknowledging her appreciation for a man who 40 years earlier had collected the breed's best available genes into a gene pool that would be tapped later utilizing linebreeding. This ability to understand that the banking process is like storing valuable priceless jewels in the vault until they are to be utilized is a talent Bingham shares with other *master breeders*.

Wind Walker was an upstanding, square dog with lovely front assembly and an exceptional head-piece. The interesting aspect of his producing record is the extraordinary quality of his offspring. With six All Breed BIS winners and 10 Specialty winners to his credit, Wind Walker has greatly influenced

Ch. Jessy V D Sonnenhohe, Doberman Pinscher bitch imported to the U.S. from Germany in 1937, was considered the ideal specimen of her breed prior to World War II. Doberman fanciers have been eternally grateful that this grande dame was obtained before Germany and the U.S. went to war, for she was a great matriarch of the breed in America. Imported by Francis F.H. Fleitmann, she was a multi-BIS winner as well as the Doberman Pinscher Club of America National Specialty winner before retiring for matronly duties. (Photo courtesy of the American Kennel Club)

Ch. Brunswig's Cryptonite won 124 BIS honors for Sam and Marion Lawrence and appears to be in line to inherit the mantle of Top Sire in the Doberman Pinscher breed, as well as Top Winner in the breed's history. Cryptonite is the grandson of Wind Walker who was linebred to Delegate, leading sires in the progression to Cryptonite. George Murray handled this amazing dog throughout his illustrious career. (Photo courtesy of George Murray)

the future of the breed through his producing sons and daughters. When his record is challenged, it will no doubt be as he himself challenged Delegate—by a member of his own family. In a continuing pattern of "great sires beget great sires," his grandson, Ch. Brunswig's Cryptonite, appears ready to move to the top of the list.

Ch. Royal Tudor's Wild as the Wind UDT, "Indy," (see color section) is the most well-known of Wind Walker's progeny. In addition to winning Top Dog All Breeds in 1988 and BIS at Westminster in 1989, Indy is also the dam of four champions with others pointed, and these offspring in turn are proving to be good producers. She was the first obedience-titled dog to win BIS at the Garden, and she won the National under respected breeder-judge Peggy Adamson (Damasyn Kennels) 10 weeks after whelping a litter! Indy was co-bred by Bingham with Beth Wilhite. She was handled by Andy Linton through most of her conformation career and by owner Susan Korp through her many obedience honors and occasionally in conformation. Wind Walker definitely represented a turning point in Dobermans in the last part of the 20th Century.

COCKER SPANIEL, PARTI-COLOR - A FAMOUS FATHER-SON SIRING TEAM - SINBAD AND DOMINO

One of the great father-son producing combinations of all times was that of the red-and-white Cocker Spaniel, Ch. Scioto Bluff's Sinbad and his black-and-white son, Ch. Dreamridge Domino. Both dogs were handled in their show and stud careers by Ron Fabis, and their contributions added more than 200 champions to their breed's gene pool. Sinbad was owned by the Charles Winders and sired 118 title holders, while Tom O'Neal's Domino added 109 more.

Sinbad was a dog of such lovely neck and shoulders that he was considered easy to trim. The trimming of Cockers requires great skill to blend the clipper work and the thinning shear work from the neck into the shoulders. But Sinbad was so extraordinarily clean there, the job was not difficult. And he threw this quality to his progeny, which was one of the many reasons he was such a popular stud.

Ch. Dau-Han's Dan Morgan winning BIS at the Camden County Kennel Club December 1959. Mr. Edward C. Doyle is the judge and Mrs. John Irwin is presenting the trophy. Dan Morgan was considered a turning-point dog by parti-color breeders. In spite of his early death he sired more than 25 champions. This was the author's first BIS win! (Brown Photo)

Ch. Dreamridge Domino by artist Michael Allen courtesy of Tom O'Neal, owner and breeder. He was the product of Dinner Date bred to her own grandsire Sinbad.

Ch. Scioto Bluff's Sinbad by artist Michael Allen for owner Tom O'Neal. The artist has captured the correct square muzzle of Sinbad, a dog whose siring record was enhanced by the excellent bites and heads he put into the gene pool. He is an example of a dominant sire resulting from the correct assembly of genes in his own genotype. He sired more than 100 champions, as did his son, Ch. Dreamridge Domino.

Ch. Dreamridge Dinner Date is pictured handled by Ron Fabis. She was the top Particolored Cocker Spaniel bitch of her day and a granddaughter of Dan Morgan. All of her 9 puppies finished their titles. (Ritter Photograph)

Ch. Dreamridge Dinner Date, black and white, was the top-winning bitch of her day. A gorgeous-headed bitch of exquisite type, her dam was the product of a Ch. Dau-Han's Dan Morgan daughter bred to Sinbad. I was eager to see her because of the cross to Morgan, and was impressed with this fantastic bitch. When bred to her grandsire Sinbad, the lovely Domino was the result. Domino was a dog with an extreme neck and headpiece he stamped on his get for generations. Yet, both he and Sinbad passed on the excellent legs and running gear they had inherited from Sinbad's sire, Ch. Hallway's Hoot Mon, a dog from the sound breeding program conducted by Jim and Beth Hall in the Pacific Northwest. Although Dinner Date produced only nine puppies in her lifetime, each of them finished easily.

To have two sires carry such important factors in perfect harmony in their bloodlines is a great tribute to all the animals in their pedigree. In-depth pedigree researchers of today will find these prepotent animals in the background of most of the breed's top parti-colors.

A Look At The Future

CH. EMPIRE'S BROOKLYN DODGER - BLACK AND WHITE COCKER SPANIEL

If one had a crystal ball with which to predict the future, it might feature Ch. Empire's Brooklyn Dodger, parti-colored Cocker Spaniel, as a good bet to break all existing siring records. Not only is this six-year-old dog on course to rewrite the record books for his own breed, he is a serious challenger for all breed honors, assuming he stays healthy.

Dodger holds the record as all-time Specialty winner for his breed with 33 bests and has already sired the top parti-colored Cocker in the history of the breed in Ch. Rendition's Triple Play, number two Dog All Breeds in 1995. Dodger is the only futurity winner who has in turn sired three futurity winners to date at the Spaniel Club.

This gorgeous dog first came to my attention when I returned to my crates after Elkhound judging at an all-breed show in Texas to find him sitting proudly on a table in the grooming area. His wonderful headpiece, neck and shoulders jumped out at me, and by the time my dog was put away, handler Jeff Wright was there to take care of his charge and graciously allowed me to go over him. Here was a dog made to be a sire. In addition to his lovely front assembly and harmony of parts, he carried an absolutely correct Cocker coat. Time would prove his ability to stamp his get with his own excellent characteristics.

No matter which bitch Dodger goes to, he is dominant for his good forequarters, even out of bitches who are not so good there themselves. A correct and typey dog, he is the product of Wright's breeding program of linebreeding to Ch. Rexpoint Flying Dutchman with descendants of his good Dreamridge foundation bitch. Jeff bred Dodger's sire, Ch. Terje's Thunderbolt, the dog credited with passing his prepotency for good legs and soundness to his son.

With more than 80 champion sons and daughters to his credit at

Ch. Rendition Triple Play is the Top Winning All Time Parti-Colored Cocker Spaniel and the son of Ch. Empire's Brooklyn Dodger. Pictured here going BIS under Judge Charles Trotter at the Umpqua Kennel Club Show in Eugene, Oregon, handled by Michael Pitts, who shared handling honors with his wife Linda. Brigitte Berg of Issaquah, Washington, is the breeder and owner. Pat Bolyard presents the trophy. (Photo by Callea)

Ch. Empire's Brooklyn Dodger, the sire of the '90s, is now the sire of more than 80 champions with 6 of the Top Ten Particolored Cocker Spaniels for 1995 his progeny. A dog of exquisite type, head, neck and shoulder, he is putting a look of great breed character into his puppies. He is managed at stud by owner Jeff Wright. (Photo by Michael)

the time of this writing, Dodger seems bound for destiny—and that destiny is to challenge the record of his ancestor, Ch. Rinky Dink's Sir Lancelot, all time top sire for the breed. In fact, it is not unrealistic for his supporters to shoot for the top of the siring list with this exceptional young sire.

Thoughts on Sires

- Home sires can be the most expensive matings.

- In addition to being born with the credentials to be a great sire, the animal must also have opportunity, timing, and quality of mates. The great thoroughbred sire, Lexington, was the leading sire more than 12 times and would have put even more numbers on the board if so many of his best sons had not died in battle during the Civil War.

- Some sires will have an entirely different show performance and breeding performance.

- If two good sires are able to be used on each other's daughters and nick, the breed is blessed with rapid improvement.

- Genetic information associated with the Y chromosome contributes to the greatness of a sire line (see Tesio).

- In assessing a sire, consider how he rates among his peers. If he is siring at a time when the breed is at a high point, and his progeny are exceptional among those good ones, he is truly the peak of the highest mountain range. If he is siring at a time when the breed is in decline and puts numbers up simply because his progeny are a little better than the rest, he is the highest hill in a rolling, low range.

- Some studs may be more or less private. If they have exceptional gene pools to share with the breed, this is indeed unfortunate and a loss to the breed. At the other extreme is the stud who is pushed in such a manner as to entice the public to pay for the dog.

- A stud who is private can be owned by one of private means or not, but it is owned by one who does not desire to have the blood of his animal spread all through the breed by those who do not know what to do with it. It might be said that this owner is protecting his stud against its future bastardization.

- A great sire must be able to produce his own virtues at the same time he blends harmoniously with the blood of other sires.

Summary on Brood Bitches and Sires: In conclusion, evaluating dams and sires to determine their contributions to the breed's gene pool is based on separating the effective breeding population of those who really produce from the general breeding population of those that merely have puppies. And, sometimes this is difficult to do because of the important factor of progeny opportunity for the animals resulting from the program. In studying thoroughbred horses and the history of Calumet Farm, it was interesting to realize the fantastic producing and racing record the farm enjoyed under the guidance of Ben Jones and the decline it suffered following his loss. Expert bloodstock people were not absolutely sure if the producing line itself weakened or if its effectiveness was greatly reduced because Jones was no longer the trainer.

The greatest of dams and sires must be in a position for the progeny to have proper opportunity for success in order to receive their just place in producing annals. *Master breeders* are able to effect a favorable outcome to ensure the best of opportunities for their producers. That is what *master breeding* is all about.

Profiling a Pedigree

When you look at an animal's pedigree, it tells you what he ought to be. When you look at an animal performing in the ring or in some other event, it tells you what he seems to be. When you look at his offspring and producing record, it tells you what he is.

The pedigree is the family tree of the animal. But it is not absolute proof that the bearer of the pedigree has the hoped for genetic makeup that his pedigree might promise, for it is impossible to know which of those greats in the pedigree are the ones whose genes actually end up in the final product. Perhaps the two or three weak areas in the pedigree are the ones with the most impact on a particular animal. Because an ancestor is present more than once does not mean you can depend on a particular trait of that ancestor's appearing in later generations. A trait is either *present* or it's not, depending on its dominance or recessiveness and what was copied from each side of the pedigree.

> "It is indeed a desirable thing to be well descended, but the glory belongs to our ancestors."
> —Plutarch, Ancient Greek

Pedigrees—genetic blueprints—have an honorable history dating back to ancient clay tablets in Babylonia more than 6,000 years ago. These ancient artifacts were pedigrees of horses indicating traits thought to be inherited.

The Talmud contains ancient Hebrew laws that seem to recognize that hemophilia was not only inherited but carried by the mother, as it warned against circumcision of later sons if earlier ones had been lost. In spite of Biblical advice regarding family tree activity, horse breeders remain the ones to whom we are indebted for early efforts at keeping pedigrees.

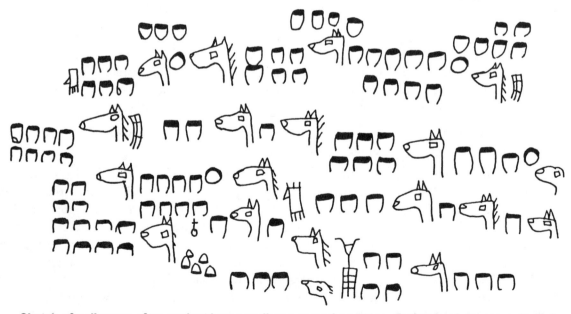

Sketch of a diagram of an ancient horse pedigree carved on stone. Dating back to approximately 3000 B.C., archaeologists believe that the manes indicated the status of the horses and the head forms were representative of specific types. The concave head was a horse that could very well represent the progenitor of the Arab, with the more "Roman" head indicative of other blood. (Artistic impression by Vivian Casillas)

PATTERNED PEDIGREE

This pedigree of Ch. Vin-Melca's Debonair is an example of a patterned pedigree. This young dog finished his championship in puppy coat under Mrs. James E. Clark. It will be interesting to see what his future role, if any, will be in the progress of his breed.

This patterned pedigree returns the full brothers Buckpasser and Smuggler as three of the four great-grandsires. The fourth one is Barnstormer, son of the sister to Buckpasser and Smuggler. Furthermore, the very tightly bred Ch.

Vin-Melca's Before Dawn, multi-BIS winner and Westminster Group placer, is in the same slot in this pedigree on the sire's side and the dam's side.

To further interest you (or complicate the matter) Dawn's dam, Morning Star, was from the same bitch as Victoria—the good producer Ch. Hedda Gabler, another daughter of Howdy Rowdy! Not only does this pedigree represent pattern breeding, it is also interpretative of the author's expression —closebreeding.

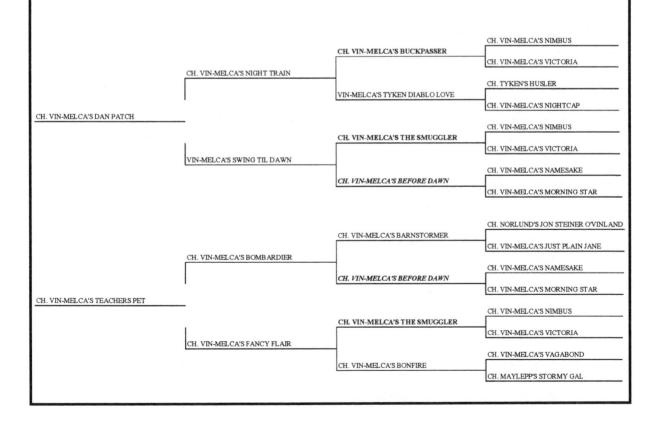

Like the sagas of the Vikings, early pedigrees were passed along by word of mouth. Horse traders memorized them to improve their sales pitch as they practiced their trade. Authenticity was added to the practice of keeping pedigrees once they were put on paper. When stud books maintained by breed registries came into use to verify pedigrees, they gained even more credibility. The Foxhound people who claim to be the first to keep true registries and pedigrees among dog fanciers have a valid claim based on both records of dogs and the fact that the owners were already in the habit of keeping them for their horses.

The study of a pedigree is an attempt to make *order* out of what could be called *disorder*. It recognizes the genetic fact that every living thing is the sum of all its collective ancestors—for better or for worse. Some pedigree analysts believe that each generation reshuffles all the genes from previous generations. Although the animal always inherits the same number of characteristics from each parent, it does not inherit the same quality of individual characteristics.

A pedigree of just names—no matter how famous—is of little value until you learn to put traits, both good and bad, with those individual names. Therefore, the annotated pedigree giving much more information on each animal is of great value. The first requirement of the pedigree is to contain four, preferably five, generations of the names of the individual ancestors. The next requirement of the pedigree is an indication of the performance records of the animals. The ultimate pedigree has traits and characteristics, both good and bad, as well as producing information and advice.

The in-depth analysis of a pedigree will be both quantitative and qualitative. In the first instance, it is to recognize that a name occurring over and over in a pedigree has more weight than a closer name that only appears once. This is in accordance with Galton's Law. In the second case, it is to recognize that the name of a great sire and/or dam that appears a number of times in the pedigree does not mean that each contribution of that particular animal is the same. In fact, even prepotent sires and dams have a wide range of characteristics and aptitudes that can be contributed to ensuing generations.

Remember that good dogs and those who are not so good can and do come from the same pedigrees. That is why I worry about mediocre dogs from well-bred pedigrees, for pedigree *junkies* who come later think they have a better animal than they do in fact have. They have an unwarranted sense of value, based on paper, than the living dog deserves. In the '60s, there was a lady who had the most incredible ability to recite pedigrees. She could rattle off the names of sires and dams dating back into the mid-1800s when the concept of the first purebred Elkhound was in its infancy. Yes, she really knew some names. What she did not know was what the dogs were like—even a generation or two back.

Knowing names in pedigrees is all well and good, but it has little value if you have no knowledge of the characteristics, qualities and weaknesses of the individual animals and their families. The purpose of studying pedigrees is to assist you in getting the classic names in proper order into your pedigrees as often as possible. It is designed to help concentrate the best possible genes in the end product. The pedigree helps give direction to the search for valuable traits resulting in a product that breeds true. To do this you need a working knowledge of the individuals in the pedigree for at least four or five generations. Know what each name represents. The more one knows about the qualities and the limitations of the animals, the more likely one is to improve on the pedigree of the next generation. That is why you should use great caution when using animals whose other family members you know nothing about. When you make a decision to import an animal for breeding purposes, make sure you have in-depth knowledge of animals in the pedigree as well as brothers, sisters, cousins and other relatives.

Here are some ways to brainstorm a pedigree:

- Prepare a synopsis of the qualities of the individual whose pedigree it is. Acknowledge both strengths and weaknesses.

- Do the same thing with very close ancestors. The closer the ancestor, the more in-depth information you should try to get. Give more credit to an outstanding sire and dam than to an outstanding great grandsire.

DOGS OF DISTINCTION — PERSONS OF PROMINENCE

Actress BETTY WHITE with CH. VIN-MELCA'S BEFORE DAWN, dam of Ch. Vin-Melca's Bombardier, grandam of Ch. Vin-Melca's Marketta. (Photo by Jeradine Lamb)

Pay attention Pat, CH. VIN-MELCA'S CALISTA seems to think as she sees friend BILL COSBY approach with congratulations on the 1990 Westminster Group win. (Photo courtesy of Ashbey)

Up, up and away. The author and CH. VIN-MELCA'S BOMBARDIER, sire of Ch. Vin-Melca's Marketta. (Photo by Deidi Kramer)

CH. VIN-MELCA'S VAGABOND, Norwegian Elkhound Dog of the Year, 1970. (Photo by Ludwig)

CH. VIN-MELCA'S NIMBUS as sculpted by Ric Chashoudian in 1978. (Photo by MikRon)

CH.VIN-MELCA'S MARKETTA, Norwegian Elkhound, pictured in the BIS class under Judge Walter F. Goodman at Westminster in 1994. (Photo by Backstage)

CH. DIOTAMA BEAR NECESSITY, H.C., First Bearded Collie to win the Westminster Group. Owned by Pat McDonald, Susan Ly-brand, Karen Kaye, Linda Swain and Pat Hyde. Handled by Mark Bettis. (Booth Photo)

CH. REVELRY'S AWESOME BLOSSOM, Lakeland Terrier. (Photo © by Chet Jezierski)

Afghan Hound CH. KABIK'S THE CHALLENGER, bred, owned and handled by Marguerite & Chris Terrell. Dog of the Year, BIS Westminster, 1983. (Fox & Cook Photo)

COLLEEN R. WILLIAMS with CH. EASY SOUTHERN'S FORTY-NINER (FRISCO), Golden Retriever. Below: A typical Southern Golden Retriever puppy bred by Clark and Colleen Williams.

Afghan Hound CH. TRYST OF GRANDEUR. Handled by Michael Canolizo. Awarding BIS is Dorothy Welsh. Dog of the Year, 1995. (Bernard Kernan Photo)

JULIA GASOW in the 1960s with CH. SALILYN'S ARISTOCRAT, Springer Spaniel. Dog of the Year, 1967. Author's choice as Dog of the Century. (Booth Photo)

JULIA GASOW in the 1990s with CH. SALILYN'S CONDOR, Springer Spaniel. Dog of the Year, 1992. Westminster BIS winner, 1993. (Booth Photo)

CH. DON-LEE CHOWTIME, Chow Chow, owned by Desmond Murphy & Susie Donnelly.

Below: AM/MEX/INT SBIS CH. CARMAS DRIVIN MISS DAISY, Saluki, with handler Andy Linton. (Rich Bergman Photo)

Left: CH. CHANGA'S DAN PATCH JC, Basenji. Owners: Keith & Tracie Nichols, June Young, Cecily Rappe. (Photo by Michael Work)

INT. CH. RAZZMATAZZMANIAN STRIPPER, Chinese Crested, owned by Mary Dee Lindmaier.

CH. LIBRA MALAGOLD CORIANDER, *Golden Retriever. Centennial Sporting Group winner. Owned by Connie Gerstner. (Booth Photo)*

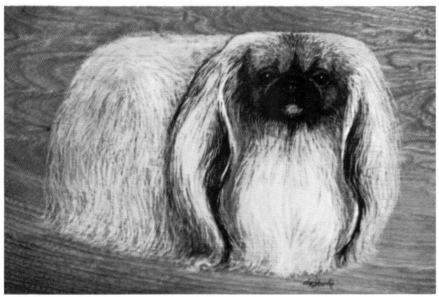

CH. CHIK T'SUN OF CAVERSHAM, Pekingese, owned by Mr. and Mrs. Charles Venable. Held BIS record for two decades. (Photo of a wood etching by Dale Gourlie from Kennel Review Magazine)

CH. ROYAL TUDOR'S WILD AS THE WIND UD ROM TD, Doberman Pinscher. Dog of the Year, 1988. Westminster BIS, 1989. Accomplished obedience performer. Handled by Andy Linton in conformation and Susan Korp in obedience. (Photo © by McNealy)

CH. ALTANA'S MYSTIQUE, German Shepherd Dog. #1 Dog All Time All Breeds with 275 BISs. Handled by James Moses for owner Jane Firestone. Breeder was M. Charleton. (Photo by Vicky Cook)

- Try to determine the heritability of traits with close ancestors. Make lists of pluses and minuses of the individuals.

- Take a hard look at siblings of the individual to assess how they resemble him or her.

- Try to get some producing records on the tail female line and the tail male line.

- Consider the degree of inbreeding, linebreeding, and/or closebreeding in the pedigree you are studying.

- Study pedigrees of prospective mates with the individual you have in mind.

- Seek out progeny of other breedings that are similar to the one you would be making in the above step to see how they turned out. If a half-sister of your bitch was bred to the same dog, what were the progeny like?

- Ask yourself, "Does the pedigree seem balanced and does it feel right?" Sometimes this balance is achieved by putting brothers or sisters into the same slot on both the topside and the bottomside of the pedigree. (See pedigree Ch. Vin-Melca's Debonair). Sometimes it is achieved by complementary proportions of inbreeding and linebreeding; by complementary proportions of exotic, elegant type and sound, honest animals; and sometimes the ultimate in balance is achieved when the great producers in the breed relate to each other in balanced genetic combinations they return to the progeny through both the sire and the dam. Such pedigree credentials would seem impeccable, but still your common sense will be your most valuable asset in reading a pedigree, just as it is with everything else associated with breeding.

You should be able to work with your pedigrees so you develop a degree of predictability as to what can be expected in type, quality, head characteristics and other traits. The important thing for you to accept is *degree* of predictability as your aim, as no one, at least for now, can predict for sure what the product of any proposed pedigree will be. In responding to the fact that people feel unjustly secure when they consider the study of mathematics as exact, Dr. Albert Einstein said: "Concepts can only acquire content when they are connected, however indirectly, to experience." Use experienced and knowledgeable people in your breed to help expand your pedigree research.

An important element for the astute dog breeder to consider when evaluating pedigrees for a long-term breeding program is if the animal will fit well with those already in the line and the pedigrees of the future. Sometimes this determination is not possible until after the animal has gone on to Valhalla. The animal I have in mind is one that acts like connective tissue, pulling the pedigree together so to speak. It might be said that his genetic ingredients mixed well with other pedigrees. Sometimes an animal is so extreme it is unable to become a productive component in the pedigree of the next generation. Using this animal in your breeding program would have only short-term benefit, at best.

The Norwegian import, Ch. Tortasin's Bjonn II, was the ultimate in connecting tissue perfection in a pedigree. As previously stated, his younger brother, Ch. Viking C.D., came to the Pacific Northwest a few years after Bjonn came to the Northeast. Viking was a more masculine dog than Bjonn, and out-produced him in the first generation. It was interesting to see how the Viking sons and daughters went on to produce even better as long as they were taken to animals down from Bjonn. If the linebreedings that were to follow concentrated more Bjonn than Viking, the results were superior. In the final analysis of the pedigrees, Bjonn out-produced his brother in later generations, even if not in the first. The visionary breeder prefers this always over the dog who seems to have a positive influence on the first generation only.

Sometimes these sires will not be appreciated early on in their stud career, and they may not be respected during their lifetime. In Bjonn's case, he was already an older dog when he came to the United

States. Because his progeny did not win big early, by the time his influence was obvious, it was too late. Thirty-five years ago, breeders did not have access to semen storage. If an animal did not get into the pedigrees before his death, he did not get in them at all.

Breeders who attempt to duplicate the pedigree of a great dog with a breeding that appears to be identical are more often than not disappointed in the results. Just because all the names in the third generation are alike does not mean the same individual genetic messages were sent down through those ensuing generations. The fact is that you can actually duplicate the pedigree of a great one (as is done with repeat breedings) only to get different results because the genetic messages sent on by the very same players were different messages.

When the best individuals in your pedigrees are getting further and further back in them, an infusion of new blood from outstanding gene pools is absolutely necessary. **Do not allow a wasting away of your line just to keep "homebreds" in it.**

Unfortunately, the unlimited number of potential genetic combinations that can result from the bringing together of two pedigrees means you do not know until the mating if the results will be favorable or unfavorable, or a combination of both. That is why profiling pedigrees can be such a valuable tool to you. It assists you in making the important decisions in *weeding your genetic garden.*

Part III

W I N N I N G

Means Hard Work

Kennel Facilities and Management

The word *kennel* is thought to have originated in France. It was first used to describe a pack of hounds and later their housing. The man/dog relationship that started with primitive people resulted in the twosome learning to live together early on, so it was quite natural that over the centuries man would construct special quarters for his four-legged friends.

The most lavish kennels I researched belonged to the Tang Dynasty Emperors of the 7th Century. These amazing kennels housed 2500 *couples*, as dogs were counted in antiquity. These 5,000 dogs were attended by 10,000 huntsmen or caretakers in splendid kennels of sporting dogs used for the hunt. According to an official AKC publication in 1935 (*Non-Sporting Dogs*), Chow Chows were used as game animals and were considered excellent pheasant dogs during that era.

No animals have been the benefactors of more royal treatment than the Russian Wolfhounds owned by czars and members of the Russian nobility. Housing hundreds of these magnificent hounds, known today as Borzois, was the source of great pride and their masters held huge hunts to showcase them. Participating in these exciting events was proof that you were a member of the inner circles at court.

Throughout Europe some breeds were privileged to belong only to those at the top of the class system and were housed in accordance with their masters' status, while others were cottage dogs of the working classes. In essence, dogs more or less lived in the same circumstances as their masters with kenneling to reflect their masters' means.

Reference to George Washington at the beginning of the book touched on early American dog breeders and their love of fine dogs. Americans have a tradition of dog breeding with roots to the more practical breeds that brought game to the table. It was natural for this association to evolve in time to

> "I am a great believer in luck, and I find the harder I work the more I have of it."
> —Thomas Jefferson

a dog-breeding and a dog-showing society. Just as Americans always represented a cross section of every background in the world, so did their dogs. Furthermore, their dogs' kennels were to come in all kinds ranging from spectacular and huge to a yard with a garage or even less!

There was a time during the early decades of the 20th Century when most American show dogs were raised in splendid and luxurious kennels staffed with kennel masters and kennel maids to care for their highbrow charges. The famous Sand Spring Cocker Spaniel Kennel of Somerset Hills, New Jersey, not only employed a kennel manager with several kennel boys and maids, it also utilized the services of a full-time secretary.

An ongoing series of articles starting in the 1920s in the *American Kennel Gazette* provides a permanent record of many of these establishments and is available to the researcher of today. Written by the talented Arthur Frederick Jones, these articles appeared intermittently for more than 30 years. His personal presentations of these famous American kennels portrayed the fanciers as people of tremendous wealth who spared nothing in providing their animals with the best of facilities. Many of these gentried dog lovers lived life-styles of the rich and famous like heroes and heroines of F. Scott Fitzgerald novels. It was a time of great opulence.

Jones' article on the Far East Chow Kennels of L.R. Zufferer enticed me to ponder if Zufferer was attempting to rival the previously mentioned Chinese emperors when he built his palatial reproduction of a Chinese temple for his dogs in the 1920s. Described by Jones as a true lover of dogs, Zufferer was credited with accumulating bloodlines of great splendor to match the splendor of the place itself. The Chinese motif was carried throughout both the exterior and interior of the structure. The kennel building was 214 feet from end to end with two wings of 84 feet each! It required great bracing and architectural magic to get it built the way Zufferer wanted it. Located in Columbia, Pennsylvania, this masterpiece featured reproductions of Chinese lanterns, pagodas, art, furniture, rugs and other furnishings.

All meat and dairy products were raised on the premises and slaughtered there to assure absolutely pure food. One of the many kennel maids did nothing but bathe dogs all day and clean the eyes of every dog with boric acid. The dogs were fed three times a day, with puppies enjoying five meals. Their morning meal was shredded wheat and milk, at noon they received buttermilk, and the main meal in the evening featured fresh vegetables and meat from the farm. The meat was served alternately cooked and raw.

The Firenze Kennels of Colonel M. Robert Guggenheim were located on 1,100 acres of prime Long Island real estate. Bedlington Terriers were the main occupants at the time of Jones' interview. In addition to the great numbers of Bedlingtons, there were also 20 Pointers, a dozen Wire Fox Terriers, 20 Springer Spaniels, three German Shepherd Dogs, and a number of Labrador Retrievers. Imagine such extensive kennels that you could easily house and care for 50 dogs that weren't even the primary breed!

The puppy house had once been a bowling alley and always housed about 50 puppies. The estate boasted its own separate kennel cook house, as did many of the great kennels of that day. It was both a convenience for the kennel workers and a fire preventive measure. The kennel was managed by the Englishman Edward "Ted" Ward, who accompanied 26 of his employer's Bedlingtons to the 1927 Westminster show. Ted was the great-uncle of two-time Garden winner George Ward. Ted's brother George and George's son Ted were the grandfather and father, respectively, of our modern George, who chuckles at the Ward family tradition of sharing names. Living in Toronto, Canada, in 1927, the senior George and his son Ted came to New York that year to assist their relative in showing Guggenheim's string of dogs. It was reportedly an impressive sight at the Firenze benches. Prior to the concentration on the Bedlingtons, the Colonel's kennels had housed and bred more than 65 Bulldogs, all of exceptional quality, as well as any number of other breeds. It was said that if all the dogs from over the years at Guggenheim's kennels could be brought together in one giant dog show, it would have constituted one of the finest all-breed dog shows ever held in the United States.

The same could be said about the kennels of Mrs. Geraldine R. Dodge a couple of decades later. Her Giralda Farm was not only the site of America's most extravagant dog show, Morris and Essex, at one time or another it housed famous best in show and group winners in more than 85 different breeds.

Not only did many of these great kennels have their own cookhouses and food production systems on their estates, they also had benches and judging platforms for the employees to use to simulate ring experiences and conditions in the training of the show dogs. Indoor practice rings were also features of some of the kennels profiled in the articles.

Mrs. Florence B. Ilch's well-known Bellhaven Collie Kennel on the banks of the Shrewsbury River in New Jersey was one of many kennels whose inside pens were formerly stalls for horses (about 12 feet by 12 feet). A former stable was used by Lina Basquette in the glory days of her Honey Hollow Great Danes in Chalfont, Pennsylvania (1950s and 1960s). At one time she housed 100 Great Danes.

Mrs. Ilch imported several animals from the respected Laund strain of William Stansfield in England. Her kennel manager, Mike Kennedy, was one of the first I could find on record as oiling coats. Mr. Kennedy trained the dogs and cared for them, but the Ilch family was involved in showing the dogs. Her Laund Loyalty of Bellhaven was Best in Show at Westminster in 1929.

Mrs. A. S. Moffit, of Poughkeepsie, New York, was proud of the fact that her Rowcliffe Cocker Spaniels were both bench show winners and field trial champions. So dedicated was this good lady to keeping the Cocker a dual dog, she organized the Hunting Cocker Spaniel Club in 1924 and later purchased her own game farm where her dogs were trained. More than 4,000 pheasants were raised on these spacious acres every year, so the Cockers had their work cut out for them.

These large kennels were well staffed and managed by experienced dogmen, usually from England. In addition to the knowledgeable kennel manager, who usually prepared and handled the dogs at the

The founder of Grandeur Sunny Shay with the glorious Afghan Ch. Shirkhan of Grandeur on the occasion of his 1957 Westminster BIS, the first in history by a breeder-owner-handler. (Photo courtesy of The American Kennel Club)

Afghan legends Ch. Shirkhan of Grandeur and Sunny Shay—pictured winning BIS at Bronx County Kennel Club the same year he became the first hound to win BIS at Westminster. Shirkhan is credited with putting Afghans on the map both with his own persona and his ability to influence the gene pools of ensuing generations. A quarter of a century later, Shirkhan descendent Ch. Kabik's The Challenger revived the Shirkhan look to become Top Dog All Breeds and BIS at Westminster. Four decades later, Ch. Tryst of Grandeur also became Top Dog All Breeds. (Photo courtesy of Dennis Sprung)

GRANDEUR KENNELS TODAY

Grandeur Kennels' parking area leading into the reception room and grooming areas. All runs are inside-outside, offering dogs protection from all extremes of weather. Additionally, the facility features several large outdoor exercise paddocks. Its splendor earned it the coveted Archi Architectural Award. (Photo courtesy of Grandeur Kennels)

Another view of Grandeur. This modern state-of-the-art kennel is a premier showcase kennel in the US. This view looks across the grass outdoor practice ring that features bleachers for spectators. The downstairs area behind the tree contains the trophy room, whelping rooms, the indoor practice ring and the kennel offices. (Photo courtesy of Grandeur Kennels)

shows, there were also plenty of kennel workers to help with the many chores involved in running such huge establishments. Because hard pad and distemper were more life-threatening to dogs, until after World War II when vaccines were developed, the kennels usually featured isolated puppy facilities as well as separate areas for all dogs going to shows. Both World Wars served to bring all kinds of people together in a dedicated common cause. Such intermingling of the classes of people spilled over into all walks of life. During the post-World War II era these palatial kennels and estates were no longer the norm, and today it is definitely the smaller operation that has evolved as the current home of most American dog show bloodstock.

Today only a small handful of kennels would come close to the pre-World War II country estate life led by American show dogs. A state of the art kennel such as the fabulous grandiose that is Grandeur is an exception to the rule. Established by the incomparable Sunny Shay in 1941, the Grandeur line has been carried on by Roger Rechler in a fashion that does justice to its name.

This modern kennel is located on Long Island and boasts a staff of five under the careful supervision of manager-handler extraordinaire, Michael Canalizo, who works in close cooperation with Rechler in planning the breedings and show careers of the dogs.

The kennel's most well-known early star was the magnificent Ch. Shirkhan of Grandeur, the first Afghan to win Best in Show at Westminster, as well as the first breeder-owner-handled dog of any breed to attain this high honor. This dog not only became the foundation sire for Grandeur but also for any number of outstanding Afghan kennels throughout the country blessed with heavy doses of Shirkhan in their gene pool. Ch. Kabik's The Challenger, also a breeder-owner-handled Westminster Best in Show winner, is credited with bringing the Afghan Hound

Current champions of Grandeur, from left to right, include an absolutely beautiful array of Afghans: Shahadow, Shahkira, Blu Shah, Shahkhan, Shahrp and Shahpphire. (Photo courtesy of Grandeur Kennels)

back into prominence in the early 1980s and has several crosses to Shirkhan. "Pepsi,' as he was fondly called by the fancy, was the product of Chris and Marguerite Terrell's excellent breeding program in Anacortes, Washington.

Shirkhan's major influence was in putting the true houndy look of this exotic Eastern breed on an animal with a square profile and desired definition of hip bones. Four decades later, Afghan fanciers still seek the "Shirkhan" look. With 12 crosses to Shirkhan in his pedigree, Ch. Blu Shah of Grandeur marked the renaissance of the name Grandeur, and in 1995, Ch. Tryst of Grandeur (see color section) became the number one dog all breeds, all systems. By mid-1996, Tryst had broken the All Time BIS winning hound record with well over 130 red, white and blue rosettes to her credit, and still counting. Her many accomplishments include the Westminster Group and three Quaker Oats awards. She is representative of a splendid blood line and an elegant kennel facility that has few if any peers in architectural structure.

Most of America's top dogs today are raised in breeding programs that are relatively small with kennels that accommodate about 20 animals. Kennels of 100 dogs or more are rare indeed. These smaller breeding establishments are often operated by family members as a family-shared activity and/ or by singles and married couples as an activity to take the place of the family unit. Some represent very precious pockets of dedicated dog people who have committed a lifetime to the breeding of pure-bred dogs.

The small kennel concept has its honorable background in the British Isles where historically so many of the great lines and their stars were developed. It is hard to find better "dog people" than the

Proper kennel facilities include adequate security and isolation areas for bitches in season. Such facilities will insure that male dogs are not in close proximity and therefore not unduly thrown off their regular routines. (Cartoon by Mary Jung)

traditional English lady in her tweeds and sensible shoes who knows her stock well and concentrates more on her bloodlines than on show records, or the dedicated terrier man who is horrified at the idea of doing anything that requires electricity to a terrier! The hands of these people are the testimonial to their skill and craftsmanship.

No matter whether your well-bred dogs are housed in lavish kennels or not, the importance of the kenneling is that it be safe, sanitary and comfortable in all seasons and conditions to provide the animals with a secure environment. Good kennel management starts with making sure that all fencing on the perimeters of the property is escape proof and protected against children or workmen or anyone capable of letting an animal loose accidentally. Such fencing must be high enough and strong enough to contain animals on *both* sides of it, as it would be as important to keep large animals away from your toy dogs as to keep the little dogs inside. This perimeter fencing should be buried in the ground to prevent escape by digging out. Safety is part of the dogman's skills, whether it involves checking the fences for a loose piece of wire that could damage an eye or a board in the fence that is weakened, as well as safe latches on gates.

Good animal husbandry must answer these questions: How will bitches in season be maintained separately from dogs? Where will bitches be housed when whelping their litters to protect their sanctity? How will feces be disposed of and sanitation controlled? How will regular, proper disinfecting be accomplished? How will dogs be groomed and prepared for shows?

There are many right ways to do these tasks. The important thing to keep in mind is to adapt your facilities to meet the personal needs of your breed of dogs, the environment in which they are living and your own schedule. You are trying to achieve whatever system works best for you and your situation. Your facilities must work in concert with your attention to detail to provide the ultimate setting for your dogs.

Attention to detail and hard work are the two major ingredients required by an efficient, smooth-working kennel facility. If you are building a kennel from scratch, plan it carefully to avoid making mistakes you will have to live with later. Pay special attention to such things as drains, ventilation, noise control and exercise facilities. For example, I favor more rectangular paddock areas over square ones for they encourage maximum exercise by the dogs. Base decisions on your available acreage.

Many small breeding establishments are not kennels in the true sense of the word. They lack rows of runs and a separate kennel building. Instead, the dogs are moved in and out in sets, taking turns with their kennel mates. Although this involves a great deal of work in moving the dogs, the upside of it is that the dogs receive individual attention several times a day and are not likely to be reduced to human contact only when being fed, watered or sanitized.

In handling your animals on a day-to-day basis, it is vital that you keep in mind that no two animals are alike. Each must be treated as one of a kind at the same time he is one of many. Do not allow the dominant animal to monopolize all of your attention while the more submissive ones get too little of it.

If you need to hire part-time kennel help, you might want to contact local high schools for the names of some promising and responsible teenagers. Make sure such youngsters have a clear picture of your expectations and the needs of your animals, as well as emergency plans and phone numbers. In planning and operating your kennel, the importance of consistency and safeguarding cannot be emphasized too often. Preventive measures can save you heartbreak, money, veterinary bills and, most of all, your animals. While on the subject of veterinary bills, it is absolutely necessary for the success of your breeding program and kennel management to have a competent veterinarian who understands your special needs as a breeder.

It is not the most luxurious kennel or motorhome or the biggest assortment of equipment that makes the quality kennel. Nor is it the number of dogs. It is the quality of the animals that makes the quality kennel. As long as the dogs are housed safely in comfortable, clean, sanitary and secure kennels, they are *well-kenneled*. It's what's in the kennel that counts!

Picking Puppies

Analyzing litters is a somewhat subjective process under the best of circumstances. Your job is to be as objective as possible while doing it. Personally, I like to grade puppies on the ground and running around. It doesn't matter to me if they are in a familiar place or not as there are advantages to both. If at home they are in surroundings they know and will be confident as they play and run around. If in a strange yard or exercise area, the more confident, outgoing puppies will quickly identify themselves.

Although I have known people who have put puppies on the table to begin evaluation, I never do this until I have seen them on the ground. Since your goal in grading a litter is to find the best ones for future potential in the ring and breeding program, you may not have to put all of them on the table. The other end of that goal is to select the least promising in the litter for sale to pet homes. At the same time, you need to allow time to evaluate the ones in the middle who do not readily fall into either category.

> "How beautiful is youth, how bright it gleams with its illusions, aspirations, dreams!"
> —Longfellow

First, observe how the puppy—or puppies—comes out of his crate, his pen or his yard. Keep in mind your initial impression of his assurance, quality, strength, balance and grace. Did you like this puppy at first glance? Do you want to take him home?

Next, watch the puppy from every angle: side profile; length of leg in relationship to length of body; shoulder placement and set on of neck; how he uses himself. If he has some glaring fault—very light eyes or poor tail set—it does not much matter how the rest of him is conformed. If you are picking a show dog, he cannot have things you cannot sell in the ring or characteristics the judges will not accept. Overall balance is essential in a puppy at the "right" age for that breed or that line. Eight weeks of age is a good time to evaluate my line, and I try to sort them before they start changing at 10 weeks.

A lot of good puppies will toe out a little even if the shoulder is laid on correctly and laid back correctly. If the puppy is wide enough in the chest, this will straighten out with age. The fact that the chest will drop and fill in will right this wrong if other things are right. The rear on an Elkhound puppy—I have heard differently from those in other breeds—rarely changes, but fronts will. Toeing in is a different picture, although some puppies grow out of this with exercise and chest development. I am personally wary of puppies that toe in. Disregard the puppy who seems to have both front legs coming out of the same hole.

A litter of Norwegian Elkhound babies at puppy-picking time. (Photo by Joan Ludwig)

Watch the puppy move around the yard, especially from the side. Puppies will sometimes have trouble changing from one gait to another, especially when slowing from a run to a trot or turning sideways. Forgive this in a clumsy, uncoordinated puppy. However, side-gait ability, when the puppy is running free, will not be impaired and will remain rather constant from puppyhood to old age. Fronts coming at you can go through a lot of changes and are a different matter. Standardbred colts trot effortlessly even as youngsters while being ponied. In fact, the straighter-fronted quarter horses ponying them have to canter to keep up. The same seems to be true in dogs. If they move effortlessly from the side as babies, they always will.

Puppies that experience unsound movement or tenderness in their ability to take stress or exercise do not grow out of it—in my experience. *Avoid making too many allowances for your puppies or you will spend your life trying to adjust to their shortcomings.* You are looking for a well-constructed baby version of the athlete—supple, light on his feet for a "growthy" youngster, aggressive, outgoing, confident, and showing youthful coordination.

Avoid big, overdone puppies that are excessively clumsy, overly boned, and heavy footed. This does not mean to eliminate a large puppy that is right. But make sure you are picking him for right and not just for large. Sometimes very large dogs get their size because they are poorly conformed. Breeders of giant breeds have to be alert to this problem. A tall, leggy puppy, well put together, is a find in my breed—and in a number of other breeds in which the standard calls for a square animal.

If the puppy has a lot of angulation, excuse his inability to control himself more than you would a puppy with straighter angles, as he has to grow into handling the angulation. Sometimes this puppy will appear cowhocked standing. Nothing in the world has more potential than a leggy, short-loined puppy that is well angled and also coordinated. Such a puppy will be true both moving and standing.

Cowhocks are less objectionable to me on very angulated youngsters who straighten them out when they move. In fact, in judging my adults, I can live with a slightly cowhocked look *standing* on a well-angled dog *if* it moves with no look of cowhocks. *Totally unacceptable* to me on both puppies and adults are straight stifled, poorly angulated rears that are also cowhocked. They are pets. In a perfect world, only cows would have cowhocks. In trying to achieve perfect animals from imperfect parents, these are some of the allowances I make in picking puppies.

Everything is relative—not just cowhocks. Take the subject of size—and I am not just talking big. A superbly well-balanced puppy may look smaller than the others—though in fact he is not. Beware of thinking a good puppy is too small until you have actually taken measurements and compared him with his brethren. For many years, I kept exact measurements on puppies and followed them through adulthood. Some of the smaller ones were always small; some of the bigger ones were always big; but many of them do not categorize themselves. Sometimes the larger puppies get their impressive size because they were poorly formed, a fact that becomes more evident as they grow and mature.

Some puppies, and adults, too, for that matter, will appear smaller than they are because they are in perfect balance. Vagabond was such a dog. Even though he measured 20 ¾ inches, he did not look that big. Other dogs with great carriage and length of neck will appear larger than life. Some of these dogs will amaze you when you measure or weigh them. Bombardier was such a dog. He looked bigger than all outdoors but measured 21 3/4 inches and weighed 57 pounds.

Ch. Vin-Melca's Bombardier looked gigantic but, thanks to his well-laid-back shoulders, measured exactly 21¾ inches. Carriage and length of neck contributed to "his look." (Photo by Steve Ross)

Back to size for a moment—even though you know a line well and have worked with it for years, animals will come along from time to time that fool you. The Smuggler dog was such a dog. As an eight-week-old puppy he was quite lovely—square, up on leg and well balanced. In the 6-9 puppy class against his brother, Buckpasser, he looked squatty and dumpy compared to Bucky's leggier, more correct hunting-type look. By the time he was a year old, he had come up on leg and was a magnificent youngster who then matured into one of my all-time favorite dogs. Patience and puppies go together! Even the glorious King Salmon starts out as a small fry.

When you pick your puppies for leg length in a square breed, there are two things to keep in mind. Yes, you want that high on leg, short-loined puppy, but make certain that the *leggy* look is achieved by correct structure and not open angles. Put the puppy on the table with someone to assist you in keeping him still. Place a finger from your right hand at the top of the shoulder blade, find the point of the shoulder with your left index finger, and extend your left thumb to the elbow. If you get close to a 90 degree angle at the shoulder point with the elbow well back under the blade, you know your leggy puppy is truly leggy—not straight angled. If you select for the obliquely placed shoulder that extends far into the back, it will make a good back appear even shorter.

Puppies spend the early months of their lives growing up and the rest of their lives growing around and down. Although, if you catch them right at eight weeks, you can pretty well get the silhouette they will grow back to later; after that, they will shoot up and look ungainly and coltlike during different growth spurts. Many times over the years, I have seen breeders make the mistake of selling puppies that appeared gawky to keep the ones that looked like miniature Elkhounds. Later, the ugly duckling fable came true and, alas, the good ones got away.

In judging puppy rears, look for hocks low to the ground with width across the beam—from hipbone to hipbone. Look for ease of handling that rear. An important part of that picture as you look at the puppy in a square breed is the distance between the front and the rear, i.e., is the puppy short across the top?

Over the years, I have heard many breeders and experts say they pick them when they're wet. About the only thing I look for, other than the good health of a newborn or obvious mismarks, is if the shoulder blades tilt toward the tail and the closeness of the blades to the tail. The next thing to study is if the neck in front of the desired short back is of good length.

If a puppy has the right angles at each end, with well-placed shoulders, is short of back with good length and rise of neck, it should be well-coordinated and athletic. If the back is short and the neck is also short, you will have a "stuffed" look to the puppy and it will lack the basic athletic ability of the aforementioned one. Correct back length and coupling, accompanied by correct angles, usually ensure a good topline.

Evaluating heads is a breed-specific matter. The best-headed Cocker Spaniel puppy will have a very domed head at birth as well as at eight weeks. The Norwegian Elkhound head must have a relatively flat skull with adequate width between the ears. There must be plenty of fill under a very dark, oval-shaped eye. If the puppy eye is still somewhat blue, wait until the eye is totally brown before evaluating it, and then do it in the sun. Some feel that the eyes of their breeds darken with age, but this is not true of Elkhounds. In my personal experience I have never seen light eyes darken. Brittany fanciers tell me the eyes of their puppies will darken well into adulthood, as can those of other "self-colored" breeds.

By eight weeks, the ears should be showing some mobility toward coming up, although larger-boned, heavier puppies will be slower. Some of these puppies will not get total control of the ear until they are several months old and have been through the teething stage, but you can get a handle on it at a much earlier age. If the ears are just hanging houndlike and not starting to come up some at the set on, you could be in trouble.

You should perfunctorily check the bite. The best puppy bite in my line is one that appears slightly overshot, as the lower jaw continues to grow. Puppies with a perfect scissors bite—or worse, a level bite—indeed bear watching. I have never seen an undershot baby Elkhound puppy. In discussing this problem with breeders of other breeds, most agree that puppies with undershot jaws rarely straighten out. Nonetheless, this is a breed-specific matter and you should make sure you have done your homework before you bet the farm on the puppy you select.

In evaluating the head, the entire look must be one of great quality in a puppy face—intelligent, and curious. The males must be masculine and the bitches feminine.

A 7-week-old Vin-Melca Norwegian Elkhound puppy showing a wedge-shaped head with a flat skull and correct fill under the eye. The puppy ears are showing mobility and signs of "coming up," especially the left ear. It is a correct and intelligent "puppy" expression. (House Photo)

Another important part of the look of breed type along with the head is the tail. In fact, the look starting from the head, down the neck, and across the back to the tail is a vital part of the picture of breed type.

The Elkhound has a flat croup with a high-set, curled tail. These tails are active right from the beginning. Nursing puppies wag them and use them in their scramble to the nipples. As the puppy starts to walk around, the tail starts to curl. At eight weeks, the puppy tail will be about what it will be at maturity. Tails can do some strange things, along with ears, when the puppy is stressed during teething or illness. However, if the tail is good at eight weeks, it will be good later. Loosely curled tails have a chance to make it *if* they are set on high. Learn the correct tail set for your breed well enough to evaluate the puppies at the age when you are picking them.

Color and coat texture are also breed-specific traits that complete the picture. Elkhounds are born black, and if you do not know this with your first litter, you may worry unnecessarily that the neighbor's black Labrador Retriever got over the fence! They start to silver-in while still in the nest and, by eight weeks, will exhibit a baby version—more or less—of what their color will be. Their legs will be clean with only a little sootiness at the knees and their undercoat will not show any yellow or brown. Enjoy! For in a few weeks they will turn beige all over, and you will now worry if it was the yellow Lab instead who did the dirty deed.

Stay tuned, for your patience will soon be rewarded by the appearance of black guard hairs forming a saddle and protective puppy coat, gray undercoat, and correct harness markings. The Labradors behaved themselves after all, and all is well with your Elkhound litter. Nonetheless, these constant changes on Elkhound puppies contribute to difficulties determining what the eventual mature coat will be. If you are fortunate to have a flat, smooth-lying puppy coat, you need never be concerned. That puppy will grow up to have the correct Elkhound coat—with a desirable harsh outercoat for weather resistance and a softer undercoat for warmth.

The typical fluffy puppy coat can go either way on the adult. In evaluating this puppy coat, you must factor in strongly the coats of the parents and grandparents. If they have the correct coats, in all probability your puppy will lose his fluff at the appropriate time in his life and grow a correct coat. This is an area of grave concern in this breed. Far too many Elkhounds are open-coated with the accompanying problem of all one kind of coat and sometimes all one color all over. The correct Elkhound coat must show contrast to differentiate guard hair from undercoat.

Once you have made your decision at the crucial eight-weeks stage, realize that the puppies will go through a lot of changes as they grow. Be patient and give them the opportunity to grow into themselves. Don't expect them to look like perfect miniatures. Make sure you are not picking the puppies when they are too fat, as some faults (long loin for example) will be minimized with weight. Above all, do not get so caught up in details that you miss the whole. Take it from an aspiring judge, that also can happen to you from the other side of the badge if you're not careful.

Will you make mistakes no matter how expert you are? Indeed you will. Two dogs that I "missed" were just too much for me at the eight-week selection age. My choices usually run to the slower developing, balanced-type puppy. Such a puppy is not plush or awesome. The first one I missed was Howdy Rowdy who ended up with me because Dr. John and my good friend, Gladys Tangen, loved this puppy and felt he had a future. They were right! The second one was Bombardier, who was the favorite of Joe Sealy, a young man who was working for me at the time. Since I needed good help to care for the dogs, I kept "Joe's puppy" for him. Gladys had been in Elkhounds a lot of years, so for her to outguess me was one thing. For Joe, who was totally new to dogs and was enjoying his first experience with a litter, to outguess me was something else. The message is clear, sometimes the good ones get away. You might want to track your dogs later to see how they grow up so it can assist you in reducing your mistakes in grading future litters. Many breeders seem perpetually concerned about the possible dilemma of letting the best puppy get away. "What if I lose the best one?" you hear them say. What's worse than breeding a great one and letting it get away? Breeding a poor one and keeping it.

Your learning will continue to occur in the grading of stock just as in everything else associated with breeding dogs. The following story is an indication of one of the many ways this happens:

> More than two decades ago, a young couple living in an area remote from other breeders purchased a compatible breeding pair from me. After several years spent advising them via letters, commentary on pictures and film and endless hours of long distance calls, it was with great anticipation that I made my first visit to compare the resulting progeny with their first cousins at home in California. Imagine my surprise when the two animals presented to me out of the excellent dam and sire I had sent them bore little resemblance to their close relatives in Carmel.

> The mystery was solved the next day when a gathering of the couple's newly formed circle of first-time Elkhound owners provided the answers. The four animals they had sold as pets were extraordinary two-year olds while the two they had kept were anything but. In spite of all attempts to advise them from afar, they had chosen "cutesy little puppies" that grew up to be "cutesy adults" and had sold what they considered the "ugly ducklings" of the litter for pets.

> Our mutual lesson was a reminder to avoid perfect miniatures. People buy their animals and start a breeding program and the original breeder, the *master breeder*, hardly

recognizes his own dogs in just a few generations. The explanation for the resulting animals to stray so far from the original source has to do with the selection procedure.

Getting back to the matter of picking puppies, the aforementioned criteria would work as a basic starting point for anyone breeding a square dog, which many breeds are. Then breed specific characteristics must be adjusted to suit the dictates of the given breed. This is where your mentors will serve you well, for no one in the world knows how to pick puppies in the breed as well as the breed experts. Keeping this in mind, here are a few puppy-picking pointers from some *master breeders*.

The Experts Tell You How

Charlotte Patterson also works with a square breed, the Pug. Her fabulous line of **Ivanwold Pugs** has long held its own in the strongest of competition including Westminster, national specialties, and all-breed competitions. Charlotte uses a system she considers gradual in selecting her puppies.

Obvious pets she can spot at birth. Since Pugs are a "head" breed, as soon as all her puppies are

A correct Ivanwold Pug head at two months of age before the puppy fat sets in to create optical illusions. If one drops an invisible vertical line through the middle of the head and a horizontal one across the bridge of the nose and through the center of the eye, it will divide the head into four equal quarters. Although the longer ear of the puppy may not have the tip at the line, in the mature Pug the tip of the ear will be at that line. Note the strongly boned legs, good feet and dark black mask and ears. The correct Pug has a round head on a square body. (Photo courtesy of Charlotte Patterson)

delivered and pronounced in good health, she feels the bone structure of their heads by placing her hand around the head. When the puppies are up on their feet at six weeks or so, she starts evaluating to make sure the "right things are in the right place." For Charlotte, this means evaluating body structure, legs, and tail set. This is a good time to re-evaluate heads with the focus on underjaw. She warns if you wait too long to grade the heads, the puppies will accumulate puppy fat that may create some optical illusions.

By the time the puppies are five months of age, Charlotte has pretty well decided on her choices. The ultimate in a Pug head is one that divides into four quarters. This perfect division is achieved by an invisible vertical line down the middle of the face with an invisible horizontal line dividing it equally across the bridge of the nose and through the center of the eye.

In the mature dog, the tip of the ear is right at that line, but in a puppy the ear is a little longer. The upper lip will line up sideways in a simulated smile on this correct head. It is an affidavit that the puppy has adequate underjaw and chin to accommodate his broad, wrinkled skull.

Carroll Gordon Diaz began breeding her **Page Mill Beagles** in the 1950s. Since Carroll breeds only one or two litters a year, she prefers to raise her puppies for several months before making her final selection. She begins her in-depth preliminary evaluation at eight weeks.

Carroll looks for round bone and no sign of a

Beagle puppies from the cooperative breeding program of Manahound and Loverly. Their grandsire was Australian Ch. Manahound Matchpoints. Note the soft pleading expression and correct Beagle muzzle. The puppy on the left in the wagon was Best of Variety at the National Specialty Sweepstakes in 1991, Ch. Loverly Dancing Lady. (Photo courtesy of Liz Rosbach, Jerry Vavra Photography)

crooked front. Early on she observes length of neck in relation to back, wanting the former long and the latter short. She looks for width across the rear and good angles to accompany it.

Then she proceeds in her grading process by comparing her puppies in an elimination contest. By eight weeks she gets a good impression of the puppy's head and ear set as well as eye and correct soft expression.

Because Beagles can produce either 13-inch or 15-inch animals in the same litter, her eye is always tuned to search for the dream come true, a little male who will stay under 13 inches, as it is usually the bitches that qualify. Over the years, she has disciplined herself to keep only an exceptional dog puppy.

She cautions newcomers against too much emphasis on markings. "Some very good ones can be missed in the search for flashy markings."

When **Myrtle Klensch, Salutaire Manchester Terriers,** told me it depended on whether it was a toy or a standard and then if the breeding was mixed toy-standard breeding as to what age she preferred to select, it surprised me. She does make her first grading at eight weeks for color and black thumbprints and her final selection at three months for standards and at four months for toys.

The eight-week grading finds her avoiding too much thumbprint, for it can be overdone as the leg blackens. Although she doesn't believe in a lot of mixing of toy and standard breeding with the Salutaire Manchesters, she laughs about the fact that the top winner, Ch. Salutaire Surely You Jest C.D. (Jessie) was from such a cross. Because the fronts on the toys are so "iffy," Myrtle likes to wait until they are four months to make her final selection. Three months of age works for the standards. She selects for the overall look, and is careful to avoid coarse heads and light eyes.

Florence Males is another breeder who has found eight weeks the best age at which to grade litters from her **Weeblu Silky Terriers.** She looks for temperament and personality while observing the puppies running free. This gives her an opportunity to evaluate outline from head carriage to tail carriage as well as the best overall picture.

Her breed specific criteria include these attributes:

Puppy picking personified in the form of BIS Ch. Weeblu's Trailblazer of Don-El ROMX, the stud-fee puppy selected by Silky Terrier breeder Florence Males from a litter sired by her well-known BIS winner Ch. Weeblu's Blaze of Joy ROMX. Even at eight weeks of age, Trailblazer exhibited great carriage and strength of character in his well-balanced baby form. Coat texture and head to come at maturity were already showing promise, as was a strong youthful topline. *Master breeders* develop such puppy selection skills, as evidenced by Florence's choice, as they progress in their breed. (Jayne Langdon Photo)

1) A puppy coat that shines, for it is indicative of the correct texture at maturity. One word of caution is to avoid bathing the puppy before selection so it will have its natural sheen.

2) Good tan to go with whatever blue the puppy will be. Without the texture, you have no *silky*. Without the tan, you have no *terrier*. Secondary choices include eye shape and ear set. Ch. Weeblu Blaze of Joy was a dominant sire selected from such breeding methods and the start of three consecutive generations of BIS Silky Terriers.

Dr. Jacklyn Hungerland agrees with one of my idols, the late Beatrice Godsol, that you can pick them when they're still wet. Jacky provided a chuckle when she related the story of coming home after a new litter of her **DeRussy Standard Poodles** was already dry and finding herself unable to form any opinions!

Jacky's Standard Poodles have been famous for decades. In 1969, Frank Sabella handled Ch. DeRussy's Lollypop to Number One Dog All Breeds for owners Frank and Susan Dale. Jacky evaluates the newborn puppy for overall balance and head while it is still wet. "The head should be shaped like a shoe box," she shared. She assesses each puppy for bone and breed character, zeroing in on its angles. "You can see every angle when they're wet."

Once the little babies get on their feet, their mistress starts looking for exaggeration all over. The biggest mistake newcomers make in her breed is looking for the finished product in an eight-week-old.

Longtime **Rose Farm Dachshund** breeder **Dee Hutchinson** watches her growing puppies carefully while they are running around and playing. As she sees something in a particular puppy that does not satisfy her demanding criteria for show and breeding stock, she makes that puppy available to a pet home. She doesn't make any final decisions until the puppies are about 12 weeks of age.

Hutchinson insists on good temperament and general soundness in her stock. While grading a litter she looks for overall balance of the picture that she wants. To achieve this look the puppy must have good upper arm and front assembly as well as a short loin.

Perhaps it is because the breeding of Dachshunds requires in-depth knowledge of front assembly that accounts for the fact that some of our best judges such as Dee come from their ranks. If you are trying to learn more about the oft-misunderstood front assembly, a Dachshund expert can help you pick puppies as well as help you become more educated in appreciating their structure.

Lois Thomasson exemplifies the "unsung-hero" breeder who has maintained a select gene pool over decades while keeping a relatively low profile. Yet her **Fleetwind Irish Wolfhound** breeding program has produced more than 60 champions and has served as resource breeding stock for other kennels whose extensive campaigns and wins give them a high profile. I hold such people as Lois in the highest esteem.

Ten-week-old Irish Wolfhound puppies bred by Fleetwind Kennels. Notice the bone and substance, length of legs and tail along with the scope of body. Also important is the breadth and shape of the muzzle and skull. (Photo courtesy of Lois Thomasson)

Lois Thomasson's Fleetwind Irish Wolfhounds are based on the work of Mrs. Alma Starbuck, her mentor. Here is an Irish Wolfhound of the 1930s from that line. Ch. Macushla of Ambleside, shows the excellent type that is still appreciated today. (Photo courtesy of American Kennel Club)

Indeed, the size of the Irish Wolfhound and the size of the litters prohibit a breeder from raising all of the puppies. As Lois says, "You simply cannot run them all on." So she tries to start sorting them out in earnest by 10 weeks and get them into their new homes by three months of age.

When they are 10 weeks, she is very keen on their frame and outline and the accompanying bone. Though the youngsters may not have tuck up, which will come later, they will have outline and range. "A tall drink of water" is how she describes these unfinished youngsters who have lots of room for growth. Thomasson does not want her Wolfhound puppies to be compact or cobby under any circumstances. She prefers them to cover a lot of ground and have both long bodies and long tails to give a lion-like impression.

Although the six-week-old puppy has a cute face, by nine to ten weeks the muzzle begins to lengthen and will continue to do so as the youngster grows. The upper jaw develops much more rapidly than the underjaw so breeders must not be alarmed if the young puppy is somewhat overshot as this will correct later. Lois likes to put her hand around the foreface to check it for length and strength. She looks for clean lines, level planes with little stop (but more than a Deerhound) and with length to the head, which is the index of the breed.

She eliminates any with undershot mouths or those who are undersized for their age. "In our breed they don't catch up if they are small at three months."

Although fuzzy puppies may be precious, Lois cautions the aspiring Wolfhound breeder to select for hard puppy coats or even *no* coat over the cute fuzzy ones, as they come into correct harsh coat later. Most of all, she wants the puppy to look and act like the potential hunter-companion it was bred to be.

Bull Terriers are a difficult breed to grade as puppies, and even such great breeders as Raymond Oppenheimer himself could make mistakes in missing a good one, according to Oppenheimer's well-known disciple, **David C. Merriam, Broadside Bull Terriers.** The master of the magnificent Ormandy line of Bull Terriers in England, Oppenheimer served as the absolute in mentors for this breed for five decades before his death in 1984. We are indebted to David for sharing some of his wisdom with us.

The first serious look at the litter would come at about six weeks, when you would study to find the rectangular full head that promises to mature into the ultimate of this "head breed." Although you could not have any degree of certainty that you were right on the good ones, you would certainly be able to eliminate those with weak and snipey heads.

Just how unique is the head of the Bull Terrier is answered in this picture of a newborn nestling in an incubator while his dam delivers the next whelp. Notice the incredible amount of substance to the head in front of the eye—the fill, breadth and strength. (Photo courtesy of David Merriam)

After you have eliminated these obvious pets (and Bull Terriers do make wonderful pets for the discerning owner), you must now raise your puppies until you can feel secure about their mouths. Merriam relates that mouths are a controversial subject, for it is very difficult to get the correct head and correct mouth in the same dog. Although a scissors or level bite is preferred, breeders are sometimes forced to deal with a reverse scissors. They are not forgiving of a mouth that is off more than that. Youngsters with level mouths may end up in a reverse scissors later, and breeders must guard against this. Like all other breeders, Bull Terrier breeders have to make trade-offs to get the traits they desire, especially the unusual head.

Although the front view fullness of the basic egg-shaped head may not change much as the puppy matures, the correct profile can come on and mature into the desired Roman finish. Look for eye placement that exhibits more foreface in front of it than skull behind it, which also contributes to the Roman finish. Such a triangular and piercing eye will have the "varminty" look so identified with the breed.

Once the puppy has been evaluated for head, eye, and Bull Terrier-essence of type, running gear and strength of topline are brought into the equation. To complete the picture, the ideal puppy will be off square with good strong bone and a marked air of confidence.

A pair of closely related Wolfpit Cairn Terrier youngsters with typical correct heads that will grow furnishings as they mature. Although one is a light silver with dark points and the other a dark brindle, the make and shape of the heads is the same. (Photo by Marjorie Shoemaker)

Lydia Hutchinson is one of the terrier greats in the United States today. It has been 48 years since a 10-year-old girl and her parents started showing their first Cairn Terrier, a grandson of their original bitch. Together, this family has owned and/or bred some of the breed's greats—producers, show dogs, and well-adjusted family animals. Her dedication to her own breed, to terriers, and to dogs in general is well-recognized by an appreciative dog fancy. For **Lydia Hutchinson** of **Wolfpit Cairn Terriers** is one of those rare ones— *a dog person's dogwoman.*

Lydia likes to select her puppies between 10 and 12 weeks of age, as before that their movements and temperaments are not as predictable. At this point, she starts picking those that go to pet homes because of obvious conformational defects that will in no way affect their ability to be super family dogs. She cites a recent cowhocked puppy that went to a pet home because this is "not common in the breed" and she was not of a mind to open the door to it.

Hutchinson's bottom line in her breeding program is structure that produces the soundness so necessary to a working terrier. Therefore, she places a high priority on an animal with a hard weather-resistant coat and a confident attitude. She wants the expression to be alert and sparkling, mischievous but not evil or mean.

In assessing puppy heads, Lydia looks for a good stop where your thumb fits nicely and a muzzle that is slightly shorter than the skull. She warns newcomers to the breed that puppy muzzles and skulls can broaden as they mature, so don't discard a good one because he seems a little narrow in the head. However, he *must* have the correct head profile showing the muzzle length to skull as four is to five with the decided stop. Although the Cairn has a foxy expression, the head is actually shaped considerably more rounded than that of the fox and should not have a snipy muzzle.

The set-on of the tail is important to the look of the breed, and Lydia warns that the actual carriage of the tail can go through some interesting changes while the puppies are teething, but eventually should come back to its correct 12 o'clock toward one o'clock carriage if it is set correctly. Lydia emphasizes the message often heard from *master breeders*—allow puppies to go through the gawkies as your patience will be rewarded later.

The breed's All Time Top Sire was her parents' dog, Ch. Cairnwood's Quince, with 51 champions. His double great-grandson recently tied the record. Lydia's family is now 17 generations away from the original dog with well over 120 champions from this small-but-select breeding program. Today's standard-bearer for the kennel is Ch. Caledonian Berry of Wolfpit, a back-to-back BIS winner and the breed's all-time record holder of specialty wins. Already the sire of 13 champions, he is well on his way to recognition as a producer and will no doubt give Lydia a number of opportunities to put her puppy-picking skills to the ultimate test.

Betty-Anne Stenmark, King's Mtn. Dandie Dinmonts, evaluates width of skull on her newborns and length of body then begins the gradual grading of her litters that allows her to determine pet quality by eight to eleven weeks of age. Sorting out the best show prospects is a slower more arduous task.

Puppies that appeal to Betty-Anne are the streamlined ones with the "arrow" look that will grow into the low-stationed, long-bodied adults blessed with the correct graceful curvature of silhouette. The highest point of the arch over the loin is in the middle of the loin, curving slightly downward toward the low point of the shoulders in front of the arch and sloping slightly downward toward the set-on of the tail behind the arch. This is a similar topline to that of the Borzoi, and in the Dandie Dinmont does not always stabilize to its permanent form until adulthood.

Following all of the *master breeder's* criteria for picking a Dandie Dinmont Terrier puppy resulted in the selection of King's Mtn. Montizard Edition at age six months by Betty-Anne Stenmark, who co-bred with Douglas Young. At this age the puppy has met his breeder's exacting standards for a show prospect and appears ready to test her decision-making abilities in the puppy classes. (Photo courtesy of Betty-Anne Stenmark)

Another factor that complicates the grading of puppies concerns the desired length, *twice* as long as tall, less one to two inches. Since this measurement is taken in this breed from the *top* of the shoulder blade to the set-on of the tail (rather than from the *point* of the shoulder), this is a very long dog indeed. Betty-Anne says that in grading puppies one has to hope that the choice of a puppy with great length of body will be one that remains low to the ground with the desired "weasly" outline, hallmark of the breed. Like breeders of other achondroplastic breeds, Stenmark places great emphasis on the correct front with the correctly laid back shoulders matched by upper-arm angulation and elbows close to the body. She defines the "wrap-around front" that allows the forearm to support the weight of the body as typical of achondroplastic breeds. Betty-Anne also emphasizes that terriers with so-called "terrier fronts" are the long-legged ones, not the short-legged ones.

In evaluating heads, she wants one that "fills the hand" and meets the required square skull created by measurements that are about the same from ear to ear as they are from stop to occiput. As Dandie breeders have worked hard in recent years to achieve the ideal blocky head, with muzzle to skull proportion of 3:5 (as viewed from the profile), they have had to pay more attention to bites. Betty-Anne wants her puppies to be a little overshot at a young age, as this accommodates the continued growth of the underjaws as they mature.

Since she has known bites in her breed that were perfect with the correct scissors at five and one-half months (adult teeth) to become even at six months and then go undershot to a reverse scissors at six and one-half months, this very conscientious breeder does not let her show prospects go to their new homes until they are past this age and the bite is definitely acceptable.

Betty-Anne wants her breed to be practical for family ownership as well as for the work it was bred to do and warns that a profusely coated puppy becomes a difficult adult to groom. If the dog has the correct double-coated mixture of hard coat and soft hair, the average owner should be able to care for it utilizing regular plucking and grooming. The silky topknot and ears with softer hair complete the picture of the natural look.

The Dandie Dinmont is a breed that requires "an alpha owner with a soft touch" and Betty-Anne wants her puppies to be house dogs getting all the right "vibes" from their owners to develop fun, show dog temperaments. They must be willing to condition the animals so that they are lean and athletic, allowing them to mature into their full potential. *Master breeders* are as selective about potential owners of their dogs as they are about their breeding stock!

Tommy Oelschlager, Kontoki Siberian Huskies, likes to pick puppies running on their own at nine weeks. His eye is drawn to the one that is the smoothest and most agile. Like many of the best breeders, Tommy believes puppies come back later to the movement they displayed at that early age.

Tommy's line is built upon that of the outstanding breeders, Kathleen Kanzler and Anna Mae Forsberg. I always considered Anna Mae a personal loss to the Norwegian Elkhound breed, as her parents, Ragnar and Ingrid Forsberg, were Norwegian Elkhound fanciers and her kennel name, Savdajaure, reflects her Norwegian ancestry.

Two important dogs that Tommy linebred to were Ch. Innisfree's Pegasus as well as the Westminster BIS winner, Ch. Innisfree's Sierra Cinnar, all-time top sire. His Ch. Kontoki's One Mo' Time was not only from this line but clicked with it too.

While Tommy evaluates puppies for overall soundness, character and athleticism, he also emphasizes the elements that give the animal its Arctic look. These features are an absolute *must* and include the obliquely set eye and a small, high-set ear. Furthermore, he prefers the puppies have too little coat than too much, as the latter is a sure sign of the undesirable open coat to come.

Tommy Oelschlager and a typical Kontoki Siberian Husky puppy exhibiting the Arctic features of eye, ear and expression so vital to the breed. *Master breeders* combine the fine art of selecting for the ultimate in breed type with the exacting science of breeding for the correct structure to carry that type at work. (Photo courtesy of Kontoki Kennels)

Tommy looks first and last for those qualities that would enable the animal at adulthood to do that job for which it was bred. This is how he selected the most recent star, Ch. Kontoki's E.I.E.I.O. (Donald) who is now the winner of 60 All Breed BISs—a new record for the breed! This all-breed winner sports four crosses to the breed's all-time winning specialty dog, Ch. Kontoki's Natural Sinner.

Connie Gerstner (Miller) was extremely fortunate to have an advisor in her original breed, *Alaskan Malamutes,* who helped her acquire exceptional skills in selecting puppies—skills that apply to the *Golden Retriever,* the breed with which she would soar to such stardom as winning the Sporting Group at the American Kennel Club Centennial show in 1984. So attached was Connie to both of her breeds that she combined their names to achieve the kennel name of **Malagold.**

Connie checks each newborn Golden for a certain feel of heftiness and solidity. When the litter is all on the ground and the puppies are dry, she checks for the breadth of head and muzzle. She feels that this examination is most productive when the puppy is on its back, for that is the view best suited to her process. Gerstner checks her puppies on their backs during their growing stage for a second reason, that of ascertaining temperament and strength of character.

At five weeks, she starts pairing puppies off and comparing them, picking one with which to compare the next one, and so on. By seven to eight weeks of age, she evaluates their movement, assesses toplines and notices how they handle themselves. This study includes angulation and structure.

She avoids fluffy puppies and selects for rough coats that will grow into the correct Golden Retriever for field work as well as the conformation ring. She is wary of the shiny coat as it will be too soft and lack undercoat. She avoids puppies that are too narrow all over and especially in the head. This narrow look is sometimes accompanied by a head that is too pointed at the skull. Connie laughs that growing Golden puppies sometimes will seem wrinkled far beyond their age but, in time, the head will broaden and fill in the wrinkles.

Artist Katie Ropar, of Cincinnati, Ohio, has produced this exceptional work demonstrating Connie Gerstner's method of handling a baby Golden Retriever during the evaluation and selection process. (Courtesy of the artist, from her collection of Golden Retriever paintings)

Using these methods of picking puppies long distance helped breeder Cheryl Blair select Ch. Libra Malagold's Coriander (see color section) from a litter sired by Connie's Ch. Malagold's Summer Chant. Unable to grade the litter herself due to a scheduling conflict, Connie consulted with Cheryl by phone to arrive at the choice of this puppy who became a multi-BIS winner. Coriander was E.W. Tipton's choice as the winner of the Sporting Group blue rosette at the American Kennel Club's Centennial Show in Philadelphia in 1984. Selected as a Hall of Fame showdog and sire by the Parent Club, he was the National Specialty winner from the Veterans Class at the age of nine.

The ideal Golden Retriever is a multi-purpose, strong, working animal that is also a marvelous companion. Gerstner keeps such ideals foremost in all of her selection processes, whether in the choice of dams and sires or in the selection of puppies. It is no wonder this *master breeder* is held in such high esteem by her fellow Golden Retriever breeders.

Summary: Sometimes breeders find themselves in the unenviable position of having sold dogs for pets that later turn out better than the ones kept to show. Apart from the obvious cause of simply missing a good one there are two reasons for this dilemma. The first reason is associated with a lack of attitude and confidence on the puppies kept by the breeder while the ones sold as pets have plenty of show personality. This means more concentration is needed on socializing puppies, and they are getting a better show environment in their pet homes than you are providing for the ones you kept to show.

The second reason for missing your best puppies on a regular basis and having them end up in pet homes has to do with mistakes in your selection process. Perhaps you're picking the most plush and need to heed the advice of experts who say that too little coat is better than too much. Perhaps you're trying to find the perfect miniature in your baby puppies and haven't allowed them in your mind to go through the awkward leggy stage. This is especially likely to happen in a medium-size or larger breed that should be square. Have you ever looked at the pictures of some of the world class athletes when they were age 13?

It is important in selecting puppies to know when to be forgiving. If a puppy with exceptionally well-constructed neck and shoulders and correct return of upper arm is let go because he is a tad high in rear at selection time, a crucial mistake could have been made for that puppy could very well "let down" in the rear later and correct his topline! The breeder has to develop a feel or willingness to accept what appears to be a fault in a puppy in order to keep the animal with the desired virtues. Learning what allowances to make so that your pets don't routinely end up better than those you keep is part of the *master breeder*'s expertise.

Ours is a society based on instant gratification. Yet in the area of picking puppies, success is based on delayed gratification. Heed the words of the great Greek orator, Pericles: "Wait for the wisest of all counselors, Time."

Raising Puppies

It is time to remind you that there are many behavior experts out there who have much more validated information and knowledge on the subject of raising puppies than I. This effort is not in the same world as theirs, and their works should be required reading before you ever consider breeding a litter. Other required reading should include some of the results of surveys such as that conducted by Linda Johnson, a Vermont breeder of Rottweilers, reported in the *American Kennel Gazette* (February 1987).

Linda's survey encompassed approximately 25 breeds and questioned breeders' financial investments in their litters. The survey factored in a number of variables, including number of hours spent with the animals as well as all investment in the costs of the litter. Her survey produced an overall picture stating that it costs the dedicated breeder about 2,500 dollars to raise a litter after all income on puppy sales is factored in. So, if the breeder keeps one puppy from the litter it is worth approximately 2,500 dollars. Indeed, the raising of quality puppies is anything but profitable. Linda pointed out that her survey was not meant to discourage new breeders for they are needed to perpetuate the good of breeds in the future. "However, it is imperative that they be educated and prepared for what lies ahead of them."

Once you get a litter on the ground and the contented dam is quietly caring for them, you get a few days' respite. But soon you must start handling the infants to accustom them to human contact. This imprints trust in people and begins socialization right from the start. Start feeding them very early from your fingers, even though the dam has plenty of milk. This emphasizes the bonding process with people. I turn them on their backs and stroke their tummies right from the start. Dogs that grow up to be show dogs are going to be handled by any number of people in their lifetimes, so the sooner they develop total confidence in people, the better. The more natural you can make things seem to the babies as they grow, the more confidence they will have both in the show ring and in pet homes.

Leash breaking of puppies can be facilitated by starting them early on a thin lead while walking their dam on another lead. The puppy naturally follows its mother and is rewarded with nursing time-outs. Such sessions soon result in lead-broken puppies that were never traumatized. The leash becomes a natural thing associated with nurturing.

Just as important early on is getting the puppies accustomed to their crates and helping them identify the crate as a safe haven. Putting them in crates in vehicles at an early age, taking them to schools or parks or other areas where people will handle them and other similar activities is a positive learning experience that will pay off later. My personal belief is that the time you spend with them as little babies reduces your work later. Usually puppies who are accustomed to being in vehicles from the beginning will not fall victim to car sickness as adults.

Placing the puppies on tables and standing them, even if you have to hold them up, is a good practice to start early. Stroking and gentle brushing is a pleasant experience for them. Hold them in your lap while you watch television and handle them at every opportunity to get a jump start on their education. To accustom them to traffic, walk them early on beside an older, confident and calm dog so that they can imitate its behavior. Spend time working with each puppy early because a puppy is most impressionable from the time it opens its eyes until it is about 16 weeks of age—five minutes now is

Puppy Sweepstakes winner Nordic's Viking of Kee Note at the Nor-Cal Keeshond Club, September 1980, handled by his breeder-owner Rondi Tyler, who co-owned with Carl Tyler. After the author completed the assignment, Keeshond fanciers teased her about selecting a Dutch dog with a Norwegian name. (Callea Photo)

worth an hour later. So take them with you whenever and wherever you can. This early work will increase their ability to achieve the ultimate in their genetic potential because it is true quality time.

Although you want lots of exposure and handling of the puppies right from the beginning, do not interpret that to mean overtraining. The main idea of all this exposure is to develop a confident and trusting puppy, not a well-trained mechanized baby show dog. Puppies, like children, need to enjoy their youth. They benefit from game playing and horsing around just as children do. And the breeder also benefits from watching their game playing and enjoying it. Not only is it fun, but it helps sort your puppies. You do not get much else done when you have a litter, but if you are a true dog person, you accept that as part of your investment in them. In the raising of puppies like in the raising of children, don't be too obsessive about cleanliness, for puppies will get muddy and dirty just like kids. This is not to be interpreted as an endorsement of laziness in matters of sanitation. It is simply to say that it is impossible to keep puppies perfectly clean and you can drive yourself crazy trying to bathe them every day.

Perhaps the biggest temporary benefit of the puppy is that delightful gift of Mother Nature known as "puppy breath." It would be a big seller if one knew how to bottle it! Enjoy it while you can, for they soon grow out of it and into the brat stage in which chewing and other by-products of puppyhood abound.

Taking puppies to matches and fun events should be part of their early experiences. Let them enjoy it and have fun, for if they have fun right from the beginning you might have a happy show dog for life. Subjecting them to a variety of early experiences prevents them from falling apart later, for they know what to expect. Don't take matches seriously, for that is why they are often called *fun* matches. Puppy sweepstakes held in conjunction with specialty shows offer you twice as many opportunities on that day for your puppy to learn. Take advantage of these opportunities while your puppy is in the puppy stage, for some breeds will go through a period later where their adolescence may take them out of the ring for a while. Since puppies should not be campaigned heavily before they are ready, that works out in their best interest.

Most of all, use the youth of your dogs to encourage them having an upbeat attitude as they grow into adulthood. People are not the only ones who benefit from proper motivation during their early days.

Behavior

Any discussion of behavior almost always leads to what is inherited or what is learned—one more area in which to investigate the heredity versus environment debate. Since this question perplexes human psychologists as much as dog fanciers, there are no set formulas by which to determine behavior.

After observing many puppies for half a century, here is an idea for you to consider. A certain percentage—for the sake of argument, say 60 to 80 percent—of the puppies are preprogrammed to become the products of their good behavioral environment and will show that influence throughout their lives. Their positive experiences will produce good temperaments.

Another 10 to 20 percent fall at each end of the vast majority of these well-adjusted puppies who are influenced by their environmental education. At one end are those 10 to 20 percent of the puppies who will be well-adjusted, even-tempered animals no matter how much or how little socialization they get. At the other disastrous end is the thankfully smaller percentage who fall into the sad category of no matter how much you work with them, socialize them, give optimum positive reinforcement, they will never have the strongest of temperaments. The wise breeder will see to it that these animals are culled—removed—from the breeding population.

Sometimes what one considers acceptable behavior in an animal another would not. In a way, it is like looking at an abstract painting—one has to decide what one likes. Over the years, some older couples purchasing a puppy have requested a "laid-back" dog. Since I prefer a male dog to be more on the muscle, it is fairly easy to pick their puppies out of litters: It is a lazier youngster than its brothers and sisters. Young active families prefer a more energetic dog, another personality trait that is noticeable rather young. Some people want a dog that is easily trained. Even though this is somewhat against the natural independence of the Norwegian Elkhound, a few are more tractable than others.

The breeder must make it his responsibility to choose carefully the appropriate match of puppies and prospective owners. It is also the breeder's responsibility and in your best interest to avoid dogs in your gene pool—as well as that of the breed—that exhibit abnormal behavior.

Although some might consider behavior a cause-and-effect relationship, the puppies nonetheless are affected by hereditary predisposition in regard to temperament. The dam provides a warm and peaceful environment in the womb. Once the puppy is on the ground, environmental influence is ever-present, from the maternal behavior of his dam to the world around him as he grows. Good-natured dams have an opportunity to imprint their progeny in the nest and do. But so do bad-natured dams imprint their puppies. Early puppy behavior is a copycat activity as the puppies interact with their dam, their littermates, humans and other animals that come into their lives.

The instinct for play is present in all mammals, and such play activities reduce boredom. Furthermore, they simulate activities that the animal would do in the wild. Puppies stalking toys are simulating instinctively the predator at work to feed his family. Growling and mock battle simulate a male adult fighting for his territory and his mate—the male dominance thing.

Little baby, puppy dogs mounting their toys or herding their littermates are responding to those instincts buried in their heritage. Such instincts usually relate to survival or to assert their ability to do the job for which they were bred.

Animals that are big-time game players are often the more assertive ones. They are the first puppies out of the whelping box. They rapidly learn how to do things and may later be the ones to open the crate door or the gate or pull a number of other innovative tricks on you. Dogs who nuzzle you or clean the ears of their kennel mates are practicing grooming and showing affection.

Remember that an animal in the kennel is out of its natural environment. Although there are many breeds far removed from the wild-dog state who would not be comfortable except in the lap of luxury, other breeds still remain primitive and close to nature in some of their habits. Some Arctic dogs fall into that category, and some of them must either simulate activities in the wild to some extent, or they will become uncomfortable in their unnatural environment.

Some rather harmless simulations include circling before lying down, chasing tails, howling at a full moon, wrestling with playful growls, shaking toys and possessions hard enough to pretend it is a kill, and certain forms of digging.

Behavior is defined as a way of acting, but often in the case of animals it includes reacting. Again, I do not know what factors are heritable and which are not, but some dogs seem more affected by loud noises than others—reacting to public address systems, air-conditioners and other machinery in a negative manner. A frightened animal's instincts are to fight or take flight, and he will often follow those instincts when frightened. Normal behavior is to recover. When a dog is too sensitive to adjust to the demands on him, perhaps he belongs in a quieter, more soothing situation.

Dogs are creatures of habit, and once they accept a routine they become comfortable with it. All of us know dogs who adjusted so well to the hectic schedule of being a top show dog that they missed it when it was over. They had a marvelous ability to adjust to any environment or event in which they participated, took all the traveling in stride, enjoyed the ever-changing schedule in their eating, sleeping and exercising habits, and actually thrived on it.

Others are stressed by flying, unhappy with confinement, and never do adjust to a madcap routine. Depending on the degree to which their adjustment problems deviated from desired behavior, you must decide if they are of use in the breeding program. Certainly there is a vast amount of difference in a frightened animal that is a total spook and one that is simply bored or turned off by some of the elements that exist in the show place. Never forget that any animal will exhibit abnormal behavior if he is in pain—severe hip pain caused by dysplasia is an example. Super sensitivity to noise is another.

In trying to figure out how a dog's mind works, it is easy to understand that many behavioral vices are created because the animal is bored. When boredom becomes intolerable for the dog or the animal's temperament does not allow him to adjust, a number of bad habits ensue. Those bad habits include, but are not limited to, the following: chewing of fences and kennel walls, frantic circling or barking, wild pacing, and semi-hysteria.

Ways to Relieve Boredom

Dogs are a lot like children. They will test you to see what they can get away with, and they need lots of exercise and activities to keep them out of trouble.

No dog should be in the same kennel area day after day, month after month, world without end. Dogs need to be moved into different areas with different companions to keep life interesting. Run some of them in the large yards while others are in runs, and keep moving them around. The constant handling and alternating of the dogs is good for them, and it is especially important to do some of this at feeding time when they are the most active. Another time you get mileage out of alternating them is in the early morning when you start putting them out. The idea is to get a few of the dogs running in sets to stir up others and then rotate them. The idea is to wear them out.

Provide plenty of interesting diversions. Tubs of water, hurdles along fences they have to jump when they are running the fences, and any number of articles and imaginative equipment around will keep dogs from being bored. I once had a hyperactive squirrel flying from tree to tree in my back exercise area. He kept them all running.

In other words, try to picture yourself in their paws—make life interesting for them and keep them guessing. It keeps them both physically and mentally fit.

Bad Habits to Select Against

The Picky Eater Syndrome: This is not about the dog who misses an occasional meal due to an upset in his routine or a bitch in season. This is about animals with such fussy appetites that they ignore good food and well-balanced diets to eat what is appealing to them. They remind you of a kid who will eat junk food or Beluga caviar, but nothing in between!

This behavior can drive you crazy. Naturally, they will not starve themselves to death, but they will not eat enough to stay in peak condition either. Although this will sometimes happen with young dogs who grow out of it, I mean really fussy eaters who beget more fussy eaters.

Try to select easy keepers as dogs that are picky will become a problem during times of stress. Furthermore, because of their bad eating habits they can become malnourished unless their owners are prepared to stuff them with vitamins and/or food. I believe that picky eating habits are somewhat heritable.

As the puppy goes from nursing to eating on his own he will be establishing a lifetime habit of eating patterns. The puppy who learns to enjoy a diversity of food while young usually keeps these habits all his life. Due to their distance from the wild dog, some breeds are more prone to this picky-eater problem than others.

Side-Sucking, Paw Chewing and Licking: Although I had seen side-sucking in Dobermans as a teenager, I had never known a Norwegian Elkhound to do this until the mid-seventies, when one of my bitches started sucking on her loin area overnight. Every morning her side would be wet and even though I sprayed her with the appropriate repellents, it did no good.

Eventually, the bitch wore her hair down to the hide, creating a large pink area discolored by the chemical activity of her saliva. It is a most unattractive habit and similar in a dog to cribbing in a horse. Although it can be caused by boredom, it is also a trait that runs in families. Evidently, the problem is much worse in areas of high humidity or areas with high flea infestations.

Other self-damaging actions dogs can do to themselves include unreasonable licking and chewing of the paw or toe. Although some of these bad habits are the direct result of boredom, if the dog is obviously not bored, consider that you might be enabling a problem to start in your line and act accordingly.

Tufts University Veterinary School is studying lick granulomas as an obsessive-compulsive disorder that may in part be caused by genetic predisposition brought on by stress and anxiety. The university put out the word in the fall of 1995 that it was collecting and processing information through behavioral and pedigree analyses of families of dogs affected by this problem. Such efforts deserve the support of the fancy in a cooperative effort to provide much-needed answers.

Excessive scratching can fall into the behavior category or can be the result of true skin problems. Either way, unreasonable scratching is another problem with which the breeder must cope.

Dirty Personal Habits: Nothing in the world is more disgusting than animals that will do their droppings in areas of high traffic and then run in it. Usually this area will be at the front of the run near the gate, and before you can get in there to clean, they have it all over them. It is not my aim to be unkind, but some breeds are more prone to this ugly habit than others. Most dogs will try to evacuate far away from where they spend much of their time. Such clean animals will try hard to avoid getting in their own messes. In fact, as all professional handlers know, some of these animals have a hard time adjusting to relieving themselves in an exercise pen for that very reason.

Other dogs seem to have very little concern for the sanctity of their home and will foul their own crates even when properly exercised. Breeders need to consider it an advantage when animals are naturally clean. With such animals, crates will stay clean unless they are sick—or heaven forbid—not properly exercised.

The eating of feces is a different matter. It can be just a disgusting habit or an indication of a nutritional imbalance that requires veterinary advice.

Head Shaking: Head shaking that is not a physical problem can be due to discomfort with the lead. This discomfort is sometimes a minor temporary problem with a youngster new to the lead. In that instance, the dog views the lead as a nuisance and usually gets over the head shaking in time.

If the discomfort is due to a long-running distaste for the leash caused by a bad early experience to the dog, the lead has become a negative symbol. Your job is to prove to the dog that the lead can be a pleasant experience. Keep the dog on lead in the house, make fun experiences part of the leash, including tying the dog where you can see it and feeding it on lead. With patience and kindness you should be able to overcome a sensitive dog's objection to the lead.

When head shaking on lead is caused by tonsil problems or pain in the ear, the dog is experiencing real discomfort and will need to see a veterinarian for treatment. Fox tails in the ears are a major concern in the West. When head shaking occurs off the lead, it is a signal that veterinary assistance is required to determine the nature of the disorder. You should clean the dog's ears and make a routine check before seeing the vet. I have encountered a few dogs over the years whose head-shaking problem while on lead I never solved. It was simply an unexplained habit.

Noise Anxiety: Temporary fright from loud and unexpected noises, such as a backfiring truck, is not unusual. It becomes a concern when the animal does not recover in a reasonable amount of time.

Some animals are susceptible to noises and can become almost neurotic when confronted with the noisy confusion of a dog show and its blaring public address system. Animals hear much better than humans and it is difficult to know if some well-adjusted dogs hear too well for their own good, reacting negatively to any loud noises. Perhaps constant exposure to taped noises or the radio in the kennel will help. Nonetheless, a dog who is supersensitive to noise will be a problem child in the dog show environment.

Rock Chewing: Is uncontrolled rock chewing a learned bad habit, an hereditary tendency, or an indication of a nutritional imbalance? If you have seen a young dog with his teeth as worn as those of a normal 12-year old, you know what I mean. If you run into this problem, try to figure out which it is, especially if it is because of boredom. Dogs are like people. They need help to break bad habits, but it can be done.

In dealing with vices you will have to stay one step ahead of your animals, as did the handlers of the great race horse, Man O' War. Because "Big Red" always ate too fast and horses are susceptible to digestive tract problems, such as colic, his grooms were forced to figure a way to deal with this potential life-threatening situation. Their solution was to put a bit on the champion horse while feeding him, thus forcing him to eat more slowly. The great Man O' War was spared from falling victim to severe problems and lived to a ripe old age in Kentucky's blue grass country.

The aforementioned bad habits are a small sample of the many potential ones that exist. The point is for you as a breeder to recognize and identify bad habits in your dogs and deal with them accordingly. If they are habits caused by the environment, you should alter your regimen so that you can eliminate the causes. If they are problems caused by heredity, again you must identify them and deal with them. Some problems are caused by a combination, which once again requires you to act upon them in a responsible way.

Above all, keep in mind that the best relationships between you and your dogs occur when you have the least problems. Remaining vigilant in all areas will enhance the lives of both you and your dogs.

Conditioning and Nutrition

Dogs aren't the only ones who seem to be the most influenced by experiences in their youth. People fall into this category and for that reason I would like to share a story that happened at the Chesapeake Cocker Spaniel Specialty decades ago. Mrs. Thelma Blair of Blairwood Kennels was grooming a buff dog on top of her crates. I think the dog was named Broomstraw, but that's not relevant. What is relevant was the message she sent home with a budding dog person. As she worked and prepared her dog for the ring, this glamorous lady advised that although she could not control whether she had the best dog at the show, she could certainly control whether or not she had the best-conditioned dog at the show.

Eureka! Here was a lady who could tell it like it was. Even if your dog was not as good as those of your competitors, if you had it in the epitome of health and proper condition with every hair in place, you could be competitive. My first Norwegian Elkhound bitch was somewhat long and swaybacked, but maybe she would be able to seek a championship if she were in super condition. So this bitch and I began a regular jogging routine that in time muscled in her back and body. This not only helped the softness of the back, it also caused her to "body up" and appear shorter. And in time we were able to add the word champion to her name. This conditioning process and learning to show her better had amplified her somewhat-limited ability to reach her full potential and beyond.

Now conditioning is no substitute for quality. But it certainly enhances what the animal has and helps it reach the upper limit of its potential. It can make a marked difference in the performance of the animal in the ring. Over the years, Mrs. Blair's advice has been a guiding factor in the conditioning program for the Vin-Melca dogs. And more than one judge has indicated an appreciation for the condition my dogs were in when presented to them.

Many people showing dogs interpret conditioning as the care of the coat and having the animal in correct weight. These well-meaning folks don't understand that the reason someone else's dog is out-

The author's first Norwegian Elkhound bitch. In the picture on the left, she was overstretched and soft-backed. After several months of a conditioning program and handling classes to learn how to pose her, the picture on the right tells the story. These pictures are over 45 years old, and Ch. Ulf's Madam Helga C.D. is in the extended pedigree of every dog to carry the Vin-Melca prefix through her daughter, Ch. Vin-Melca's Astridina, maternal grandam of Ch. Vin-Melca's Howdy Rowdy and Ch. Vin-Melca's Vagabond. (House Photos)

performing theirs on an extremely hot day is that the other animal not only looks in condition, it is in condition. To be in condition is to be fit with lean, hard muscle.

A fit animal is more able to perform under all conditions of weather and environment. He has the "bottom" for a stretch run when his competitors are starting to look tired, and he has a better attitude while sustaining the stress and rigors of the campaign. When he is fit he is better both physically and psychologically. He has reserves that can be called upon when the going gets tough.

Proper conditioning starts out slowly and progressively increases the animal's ability to handle exercise. A program of long, slow jogs gradually increases the dog's oxygen delivery system while building muscle strength and developing smooth coordination. All of this adds up to helping the animal resist fatigue. When a dog goes out and shows happily at first, then later gets sour, you can suspect he is experiencing fatigue. Because he isn't feeling well while performing, he is discouraged from trying as hard the next time.

Occasionally, you will hear someone say that of course his dog is in top condition because it has three acres to run in. Often what they don't realize is that he has three acres to sleep in! Because of their high energy that keeps them on the move, terriers seem to stay in excellent shape on their own in runs. And active toy dogs will firm up and stay in condition running around in the house.

Although the requirements of each dog and each breed are different, it seems that the better-built dogs thrive on more work. Perhaps this is because a dog that is made right requires more work to feel the same effects of stress than one not made quite so right. Straight-angled dogs seem to require less work to stay in shape, for they are laboring and experiencing muscle-building stress with each step. For them, the accumulative effects of exercise are not unlike those of the weight-lifter who has worked out for a long time. Soft-backed dogs require more work to fill in the topline. Actually, poor conformation can prevent a dog from being in the ultimate condition at the same time good conditioning will help overcome some conformational flaws.

Because working with your dog is a bonding activity, you might want to start out with long walks and slow jogs. When the dog's exercise tolerance has been increased, mix up the sessions on foot with some beside a bicycle or automobile, being extremely careful in each case to prevent possible accidents. Another alternative is a jogging machine which has the advantage of being useful no matter what the weather conditions. Walk the dogs up the jogger with rewards and encouragement several times before turning the machine on. Take care not to use force, and if your experiences are like mine, there will be a few dogs you never will get to go on a jogger. Accept that and use other forms of exercise rather than souring your dog.

Varying the way you exercise the dog and the places you do it helps keep the dog interested and reduces boredom. In all activities try to make it fun for the animal. No matter what form of exercise you pursue, check your dog's feet often. Although dogs in the peak of condition may not require any

The ultimate in conditioning with a well-designed regular exercise program is nothing new as shown here by Louis Murr bicycling Borzoi Ch. Vigow of Romanoff in 1934. Mr. Murr went on to become a respected all-rounder judge. (Photo courtesy of the American Kennel Club)

special care of the feet, it is a good idea to moisturize the pads from time to time. Hand lotion or a good skin oil can be used for this. The moisturized pad is more flexible and elastic, thus more able to absorb shock. It toughens up and resists cracking and tenderness. Furthermore, it can tolerate a variety of ring surfaces without discomfort.

There is usually a valid reason if a dog suffers from exercise intolerance. Such a dog is either unwilling or unable to perform. If he is simply unwilling, it may be nothing more than a couch-potato mentality that needs your help making an attitude adjustment. If he seems unable to tolerate normal exercise, there is usually a reason.

Maybe the dog has an obscure lameness not showing in his gait that is causing him pain. Perhaps he has a sore back or muscle problems. Perhaps he is anemic or suffering from some nutritional deficiency.

If an animal is feeling mild pain or discomfort, he's not going to feel like giving you his best effort. Sometimes the naked eye cannot detect these problems, and it will require a diagnostic radiograph. Subtle back problems cannot only go undiagnosed by you, they can also be a problem for the veterinarian to find.

Each case is different, but unusual treatments such as acupuncture, chiropractic adjustment and swimming can help get the dog back in form and become once again an enthusiastic performer. One hint that a dog's back is hurting is that he may not

The author is working one of her dogs on the beach near Point Lobos on California's Monterey Peninsula. The hard sand where the tide has gone out leaves excellent footing, good for both human and canine exercising. Furthermore, sand, like snow, is a good surface to study the tracks a dog makes to evaluate if the animal is tracking true. (Jayne Langdon Photo)

cover ground with the same effortless stride you are accustomed to from that particular dog. Another is stiffness or unusual action in the hindquarters.

A dog suffering in his joints or bones will appear reluctant to stand squarely with his weight properly distributed on all fours. He may "rest" a hind leg rather than planting it. Sometimes hind leg trembling will indicate neurological problems as well as muscular or joint stress.

If the dog has a vague hard-to-diagnose problem converting enzymes to energy, try a blood serum test to measure enzymes and an adjusted diet and exercise program to rectify the problem. Improvement should be gradual but steady. A blood count will show if an animal is anemic. It is my understanding that the total red cell volume will increase with exercise in a well-conditioned and fit animal.

Peak condition cannot be achieved without good nutrition and utilization of a proper diet by the animal. If a dog does not seem to be thriving on what appears to be an optimum diet, it means that the digestive system is not working at its most efficient level. This could be caused by parasites or by a metabolic disorder. In either case you will need your veterinarian's help. Like an engine consuming too much fuel, it's time for a tune-up.

Regular stool checks should help you and your veterinarian keep the dog parasite free. Keep in mind that tapeworms might not show up in stool checks, so watch for worm segments when you pick up droppings. If you have had flea problems it might be best to worm for tapes routinely.

When it comes to nutrition, all dogs are not created equal. What is proper nutrition for one is not necessarily for another. Your best advice is to work with someone who is an expert on the requirements of your breed in selecting the optimum diet for your dog. The perfect diet for the dog is the absolutely correct combination of all nutrients for that individual. When there is too much of one nutrient and too little of another, it is out of balance. When you realize that the elements sodium and chlorine are toxic in their individual form but when bonded together chemically in the correct formula, they constitute table salt, you can recognize the importance of having the correct balance in the dog's diet. Not only will the perfect diet vary for dogs from breed to breed, it will vary from dog to dog. Adjustments have to be made for the amount of work the dog is doing and the stage of its life cycle.

To get your animals in the best condition will require some work on your part to research their nutritional needs. For example, if cleft palates have become a problem in your line, you might want to study the use of folate supplements. Lack of adequate folate in the diet is also implicated as a cause of other problems suffered by the in-whelp bitch. Infertility in the male can be caused by a zinc deficiency among other things, and so on.

Don't fall into thinking that if a little is good, a lot is better. Such thinking can lead to imbalances in the relationships of nutrients to each other. For example, there is an interesting relationship in the minerals calcium, phosphorous and magnesium. Too much calcium can cause excessive loss of phosphorous and vice versa. Magnesium can help regulate the relationship. But the secret is that all nutrients must be in balance. People make a mistake in thinking blood tests reveal all answers to these problems. Unique cases involving nutritional imbalances require the help of hair analyses to assist in solving them.

Getting into the nutritional mode could benefit you as well as your dogs, for your studies might turn up some solutions for your own problems. And if you have a dog in the best condition, it will be a plus if you are too. The total show dog in excellent condition should look as though he could leave the ring and bay up a moose, bring down a stag, jump into chilly waters to retrieve fowl, drive cattle, or whatever job he was bred to do without missing a beat. Why not his owner too?

Random Nutritional Hints

• Do not overfeed nor over-supplement in hopes of getting bigger and better dogs. The dogs do not necessarily grow any bigger even though they may reach their size more rapidly, which is not in their best interests.

• Different animals have different needs. If it appears you are dealing with a line in which fertility is poor, it could be that the individuals in the line have a metabolic need for more zinc than their diets are providing. Lowered resistance to disease could also be associated with zinc deficiency. Low levels of zinc are associated with lower levels of growth hormones and testosterone in the male.

• Low levels of Vitamin E can contribute to poor tone of the uterus in the bitch.

• Low folic acid levels can cause placenta and pregnancy problems.

• B-6 and potassium can benefit bitches prone to pregnancy toxicity.

• Cataracts are associated with deficiency of riboflavin, Vitamins C and E.

• Magnesium can help treat severe diarrhea and vomiting. It also helps in the absorption and metabolism of other minerals.

- The B-Complex helps relieve stress.

- Manganese may be beneficial in the treatment of epilepsy and diabetes.

- Optimum health requires the dog to have the correct amounts of all nutrients in balance for that animal. Dogs, like people, do not have the same exact needs. Working with your veterinarian and doing your homework will help you achieve the correct nutritional program for your animals. Animals have varying needs during the course of their life cycle and according to the stress in their lives. Reproduction and periods of growth require appropriate nutrition to minimize associated problems.

- Red Raspberry (Rubus idaeus leaf) is a blood tonic that helps the bitch regulate hormones and tone her uterus.

Problem Solving: When Bad Things Happen to Good People and Dogs!

Problems are a part of life. Whether on the road, at a show, at home in the kennel, or anywhere else that our day-to-day trip through life may take us, problems are there. How we deal with them varies, but here are a few things that have worked for me.

The most important thing to remember about a problem is to prevent it from happening. If it cannot be prevented, deal with it in a rational manner. If it cannot be dealt with immediately, back off—unless it is an emergency. Leave it alone for a while, and maybe it will take care of itself. Often you can look at it later with a fresh approach.

One thing to remember is that you have to be adaptable. No one solution will work for everything or for everyone. Furthermore, the solution that works for someone else may not work for you because we all have different needs.

In April of 1960, I faced a potential disaster. My Ch. Vin-Melca's Astridina suffered a heat stroke at the Old Dominion Kennel Club show in northern Virginia. The weather had taken a sudden trip to the top of the thermometer. The heat, combined with the humidity, suddenly turned a spring day into a scorcher—weather usually reserved for July and August. When the bitch went down, it was my good fortune to be set up with Harold Correll, the holder of the AKC's first license ever granted to a professional handler. Mr. Correll immediately threw icy water all over Astridina, helped administer an ice-water enema, and in a few tense minutes, the bitch was fully recovered. She suffered no after effects. This great gentleman had saved the life of the bitch destined to become the maternal grandam of Vagabond and Howdy Rowdy.

Being alert to your animal's well-being and responding before it is a *Red Alert* is best. Astridina gave no outward signs of being in such stress. She was not laboring with her panting and her eyes looked normal. She had, however, just come out of the ring after working hard in the noonday sun. She had been returned to the shade and watered in her wire crate. I saw her fall down and was able to get help immediately.

Ch. Vin-Melca's Astridina, saved for posterity by quick-thinking Harold Correll, went on to become the maternal grandam of Ch. Vin-Melca's Howdy Rowdy and Ch. Vin-Melca's Vagabond after recovering from a heat stroke. Second only to prevention itself is immediate correct emergency response to Red Alert situations. (Photo by Ed Heath)

Thankfully, a quick recovery was possible. It was one of my all-time great learning experiences. I now know that nothing is more dangerous to dogs than heat—especially if it is sudden and unseasonable. It taught me to recognize the difference in our cooling systems, watching for any sign of heat stress—excessive panting, glassy eyes, or general malaise—and acting accordingly. Over the years, a number of methods have helped dogs during times of extreme heat:

- Fans giving constant cool breezes, generators are helpful at outdoor shows;

- Ice packs previously frozen and put into zippered pillow cases under the dog;

- Teaching dogs to lick and eat ice at an early age so that they routinely have it in their crates at shows;

- Standing so your shadow covers the dog when you are in the ring on a hot day;

- Heading for the shade of the tent whenever possible;

- Using water guns that have been submerged in ice chests to cool off dogs while in the ring, squirting ice water in the dog's mouth, on the pads, and other areas that will help lower body heat.

A different kind of problem occurred when Vagabond was 13. He developed an ulcer about the size of my fist near the base of his tail that resisted every known method of treatment. He continued to lick it and agitate it, causing it to become so inflamed and nasty that it began to look as though his tail would have to be amputated. The problem had been ongoing for several weeks.

Since amputation would be a last resort, Dr. John decided to try something drastically different—something that would draw out the moisture and inflammation, prevent or reduce licking, and shock the problem. We began to pack the ulcer with Vitamin C powder which drew out the inflammation. When the dog licked the ulcer, the taste was not good, but the Vitamin C would only help him anyhow. It was nothing short of a miracle. Within 24 hours the ulcer began to dry out and heal. In a few days, new skin was forming and soon the hair grew back.

The following year, Vagabond returned to Westminster for the 1981 Parade of Champions, becoming the oldest dog, at 14, to appear on the Garden floor. He lived until he was almost 18 and never had another recurrence of the problem.

Crates and Associated Problems: At the Del Mar thoroughbred yearling sales many years ago, a $250,000 Pretense son had just been sold. I liked him so much that I followed him back to his stall. I had already spent a lot of time studying this youngster, for I always felt empathy for his half-brother Sham who spent his three-year-old year chasing Secretariat. Face it. In most years Sham would have been the champion three-year-old—but not in 1973.

The kids working for the buyer of this gorgeous colt were trying to load him. To my horror, they did not seem to have a clue as to how to get the colt into the trailer. Now this is amazing to me—a quarter-of-a-million-dollar colt being mishandled by kids making minimum wages who did not know how to load a colt. The insurance company would have been appalled. It did not take long for my friend who worked for the California Thoroughbred Breeders Association to give them a hand and avoid a disaster.

You, the owner, breeder, handler, or lover of a wonderful dog, must always be one step ahead of the

Fourteen-year-old Ch. Vin-Melca's Vagabond participating in the 1981 Parade of Champions at Westminster Kennel Club. As he moved through the spotlight, Roger Caras, "The Voice of Westminster," pronounced him the oldest dog to appear at the Garden.

person who is in a position to hurt your animal inadvertently. This person can be the nice guy who does not know any better. He can be the fence builder who left a wire loose that could poke out an eye, your dog's baggage handler who dropped the crate at the airport, the show committee's volunteer who forgot to secure the mats, or any one of a number of good people with good intentions.

Your job is to prevent something from going wrong. Walking your dog in an unknown park after dark is an example. A few years ago, it seemed to be the town sport in a number of Rocky Mountain city parks, open to dogs on lead by the way, to break bottles against trees. When an unsuspecting dog owner allowed his dog to lift his leg on a tree, he discovered that the dog had a cut pad. This kind of glass pollution is something you have to alert yourself to all the time. Your dog is always barefoot. Glass pollution is forever and is the waste generated by people. A lot of human waste is dangerous. Human beings are the only animals that produce waste that is not recyclable.

Your job is to find the burrs, thorns, hot concrete or blacktop, glass, or anything else that can harm your dog before a mishap occurs. If you cannot pick your dog up and carry him through the hot asphalt parking lot, walk him close to parked cars that throw enough shade to give a cooler spot on the unrelenting hot surface. Wet his feet before doing it.

In other words, like the parents of a toddler, you must always look at every situation, every environment, every possible scene to determine what and how it can harm your dog. Act accordingly and you will limit the bad things that can happen to you and your dog.

Dangers like this burning cigarette pose a serious problem to your dog who is always barefoot. (Photo by Deidi Kramer)

When you use bungee cords to secure crates in your vehicle, turn the ends of the bungee out so that they cannot stick your dog in the eye. When you pick up a dog at the airport, make certain the air cargo doors are closed before you attempt to take the dog out of its crate. In other words, use common sense and all should go well. You will reduce the number of things that can go wrong.

When you visit friends over a show weekend, resist the invitation to turn your dog loose in their yard. Even if you are tired and hate to walk in the dark and cold with your dog, it only takes a wrong jump or turn in a strange yard to pull a muscle. A friend of mine put a dog in what appeared to be a safe run, only to have the dog pull a toenail—the BIS winner was out for a week. The dog of another friend pulled a toenail in a new crate. Things will happen. You can reduce the incidence of accidents by being alert.

There are fewer smokers than there used to be; however, be alert for the unthinking person who tosses a cigarette where your barefoot friend could step on it: Ouch, another unnecessary hurt for your dog. It did not have to happen.

An ounce of prevention will find you checking for possible hazards in crates, show buildings and rings, kennels, motels, vehicles and every other place you might end up with your dog. The cure is often worse than dealing with a missed ring call. Be aware: protect and prevent. Watch for yellow cautions so that you do not suffer Red Alert.

Dealing With Difficult People: Not all of your problems will be actually associated with the dogs themselves. Sometimes you will have problems with people. Most of the time you will be able to deal with those problems just as you deal with other problem people in your life.

If you show people who are overly stressed that you care and deal with them in an understanding and compassionate way, they will usually respond and all will work out.

Stressed-out people are a product of our times. All of us have been there at one time or another. Lest you think that the dog fancy has more than its fair share of these people, take it from a school teacher that there are plenty of them in other walks of life. If you think Junior Showmanship moms are difficult, or kennel blind people who look only at their four-legged kids, try Little League moms and dads and PTA politics. And so it goes. The main thing to remember is that your common sense will serve you well in resolving the conflicts you encounter in the world of dogs. For situations in which you are forced to deal with genuinely evil people, you must act accordingly.

Not only is my mother a wonderful parent and beautiful lady, she has always been a good role model. A favorite saying of hers that is always with me is, "There's a lot of good in the worst of us and a little bad in the best of us." For the most part my mother knows what she is talking about.

There probably is a little meanness in all of us at times—and it sometimes comes out in times of stress. We feel bad about it and make the appropriate apologies and ask forgiveness. Truly mean people are different. They are mean to the bone and full of toxic emotion. They try to hurt others and get a high from it, often without realizing what they are doing. Fortunately for us, there are not many of them in dogs. Dogs have better taste than that!

If you should meet these rare people, prepare to deal with them. If someone treats you mean once, assume it is a flare up or stress. If the mean behavior continues and you realize it is a way of life with them, "lay it on the line" and "meet them head on." Come right back at them when they say something vicious about someone else, otherwise they will assume you agree with them. Draw the line and let them know early on where you stand. Do not let them intimidate you. People who talk viciously about everyone else to you will talk viciously about you to everyone else.

In our world of dogs, judges are special targets of such people, people who criticize every action and decision a judge makes. The intimidator counts on people not communicating with each other about them. Maybe he figures you are too embarrassed to admit he tried to push you around.

The good guys are uncomfortable with themselves when they enable an intimidator. Once the good guys decide to stop enabling, they feel a lot more comfortable. Sometimes it is tough to be the only one or the first one who stops enabling rude and unsportsmanlike behavior. Even if it is a tough job, somebody has to do it.

In addition to intimidators, watch out for hate mongers, poor sports, vicious gossips, and parasitic people who will drain all your energy without ever putting anything back into the relationship. In short, try to keep positive people in your life, and if you are thrown into the company of negative people meet them head on. Above all, remember that gossip is not gospel.

Once that sort of person gets it, forget it and accept an apology if it is offered. If an apology is not offered, ignore it. Sometimes those who set good examples spill over on others. Being kind to those who are negative may rub off on them. This just proves that my mother was right: "There is a lot of good in the worst of us."

Time Management

Many people may have more money than you do, more resources, more ability, or better connections. But nobody will have more time, because we are all dealt the same cards on that issue—24 hours a day. Achievement in any field is about making the most and wisest use of your 24 hours each day by getting the most mileage out of what is available to you. And face it, time flies even when you're *not* having fun.

Many of us do not realize that what Benjamin Franklin preached before the American Revolution is still true today: "Time is money." Nowhere did I see better examples of ignoring this old adage than during the endless hours I spent in my years as an educator attending boring, unproductive teachers' meetings.

> "It is wonderful how much may be done if we are always doing."
> —Thomas Jefferson

It did not take long to realize that, although I was forced to attend the meetings, I was not forced to sit there doing nothing. So grading papers during the meetings became standard operating procedure. To avoid disturbing the speaker, I sat in the back behind others and did my work unobtrusively and as quietly as possible.

Over the years, the schedule of increased numbers of dog shows, coupled with the five-day teaching week required innovations for me just to run in place. To put things in perspective about the ever-increasing demands on people to try to get the same things done, look at these statistics: In 1970, Ch.

Vin-Melca's Vagabond became Top Dog All Breeds All Systems and attended 87 shows. In 1990, just 20 years later, his granddaughter, Ch. Vin-Melca's Calista, was runner-up to the wonderful Bouvier des Flandres, Ch. Galbraith's Iron Eyes for Top Dog All Breeds and competed at 120 shows! Now, there are still just 365 days per year, so if you are not getting the most out of your time, it will be costly.

Even though time is not money in the purebred dog world, it is success. Franklin is still right today. It means getting the most out of your time by learning ways to combine activities, utilizing even farfetched sources and ideas to help you get your jobs done, and learning to do more than one thing at a time.

How many of you work like crazy on the day before you are getting ready to go to a dog show? Not only are you superbly efficient in your employment to get details at the workplace covered while you are gone, you are most effective at home getting organized and being productive. What if you worked like that all the time? Would it reduce the time you waste in life and increase your productivity? In following the good example set by Franklin and Jefferson, it is wise to remember they were able to accomplish so much because they practiced self-discipline and stayed focused.

For example, the telephone can rob you of more time than almost anything that comes to mind. You must learn to keep your conversations short and on target. Visit enough to be civil, but avoid long-winded conversations that rob you of your time. Keep a phone near your grooming area and work on a dog while you talk. Make calls that can sap your time while on hold early in the morning before airline, rental car, and other phone systems back up. Call friends early in the morning because you will be able to get to the point quickly as they, too, have to get to work. In other words, budget your phone time which will also save on the phone bill. One wonders if Ma Bell and associates have any idea the contributions to their economy made by the good dog people of America!

Television: Another ongoing thief of your valuable time is television. Since many television programs require little concentration, do something else while you are watching them. Going through mail, logging your show campaign for the next month, working out the pedigree on a potential breeding, and stacking a dog in front of the television set are a few activities that come to mind.

Keep a television in your grooming area; then you can work on your dogs at the same time you watch. Highly recommended time could be spent on the grooming table during Monday night football. For one thing, the excitement of the game causes lots of fan participation and noise not unlike that in a high-profile dog show. For another, if you just showed the dog on Sunday, it is a good time to go over the dog thoroughly, making sure you see standing exactly what the judge saw. If you see areas on the dog that need a few hairs removed or to be brushed in a different manner than at yesterday's show, it is best to see it on Monday night instead of hoping you will pick up on it during the confusion of next week's dog show. Furthermore, Monday night seems a good time to give the animal a good going over that is more than just grooming. Check his teeth, ears, eyes, and pads to make sure all is well.

Socializing. Take puppies and youngsters with you everywhere—if they will be safe in your vehicle—and work them a few minutes here and there. Chaperoning and attending athletic events after school is part of a teacher's job description. Games usually start about 30 minutes after school is dismissed. While I was still a teacher, I would run home, pick up a couple of young dogs, and return to school to work them on the sidelines during games. They got much more exposure than they would at a match or regular show. They do not know it is not a judge going over them. And it is good public relations for your breed.

Volunteer to attend an elementary school with a litter of puppies and help the teacher put on an intriguing educational event. It is good for you, the kids, and the puppies. Such child-oriented activities can lead you to meet the families and often lead to securing pet homes for dogs you would like to relocate. A friend used to kid me that "there are more Elkhounds in homes in Carmel, California, than there are in Oslo, Norway." This might be a slight exaggeration, but some of my retired dogs, or yearlings that did not measure up to their early promise, did end up in pet homes where they were much loved. Placing them with the right kind of people—neutering them is part of the equation—helps you keep the dog population manageable and is certainly in the best interest of the dogs.

Most California shows are outdoors. It is not difficult to park outside the show limits, put out your awning, and set up camp. During the day, puppies can be put in pens and/or lead-trained to make valuable use of your time. One show that was great for this was near a flea market. Many people handled the youngsters on their way to this event.

When guests come to your home, let them spend a few minutes handling your animals. They know you are *kooky* because you are in dogs. So if they like you anyhow, they will not mind. Such brief encounters for your dogs can have an excellent effect on their socialization.

When you have to run errands at the supermarket, the bank, etc., take a dog along to work for a few minutes. One tip on supermarket timesaving is to go when there is less traffic. The 24-hour supermarket is perfect, for if you go in the early morning, everyone is in a hurry to get out of the store. If you meet friends when you go, they will say, "Hello," but they will not want to stand around for a time-consuming visit because they have to get to work, too. The same is true of late shopping. They have to get to bed.

Try to run all your errands at the times when you spend the least time in line. Somewhere I read that Americans spend several years of their lives waiting in lines—the less you do this the more time you have for productive activities. When you know that standing in line will be unavoidable, take your magazines or a book with you.

When you are commuting, listen to educational tapes, relax or get in touch with yourself. I used to plan my breedings driving the endless miles between Northern and Southern California on Interstate 5. Try to make time-consuming parts of life into your own personal survival system. It seems incredible that I once considered sleeping on the red-eye flight a personal bonus because it was efficient use of time for one who didn't sleep much anyhow.

Get into the habit of throwing out your junk mail without wasting a lot of time on it. Try not to handle papers more than once. If you have to make calls that you know will land you *on hold* with an automated phone system, have busy work to do. Pay bills, make your grocery list, address Christmas cards, or whatever.

We live in a chaotic world where just getting through the day can be rather demanding. When you add the all-consuming life of a dog addict to that of just an average human being in this modern world, the result is a person who is overworked every day. Trying to figure out the ways you can maximize the use of your personal 24-hour day will benefit you and your dogs.

Records: And Other Such Stuff

Health certificates, breeding arrangements, contracts, registration papers, tax records, pedigrees: Sounds like a horror show. Especially to someone as disorganized as I have become since I have been out of the classroom. All of the above are necessary evils that we have to deal with whether we like it or not.

Keeping it all in your head just does not cut it. Even though many of us are good at keeping things in our heads, apart from pedigrees and a few special registration numbers, we just cannot do it all. Actually, I, for one, could remember a favorite dog's registration number but not my own social security number. I could quote its pedigree for six or more generations but forget my own birthday. Nonetheless, the message has to be, "Keep workable records."

The first place to start is with a system of recording information needed for tax records so that you and the IRS are on the same wave length. Unless you are skilled in this area, it is best for you to go to a good tax accountant so that everything is done correctly. Then it is a matter of keeping all income and expenses to turn over to the tax accountant at the appropriate time. Using a compatible computer software program facilitates record keeping.

Health certificates and all health records should be kept in a file separate from other records, using a separate file card or page for each dog. The health record should include a history of any bitch's heat cycle, worming records, immunization records, eye certifications, x-ray information, and other health information that will help you breed better dogs. Records of booster shots are easier to keep if the annual ones are given at the first of every year. Then you always know when they are due.

Review your records over the years to see if you are having recurring problems. Maybe the great-granddaughter of your first champion has low thyroid—you have not seen it in years, but in researching your records, there it is.

Especially important are records on the breeding habits of your animals. If a given bitch is an early breeder, you should be on the lookout for that peculiar trait in her descendants.

No one is in a worse position to give advice on contracts than I am. All too often people have talked me out of their honoring a contract with me. Maybe that is why I should give the advice: "Don't do as I do. Do as I say." Write the agreement down so that everyone knows what is expected. Be reasonable in your expectations as too many strings aren't in anyone's best interest. My personal best long-term relationships with people have been based on our mutual word, which was our bond.

Keeping good records on a well-known stud is especially important. As his progeny come of age, looking at your records will help you decide which bitches do well with him. You may find a pattern or nick to his producing ability sooner than expected if you are on top of the records of his offspring.

You can obtain a record-keeping booklet from AKC, or you can develop your own system. Be certain that they are available and current. Make sure all dogs are readily identifiable. This will facilitate proper dispersal of your animals if something should happen to you as well as satisfy AKC requirements. You might want to set up a plan that will provide for your dogs. Some breeders have this provision in their wills. Others add it as a codicil.

To the true-blue breeder, some of the best record keeping will involve pedigrees. Breeders hoard pedigrees for decades, often on dogs that they never used—dogs that have long disappeared into the sunset. The hardest thing I had to part with when I left California to move to Tennessee was the huge file, titled "Breedings Never Made," that contained wonderful figments of my imagination. Never mind. I think they were stimulating and looked good on paper. Nowadays, those of you who are computer-literate can play that game—and have a lot of fun with it.

A calendar to plan your show schedule is essential. Enter the name of the club and judges. Indicate when you mailed your entries and other information involving the trip. You can use the same calendar to indicate your placements and make an end of the year record later. Some people like to write notes on the kind of dog the judge preferred—"likes side gait"—"death on bad fronts," etc. In fact, I have been told that there are computer whiz kids that have every bit of information imaginable recorded on judges, shows, and competitors' dogs!

Keeping too much information would overwhelm me, but perhaps too much is better than not enough. The main thing is to have the important information where you can locate it without wasting time. That is what it is all about. In theory, keep it simple and do not get bogged down in it. As a result, you have more time for personal work with your dogs.

In realizing that *winning means hard work*, much thought must be given to the commitment necessary to become a *master breeder*. Much of your life will be sacrificed to this commitment and it's not for everyone. It's a personal choice each person must make.

SALES CONTRACT

Breed_____Sex_____

Reg. No._____ Birth Date_____

Sire_____Reg. No._____

Dam_____Reg. No._____

On this date, _____, the above described dog has been

sold as _____ to the following individual(s):

Name_____

Address_____

City_____State_____Phone_____

for the sum of _____, payment in full (in accordance with the
terms of agreement as provided on the reverse of this contract.

****
Seller guarantees said dog to be in good health on date of sale.

The purchaser agrees to take this dog to a licensed veterinarian of his choice within 48 hours for a health check. Should the dog be determined to be in ill health, the cause of which is clearly attributable to the seller, the dog may, upon presentation of a written diagnosis from said veterinarian, be returned for refund of purchase price or for another dog of equal value, the choice of which to be determined by the seller.

In addition, if the dog should develop a major communicable disease (i.e., distemper, leptospirosis, hepatitis) within ten (10) days from the date of sale, the seller must be notified immediately and will provide instructions for refund or replacement as specified above.

Any veterinarian's diagnosis shall be subject to confirmation by a veterinarian chosen by the seller. Should said veterinarian not concur with the diagnosis, the matter shall be presented to a third veterinarian mutually agreed upon by the seller and the purchaser.
****
Sold by_____

Address_____

City_____State_____Phone_____

_____   _____
Signature and Acceptance of Purchaser   **Signature and Acceptance of Seller**

Master Breeder Robert G. Wehle and his Elhew Pointers

Bronze sculpture of the classic Pointer Elhew Snakefoot by his *master breeder* Robert G. Wehle is one of many sporting bronzes by the artist on display at the Lime Rock Gallery in Sackets Harbor, New York.

For an outstanding breeding program that produces generation after generation of easily trained, quality puppies that grow into outstanding bird dogs of sound mind and body, consider the Elhew Pointers of *master breeder* Robert G. Wehle. For six decades, Wehle's breeding program has accounted for one National Champion after another dominating American field trials with brilliance and beauty.

Furthermore, these super dogs are so treasured by their owners that generation after generation of owners return to Elhew to acquire classic dogs as their fathers and grandfathers before them have done, allowing them to continue this family field tradition.

Hunting enthusiasts are always amazed when they visit the estate in Henderson, New York, to see the eight-week-old puppies walking with their master freeze into point. It is as natural for them as breathing. Wehle's closebreeding dedicated to using only the best has led him to perfect a strain concentrating on the essence of true Pointer type coupled with the hunting abilities of the exceptional bird dog. His dogs are noted for their exquisite Pointer heads, conformation and athleticism, temperament and trainability.

This extraordinary man's skills extend beyond his ability to breed and raise the classic Pointer into the arts—he is both a writer and a sculptor. The dog portrayed in the illustration above is National Champion Elhew Snakefoot, model for the sculpture and the subject of the book, *Snakefoot -The Making of a Champion.*

PART IV

W I N N I N G

MEANS HAVING FUN

The Dog Show and its History

To dog people, the showplace is where the dogs come to strut their stuff. Some people consider the dog show as a subjective pseudo-sport somewhere between judging figure skating and beauty pageants. The dog show is surely one of the few places left on earth where civilized battles can take place. Since antiquity, man has utilized both the horse and the dog to serve him. It was inevitable that man's innate spirit of competition would lead him to prove whose animals were the best through horse races and dog contests. Certainly the dog show was more acceptable to the gentry of Queen Victoria's day than such competition as bull-baiting or rat-killing for dogs. Over the centuries, these competitions have evolved into international events in which breeders showcase their best in their efforts to improve their lines, as well as the breed itself. Consider the focus on the thoroughbred that has resulted from The Breeders Cup, now in its second decade.

When the automobile reduced the primary importance of the horse to the family, more and more

> "All the world's a stage, and all the men and women merely players..."
> —Shakespeare, from *As You Like It*

families turned their interest in animals to their dogs. Americans had a traditional interest in dogs for the sport and the hunt, so it was logical that they would embrace the idea of the bench show. These early sporting dogmen used to meet in New York's Westminster Hotel to discuss the merits of their various Pointers and Setters, and eventually they decided to follow England's example and stage their own show at Gilmore's Garden on Madison Avenue. Two such shows had already been held in Memphis, Tennessee, and Philadelphia, Pennsylvania. Westminster held its first show May 1877, and in those early years it was entirely a "man's" world. To this day, Westminster membership is prized by dogmen all over the nation.

One breed that had caught on by the last part of the 19th Century with both men and women was the French Bulldog. An interesting chain of events led to one of the most unusual dog shows ever held in the United States—that of the French Bulldog Club of America in 1898.

For a number of years, there had been on-going controversy over what kind of ear these small bulldogs should have, rose or bat. This argument had not started in the United States but in Europe, where the rose ear was preferred. Nonetheless, American fanciers stood firmly by their choice of the bat ear, rightly believing that this feature gave the breed a large degree of its individuality. Therefore, these fanciers had been offended when the English judge who passed on the breed at Westminster in 1897 had favored rose-eared dogs, which they believed to be toy English Bulldogs and not true French Bulldogs at all, for the highest honors. The following year, 1898, the Westminster premium list offered classes for both rose-eared and bat-eared to be judged by the respected E. D. Faulkner. When their protest did not result in the withdrawal of classes for rose-eared dogs, the French Bulldog Club was incensed. From this disagreement between the two clubs emerged the first specialty show ever held for French Bulldogs anywhere!

This elegant event took place at the world-famous Waldorf-Astoria Hotel on February 12, 1898, and might very well have been the most unusual show ever staged. Engraved invitations were highly prized, and this New York Society dog show received widespread acclaim in the New York newspapers. Mr. Faulkner himself judged it and selected Mrs. Amy C. Gillig's Dimboolaa as his Best French Bulldog. So much favorable publicity surrounded this event that everybody benefited from it, as evidenced by the fact that each year after that French Bulldog entries rose (no pun intended) in this breed at Westminster, and by 1906 there were 100 Frenchies entered at the Garden. This famous all-breed club and the world's first French Bulldog Club's joint message is one that is still meaningful to us today. A difference of opinion is not a difference in principle.

In the first one-third of the 20th Century, huge kennels were built by those of great wealth who became patrons and enthusiasts of their chosen breeds. They hired expert help to run their breeding programs, manage their kennels, and show their dogs. In most cases, the kennel manager was also a talented handler. Some of these ladies and gentlemen preferred to handle their own dogs and thrived on the competition. A number of them got into the grooming and care of the animals while others became skilled handlers (after all, they were learning from the best) and showed up at ringside to waltz their well-trained, perfectly prepared charges into the ring. By 1937, more than one million people a year were attending dog shows with more than 100,000 dogs competing in them in the United States.

Tremendous growth in the dog show world took place following World War II, and the era of intensified participation by women began in earnest. Rosie the Riveter had proved she was as good as any man at doing her job in the factories while the men were off to war. Women had come of age, not only in dogs, but in everything else too. Actually, this trend had started during World War I as women's early independence expressed itself as the flapper of the Roaring Twenties. How all of this social change in America affected dogs is interesting. It eventually resulted in widespread influence throughout the sport by women at all levels—prominent breeders, handlers, judges, publishers, executives, and veterinarians—with a woman becoming president of the American Kennel Club in 1994.

The last half of the 20th Century has seen any number of changes in the socioeconomic picture in America and the rest of the world as well. By 1994, almost two million dogs competed in 8,170 events licensed by the American Kennel Club with 3,080 of them being conformation dog shows—1,220 all-breed shows and 1,860 specialty shows. The other 5,000-plus events consisted of performance contests including obedience trials, field and hunting tests, tracking, herding, lure-coursing, agility and earthdog trials. In addition to the more than 8,000 licensed events, another 13,041 sanctioned events took place for a grand total of more than 20,000 purebred dog activities overseen by the American Kennel Club in 1994. Of the almost two million animals—about 10 percent of all registered dogs—competing in these events, approximately three-fourths of their numbers vied for honors at conformation shows. The AKC licensed 2,642 conformation judges to handle these amazing numbers (Fall 1995 statistics, courtesy of AKC).

Such staggering statistics reflect the growing interest in purebred dogs as a sporting hobby. There was no information available regarding the number of people involved with their dogs in these activities in 1994, or how many people attended them. Using the previous statistics that indicate for every dog that competed, an average of 10 people attended the events, assume that somewhere in the neighborhood of 20 million people attended performing dog events and dog shows in 1994.

Just what these numbers mean to us as fanciers is unclear. Americans have always been addicted to sports, but some fans are becoming turned off by the outrageous salaries paid to star athletes. Although these "humongous" sums of money pouring through professional sports may be good for the athletes and the owners, just how good it is for the American sports fan is another matter. Millions of sports fans who cannot see the games live in a stadium are glued to television sets in what has become the ultimate couch-potato sport, that of the removed spectator becoming more removed all the time as teams relocate from one city to another in increasing numbers. Such continued relocations of both teams and athletes cause fans to question their loyalties. And, that is where the dog show enters the picture, for the dog show offers people the opportunity to participate as well as observe.

Dog shows are a participant sport that offer healthy competition for all ages from all walks of life. All you need is a good dog and a little training and you are ready to play. Dog shows offer an outlet for people's natural competitive drive and they can play a little or a lot as life styles and desires dictate. The wonderful element of performing dog events is that everyone in the family can get involved. It becomes an activity that gets you off the couch and into action. No wonder as sports fans get more and more removed from the game itself, dog shows get more and more popular. And that is in the best interest of the entire fancy.

For the truth is, the same temperament that makes the perfect, well-adjusted show dog also produces the perfect pet. Therefore, as we enter the 21st Century, the fancy must figure the best ways to deal with the explosive growth of the game—ways that are good for the order and in the best interest of all. The monumental changes that we will experience in the next 50 years may very well be even more radical in all walks of life than those we have seen in the last 100 years.

Yet, even as we appreciate the dog show as an attractive setting to draw potentially responsible pet owners into our circle in their search for quality animals and our search for quality homes, the fancy must never lose sight of the true reason dog shows were begun—for breeders to take their best and compare them with the best of others in a continuous effort to select the best breeding stock. If you are genuinely dedicated to dogs, better breeding will always be the ultimate goal as you seek dog show honors. The most effective use of this concept is achieved at the shows in which the best compete against each other. To refute the professional football coach—*winning is not the only thing*. In essence, dog shows should and do encourage breeders to breed better dogs.

Evaluating Master Judges

When you evaluate a judge, you are comparing your opinion with that of the judge. Ask yourself if your personal definition of a good judge is one who always puts up your dog and if a bad judge is one who puts up another dog. If so, perhaps you need to examine your own thinking.

The truth of the matter is that you seldom see your own dogs as others see them. Therefore, when they don't win, the judge is either "political" or "stupid" or both. And you seldom look at your competitor's dogs as you look at your own. Therefore, when they win you are incensed. With all of these human contradictions built into each and every one of us, it is a wonder that you agree with the judges as often as you do.

These contradictions of human nature are not limited to the world of dogs. A number of Dallas Cowboy fans thought Deion Sanders was a worthless, showboating, overpaid San Francisco Forty Niner, who became great only when he joined their team. All of us have known handlers who thought particular dogs were not so good until they ended up on their strings!

Total objectivity is not possible in the world of judging dogs because the interpreting and applying of the standard to judging involves a certain degree of subjectivity. When you evaluate judges you are also being subjective to a greater or lesser degree. The important factor for all in the equation is to be fair as well as knowledgeable.

"How can he like both of those dogs?" was a question I heard asked of a Sporting Group judge who placed two rather different Cocker Spaniels in the same group a couple of years ago. Now this outstanding judge being questioned by the discontented ringsider is an expert on Cocker Spaniels and one of the best judges in the ring today. In my eyes, he ranks right up there with many of the *master judges* who have gone on to their greater rewards. Perhaps to the untrained eye it appeared he did not know what he was doing.

But his was a very trained eye blessed with natural artistic ability and intricate knowledge to augment it. The one dog was a compact and typey dog somewhat smaller than some of his brethren, yet correct and very much within the standard. The other dog was a leggier, more sporting type Cocker who was overall more dog yet still within the standard. There is room for and need of both these lovely dogs in this breed. Just as a football team needs fullbacks and halfbacks to be a team, so does a breed need its different kinds of players all on the same team to be complete. For although the good animals in a breed need to be of a like type, there is still sufficient room for enough variables within that correct type to prevent the good ones from being monotonously alike.

Slight differences in strengths and virtues make it possible for breeders to effect their corrections within a similar framework as they seek continued progress within their breed. Certainly this is true until that day when the ultimate dream comes true, a world full of absolutely correct dogs of exquisite type and sound mind and body that are all alike. When that day happens, dog shows will cease!

In the meantime, breeders need to consider the dog show the test of their applied studies in their chosen breed. They know what is required of the correct animal and its presentation by the educational system. They are totally prepared for the ultimate performance that will test to see if they have done their homework.

The exacting drill of the dog show is the feedback all of us who are students and would-be *master breeders* need to test our work. For in spite of the old saying that "practice makes perfect," practice without feedback does not make perfect at all—what it makes is permanent. That is why judges and breeders alike need the continuing education of the dog show and its associated activities to help them achieve expertise.

Because judges are human and subject to human frailties does not mean they are crooks or morons. They are expected to maintain a demanding schedule and at the same time render difficult decisions under sometimes stressful conditions. In evaluating the litter sired by Ch. Vin-Melca's Bombardier out of Ch. Vin-Melca's Calista (Sarah), it took me almost two years to decide which one was my first choice, and even then there were times when watching them in the yard gave me second thoughts. And this was dealing with animals whose virtues and weaknesses, heritage and nuances, were familiar to me. A judge's decision must be made in matters of minutes and administered accordingly.

And, most of all, *master breeders* and master judges need to keep their perspective to keep reproducing and appreciating works of art. Because some of the critics of their day did not prefer a certain Beethoven composition did not mean that it was not magnificent. Perhaps they were in a Mozart mood that day. Yet, they loved Beethoven's next masterpiece.

Handling

"You start handling the dog where it stops handling itself." So spoke my mentor, Johnny Davis, over four decades ago as he trained students to improve handling skills at conformation classes in the Tidewater area of Virginia. Improving your skills in handling your dog requires watching and studying the skills and styles of those at the top. Such studying can be supplemented by reading and visual aids as part of your skill drill. Such training classes as those conducted by kennel clubs and professionals are excellent for both exhibitors and their dogs.

The star graduate of the George Alston school of handling wins the 1996 Westminster Kennel Club Show as daughter Jane Alston-Myers handles the wonderful Clumber Spaniel, Ch. Clussex Country Sunrise to BIS under Judge Roy Holloway, with Ronald H. Menaker, show chairman, and Chester F. Collier, club president, presenting the trophies. Owned by Judith and Richard Zaleski, the Clumber won the Sporting Group under Judge Everett Dean. Doug Johnson, who shared breeding honors with S. Blakely and S. Stockhill, also breeds Sussex Spaniels, as the kennel name, Clussex, reflects. Jane and her husband Greg Myers are among the prominent professional handlers whose early and correct training on the road to success came from professionals skilled in the art. (Photo courtesy of John Ashbey)

There are several books written specifically to help you improve your handling skills, and they are written by such wizards as George Alston, Frank Sabella, and Bob and Jane Forsyth, who share the knowledge that put them on top in their competitive profession. Jeff Brucker has produced a video that is a good instructional tool. Sabella and the Forsyths have turned to judging while Alston's career has cast him in the role of expert teacher as well as author.

For an outstanding learning experience, consider the excellent two-day seminar conducted by this former handler and others like him. Such seminars can teach you how to train and present your dog so the judge can actually see him. Furthermore, they will help you enhance your sense of timing and coordinate your own movements with those of your dog, putting all action into the proper sequence. Alston, considered a teaching genius by those who take his clinic, points out that in no other sport can the novice compete against the professionals at any level.

FRIENDS CHERISH EACH OTHER'S HOPES. THEY ARE KIND TO EACH OTHER'S DREAMS. —THOREAU

Friends who engage in fierce competition in the ring yet enjoy a congenial dinner together after the show are prevalent in our wonderful world of dogs. Furthermore, good friends understand that the good fortune of one on a given day may depend on the bad fortune of the other.

Carroll Gordon (Diaz) is pictured here handling her Ch. Page Mill Hallmark to BIS at the Orange Empire Kennel Club in 1967. Carroll and I drove down to Southern California together, sharing ideas about breeding Beagles and Elkhounds with each other, as each of us had a BIS hound in the station wagon. We also discussed our lives outside the dog show ring: She was a professional golf instructor at Stanford University and I taught school. As a skilled handler, Carroll often advised me on how to improve my own handling skills. The seven-hour trip home after the show was cheered by her BIS and enlivened by the fact that her slip was showing. Judge O.C. Harriman had kidded her about it while the picture was being taken.

For some reason, it seems that competitive people who are genuine and sincere are the best kind of friends. They know when to give pep talks, when to listen without comment and when to give advice that may not be welcomed at that moment. Moreover, they share the most powerful trait of all—how to bring out the best in each other. This mutual sparring and sharing

contributes to the growth of both, making it possible for them to be kind to each other's dreams. Carroll's kennel is still active three decades after that trip, with the Page Mill colors currently carried to the top by 15-inch Ch. Tashwould Deja Vu, handled by Mike Kurtzner. (Stillman Photo)

Three hundred years before the birth of Christ, Greek philosopher Aristotle advised: "What we have to learn to do, we learn by doing." Alexander the Great was his pupil and he took Aristotle's teachings to heart and proceeded to conquer the known world. You, too, can utilize that advice today. Participating in training classes with good teachers is a valuable learning experience, for practice without feedback might just serve to make you more proficient in your mistakes. Therefore, taking that practice to the dog show and getting into the ring provides even more feedback. Ask mentors and qualified friends to watch you in the ring and offer suggestions to help you improve your skills. Have a friend videotape you and compare your execution in the ring with those of the stars. After studying the experts, practice "setting up" your dog in front of the mirror. Such drills will help you avoid some of the obvious handling mistakes that prevent your presenting your dog to his best advantage.

Here are a few common mistakes made by exhibitors:

- Overhandling the dog and/or obstructing the judge's appraisal of the dog;

- Misplacing legs so that the animal is overstretched or all bunched up;

- Incorrect gaiting of the dog caused by any number of handling errors. If you are uptight and jerky with your handling style, the best-moving dog in the world will reflect this.

- Failure to train and practice with the dog under conditions simulating the show environment. If you have done all you can do to breed the right animal, raise the right animal, condition and train him with proper presentation, you should be able to perform accordingly.

Before you decide that professional handlers are shown favoritism by judges, take into consideration the fact that the expert handler can take his charge and present it so well it can beat yours; but he can also swap dogs with you and take your charge and beat his! That's why studying these people is how we all learn to become better handlers and present our own dogs in the best possible light. He would know all the faults of his, and you would not see any of them. He would also know all the faults of yours, and so would the judge when he got through.

Furthermore, the true professional can be the best friend in the world to the sincere amateur, especially if that amateur shows proper respect and interest. For example, on show days the professional handler can always use an extra hand holding dogs, "running" them, and monitoring the activity at the set up, for this is his most busy, hectic time. In return, the professional is happy to give the volunteer handling lessons on his "off day," if there is any such thing when you are working with animals. You must pick a role model who is doing it right and be willing to drill on the basics to get in tune with your dog.

There is something almost mystical in the magic between a great handler and his great dog. It is a true bond. They are in tune and connected. Neither of them makes a mistake as they work together to cover whatever shortcomings do exist and feature all the virtues. They are in sync and in harmony. The best of handlers have a sensitive understanding of the dog's nervous system and psyche, thus allowing the best possible performance. They pay meticulous attention to details. In the equine world, this skilled attention to details is known as practicing excellent horsemanship, and the best handlers do this with their canine charges.

Various handlers have different ways of going about their work. Some of them will show each dog more or less the same, managing to get their charges to accommodate their methods of handling in excellent performances. The best of them will adapt their handling style to the individual dogs as they accommodate their charges in a beautifully orchestrated performance. For every minute they are in the ring accomplishing success, hours are spent behind the scenes in hard work that makes the ring performance possible. Their love of their work and desire "to go to work" everyday is what makes them both special and successful.

Accomplished handlers recognize that the best way to motivate dogs is to motivate themselves. They project confidence in the dogs, in the judges, and in the procedure. Their body language speaks positive messages to the dogs, the judges, and the ringside. They have a special feel for each dog, bringing the young ones along slowly to acquire their education. No dog is pushed harder or faster than his young body and psyche can handle. The older, experienced dog is treated appropriately to maintain his interest and keep an upbeat attitude. Care is taken to prevent him becoming bored or soured by the process. Because of these talents, they are able to get the most out of their dogs.

Over the years some of the handling greats have become involved in the breeding programs that produce the dogs that they show. In the early years of Salgray Boxers, Larry Downey and Jane Forsyth come to mind and later Stan Flowers as examples of handlers interacting with the breeding programs. Such handlers work in concert with the breeders to select stock and provide expert second opinions. Others are content to take the dogs that come to them on their own, without involvement in the breeding programs that produce them.

Top handlers know that winning is not a weekend exercise. They are big on basics, getting both themselves and their dogs in the ultimate condition. They know that what goes on during their off days is just as important as what happens on the day of the show. They realize that what goes on during those off days determines what happens on the day of the show. One of the most skilled handlers I've ever known with wonderful "hands" on a dog never made it to the top simply because he thought the dog show started when he stepped into the ring. In his opinion, the judges did not reward his gorgeous animals the way they should have. And it was no wonder, for under their coats his dogs were either mushy and soft or a rack of bones. Being unrealistic can happen to handlers just as it can to breeders and exhibitors.

Knowing how to "peak" each dog so that he is on top of his game at the big shows is another skill shared by the top handlers. Perhaps the greatest expertise possible is shown by those terrier handlers who skillfully work coats and manage to have their charges in absolutely perfect condition for Westminster in February, Grayslake and Great Western in June, and Montgomery in October. Any true dog person in search of an exquisite panorama of peak conditioning need only attend one Montgomery County Show to have a permanent picture of what is meant by the term.

Like skilled athletes and professionals in other fields, not all great handlers have the same style or form. But they all have the ability to take a good dog and make him look better. In short, unlike those of lesser skills who compete against them, they never beat themselves. Furthermore, they are aware that few people see what doesn't stand out, and their exquisite timing allows their dog to "stand out" at the precise moment the judge is looking.

In baseball there is an expression called "mental error" that describes an error not charged to a player because it is not obvious or does not fit the usual criteria for mistakes. What it means is simple, the player doesn't get charged with it because it wasn't blatant. Most of us who show dogs make our share of mental errors over the years, and the dogs have paid the price for it. The great handler seldom, if ever, does this. He doesn't clutch when the pressure is on, for both he and his dog are true champions.

Although the average weekend golfer would not expect to take on the winner of the Masters or the British Open, amazingly skilled amateur handlers of good dogs are able to compete at the top in the showing of purebred dogs. And that is one of the many attractions and fascinations of our sport. If you have an exceptional dog and you learn to present him properly, he will indeed have his day!

Inside the Ring and Out: The Sportsman's Dog Person

In his marvelous articles on great kennels more than 50 years ago, Arthur Frederick Jones wrote on a regular basis about America's great breeders and their operations. Jones was astute with his interviews as he managed to present the philosophy of these competitive sportsmen and women as well as in-depth information on their breeding operations.

Betty Hyslop, the mistress of the famous Cairndania Kennels, was quoted as saying that in the long run "our good dogs will win. Sometimes, in losing to better specimens they will bring more satisfaction than if they had beaten mediocre opposition." (May 1939 *American Kennel Gazette*) Mrs. Hyslop is a refreshing testimonial to those dedicated to the dog show as the place where fanciers showcased their stock and sought to find animals to better their own breeding programs. This grand lady has contributed to her chosen breeds' gene pool for more than 60 years, and both her Cairn Terriers and Great Danes have been noteworthy parts of classic pedigrees in the United States as well as Canada.

In essence, Mrs. Hyslop was like all top competitors in feeling exhilaration when victory came in excellent competition. And no doubt, losses to superior specimens got her personal wheels turning to see if there was a place in her breeding program for these animals. In analyzing this quotation, you can detect a *master breeder* willingly and accurately assessing the merits of the competition. When you

> "Sports do not build character. They reveal it."
> —Heywood Broun (1888 - 1939)

are showing against dogs that are better than yours, it is in your best interest to consider getting them in your gene pool.

In the November 1, 1934, issue of the *American Kennel Gazette*, Jones interviewed Mrs. William duPont Jr. at her Foxcatcher Beagle Kennel in Pennsylvania. Mrs. duPont commented that "she found much more enjoyment in breeding a good one... than in carrying off the greatest prize offered in any kind of competition." According to the article, this was the duPonts' creed in their other sporting activities as well, including Welsh ponies, thoroughbreds, saddlebreds, and hunters. This sense of dignity serves as a worthy example to us all six decades later.

Such an attitude as exhibited by these sporting breeders is what our game is founded upon—the personal commitment of trying to breed better dogs and show better dogs and may the best dogs win. The dog show is the ultimate expression of feedback on your breeding program. Honorable, knowledgeable feedback is a valuable tool today as well as yesterday. Perhaps it was because it was a "kinder and gentler" time, but in those days it was considered inappropriate to bring ill dogs to shows. Exhibitors and professional handlers alike endured self-imposed abstinence when their dogs were sick to insure they did not expose other people's animals to contagious diseases. Unhappily, today there is no self-imposed honor code to encourage fanciers to exercise a reasonable incubation period before returning to the shows. Yes, there was much good in the good old days, and, yes, things have changed.

Many people feel threatened by change and new ideas. They feel threatened by others with good dogs. Rather than feeling threatened, the true competitor will feel challenged to rise to the occasion and produce a better animal. The true sportsman is not threatened by failure. Losses can teach you more than wins can. How you handle them will say a lot about you.

Put in proper perspective, did the dog that beat you have some breed features yours lacked? Could those virtues help your line? Breeders aren't born knowing these things and the good ones will learn to fail intelligently by getting something positive out of the experience.

It has been said that the two hardest things in the world to deal with are failure and success. Perhaps the only thing worse than a poor loser is a poor winner. It is important to avoid arrogance with success, and to remember it is not your personal ego trip—*it is about dogs.*

When I stated that the dog show is one of the few places left on Earth in which civilized battles can take place, I had in mind the sparring of two exceptional terriers by great dog handlers; the faces of two talented sporting-dog handlers intent on setting up their dogs to perfection and gaiting them smoothly; the battle between top dogs and top handlers that is followed by the winner graciously accepting the congratulations offered by the loser. In the dog world, this is good form. It is the outward

WHAT IS A GREAT DOG?

The GREAT DOG, like the genius, is abnormal. He goes beyond being good—he is extraordinary. Such a dog is in a class or league of his own. He is superlative. He exudes charisma and seems to have a magnetic field surrounding him.

Great dogs have a sense of self that is vital. As the revered Bea Godsol described it: "All dogs have faults. The great ones carry them well." They are able to pull themselves together under all situations and against all adversities. They have tremendous self-confidence with just enough nervous energy to give them star quality. They take command of the ring. The great one is the combination of all the right things—everything fits on this animal as all of his parts are in harmony and proper proportion. Such a dog has the perfect combination of symmetrical contour and outline accompanied by correctly working, moving parts and body texture. Such a dog was BORN TO WIN.

In my half-century in dogs, it has been my privilege to observe many outstanding animals who were magnificent examples of their breeds. Many of these dogs have been profiled in this book, and they stand tall amongst their peers in the same way a giant of a person, who may not measure six feet in height, seems 10 feet tall! These wondrous creatures were very special, not only at the time in which they competed, but for all time. It is not possible to truly compare dogs from vastly differing eras with each other. How do you compare Rogers Hornsby with Roger Clemens? Or, Man O'War with Secretariat or Cigar?

The great ones, both canine and human, are able to compete against all competition during their stay on the top. This they will do no matter what obstacles occur on their path to the top. Some breeds have few, if any, great dogs during a given lifetime, while others have numbers of them, one after another. In those breeds blessed by numbers

Ch. Melbee's Chances Are with handler Ric Chashoudian (Photo by Bennett Assoc.)

of great ones, they will often be related, as the great ones are the most likely to beget more of the same. Great dogs are able to "lay off" for a time, return to the ring, and still own it.

Two dogs who personally appealed to this observer above all others over the years were the English Setter Ch. Rock Falls Colonel and the Kerry Blue Terrier Ch. Melbee's Chances Are. The Colonel was magnificence in orange and white. His persona of splendid presence and cooperation with his beloved master William T. (Bill) Holt, of Richmond, Virginia, was something to behold. This wonderful breeder, owner and handler of Colonel—as elegant and worthy as the dog—campaigned his treasure to become one of the first dogs in history to win 100 All Breed BISs.

Chances Are, the blue jewel that was the pride of Mel and Bea Schlesinger's Kansas City breeding program, was the ultimate show dog—a dog of incomparable breed type and energy. Together with his handler Ric Chashoudian, he became Top Dog All Breeds in about 18 months of campaigning, winning over 40 BISs in the competitive California rings. When he won all of the shows on the 1968 Cal-Ore Circuit, people were absolutely amazed.

Ch. Rock Falls Colonel and Ch. Melbee's Chances Are will always be the prototypes by which I measure an English Setter and a Kerry Blue Terrier. They were the highest peak of the tallest mountains in my lifetime in dogs. Sadly, neither one of them won the Garden.

Ch. Rock Falls Colonel, owned, bred and handled by William T. Holt. (Photo by Shafer)

visible sign that inwardly you have your act together. No less a winner than Napoleon said: "The most dangerous moment comes with victory."

With more people coming into dogs all the time, it is fitting for those already deep in the game to set an example of sportsmanship and good will. Even though your dogs will lose sometimes when they should not, they will also win a few they do not deserve. If you keep it in perspective, you realize things tend to even out. *It is important that fanciers respect the game, respect the players, respect the officials, respect themselves and their dogs, and respect the guiding group.*

Ways to the Winners' Circle

"The great golfing professional, Arnold Palmer, was once asked why he could never beat Jack Nicklaus. Palmer said: 'Because I was always thinking about beating Jack Nicklaus, and Jack Nicklaus was always thinking about playing good golf.'" This quotation from an interview in the *Nashville Tennessean*, July 25, 1995, says a lot about focus and keeping your mind on your goals.

If you can't see your dog the way the judges and your competitors do, you're going to have trouble understanding a lot of the judging decisions you will encounter. Inability to evaluate your animal and its worth is the worst thing you can allow to happen to you, for it will prevent your ever winning what the dog can achieve by coloring your campaign decision making.

If you want to find the way to the winners' circle, you must avoid self-delusion. It is bad enough if self-delusion is the result of lack of knowledge. But if you have the knowledge and still fall prey to this human frailty, ask yourself what you are accomplishing by being dishonest with yourself. You must also avoid self-defeating attitudes.

There are many ways to the winners' circle, and all of them require a dog that ranges from good to excellent in quality. One way to get your dog into the winners' circle is to engage the services of a qualified professional handler. This route is especially inviting to those whose "specialty" breeds require great expertise to present them properly. A number of terriers and toys come to mind as well as Cocker Spaniels and Poodles. This is also a choice for those in highly competitive breeds in which, in the long run, the services of a professional are cost effective. In most cases, the handler conditions the dog, grooms it, transports it, and presents it.

Sometimes exhibitors cooperate in a team effort with the professional to get the animal into the ring. If the exhibitor (owner) lacks the necessary skills to show the dog but loves to go to the shows where his dog is exhibited, the owner transports the dog, grooms it, prepares it for the ring, and then turns it over to the handler at ringside. Another variation of the team venture is for the owner to show the dog early on and then turn it over to the professional to complete its championship. Or perhaps the owner finishes the dog and it is a truly good one, so therefore, he turns it over to the professional when it is ready to be specialed.

Even though I am not a golfer, many years on the Monterey Peninsula cultivated a love of golf by association. Running my dogs beside the golf courses, hearing golf talked about expertly, even in casual social situations, and teaching youngsters whose fathers were on tour, or club professionals at the most exacting of courses does develop an outsider's appreciation for the game. That is why I referred to duffers and hackers to describe beginners.

Now the amazing thing about those beginning golfers is that it would never occur to them to take on the PGA's leaders in a round of golf. Yet dog show exhibitors routinely take on those at the top in the competitive world of showing purebred dogs. The difference is the golfers know they're not in the same league, the exhibitors often do not. So why do rookies in dogs think they should be knocking off Peter Green, Andy Linton, or Corky Vroom? Because they are looking at their precious animals through rose-colored glasses. They never consider either their lack of expertise at evaluating their dogs or their lack of expertise at presenting them. Because the competition relies on opinion (and in their opinion their dogs are the best), there are unhappy reactions to their losses until they learn better, if they ever do. Yet, if everybody who plays golf could take on the pros after a few lessons, what would it do to the PGA tour?

The competent exhibitor is able to assess his dog's potential and acts accordingly. Depending on the quality of the particular animal and its potential, he decides where he wants to go with the dog. In competitive breeds, class wins are meaningful. In other breeds, the American-bred class rarely has competition. In a competitive breed, a dog capable of making class wins but not quite as good as the ones taking the points might be of quality as good or better than dogs of other breeds taking points.

Some owners who are fortunate enough to complete their dogs' championships become disillusioned when they start specialing their dogs with poor results. Just because a dog finishes its championship does not mean it is worthy of being campaigned at the next level. If a dog experienced difficulty in completing its title, it is usually not competitive beyond that.

Perhaps the goal for a good dog is to pursue breed wins and group placements. It might even end up in a quest for groups and the coveted red, white and blue, if the animal has the quality. And a parallel to these levels can be found in the realm of the specialty show. The comparative goals might be a class win at a regional; a class win at a National or points at a regional; points at a National or a breed at a regional and at the top rung of the ladder—a National Specialty winner.

To evaluate your dog and its potential seek advice from an expert you trust, consider the competition the dog will be facing and its relative merit in that competition, decide who will handle it and set some realistic goals. And if those in the know say that the dog is good enough and you want to give it a try yourself, why not?

Just keep in mind that you're going to make some mistakes as you learn to campaign your good one, and he is going to pay the price for it some of the time. That's what good competition is all about, and it is an ongoing learning experience.

Seeking out the best competition as you learn is the best way to improve, for you have to be better yourself to compete. Furthermore, your successes in top competition are all the more precious. Before going to California in 1961, Ch. Vin Melca's Rebel Rouser rarely lost a breed, as the competition in Virginia, North Carolina, and Maryland in the 1950s and 1960s for Norwegian Elkhounds was weak. In California, she took many best opposite sexes to Ch. Windy Cove's Rowdy Ringo, handled by Harry Sangster, and his brother, Ch. Windy Cove's Silver Son, handled by George Payton. Subsequent breed-

Ch. Vin-Melca's Rebel Rouser pictured here with Judge Haskell Shuffman in 1962 when she was already the dam of three champions. A multi-group and specialty winner, her next litter after this picture was taken produced the BIS winning Ch. Vin-Melca's Vickssen, sire of Vagabond. (Bennett Associates Photo)

ings to these two dogs resulted in Howdy Rowdy and the sire of Vagabond. In essence, the better the competition in which you are playing, the more rapid your improvement should be in both your breeding program and your handling skills. You learn to stay on target and not let down.

If you are always avoiding other good dogs in your breed, perhaps you need to ask yourself why. Have you lost sight of your purpose to produce a better dog? You need to understand that your competitors are your best friends. For they help you improve your game and keep you focused, which keeps you from letting down. There are times when your strategy for campaigning your dog includes trying to protect him in the breed, and you should act accordingly. I am talking about a way of life, not sometime decisions. I am talking about long-term goals designed to help you breed the best dogs and show the best dogs for life, not a given win on a given weekend.

Advantages of the Do-It-Yourself Campaign

You've poured your lifetime's work into the breeding and rearing of good dogs. Like the gourmet chef who is anxious to have discerning guests share the fruits of his labor with approval, you are excited at the idea of sharing your creation with the best of the critics and eager to have the feedback on this particular dog. And that is as it should be, for classic feedback intensifies the learning experience and the pleasure of having accomplished a goal.

Yet, the professionals are justifiably hard to beat, for they are so skilled at what they do. Their ability to take a good dog and make it look better is something you admire. And now that you have a good one, your sporting blood entices you to accept the challenge and compete with the professionals at a higher level than the classes. You have prepared by showing a number of class dogs with successful results as you improved your skills, so you can do the job well if not expertly. And you are of the right mind-set with the right attitude as you enter into the campaign.

The first thing you have to do is make sure your dog is worthy of this effort. Knowing just how good your dog is and what kind of competition best suits it is important to your success. It is embarrassing for dogs to be put into situations in which they are grossly mismatched. Dogs that were lucky to finish their championships do not belong in the specials ring at all. Assuming your dog finished rather easily in decent competition, your next step is to try to show him in situations that best showcase him. You can not do this unless you are totally objective about your dog and those of your competitors. And if you are not sure, seek reinforcement and help with your campaign strategy by asking those who do know to guide you in your decisions. They can advise you on the potential of the dog and the type of campaign in its best interest. Even then you won't know until you try, as there is no sure way to predict whether a dog will catch on or not.

Next put these evaluations to the test. If you were told that your dog is an excellent mover with impressive side gait as his best feature, seek out shows with rings that are adequate to allow him to look his best. If he is a beautiful specimen of the breed standing but not a gifted mover, seek shows with smaller rings that require less of him. The best dogs, of course, are indifferent to ring conditions and perform equally well under all conditions.

Once you have firmly established the setting that is best for your dog, try to decide what kind of competition is in his best interest. If he is a young dog who needs seasoning, a small circuit with lots of shows in a condensed time frame is intense and will give him an opportunity to perform both in the breed and in the group. If there is a name dog out in your breed at the time, you might want to take your youngster in the opposite direction until he is an experienced campaigner.

Such a circuit gives you an opportunity to relate to your dog on a one-to-one basis that handlers seldom have the luxury to do. Since you already know the performance personalities of this dog's ancestors because you raised them, you have already made a step in the right direction. Do not allow the animal to become a spoiled brat at the same time you relish this close relationship on the road. Use it as quality time to get into his head and get the two of you in tune with each other.

It might be said that the advantages the owner-handler has with one dog help level the playing field in competing against the professionals. For the handler has to pick shows that are favorable for his entire string of six to ten dogs, not just one dog. You, the one dog owner-handler, will enjoy the opportunity of trying to choose the shows that are good for you and your dog. If you have paid your dues in the classes over the years, you probably know which judges will reward the correct profile, good headpiece, and correct coat that are your dog's strongest features. Furthermore, they will appreciate his excellent side gait.

Another advantage of the owner-handler is not having the stress of facing clients who question each decision, for you are the master of your own ship. If you made the wrong choice of shows, call it a learning experience and try to do better next time. Recognize that even though you thought you had a good game plan, it doesn't always work out that way. If your campaign with a good dog runs aground, ask others who know more than you for some advice. Maybe the time is wrong for this par-

Successful owner-handler Walter Goodman and Skye Terrier, Ch. Glamoor Good News pictured winning BIS at the 1969 Westminster Kennel Club Show under Judge Louis Murr with William Rockefeller presenting the trophy. "Susie," proof of the owner-handler relationship, was utterly devoted to her master. Goodman, also her breeder, adjudicated the 1994 Westminster BIS. (Photo by Gilbert)

ticular dog. Think like a coach working with an athlete and ask yourself what you can do to ensure a better performance. If you have an excellent dog, conditioning him well, presenting him properly, and showing him in appropriate competition will produce success. Just as in breeding, the key to all of this is being knowledgeable and objective. If you look at your competition in the best possible light, and your own beloved dogs with a more critical eye, you will have an immediate edge because most people do it the other way around. Ask yourself how good their dogs would look if they were on your leash. By denying the worth of other dogs, you put your own at a disadvantage. Be your own best judge and remember that over the long haul, luck will favor the better dog.

The best competitors and participants in our sport are those who have a sense of what is right and act accordingly. They are persistent but upbeat; they are serious and focused, yet they have a good sense of humor. They recognize that winning is hard work, and they enjoy the up times while taking the down times in stride. Because they are survivors in life as well as in this game they love, they have learned to expect the unexpected.

Winners know that it is perfectly acceptable to be enthusiastic about the qualities of their own dogs, but poor form to talk down someone else's dog. They have an ingrained sense of the meaning of Benjamin Franklin in making this comment: "You cannot strengthen one by weakening another; and you can not add to the stature of a dwarf by cutting the leg off a giant."

Winners understand that advertising openly in the fancy's publications is a fair way to promote dogs. To promise judging assignments, send unsolicited gifts or make a career of fawning all over judges is not. Winners have respect for the judge's space and time, and they do not invade that privacy. Winners understand that it's a world of competition that on a given day allows their dogs to make it to the top as an indirect result of a best friend's loss in the breed or group. Even though they enjoy the resulting win that would not have come had their friend's dog gotten through, winners feel a certain pang of empathy because they know they're not the only one with a good dog. And, because they know that many circumstances contribute to the wins and losses, they are willing to give it another try when it didn't fall their way. Most of all, they know there is always tomorrow.

To be a successful do-it-yourselfer involves keeping your perspective. And, interestingly enough, in so doing, your wins will not offend others. You understand that tomorrow will be different from yesterday only if you plan and work accordingly. You learn from your own mistakes and the mistakes of others, and from the successes of others. You pick the very best of role models to serve as examples of how to "do-it-yourself." You know that winners are the losers of today who plant the seeds of success for tomorrow. **And most of all you know that how much you succeed is determined by how well you breed.**

Friendly Rivals

A great rivalry is one that pits the very best against each other. It is a match up between champions—the stuff dreams are made of for those with sporting blood pounding through their veins. In their heyday, it was Palmer versus Nicklaus, it was Becker versus Connors, it was Alydar versus Affirmed and it was Bangaway versus the Colonel.

Your toughest competitor and best rival is also your best friend even if neither of you realize it; for he is the one who challenges you to come up with your best effort, to go beyond the ordinary to the extraordinary.

Rivalries are nothing new on the American dog scene as evidenced by one that took place beginning with millionaire tycoon J. P. Morgan's purchase of the outstanding Collie, Sefton Hero, from England over a century ago. This led to a bidding war with prominent corporate attorney Samuel Untermeyer, fellow Collie fancier, for some of England's best Collies. Checks were signed for escalating amounts to English breeders as the two participated in a game of one-upsmanship. Not only did English breeders profit from this fun-feud, but so did the gene pool of the American Collie, leading to excellent American-bred Collies down from this stock.

Growing up in the Cocker Spaniel world of the early 50s was one of the greatest of my experiences when it came to understanding rivalry in dogs. Entering into their mature years at the top of their game were longtime rivals Clint Callahan and the brothers Bain and Ken Cobb. Very youthful and "on the muscle" in their ascendancy to stardom were the flamboyant Norman Austin and Ted Young Jr. In addition to the role model lessons they taught in skill and sportsmanship, there was the strong message of how rivals act and interact. When the one has a great dog that is performing with star quality, the other is inspired to go out and come up with a competitive dog and execute its "show" performance to perfection. When one is on a roll with a fabulous animal, the other must work harder than ever to assist breeders and owners to improve in order to compete. My eternal gratitude goes to these sporting men for making an indelible, lasting imprint during those formative years. For theirs was the healthy message that rivalries can provide more than stimulating competition—they can permanently influence the breed.

One breed that benefitted greatly from such a friendly rivalry during the middle decades of the 20th Century was the Golden Retriever. The rivals involved were Lloyd Case and Harold Correll, two gentlemen who were true sporting professionals, as they squared off in the competitive show rings of the East. In addition to providing expert handling skills in the ring, they contributed significantly to the improvement of the gene pool of the breeding programs of their clients as well as conducting their own select breeding programs.

Case and his wife developed the Celloyd line of Goldens that became instrumental foundation stock leading to some of the breed's influential greats. For example, a Celloyd bitch was the granddam of Ch. Cragmount's Peter, who in turn sired Ch. Cragmount's Hi-Lo—the only Golden to win the Group in Westminster's history. Case handled Ch. Prince Alexander, owned by Elizabeth Tuttle, to BIS at my "home show," Tidewater Kennel Club, while I was still in Children's Handling (as Junior Showmanship was known in those days). It was an awesome performance that impressed this enthusiastic youngster.

Correll advised and handled for his neighbor in New Jersey, Mrs. Charles W. Engelhard Jr. of Cragmount Golden fame. The Cragmount Goldens were not only influential in Mrs. Engelhard's day, but forever, mostly down through Ch. Cragmount's Peter, who became the paternal grandsire of both the outstanding winner, Ch. Cummings' Gold-Rush Charlie, and the top-producing sire, Ch. Misty Morn's Sunset. (At the same time Mrs. Engelhard's dogs were influencing the American dog show world, her husband's classic thoroughbreds were leaving their mark in racing annals. The most notable was the remarkable Nijinsky II.) Sunset's dam Amber Lady of Tercor Farm was bred by Correll with his son Terry. Tercor was the combination of their names, and Terry went on to follow in his father's footsteps as the handler of this outstanding line of Goldens. The significant contribution pro-

Below: Greyhound Ch. Aroi Talk of the Blues and Corky Vroom were competitive friendly rivals who soared to the Top Dog All Breeds position in 1976. "Punky," the pride and joy of Mr. & Mrs. N.J. Reese, still holds all records for her breed. Georgiann Mueller bred her from Ch. Aroi Blue Tiger Blues and Ch. Aroi Talk Of The Town. This outstanding bitch won 68 BISs, and was a two-time Westminster Hound Group winner and Quaker Oats winner. (Photo by Ludwig)

Ch. Bel S'mbran Bachrach and George Bell were formidable friendly rivals for the author and Ch. Vin-Melca's Nimbus. Nimbus was fascinated by Bachrach's tail and always tried to chase it, thereby destroying his own composure. The author tried to get into the ring ahead of the Saluki twosome. This resulted in some strategic "jockeying" at ringside with George, much to the amusement of fellow hound competitors. George and Bachrach are pictured in flawless movement here at Madison Square Garden. (Photo courtesy of George Bell)

Ch. Misty Morn's Sunset CD, TD, WC, Golden Retriever, was from Harold and Terry Correll's unfinished bitch Amber Lady of Tercor Farm and became the top Golden Retriever sire in history with 119 champions. (Photo courtesy of Jackie Root)

Multi-BIS winner and Multi-Quaker Oats winner Ch. Kabik's The Front Runner, son of Westminster BIS winner and Top Dog All Breeds Ch. Kabik's The Challenger, continued where his father left off in dominating the show rings of his era. A stallion of a dog, he was owned by Mr. & Mrs. William A. Clot, and his handler Chris Terrell, who, with his wife Marguerite, co-bred him and his sire. The exhilarating competition provided by the splendid array of hounds campaigned during this era was the experience of a lifetime for all the players. Judge Edd Bivin is awarding "Runner" BIS. (Rich Bergman Photo)

duced by the amicable Case-Correll rivalry is that they advised their clients to use each other's dogs thereby merging the blood of Golden Pine, Celloyd and Cragmount into the bloodlines still being utilized by breeders more than five decades later!

My California years resulted in some rivalries that were absolutely exhilarating at the same time they were intense. The Hound Group rivalries with fellow owner-breeder-handlers George Bell of Saluki fame and Chris Terrell of Afghan fame created an appreciation of the work of others at the same time we were competing. There were some shows in which the hound group placements went to dogs who were number one in their breed all time at that point in canine history. I wonder what sort of records they might have finally put in the book if they weren't all competing during the same era.

During a five-year period, Ch. Bel S'mbran Bachrach and Ch. Bel S'mbran Aba Fantasia, Ch. Kabik's The Challenger, and Ch. Kabik's The Front Runner, Ch. Vin-Melca's Nimbus and Ch. Vin-Melca's Last Call all vied for Hound Group honors along with the incredible Greyhound piloted by Corky Vroom—Ch. Aroi Talk of the Blues. Consider the fact that in a seven-year period these dogs combined efforts to win six of the Westminster hound groups with the Eastern exhibit of handler Robert Forsyth, Ch. Sporting Fields Clansman, Whippet, knocking off the seventh one. It was a glorious array of hounds competing for the honors against each other most weekends in magnificent settings in California, Oregon and Washington.

When it comes to favorite "friendly rivals," they don't make them any better than the charming Sandy Frei and her wonderful Afghan bitch, Ch. Stormhill's Who's Zoomin' Who. First of all, "Zoomie" was down from the BIS Shirkhan daughter, Ch. Pandora of Stormhill, a bitch greatly admired with her glamorous owner-breeder-handler, Ginny Withington (Sandy's mom) in California in the early 60s.

Second, she was sired by everybody's favorite Afghan, Ch. Pahlavi Puttin' On The Ritz. "Taco," as he is called by breeder-owner-handler Karen Wagner and all of his friends, won more specialties than the law ought to allow and was still winning breeds at Westminster well into his old age. Not only that, he has been an awesome sire.

Add to that the fact that Sandy and husband, Dave Frei (the handsome anchorman on USA's Westminster telecast), were tons of fun to visit with on the circuit, and 1989 was a memorable year for Zoomie and Ch. Vin-Melca's Calista (Sarah). Today these two canine "golden girls" are enjoying home life while their grandchildren are carrying the banner in the ring. As for me, it was one of the few times in my life when there was an adequate "sports fix" available at the dog shows. (For confirmation of this, just look at Dave's Super Bowl ring.)

A personal friendly rivalry of long standing was the ongoing one with Corky Vroom that started when Corky returned to California from the Navy and was working with Harry Sangster. Early on, we showed against each other with the Elkhounds and Mrs. Bagshaw's Whippets (Canyon Crest Kennels). Corky had won his first BIS with the sire of Howdy Rowdy and was later to finish scores of Howdy Rowdy's progeny. Mrs. James Blood, with her endearing sense of humor, asked me to be the trophy presenter at the Sacramento show when Corky beat my dog with the Whippet bitch "Becky" to win the group. I handed my dog to a friend and did it!

Our first serious, hotly contested, friendly feud was in 1970, when Corky was handling the Doberman Pinscher Ch. Rancho Dobe's Maestro against Ch. Vin-Melca's Vagabond. Vagabond was number one Dog All Breeds that year with Maestro number two, and each dog won all the assorted honors for their groups. In 1973, Corky had another top Doberman going in Ch. Galaxy's Corry Missile Belle, who ended up number one Dog All Breeds while Ch. Vin-Melca's Valley Forge finished in the number five All Breed slot.

The late 70s presented us with perhaps the greatest challenge with the advent of Talk of the Blues and Nimbus, for this time we were in the same group. Not only did these two winners exchange placements weekend after weekend in California, they traveled East with Talk of the Blues winning the Westminster group in 1978 and 1980 and Nimbus winning the same group in 1977 and 1979. Both dogs were record breakers at a number of levels.

Left: Ch. Stormhill's Who's Zoomin' Who pictured winning BIS under Afghan breeder-judge Ned Kauffman on the day in 1989 when she broke the record for Afghan bitches. "Zoomie" was owned, bred and handled by Sandra L. and David Frei of Stormhill Kennels. This pair exhibited the best of sportsmanship and carry on the tradition of the Stormhill line established by Sandra's mother Virginia Withington. Today, both Freis are judging as well as continuing their breeding program. Dave has become very popular as the television voice of Westminster Kennel Club. (Booth Photo)

Right: Ch. Canyon Crest's Bakara, Whippet bitch bred and owned by Mrs. Bagshaw's Canyon Crest Kennels and handled by Corky Vroom, pictured winning the Hound Group at the Sacramento Kennel Club in 1967. Loser, Pat Craige, was asked to present the trophy to her friendly rival Vroom by club official Mrs. James Blood, much to the amusement of Judge Virgil Johnson. Mrs. Bagshaw contributed to the fun of the occasion by sending the picture to the author. (Bennett Associates Photo)

Left: Ch. Rancho Dobe's Maestro, Doberman Pinscher, pictured winning BIS under Judge Isidore Schoenberg in 1970, handled by Corky Vroom. Owned by Karen Vroom and Don Bolté, Maestro was bred by the beloved Vivian and Brint Edwards, who also bred such greats as Ch. Rancho Dobe's Storm and Ch. Rancho Dobe's Roulette. He was campaigned to #2 Dog All Breeds and #1 Working Dog by Vroom, and numbered some of California's most prestigous shows among his victories. (Photo courtesy of Corky Vroom)

Top Dog All Breeds 1990 was won by the beautiful Bouvier des Flandres, Ch. Galbraith's Iron Eyes, owned by Mr. & Mrs. N.J. Reese and handled by Corky Vroom. He is pictured winning the Herding Group at Westminster Kennel Club under popular Judge Louis H. Harris. Bred by David D. Galbraith, Iron Eyes went on to become a significant sire upon his retirement from the show ring. (John Ashbey Photo)

It seemed like every time one of us had a top one, so did the other. This incredible tempo of coincidences continued on and off for years and in 1990 we were at it again. This time Corky was on the lead of the eye-catching Bouvier des Flandres, Ch. Galbraith's Iron Eyes, to achieve number one Dog All Breeds with Ch. Vin-Melca's Calista (Sarah) runner-up to him. Again, both dogs were also Quaker Oats winners. And when I left California in 1994 for Nashville, we were still competing with the top Bouvier and Elkhound meeting again in the BIS show rings.

More than once, Corky and I roadworked our top-winning animals together in the cool of the evening after the show. One time that comes immediately to mind was using my station wagon in Vallejo, California, at two shows Iron and Sarah had split. Corky Vroom was an inspirational person in my life, for to compete at the high performance levels he set contributed continued efforts on my part to improve my game.

Ric Chashoudian and George Ward: Professionalism in dogs started with terriers long before it moved on to Cocker Spaniels, Poodles, and other breeds, and it started in the motherland of bloodstock with the English. The skills of "doing terriers" developed into a fine art that eventually found its way to the shores of the "colonies" with the expert men who came to the new world. And it was indeed a man's world, for although there have been and still are some great terrier women, it is one area of the dog game that continues to be dominated by men.

There is no greater professional nor greater dominator than the incomparable George Ward, a third-generation terrier man who showed his first dog at three years of age. George still credits his grandfather, also named George, with being the best dogman of them all; however, modern experts think "they don't make them any better than George Ward," according to his greatest fan and arch rival, Ric Chashoudian. Although they lived thousands of miles apart, George helped Ric and gave him a terrier man's education.

Some of the greatest stories involving these two men revolve around Westminster and some of the trips they made to New York together. Early on, George sent the younger man into a terrier breed ring at the Garden with the previous year's best-of-breed winner, while George elected to stay on his open bitch. (In those days, non-

Something happened to Top Dog All Breeds Ch. Miss Skylight on the way to New York as friendly rivals George Ward and Ric Chashoudian ended up competing for the Terrier Group honors at Westminster. The lovely Wire Fox Terrier bitch was edged out by Ch. Elfinbrook Simon, West Highland White Terrier, who went on to BIS. Ric is pictured with the champion. (Photo courtesy of Ric Chashoudian)

Heywood Hartley awarding Ch. Elfinbrook Simon, West Highland White Terrier, BIS at Westminster Kennel Club in 1962. Simon was owned by the Wishing Well Kennels of Barbara Keenan and handled by George Ward. Simon and Ward dashed the hopes of Miss Skylight and Ric in the Terrier Group en route to BIS. (Photo by Evelyn Shafer)

champions could compete at Westminster.) Meanwhile, he gave Ric instructions on how to use the dog he was showing to break the concentration of another competitor. Although neither won, George praised Ric for following instructions. It was a lesson Ric never forgot, and forever more, he was willing to turn himself inside out to please George.

Perhaps the greatest evidence of the meaning of this friendly rivalry took place in 1962 over the Westminster week. Ric had campaigned the Top Winning Dog All Breeds in the form of the Wire Fox Terrier, Ch. Miss Skylight, and had high hopes for her at Westminster. But something happened on the way to New York—and that something was a stopover at George's that proved to be Ric's undoing.

Dealing with the rigors of a Michigan winter, George was chipping ice out of his runs when Ric arrived. George said he wasn't planning to go to New York even though his dogs were entered. The more Ric tried to talk George into accompanying him in his truck, the more adamant George became about not going. Finally, George agreed to make the trip, and the two of them set off for New York. You guessed it! Ric went second in the group to George showing Wishing Wells Kennels' Ch. Elfinbrook Simon, West Highland White Terrier, who went on to Best in Show under Heywood Hartley.

In those days, word didn't spread like wildfire the way it does today. Imagine Ric's surprise when he found out later that the Westie had burned up the Florida circuit the month before the Garden. It seems everybody but the California Chashoudian knew who was the hot new dog to beat!

So, even though at times their rivalry played like a love-hate relationship, Ric laughs about it and says: "The truth is I love the man." And George reciprocates with equal affection and respect for Ric. Throughout their years of friendship they have engaged in the most intensive battles in the rings, resuming their best-buddy relationship out of it. No wonder they have served as super role models for a generation of young people learning to perfect their terrier skills, for they are in a league of their own.

Dee Hutchinson and Peggy Westphal: A friendly rival relationship that has endured for decades is one between two of dogdom's dynamic Dachshund fanciers, Dee Hutchinson and Peggy Westphal. Over the years they have shared breedings, social occasions, family affairs, heartaches, and joyous times and remained not only hardy competitors but also best of friends.

As the daughter of the superbly elegant Mrs. Pierce (Nancy) Onthank, Dee grew up at Rose Farm, which had been purchased to raise the lovely smooth Dachshunds Nancy was breeding as well as the standard wires and miniature longhairs she imported following the war. Fourteen-year old Dee stayed home and ran Rose Farm while her mother showed the dogs to amass awesome records for those days. Her twin sister sometimes assisted in these duties.

A remarkable element of the Hutchinson-Westphal relationship is that both of them had twin sisters, providing each of them with early childhood bonding experiences that no doubt contributed to their lasting closeness. While Dee was growing up in Mrs. Onthank's world of dogs and the highest echelon of dog people, Peggy was in another arena of the classic suburban country life—that of riding lessons, tennis at the club, and tea dances. When she married Allen she got into Dachshunds with the Kleetal bloodlines of John H. Cook.

In time, their breeding endeavors led each of them to acquire exceptional wirehaired breeding stock that was to create great improvement in the variety. Peggy's Ch. Vantebes Draht Timothy was the first,

Dee Hutchinson (photo on left, courtesy of Ashbey Photography) and Peggy Westphal (photo on right courtesy of Dee Hutchinson) have been best of friends for decades, cooperating in the best interest of their beloved breed, the Dachshund, even as they competed in the ring. In addition to sharing the dogs, they have long shared family activities and social occasions. Peggy's pursuit of artistic interests became the productive outlet for her creative talents, while Dee's exceptional skills as a well-respected judge have taken her to all corners of the world. These two "sisters" are a testimony to the bonding effect of man's best friend. It comes as no surprise that people who love dogs have warmth and affection for people too.

putting wonderful puppies on the ground, which included splendid daughters and granddaughters for Dee and her mother's Ch. Pondwick's Hobgoblin to have as mates. It was the textbook case of one marvelous sire building upon the daughters of another who "clicked" with them. Hobgoblin became the All Time Wire Sire with 90 champion progeny to his credit. The runner-up to him is Peggy's own Ch. Westphal's Shillalah-W, with 61 title holders.

In 1972, Peggy's buff Cocker Spaniel bitch, Ch. Sagamore's Toccoa, was handled to Top Dog All Breeds by Ted Young Jr. even as Peggy was becoming more interested in pursuing fine arts. She always maintained if she had done one thing differently in her life it would be "to get started earlier with my art interests." At the same time, Peggy was developing her newly discovered talents, Dee was absorbing even more comprehensive dog knowledge to augment her "natural eye" for a dog in preparation for what was to become an inspired judging career.

Today, Dee is a popular judge of five groups as well as a breeder of her beloved Dachshunds. She is also working on a breed book with her delightful husband, Bruce.

Over the years, these two *master breeders*, Dee and Peggy, have competed in the ring, become well known for their Rose Farm and Von Westphalen bloodlines and risen to the top of their respective judging and art careers, as well as enjoying their many breeding success stories. Their mutual respect and enduring affection for one another has survived all the bumps in the road that occur in long-term relationships. After several decades they still assist each other with such tasks as handling matings and tattooing puppies—another testimony to the magnetism of dogs that draws the very best people to them.

Anne Rogers Clark, Jane Kamp Forsyth and Jacklyn Hungerland: Such greats as the incomparable Anne Rogers Clark, affectionately known to the fancy as "Annie," have participated in any number of "friendly rivalries" in their lifetime in dogs. Some of these rivalries occurred in the ring during her days as a top handler while others were the by-products of breeding programs, club activities, and other happenings in the sport of dogs.

Perhaps the first significant rivalry in Annie's life was in the early days of her professional handling career with her good friend, Jane Kamp, with whom she is still a "sister" and best of friends all these decades later. Their rivalry was long before their future husbands, James Edward Clark and Robert Forsyth, appeared on the scene. These two fun-loving girls just out of their teens enjoyed playing games on each other at the same time they were banging heads in the ring. They were pioneer women in the field of professional handling, traveling together as they competed against each other and the males who dominated the sport.

Annie had been born into dogs, as her mother Olga Hone Rogers was an excellent breeder of the three varieties of Poodles and English Cocker Spaniels under the Surrey prefix, the name Mrs. Clark still uses on her Miniature Poodles and Norfolk Terriers. Mrs. Rogers' bloodlines were so outstanding that no less a breeding program than Becky Mason's famous Bel Tor line started with a Surrey foundation bitch.

Jane had discovered a life she loved and took to it like a duck to water. The two of them, Anne and Jane, were to become icons in the sport of dogs.

When Annie married the elegant James Edward Clark, fondly known as Jim or Jimbo, it brought together a twosome well steeped in the tradition of dogs. It was almost like the merger of two successful corporations, and introduced a different tempo into her life, allowing her to participate in parent clubs and other activities for which there had been no time as a professional handler.

From this turn of events emerged another "friendly rival" related to one of her favorite breeds, the Standard Poodle. Dr. Jacklyn Hungerland and Annie began to enjoy an interesting relationship that allowed them both plenty of space at the same time it stimulated and challenged them.

They came from different worlds as well as different backgrounds in dogs. Annie was an Easterner who had been born into dogs. She was the professional dog person's professional. Jacky was the consummate Californian who bred Standard Poodles for decades while raising a family and pursuing a non-doggy professional career.

Both of them were breeders of renown. The Rimskittle prefix (used on the Standard Poodles bred with husband Jim) produced the Westminster group winner, Ch. Rimskittle Ruffian, and other multi-BIS winners including the regal Ch. Rimskittle Bartered Bride. Not only had Jacky bred the number one Dog All Breeds in 1969, Ch. DeRussy's Lollypop, she had bred a number of outstanding ones that had also contributed to the breed's gene pool. Both of them were well-respected judges who had achieved any number of honors individually and collectively. Annie had been the first woman to win BIS at Westminster and won two more in rapid succession. Jacky had been the first woman to serve as a Director of the American Kennel Club. Both of them were to judge BIS at the Garden.

These were two strong, successful women who became both friends and rivals due to their differing opinions on any number of issues relating to purebred dogs in general and Poodles in particular. When the one tragically lost her beloved husband, the other was there for her. When the other suffered through a devastating bout with cancer, her friendly rival was there for her.

And it was not uncommon to see them working together for a common purpose such as the good of the order of the Poodle Club of America. In essence, they are the quintessential friendship able to be their own persons at the same time they are able to get along. They know when to agree to disagree and when not to, and the sport of dogs is all the better for it.

The message imparted by these two female forces in the dog game as well as in life itself is well worth repeating: A difference in opinion is not a difference in principle. No wonder friendly rivals are all in the family in the world of dogs.

Dr. Jacklyn Hungerland and Anne Rogers Clark (Mrs. James Edward) relaxing at a recent dog show. These two successful women have competed and cooperated, agreed and disagreed over many issues in the best interests of growth in the world of purebred dogs. Their message is a powerful one that speaks to all mankind: A difference in opinion is not a difference in principle. The sport of dogs is blessed to have such role models to inspire all who pursue excellence. (Photo by Bernard Kernan)

Westminster Kennel Club: The Greatest Show on Earth

The Ringling Brothers have long billed their circus as "the Greatest Show on Earth," but to the American dog fancy, that honor goes to the Westminster Kennel Club's annual event held at New York's Madison Square Garden a few weeks before the circus comes to town. For well over a century, the American dog show world has riveted its attention on the "Big Apple" every year when dogdom's elite meet for the annual crowning of a new Westminster winner as a finale to one of the country's oldest sporting events.

It is difficult to describe Westminster's allure. It isn't the country's largest show and certainly not its most convenient. Yet Westminster has a mystique of its own that is a rare combination of tradition, social sophistication, good theater, and camaraderie that draws thousands to its ringside every

> "The show you love to hate, and the show you'd kill to win."
> —Eugene Zaphiris prior to winning the Terrier Group at Westminster 1996, *Dog News*

year. Furthermore, 14 million television viewers enjoy the prestigious events from the comfort of their living rooms. Many of these good dog people stage Westminster parties similar to the Super Bowl celebrations of professional football fans. And that is so very appropriate, since Westminster is a "super bowl" of sorts to dog show enthusiasts.

The name *Westminster* comes from the Westminster Hotel where Sporting Dog aficionados originally held their fraternal gun dog meetings. The club also had its own kennel facilities in which to house the members' bird dogs, the most famous of which was the lemon and white Pointer, Sensation, owned by the entire club. Considered the prototype for Pointer heads when he came to the United States from England in the 1880s, Sensation is permanently remembered as the symbol of the club, and his likeness is used as a logo on catalogs and advertisements as well as on the sterling silver Best in Show bowl.

In his first year in America, Sensation is reported to have won more than one thousand dollars in prizes (no small sum in those days) before his untimely death in 1887. Although the club started as a sporting gentlemen's bird dog association, it is internationally famous today for its bench show held annually in February.

A measure of the show's status can be best understood by recognizing the number of events staged around it as part of the "Westminster Weekend," perhaps a misnomer since it starts late on Thursday and ends after the Wednesday luncheon the following week. Such events as judging seminars, awards dinners

A jubilant Eugene Zaphiris and Skye Terrier Ch. Finnsky Oliver react to a Westminster win in the 1996 Terrier Group. The European import was sired by Rannoch Skye Superstar out of Finnsky Glacier and was bred by Thea and Rolf Dahlom. American fanciers were able to appreciate this extraordinary animal due to the cooperative efforts of Zaphiris, Matthew Stander and K and M. Sainio. (Photo © by Chet Jezierski)

The author's first win at Westminster came with the R/W Particolored Variety Winner Ch. Poling's Wee One in 1960 under the lady of Pinefair Cocker Spaniels, Mrs. H. Terrel Van Ingen (Jessica). Owner Dave Poling was one of the marvelous characters of his day. This portly, twinkling gentleman from the Buckeye State made certain all of his dogs knew their name by calling everything in the kennel by the same "call" name— Sonny for the dogs and Sunny for the bitches. (William Brown Photo)

and dances, late-night parties, and any number of specialty shows simply make Westminster a must-attend event for the fancy. Junior handlers work all the previous year to qualify for a shot at the Leonard Brumby Senior Memorial Trophy awarded to the Best Junior Handler.

The first show was held in Gilmore's Gardens in May of 1877, and it was a three-day event. Later, the show was moved to the Old Garden before settling in at the New Garden in the 1960s. The Garden is the home ice rink for the 1994 champion New York Rangers, who often have a game on Sunday night before judging starts early Monday. There have been a few times over the years when the footing in the ring was chilled temporarily by cold air remaining in the flooring. In recent years, there has been talk of returning the event to a three-day format to accommodate all those who are disappointed when the entry quota is filled without them.

My first trip to the Garden was in the 1950s with my mentor, Johnny Davis. The trip started off with a ride on the Little Creek Ferry that took almost two hours to cross Chesapeake Bay. We only took a few dogs, for Davis was keenly aware that only the best should make the journey to New York in February. A splendid sight that will remain in my memory forever was that of the debonair Peter Knoop handling Len Carey's Doberman Pinscher, Ch. Rancho Dobe's Storm, two-time winner of Best in Show in the 1950s. This experience was one that Vivian and Brint Edwards, the breeders of Storm, loved me to retell when I later became good friends with them in California.

When Westminster was held in the Old Garden, all the benching was downstairs in what was probably the best classroom environment possible for a fledgling dog person. Bill Holt remarked: "Some of the best dogs are downstairs on Tuesday night," and it was a good time to study them. The benching area was much less congested with the showing and benching at two different levels.

Terriers have dominated the show since the inception in 1907 of Best in Show honors when Winthrop Rutherfurd's Smooth Fox Terrier bitch, Ch. Warren Remedy, won it three consecutive years. The Best in Show rosette has been carried off 13 times by Wire Fox Terriers with Scottish Terriers accounting for seven more such honors. All in all, almost half of all Westminster shows have been won by Terriers. Sporting and Working dogs account for the next highest numbers, although some of those Working breeds are now in the Herding Group. Only three hounds have ever won Westminster.

Westminster represents the highest honor to which the *master breeder* can aspire. To breed a dog worthy of winning Westminster is to climb a stairway to the top. It is a dream come true for any owner, handler, breeder, or judge who is part of the equation. It is the ultimate.

The distinguished gentlemen of this sporting men's club are dedicated to preserving its image as well as its tradition. Thus, there is no reason to think that this magical show will ever lose its special electricity and synergy. As they say about England, "There will always be Westminster."

The English Pointer SENSATION is recognized all over the world as the model for Westminster Kennel Club's emblem. This antique print is from the collection of Dr. and Mrs. Bernard McGivern and has a fascinating history. McGivern, a member of Westminster for more than 25 years, was gifted with the lithograph by John W. Cross Jr., Westminster show chairman for 20 years. Cross, in turn, had received it from Dr. Samuel Milbank, show chairman in the 1930s. The Westminster logo appears on items associated with the show, including the Tiffany sterling bowl for BIS pictured on page 209.

KNOWN BY THE COMPANY YOU KEEP

Being "known by the company you keep" is an expression adults often used with youngsters during my childhood to encourage them to pick friends based on academic excellence, good manners and behavior, as well as their participation in wholesome activities of the church and community. In essence, we, as children, were urged to seek out the achievers in our midst in hopes that we too could become the very best it was possible for us to be.

I would love to think that this aphorism also applies to the world of dogs, for it was my privilege to be in the very "best of company" over the years. Consider the 10 dogs who won Best in Show at Westminster Kennel Club the 10 times one of my dogs landed me in the BIS lineup. These 10 dogs are legendary to the sport of dogs, representing any number of Top Dog All Breed winners, and more importantly, a number of great producers whose exceptional performances in the breeding programs and gene pools of their breeds were vital to that breed's improvement. Their place in dog-show history is assured.

My memories of these 10 dogs embrace their breeders, their owners, their handlers, and their personal characters, as well as the contributions they have made to the world of dogs. For being a Westminster BIS winner is like winning the Super Bowl or becoming Miss America, and the dog is forevermore a special participant in the annals of this very special sport.

Baseball has its World Series and Cooperstown and thoroughbreds have the Kentucky Derby and its Museum which are permanent traditions etched in eternity. Dogdom has Westminster—and it happens only once every year.

MEMORIES ARE MADE OF THIS: Vin-Melca's first Westminster Group win in 1970. With his back to the camera Richard Bauer has Dr. Neustadt's Greyhound, Ch. Argus of Greywitch, Evonne Chashoudian with Borzoi, Ch. Kall of the Wild's Zandor. The author with Vagabond, behind her Bobby Barlow with Basset, Ch. Richardson's Padraic of Cuas, Afghan Hound, Ch. Ammon Hall Nomad with Tom Glassford; Marcia Foy with 15-inch Beagle, Ch. King's Creek Triple Threat; and Damara Bolté with Basenji, Ch. Reveille Re-Up (back to camera).

BIS - Westminster Kennel Club - 1970. CH. ARRIBA'S PRIMA DONNA, handled by Jane K. Forsyth, winning the top honors at the Garden under Judge Anna Katherine Nicholas. Owned by Dr. & Mrs. P.J. Pagano and Dr. Theodore Fickes, the three-and-one-half-year old Boxer bitch was in season and feeling a little pouty, causing her talented handler to use all of her expertise to keep her "on" and showing. Mr. Albert E. Van Court (Kippy) and Mr. Robert V. Lindsay present the trophies. Ch. Vin-Melca's Vagabond won the first of 10 Vin-Melca Hound Group victories that year. (Shafer Photograph)

WESTMINSTER WINNERS
1970, 1971 & 1972

Westminster's last two-time winner was English Springer Spaniel, CH. CHINOE'S ADAMENT JAMES in 1971 and 1972. Pictured here repeating his Westminster victory, "D.J." was the winner under judge William W. Brainard Jr. with club officials Robert V. Lindsay and Lyman R. Fisher, M.D., presenting the trophies. Clint Harris, himself now an all-rounder, handled this star that was bred by his sister, Ann Roberts, for owner Dr. Milton Prickett. Ch. Vin-Melca's Vagabond was the 1971 Hound Group representative in the finals. (Gilbert Photo)

CH. GRETCHENHOF COLUMBIA RIVER, German Short-hair Pointer, wins BIS at Westminster Kennel Club in 1974 under Judge Len Carey. Robert E. Taylor presents the trophy. Jo Shellenbarger is handling him for owner Richard P. Smith, M.D. Bred by L.V. McGilbry from his matron Columbia River Della, he was sired by Gretchenhof Moonfrost. Ch. Vin-Melca's Homesteader represented the Hound Group in this BIS lineup. (William P. Gilbert Photo)

The incredible Irish Water Spaniel, CH. OAK TREE'S IRISHTOCRAT winning BIS at Westminster in 1979, handled by Bill Trainor for owner Mrs. Anne E. Snelling under Judge Henry Stoecker. Ch. Vin-Melca's Nimbus represented the Hound Group in the BIS class. (Photo courtesy of John Ashbey)

WESTMINSTER WINNERS 1974, 1977, 1979

Judge Haworth F. Hoch is happy with his choice of CH. DERSADE BOBBY'S GIRL for BIS at the 1977 Westminster event. Owned by Pool Forge Kennels and handled by Peter Green, "Binnie" is the recipient of trophies presented by Show Chairman Robert E. Taylor (left) and Club President William Rockefeller (right). She was the first Sealyham Terrier to win the event in 40 years and the fourth in Westminster history. Ch. Vin-Melca's Nimbus was the finalist from the Hound Group. (Photo courtesy of John Ashbey)

Michael Zollo and Pointer, CH. MARJETTA NATIONAL ACCLAIM winning BIS at the 1986 Westminster Kennel Club Show. "Deputy" was owned by Mrs. Alan R. Robson, and his breeder was Marjorie Martorella. Show Chairman Chester F. Collier (left) and Club President William H. Chisholm flank the lovely Judge Anna Wanner. Ch. Vin-Melca's Call To Arms was the Hound Group participant in BIS. (Photo courtesy of John Ashbey)

WESTMINSTER WINNERS
1986 & 1989

CH. ROYAL TUDOR'S WILD AS THE WIND UDT, ROM, Doberman Pinscher, wins BIS at Westminster in 1989. Judge Muriel Freeman is assisted by trophy presenters Chester F. Collier and William H. Chisholm in awarding the Westminster honors. Andy Linton handles "Indy" for owners Richard and Carolyn Vida, Beth Wilhite and Arthur and Susan Korp. Upon her arrival in New York, the Doberman bitch appeared off her game. New York's famous Animal Medical Center treated her accordingly, and by showtime three days later all was well. The Vidas were honored by airline personnel on our mutual trip back to the San Francisco Bay Area. Ch. Vin-Melca's Calista was one of six other group winners vanquished by "Indy." (Photo by John Ashbey)

CH. WENDESSA CROWN PRINCE was the 1990 Westminster BIS winner under Judge Frank Sabella, ably assisted by trophy presenters Ronald H. Menaker and Chester F. Collier. Owned by Edward B. Jenner, "Prince" was linebred to Jenner's famous sire Ch. St. Aubrey Laparata Dragon (See Part II, Pekingese Sire of Distinction). Prince was handled by Luc Boileau, now a multi-group judge. Ch. Vin-Melca's Calista was the Hound Group contestant in the BIS class. (Chuck Tatham Photo)

WESTMINSTER WINNERS 1990, 1994, 1995

Below: Norwich Terrier CH. CHIDLEY WILLUM THE CONQUEROR pictured winning BIS at the 1994 Westminster Kennel Club show under Judge Walter F. Goodman, himself a Westminster winner. Trophy presenters are Chester F. Collier and Ronald H. Menaker. Bred by Karen Anderson and handled by Peter Green, Willum's owners are Ruth L. Cooper and Patricia P. Lussier. Ch. Vin-Melca's Marketta was the Hound Group winner. (Photo by Chuck & Sandy Tatham)

Above: The 1995 Westminster BIS winner CH. GALEFORCE POST SCRIPT, fondly known as "Peggy Sue," takes her place in the great annals of Scottish Terrier history under Judge Dr. Jacklyn Hungerland with Westminster Show Chairman Ronald H. Menaker (left) and Club President Chester F. Collier (right) presenting the trophies. Maripi Woolridge handles for proud owners Dr. Joe Kinnarney and Dr. Vandra L. Huber. It was the seventh top award for this breed at Westminster. Ch. Vin-Melca's Marketta was the Hound Group winner in the finals. (Photo by Chuck Tatham)

Spotlight on a Vintage Year - 1973

1973 was a vintage year and, just as with a vintage year in fine wines, the very best dogs competed for honors. In an era when the California competition was always strong because the show schedules rarely allowed them to "get away from each other," they were superlative.

"They" were five outstanding animals who ended up winning their groups weekend after weekend, creating a Best in Show class that would have become monotonous were it not for the quality of the dogs. Remember in those days, the Working Group had not been divided into a second group of Herding Dogs, so there were only six groups. All of them were ranked high in the Top Ten All Breeds, three of them became Westminster BIS winners, two of them were Top Dog All Breeds and four of them were Quaker Oats winners. To walk into the ring in such illustrious company was exhilarating—win, lose, or draw.

The marvelous German Shorthair, Ch. Gretchenhof's Columbia River, was the Sporting Group's representative who went on to BIS at Westminster in 1974. Handled by Jo Shellenbarger for owner Dr. Richard Smith, this magnificent-moving gundog was bred by L.G. McGilbry and was number two All Breeds as well as the Sporting Dog Quaker Oats Winner. (For photo, see Westminster sidebar.)

Ch. Vin-Melca's Valley Forge, co-owned with Gilbert B. Mirus, was number five All Breeds and Quaker Oats Winner that year. Although he had a wonderful year with 15 All Breed BISs, he was the lightweight of these five heavy hitters, but he did make the team.

Corky Vroom handled the Doberman Pinscher bitch, Ch. Galaxy's Corry Missile Belle, to Top Dog All Breeds in that competitive year. She numbered BISs at Santa Barbara, Quaker Oats, and the Westminster Working Group among her many honors. Owned by Elaine Herndon and Mr. and Mrs. N. J. Reese, Missile Belle was a splendid showdog blessed with clean lines and always "on." She was a very tough competitor in any final.

Virginia Dickson's Lakeland legend, Ch. Jo-Ni's Red Baron of Crofton, came out of the Terrier Group in his rookie year to dominate all competition, becoming number one Dog All Breeds in 1975 and winning Best in Show at the 1976 Westminster Kennel Club show to cap his career. Handled by Ric Chashoudian, Red Baron not only won everything at the dog shows of the 70s, he continues to do so today through his many outstanding descendants. Without a doubt he was destined from the beginning to become one of the most influential terriers in American history.

And 1973's perennial Non-Sporting Group star was none other than the great white Standard Poodle, Ch. Acadia Command Performance, the breathtaking white cloud who was BIS at the 1973 Westminster extravaganza handled by the talented Frank Sabella. A son of the fabulous black sire, Ch. Hausbrau Executive of Acadia, this free-wheeling, headstrong, young "stallion" was to give owner, Edward B. Jenner, his first best at the Garden. Co-owner JoAnne Sering shared the joy with Joy Tongue, owner of the sire.

The better the talent of the competition of those you face in your chosen endeavor, the more inspired you are to play your best game. In my half-century in dogs, this was absolutely the best crop of dogs it was ever my privilege to compete with and enjoy. Every Sunday night on the long drive home, I reflected on their collective greatness and was touched by being in such proximity with them. To this day, I marvel at a lineup that appeared every weekend with three eventual Westminster winners, two Top Dog All Breeds, and four Quaker Oats winners—all at the same shows. It elevated all of us to a higher plateau.

Awards and Records

Records and points are to a dog competition what profit is to business—a way of keeping score and attesting to success. Just as inflation has an impact on money, so does the increased numbers of shows have an impact on records. Yet any show record is a relative accomplishment based on an accumulation of many subjective factors. These factors include everything from the quality of the dog to the expertise of those conditioning and handling the dog's career to the relative competition the dog encounters.

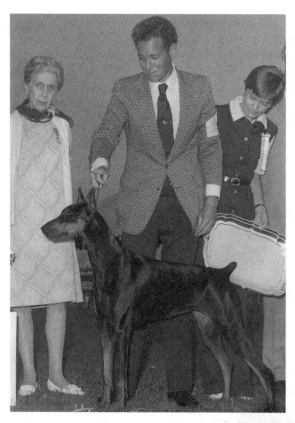

Left: Top Dog All Breeds 1973 was Doberman Pinscher, Ch. Galaxy's Corry Missile Belle, owned by Elaine Herndon and Mr. & Mrs. N.J. Reese, handled by Corky Vroom. Bred by B. Flores and Claire McCabe, Missile Belle was much admired by her competitors in a vintage year of exceptional dogs. She is pictured winning BIS at the Santa Barbara Kennel Club under Judge Mildred Imrie with Cynthia Wood presenting the trophies. Missile Belle was the first of three #1 Dogs campaigned by Vroom for Mr. & Mrs. Reese, as she was followed by the Greyhound and the Bouvier. (Photo by Joan Ludwig)

1973- A VINTAGE YEAR

Above: Lakeland Terrier legend Ch. Jo-Ni's Red Baron of Crofton started his career in 1973, becoming the dominating California terrier, a feat he continued until his retirement with the exciting Westminster BIS victory in 1976. (Photo courtesy of Ric Chashoudian)

Ch. Vin-Melca's Valley Forge was privileged to be part of the action in the vintage year—1973—as the winner of 15 All Breed BISs and Hound Group Quaker Oats winner. Sired by Ch. Vin-Melca's Vickssen X Ch. Vin-Melca's Hanky Panky, "George" was co-owned by the author and Gilbert B. Mirus. Among his more prestigious wins that year were BIS at the Kennel Club of Beverly Hills and Hound Group first at Santa Barbara to Missile Belle's BIS. (House Photo)

The magnificent Standard Poodle, Ch. Acadia Command Performance was the 1973 Westminster BIS winner at the age of two. Handled by Frank Sabella for owners Edward B. Jenner and JoAnne B. Sering, "Bart" is pictured winning BIS under Glen Sommers with Harold Schlintz presenting the Sun Maid Kennel Club trophy. (Photo by Henry C. Schley)

American-bred dogs honored by the American Kennel Club as 1937 Group Award winners gather for the ceremony at the AKC office to celebrate their honors. An early forerunner of the Quaker Oats awards, competition was based on most group victories for the previous year. Left to right, the winners were: Ch. Hugo Of Cosalta, German Shepherd Dog, winner in the Working Group, with Miss Marie J. Leary; Ch. Little Sahib, Pomeranian, winner in the Toy Group, with Mrs. Vincent Matta; Ch. Pillicoc Rumpelstilskin C.D., Standard Poodle, winner in the Non-Sporting Group, with Mrs. Milton Erlanger; Ch. Nonquitt Notable, Cocker Spaniel, winner in the Sporting Group, with Mrs. Henry A. Ross; Davishill Little Man, Wire Fox Terrier, winner of the Terrier Group, with R.L. Davis representing owners Mr. & Mrs. Forrest Hall. This picture appeared in the 1938 Edition of *The American Kennel Club Blue Book of Dogs.* In that book, Mrs. Erlanger was quoted as saying that the Standard Poodle's success as Dog of the Year in 1937 was "50 percent Rumpelstilskin and 50 percent Henry Stoecker" (his handler). Stoecker became a very respected all-rounder and judged BIS at Westminster in 1979. (Information and photograph courtesy of the American Kennel Club)

Dogs that amass records and awards are those whose qualities, showmanship and form proved them deserving. It takes a very good dog to win under all conditions and against all competition. And it takes a dedicated commitment to the task to effect it.

The most valid records are those achieved in competition in which the concentration of quality animals has depth. Dogs that put large numbers of specialty wins in the record books are impressive and should enhance the breed's gene pool.

The "run for the roses" in quest of awards became dramatically more competitive over the four decades I campaigned dogs at the top. As the number of shows increased many times over and dog shows were no longer just weekend events, it created additional challenges for those who worked during the

> "Dignity does not consist of possessing honors, but in deserving them."
> —Aristotle

week. This growth created any number of systems of rankings of dogs at all levels of breed, group, and Best in Show competition. Cluster shows brought previously smaller kennel clubs into the top echelons of dog shows in both numbers and attraction of stars. And that facet of the sport continues to change.

The American Kennel Club was a forerunner in the field when it began honoring those who collected the most wins in each of the (then) six variety groups for the calendar year 1937. Because of the domination of imported dogs in the American show rings at that time, these awards were limited to

Richard Beauchamp and the *Kennel Review Awards* were extraordinarily meaningful in the western states during the 1960s and all over the US when they went national in 1970. Beauchamp's "Winkies" were modeled after the Oscar. His innovative concepts resulted in *Kennel Review* becoming the foremost magazine of its day. Beauchamp, a knowledgeable dogman as well as a journalist, has gone on to become a respected judge of sporting dogs. He has contributed greatly to his breed, the Bichon Frise. (Missy Yuhl Photo)

Dr. Harold Shuler and the author accepting the Quaker Oats Award from guest speaker George Plimpton on behalf of Ch. Vin-Melca's Nimbus in 1978. Nimbus was #2 Dog All Breeds for co-owners Shuler and the author. (Photo courtesy of Quaker Oats)

Winkie Award winners at the *Kennel Review* Banquet, left to right: Walter Goodman (Glamoor Skye Terriers); the author (Vin-Melca Norwegian Elkhounds); Bill Trainor (president of the Professional Handlers Association); Mrs. Beatrice Godsol and Vincent Perry (all-rounders); Jackie Sinkinson (The Rectory Bloodhounds); Richard Beauchamp (publisher, *Kennel Review Magazine*); Mrs. Brint Edwards (Rancho Dobe Doberman Pinschers). (Photo by Martin Booth)

"Paper Lion" author George Plimpton, Carol Andersen and the author enjoying the festivities at the 1990 Quaker Oats dinner. It was Plimpton's second appearance on the Quaker Oats podium, and he joked that he would like to show a dog himself since he had "played" at professional football and other sports in his best-selling books. An unidentified official of the Quaker Oats organization is on the right. (Photo courtesy of Quaker Oats.

Nan Eisley-Bennett and Jeff Bennett pictured receiving the 1993 Hound Award for Ch. Vin-Melca's Marketta at the annual Quaker Oats dinner in New York City. Sired by the 1992 Quaker Oats winner Ch. Vin-Melca's Bombardier out of the 1989 and 1990 winner Ch. Vin-Melca's Calista, Marketta is believed to be the only Quaker Oats winner with both a sire and dam also winning the awards. (Photo courtesy of Quaker Oats)

The author, winner of the Ken-L Ration Biskit Hall of Fame Award, chats with Matt Bahr of the Super Bowl winning New York Giants at the Ken-L Ration dinner in 1991. (Photo courtesy of Joan H. Wood)

Kennel Review Awards dinner honoring 1970's Top Show Dogs was held in Palm Beach, Florida. The author is holding the Winkie award for Ch. Vin-Melca's Vagabond, Top Dog All Breeds. (Photo courtesy of *Kennel Review*)

Sir Cyril Richard was the guest speaker at the Ken-L Ration DOG OF THE YEAR Awards in 1971. The winners for 1970 were: Albert Greenfield's Irish Setter, Ch. Major O'Shannon (handled by Tom Glassford); the author's Norwegian Elkhound, Ch. Vin-Melca's Vagabond (owner-handled); Mr. & Mrs. Howard Sherline's Old English Sheepdog, Ch. Prince Andrew of Sherline (handled by Bob Forsyth); Mrs. Jane Henderson's West Highland White Terrier, Ch. De-Go Hubert (handled by Cliff Hallmark); Dorothy White's Maltese, Ch. Pendleton's Jewel (owner-handled); and, William & Carol Victor's Dalmatian, Ch. Lord Jim (handled by Bill Kramer). (House Photo)

American-bred dogs. As dogs bred in the United States "came of age" such restrictions were lifted and foreign-bred dogs were also eligible for these honors. The Quaker Oats Company (Heinz Company) has honored these winners at its annual dinner in New York in conjunction with Westminster since 1954. The Ken-L-Ration Awards were originally based on geographic areas of the country with the dog of any group who had the most wins being the honoree. Today, it honors the top group winner in each of the seven groups and remains one of dogdom's most coveted awards.

Irene Phillips Schlintz was the originator of the famous Phillips System of ranking dogs, which was

Harve Lubin, co-owner with Carol Andersen of Ch. Vin-Melca's Calista, accepting the Science Diet #2 Dog All Breeds honors on behalf of the team. Harve and his wife Jean are among the very special people that dogs can bring into your life. (House Photo)

first published in *Popular Dogs* in 1956. Another system highly respected was the *Kennel Review System* originated by Richard Beauchamp, who rotated his elegant awards dinners to various parts of the country over the years.

Such systems are still used by today's magazines and dog food companies in determining the top dogs for a given year. One point is awarded for each dog defeated in the show for an all breed Best in Show. The winner of a group is given one point for each dog defeated in the group. A group placer is given one point for all the dogs in that group less those breeds whose representative in the group placed ahead of it.

The Fido Awards offered by the Gaines Company are also highly treasured by their recipients. Such honors as Dogman and Dogwoman of the Year, Dog Writer of the Year, and Handler of the Year receive the Fido Trophy at a relaxed luncheon following the Westminster show. This luncheon is highlighted by comments from the Westminster Group and Best in Show judges and serves as an appropriate closing to the Westminster festivities.

It is important to recognize that records of the present and those that will come in the future were not possible for the dogs of the past. There simply were not that many dog shows. Where once it was considered a phenomenal accomplishment for a dog to win 100 Bests in Show, now those at the top have broken the 200 mark.

Because the numbers of available wins decrease as one nears the top, the competition becomes keener. Many Ken-L Ration races have gone down to the wire at the end of the year, with a couple of them ending in a tie! Such competition is healthy for the dog game, especially when all the players are fair-minded sportsmen with excellent animals. Being productive is a "turn on" and all the more so when it is deserving.

The Medicis of the Dog World

An interesting phenomenon occurred in the world of showing dogs during the last decades of the 20th Century: the emergence of patron saints willing to promote classic dogs to their true place in the greater dog show arena. Exactly how or why this situation came to be is not clear. As previously discussed, people of great wealth once maintained huge and grandiose establishments, staffed by experts, to run their breeding programs and show their dogs.

Not only did the cost of sustaining an extensive breeding program escalate in recent years, but the difficulty of finding exceptional kennel managers and adequate staff members also contributed to the demise of large breeding operations supported by high society. Instead of establishing such kennels of

If ever there was a million-dollar dog it was German Shepherd Dog Ch. Covy Tucker Hills Manhattan, for he did it all. He was BIS at the American Kennel Club Centennial Show in 1984, BIS at Westminster Kennel Club in 1987, winner of the *Kennel Review* Tournament, as well as topping all other records in between for owners Jane Firestone and Shirlee Braunstein. "Hatter" was handled by James Moses and bred by Cappy Pottle and Gloria Birch. The great gentleman of German Shepherds, Langdon Skarda, once remarked that Hatter had done more for Shepherds than any dog since Rin Tin Tin, and it was his privilege to award him several top honors.

their own, they chose to finance the show careers of potential stars that appealed to them.

Competitive sportsmen and women became to the world of great dogs what the Medici family of Florence, Italy, had been to the Renaissance—true patrons of the arts willing to support their chosen canine artistry with large sums of money. Such support made it possible for these animals to be appreciated by the public from the well-known shows of the East and California to smaller shows in more remote areas of the country.

Just as Florence became a city of great splendor, thanks to the Medicis, so did these dogs gain honors at the top with Quaker Oats awards, Science Diet accolades, and Westminster victories. They brought fame to their proud owners, their *master breeders*, and their talented handlers, as well as to themselves. Although the practice of financing worthy dogs began with such people as Mrs. Cheever Porter decades ago, it came of age in the 1980s when Mrs. Jane Firestone became the patron of the marvelous German Shepherd Dog, Ch. Covy-Tucker Hill's Manhattan, co-owned with Shirlee Braunstein, and handled by James Moses. Whereas professional handlers such as Mrs. Porter's handlers, Bob and Jane Forsyth, continued to carry their entire string of dogs, Moses went on the road with the one dog, allowing him to concentrate on the needs and performance of only "Hatter." The Manhattan/Moses team justified Mrs. Firestone's financial faith in them by scoring popular Best in

Wirehaired Fox Terrier, Ch. Registry's Lonesome Dove, pictured winning BIS at the 1992 Westminster Kennel Club Show under Judge Melbourne Downing. "Lacey" is the Top Winning Terrier of All Time and #2 All Time All Breeds with 215 BISs on her incredible scorecard. The American-bred daughter of the imported Ch. Galsul Excellence, Lacey was bred by Joan and Forbes Gordon and nurtured by Michael and Patty Kemp for eventual owners Marion and Samuel Lawrence. Handled by Mike Kemp, both Lacey and her sire (handled by Peter Green) accumulated more than 100 BISs. Westminster officials Ronald H. Menaker and Chester F. Collier complete this picture. (Chuck and Sandy Tatham Photo)

Ch. LaShay's Bart Simpson, B/T Cocker Spaniel, was piloted to Top Sporting Dog All Time with 106 BIS victories by Bob Covey, long-time Cocker breeder/handler, for owners Samuel B. and Marion W. Lawrence. Bred by Sherry Marley, he was sired by Ch. Tamra's Top Gun, who was also campaigned by Covey. Pictured here winning BIS under Judge Charles E. "Chuck" Trotter with trophy presentation by Mrs. Egon Frese. (Photo by L. Sosa)

Doberman Pinscher Ch. Brunswig's Cryptonite became the All Time Top Working Dog for owners Samuel B. Lawrence, Donna Anthony and M. Schmid with 124 All Breed BISs. Sired by Ch. Beaulane The Nite Ryder, he was bred by R. G. and P.K. Farrer from their Brunswig's Zephyr. He is pictured here with handler George Murray winning the esteemed DPCA National Specialty under Judge Betty Moore with Nancy Heitzman presenting the trophy. (Mikron Photo)

Show wins at the Westminster Kennel Club and American Kennel Club Centennial shows as they amassed more than 100 Bests in Show in the 1980s. Later, Ch. Altana's Mystique (see photo in color section) and Moses combined forces with Mrs. Firestone to achieve the ultimate All Time BIS record of 275 shows!

The most well known of the Renaissance patrons was the famous Lorenzo dé Medici, known throughout this period as Lorenzo the Magnificent. It might be said that Sam Lawrence was to three great dogs what Lorenzo was to Florence, and just as Lorenzo helped make it possible for the likes of Michelangelo and Raphael to achieve immortality, so did Sam and his lovely wife, Marion, help put three outstanding animals on record for all time.

At the top of their personal list was the wonderful Westminster-winning Wire Fox Terrier, Ch. Registry's Lonesome Dove. Known to her adoring public as "Lacey," she is the Top Winning Terrier of All Time and number two All Breeds with 215 all-breed BIS wins to her credit. The Top Working Dog of All Time is the Lawrences' Ch. Brunswig Cryptonite with 124 BIS honors. This outstanding Doberman Pinscher may well end up both the top winning and top producing dog in his breed as his records continue to climb in the latter department (see Sires). Also topping his group is the black and tan Cocker Spaniel, Ch. LaShay's Bart Simpson, with 106 red, white and blue rosettes contributed to the Lawrences' laurels.

In addition to their fine collection of four-legged classics, the Lawrences are well known in the art world for their excellent collection of American Impressionist paintings. Their support of the Cornell Fine Arts Museum is legendary in Winter Park, Florida. No wonder we think of them as modern Medicis.

Dealing with Stress

Stress is a part of living the active life. It is a by-product of the modern world itself, and even more so to those who take on such extracurricular activities as caring for animals and exhibiting them in addition to a full-time job. Yet the stress that taxes one person or dog can be exhilarating and uplifting to another. And nowhere is that potential more evident than in the show world.

Have you ever noticed how happy everyone is at the first show of the New Year? Before the holidays everyone seemed burned out and glad that the year was coming to an end, yet just a few weeks later they are on a high and eager to be back in action! It might be said that after a holiday layoff spent with family and friends, both dog people and their dogs are ready to get back to their real family on the dog show circuit. This is because our magnificent obsession can provide the most exhilarating kinds of stress at the same time it supplies the healthy outlet for it—the dog show. Not many people love what they are doing the way dog people do.

Stress comes in a number of different forms for both you and your dog. Just the constant change in routine can be stressful unless the players learn to "go with the flow" and get in tune with it. Such stresses for man and dog are physical demands caused by their environment and schedule. Animals will sometimes become more affected by it than their owners, going off their feed, refusing to perform and showing even worse signs of anxiety.

Stress can be provoked by shipping or traveling, and some animals never do willingly accept it. Disease, fever, pain, abnormal metabolic and other bodily functions can cause discomfort and stress. If either you or your dog has trouble recovering from minor physical ailments, you can suspect stress as the psychological culprit preventing a return to normal.

Perhaps the best way to deal with stress is to stay upbeat and positive, thus making stress work for you instead of against you. Rather than spinning your wheels worrying about things over which you have no control, utilize your energy to plan your breedings, condition your dogs, groom your dogs, plan your advertising, and in general, do positive and productive things. The physical activity of campaigning a dog can be energizing, for the more you do, the more you are able to do.

Nothing in the world will sap you of your energy more than wasting it for negative reasons. Even if others have treated you unfairly or even hate you, rest assured that it will cost them a lot more than

QUALITY TIME WITH YOUR ANIMALS

One of the side benefits of an intensive campaign is that it can give you some real quality time with a given animal. Quality time with your animals is much like quality time with your kids. If you get so busy in the daily routine of supporting them through your job and the physical care of them in your daily chores at home that you have no time to relate to them one-on-one or have fun with them, you're not getting quality time with them.

The reason an intensive campaign affords quality time with a given animal is that you are spending all your available time with that one creature. This dog becomes everything from your best buddy and dearest friend to a father confessor. The dog is in the motel room with you, riding in the front seat of the rental car, eating "doggy bag" leftovers from all over the country, and any number of other activities that accompany gypsy life.

My personal zenith in such a relationship came when I was campaigning Ch. Vin-Melca's Calista, whom I called Sarah. First of all, it was a good time for such a focused friend as Sarah because of the personal stress that goes with a mid-life crisis. Second, she was the warmest, most responsive personal pet in my life. Not only did she listen to my troubles, understand them, and offer moral support, she made me forget those troubles and enjoy life. Running Sarah on the beaches of Carmel was a personal high, and some days we were running up to five miles. Not only was she in splendid condition (she also worked alongside the bicycle), she had me in the best shape I'd been in for years!

Sarah was fun to travel with and got so she knew what I was thinking before I did. Most of all, she was the most generous of animals, giving more than one could ask for in any endeavor. Everything she did was beyond the line of duty—keeping it together in 100-plus temperatures in dreadful conditions just as lovingly as on the best of days. She was the total trooper.

In Alaska where she spent her first 18 months with co-breeders Fred and Dody Froehlich, she developed her skills as a canine athlete by working moose and clearing six-foot fences. At the same time she was a show ring glamour girl, she was truly a dog.

Today, she is adjusting to life in Tennessee while enjoying her kids and grandkids. She puts new life into the phrase, growing old gracefully.

Jimmy Moses developed the same kind of relationship with Ch. Altana's Mystique, #1 Show Dog All Times with 275 All Breed Best in Shows and 30 Best in Specialties. This lovely German Shepherd bitch was already five years old when Jimmy got her, and she was not all that thrilled with taking her act on the road. In fact, she gave Mr. German Shepherd himself a few anxious times after he acquired her for his client, Jane Firestone, because he was not sure he could develop the gorgeous bitch into a real show dog. If ever a relationship between a dog and a man rewarded patience and bonding, it was the Moses/Mystique twosome.

The "games people play" entered an ethereal level with Jimmy figuring out how to get into her head and keep her psyched. He added Coco, a Corgi, to the team as a traveling companion and canine confidant. Many was the time after a show was over that Jimmy and his assistant could be seen still in the arena playing games with Mystique. One of their favorites was hide-and-seek with the assistant popping out of unexpected hiding places to reward "Steekers" with a treat. As the game playing progressed and new ones were added, dog show fanciers all over the US were treated to the sight of man and dog coming together in the ring in total harmony. Their success was the beautiful result of quality time at its best.

No doubt the resulting record will live as a permanent testimony to Jimmy's ability to be the coach and field marshal. He kept this great bitch showing until her retirement, where she still has Jimmy under her thumb—oops, paw. Mystique had the genetic and physical credentials (genotype and phenotype) in being BORN TO WIN, but without Jimmy Moses, the dream could not have come true.

it does you; unless you make the mistake of giving in to it and allowing it to have a negative impact on you. Hostility is hard on those who harbor it, so avoid doing it because you need that energy for better causes. To stay positive even through the down times is to be your own best friend. And if you find it difficult to get through some of the down times by yourself, talk it out with a good friend who is also positive. Such sharing not only relieves stress, it bonds friendships and puts you in a position to help your friend when that person needs it.

Perhaps the biggest contributing cause of stress that is often overlooked is inadequate nutrition. The bodies of both dogs and people require excellent nutrition when subjected to stress. As stress increases, so do nutritional needs. Of particular importance during times of stress is the replenishing of lost electrolytes. Extreme physical stress for both canine and human athletes demands it. Marathon runners gulp down fortified liquids during their races, and professional football players use Gatorade picker-uppers during time-outs and other moments off the field.

Electrolytes are contained in the body's fluids and tend to combine with each other in their solid form and separate when in water. They are also referred to as minerals or trace minerals, and they are constantly carried throughout the body by fluids as they perform their duties. They are contained both within and outside of the cells.

An early sign that you are losing electrolytes in times of extreme heat and/or exertion is the taste of salt you get from the perspiration you are producing. A severe leg cramp in hot weather can result from sudden potassium deficiency and dehydration. Magnesium and other nutrients are lost anytime there is severe diarrhea. That is why supplementing with magnesium will help an animal recover more rapidly following a bout of it. Since magnesium is necessary for proper enzyme activity to take its rightful place in the metabolic process, as well as for its role in the functioning of the neuromuscular system, a deficiency can cause a variety of problems.

For the most part, the average diet will provide sufficient amounts of these nutrients. It's when the animal is placed under stress that excretory losses throw it out of balance. Dehydration can cause such losses. When campaigning a dog under stressful conditions, you might want to utilize a skin-pinch test of your own, always checking the animal in the same place such as the top of the head. See how long the skin stays up, and if it is staying up longer than usual recognize that you could be dealing with dehydration. Do your test in stress-free times while petting the dog so that you have a personal norm to measure it by when stress occurs.

Sick animals and newborn puppies are especially susceptible to severe dehydration. During the original outbreak of the parvo virus in the early 1980s, many dogs were saved that would not have been otherwise thanks to intravenous fluids that kept things in balance during the stress of the virus. Red-alert, severe dehydration such as heat stroke and rapidly failing puppies calls for immediate replacement of fluids and electrolytes.

Man and his best friend are social animals. Therefore, extreme isolation and its opposite—overcrowding—can place demands on their well-being. When either of them is placed into a no-win situation of intolerable stress, the result can be extreme adrenal breakdown. Such unusual physical demands are not the norm. It is wise to recognize that social health is achieved by the perfect balance of mingling in comfortable activities with others and peaceful quiet time to allow adequate rest.

That is why both dogs and people who learn to rest during campaigns will display more endurance down the stretch, for they are using the stressful times as exhilarating experiences rather than debilitating ones. At the same time they are able to relax and recuperate. Owners who set realistic goals prevent undue stress caused by trying to achieve unrealistic ones. They don't waste themselves worrying about or responding to things over which they have no control. Their own psychological well being rubs off on the dogs.

Campaigns for you and your dog can be more stressful today than ever before if for no other reason than it takes more shows to end up in the same place. Take time out to remember when you loved showing dogs and ask yourself what happened. Did you become so involved in the process that you lost sight of what got you into the process to begin with—the dogs? If so, then it's time to revitalize and re-energize. Keep focused on your own personal soundness of body and mind as well as that of your dog.

Historically, mankind has had a work week and a time out for meditation, rest and recreation on the weekends. It is the traditional framework by which you clock yourself in this stressful world, and one of the many reasons your avocation has to be giving you the right outlet on weekends. That satisfaction is what makes it possible to deal with the continued stress, and keeps your body from getting out of "sync."

Traveling with Dogs

Most of you will start out with one or two dogs in a small car or station wagon, then work up to anything from a mini van to a maxi van or even a motor home. At some point in every dog person's life, you stop shopping for a vehicle for yourself and shop for the vehicle for your animals. And, that is as it should be. You are on the road by choice. Your dogs are there because it is *your* choice. If you are going to take them into all kinds of weather and under all conditions, it must be made comfortable for them.

Aside from using your common sense to select a vehicle that is comfortable and can be kept cool in hot weather, there is not a lot I can tell you that you do not already know. But here are a few tips that might be of some use to you:

- Keep masking tape and aluminum foil in your vehicle in case you are in a situation in which your tints or shades are not doing the job. In an emergency they can be put on your windows to reflect the sun.

- Always keep your ice chests full of ice in hot weather. Keep bowls of ice in your dogs' crates.

- To avoid dogs getting away from you when you let them out of their crates, shut your van doors. Use your body to block them.

- Start your youngsters out by taking them on short trips around town to avoid motion sickness. Feed them in their crates in the vehicle as it sits in your driveway. This should be done only in comfortable weather.

- In case of motion sickness that is persistent, give the animal something for motion sickness about one hour before you start your trip. Use either a commercial over-the-counter medication or B-6. B-6 is a natural remedy for nausea.

- When driving long distances, stop every three hours or so to walk the dogs and wake yourself up. Use regular roadside areas where you are safe and the dogs are accepted. Clean up after your dogs.

- If you get sleepy pull into the parking lot of a 24-hour coffee shop, lock your doors, set your alarm, and take a 15-minute nap. Let a dog loose in the van for protection. When the alarm goes off, go in and get coffee and start out again much more alert.

- If you must smoke, do not smoke in your vehicle because the smoke is bad for your dogs.

- Do not let the vehicle get too warm as it makes you drowsy and it is bad for the dogs.

- If you leave a show late and have a long drive ahead of you, drive for a couple of hours before you stop to eat. If you have a long trip ahead of you save the fine dining for another time and get quick service or take out.

- Listen to radio programs you would not ordinarily select. Because they are somewhat out of your comfort zone of favorite music, they will serve to stimulate you instead of relax you on long drives. Consider a lively talk show or music you do not usually prefer. At one time that was country music for me late at night. Just listening to the words kept me laughing and alert.

- If you find yourself nodding, pull over. Nothing is worth risking your life for— not to mention that of your dogs.

Traveling the Skies

Nothing in the world is more of an anxiety trip than flying with your dogs, for the fact is, any dog other than a toy dog that fits under the seat is out of your hands and in the hands of the airline. So your job is to make sure those hands are as capable as possible.

The first step when you are flying is to reserve the flight for your dog as well as for yourself, and to make sure you have an up-to-date health certificate for each of the animals making the trip. Have signs on your crates that say: **"Do Not Leave in the Sun."** Even though you may never fly during the day it helps get the message to the cargo people and may help save some other dog from discomfort or worse. Also, mark your crate so you will know it is yours. I use red reflecting tape on my kennels, and I can watch them being loaded from inside the terminal.

Each crate needs two containers filled with ice just before departure. Give yourself plenty of time to get to the airport so you will arrive at least one hour ahead of time.

If you are flying from May through September, fly at night. For one thing, you are less likely to get backed up on a runway. For another, there is no danger of your dog being left in the sun and it is cooler. Pillow cases with zippers can be filled with freeze packs to keep the crate cool. Fly non-stop whenever possible.

Get to your gate early so you can make contact with those who handle the boarding process. Politely inform them you have a very valuable show dog on board, give them the claim number and ask them to stay on top of it. The dog should not be brought out until just before boarding, so do one of two things:

1) Get on board and have a seat located near the area where the dog will be—you can see them load the dog immediately before takeoff. If they do not, go to the

---

A FLYING EXPERIENCE

In 1981, 14-year-old Vagabond and his grandson, Nimbus, were going to the Garden. Vagabond had attended the first *Parade of Champions* in 1976 presented by Westminster Kennel Club—previous Group and BIS winners—and was once again participating in this marvelous exhibition of the old-timers. Nimbus, after laying off for two years, would be competing.

The major problem was that I was afraid to fly Vagabond at his advanced age and finally came up with the super solution: Flying Tigers, out of San Francisco, would fly me with the two dogs as cargo. Thus, I would be right there with Bond and Nimbus. With a skeleton crew at the top of a fireman-type ladder with me and my dogs at the bottom of a 747, off we flew to New York. The absolutely amazing thing was that both dogs were asleep before the plane finished taxiing down the runway for takeoff. I sat on my train case with my flashlight and a book while the two of them slept soundly. It was not the only time over the years I envied them their crates with soft bedding!

Vagabond showed like a million bucks and Roger Caras announced that he was the oldest dog to appear on the Garden floor. Nimbus blew up in excitement at the crowd's applause causing Judge Louis Auslander to remark: "I thought he was going to put you in the stands."

The moral of this story is that dogs can become frightened by the handling of them at airports—to the holding areas and aircraft and back to baggage claim—not the actual flying itself.

PS: We flew back on a commercial airline.

captain in the front of the plane—the plane will not take off until you are in your seat—and ask the captain to determine if your dog is on board.

2) Wait in the boarding area until you see the dog put on board. Then you can continue to ask airline personnel to call the cargo people or whatever until the dog is loaded.

Show your appreciation and gratitude when airline personnel cooperate to care for your dogs. Every positive experience helps all of us. Some years ago, I was taking a Northwest flight and never saw the dog loaded. When I arrived at the gate, unknown to me, the dog was already on board. Nonetheless, I did not see it so I kept asking and asking. Finally, one of the cargo gentlemen was kind enough to crawl into the plane, tear a piece of my red reflecting tape off the crate, bring it to me and tell me the dog's name. (It was on the crate.) He was all smiles and an obvious dog lover. Since then, Northwest has come up with an ingenious idea other airlines would be wise to utilize. Just before the aircraft's doors are closed, the cargo person comes on board, locates you in your seat, and gives you proof your dog is on board. They use a claim ticket with tear-offs on the crate.

Priscilla Benkin and the American Dog Owners Association, under the guidance of Gordon Carvill, have made remarkable strides to improve flying conditions for animals. Given their good work I hope the time will come when there will be no horror stories involving airlines and dogs.

Motels

Renting a motel room is not a license to trash it. More and more motels are closing their doors to dogs because of the owners. Leaving tubs clogged with dog hair and messes all over the grounds do not make motel managers happy. Furthermore, those actions are plain bad manners.

Always walk your dog away from the main areas and have tools to pick up any droppings. Dispose of them accordingly. Keep your dog on lead. If you are using exercise pens, do not damage the lawns.

Unattended dogs should not be left loose in rooms. Tragic things can result. Crates protect them from mishaps. A maid could open the door and let a loose dog out accidentally. Two tragedies of dogs dying because they were left in rooms unattended come to mind. One dog was electrocuted chewing on the room's wiring. Another dog got into his owner's diet medication and ate a whole bottle of amphetamines. You can never repeat the old ounce-of-prevention adage often enough, for things can and do go wrong, sometimes even when every precaution is taken. If you can avoid them by thinking ahead, it is in your dog's best interest.

Advertising

Webster defines advertising as a way to call attention to; make known to the public; a message to promote a product and a public announcement. Designed to inform, influence or persuade, advertising is as American as apple pie. By the late 1980s, Americans were spending more than $130 billion a year on advertising.

Yet advertising did not originate in America. It dates back to the ancient Babylonians of 3000 B. C. who used outdoor signs above their shops to solicit business. In case you ever wondered what happened to Babylon, today it is Iraq. The Greeks and Romans also used such advertising measures. Because few people read well in those days (some things never change) symbols were used to deliver the advertising message. The boot, for example, advertised the shoemaker. Later European cultures hired "town criers" to go through the streets and deliver their messages.

It is wise to remember that people who advertise have something to sell. They want you to buy their products and ideas. Politicians advertise to get votes. Consider the blitz of advertising shortly before election day in November. It's mind-boggling. Dog people too have a sense of timing, as the ads appearing before Westminster or a National Specialty would verify. There is nothing wrong with it as long as it is done in good taste and the product is worthy. The good salesman should sell only good products.

Nothing in the world is more of a "turn off" than an ad that brags about an animal making a win

Frank Sabella's sensational thank-you ad that appeared in *Kennel Review Magazine* was an eyecatcher as the white cloud, Ch. Acadia Command Performance, Standard Poodle, sails through the air. Sabella had won one of his many Winkie Awards (dogdom's Oscars) and chose this form to show his gratitude to the fancy. Such beautiful presentations enhance both the dog and the publication. (Photo courtesy of Frank Sabella)

over <u>(fill in the blank)</u> which does everything but name the defeated dog. Such tasteless advertising is usually rejected by dog publications, but occasionally one will slip through. To be happy that your dog won in good competition and to state it accordingly is one thing; to try to imply which dogs were defeated is another.

A second mistake advertisers must avoid is running bad pictures of their dogs. If you don't know the difference, allow the editor or publisher to help you decide which picture is the best. If your dog is not photogenic standing in the usual win position, consider getting action shots of him for your ad. Some good dogs never cooperate for standing pictures and are best served by action shots. And such pictures are a nice change of pace.

Have you ever opened a dog publication to find three different dogs of the same breed boldly claiming to be number one for that breed? If you are going to make such claims in print, spare yourself embarrassment by naming the system by which you have made your claim. Do not make claims that cannot be substantiated.

Magazine and newspaper advertising account for approximately one-fourth of the money spent on advertising in the United States. Television, direct mail, radio and outdoor signs account for the rest. Most dog advertising is done through newspapers and magazine advertising. Your local newspaper can be helpful in selling your puppies to pet homes, especially if utilized in conjunction with educational advertising messages such as "Purebred Dogs-Buy From A Responsible Breeder" sponsored by dedicated kennel clubs across the country in their attempts to educate the public.

Sarah WAS the teacher's pet and everyone else's too, as her personality endears her to young and old. Since it is my personal belief that all show dogs are essentially pets (although all pets are definitely not show dogs), I loved the satire of this ad, mainly because one of her detractors had been proclaiming loudly all year that Ch. Vin-Melca's Calista was "nothing but a pet." Sarah became the winner of 66 All Breed BISs and the mother-daughter combination of Sarah and Marketta won four Westminster Hound Groups. Nonetheless, she is still the greatest of pets at 10 years of age. Ads like this are a fun break from the usual show ring picture. (Photo by Deidi Kramer)

An important advantage about advertising your show wins through newspapers and magazines is that this method of advertising is equally available to all who can afford it. Most people campaigning dogs at the top budget advertising into the expenses of their campaign. For those who show selectively rather than the hard-knocking week-in and week-out campaign, an occasional ad fits the budget and keeps the dog in the public eye. Another benefit of advertising your dog is that advertising is open and "up front" and does not require becoming involved in social climbing to promote your dog. The busy breeder-exhibitor working to support his animals and show them enough to compile a record rarely has time for a hectic social life—even if he has the money.

Exactly how much influence, if any, advertising has on judges is unclear. When he was number one Dog All Breeds All Systems, Ch. Kabik's The Challenger (see photo in color section), Afghan Hound owned, bred and handled by Chris and Marguerite Terrell, was advertised lightly. Fair-minded judges who are competent and confident do not go out of their way to beat dogs who are advertised nor do they go out of their way to put them up. Advertising aimed at bringing an excellent sire's credentials to the owners of prospective mates is usually best served by breed publications. Many owners who don't get to see their dogs in the ring often enjoy seeing them in print. And the magazines are enhanced by having the pictures of the top dogs displayed in them.

It is advertising that keeps these many well-done publications in business and available to the fancier. Many of these publications are time-honored parts of our overall involvement in the sport of dogs. Publications have sponsored events and a myriad of activities for dog fanciers. They bring messages to the consumer about new processes available to handle old problems, as well as alerts about possible threats to the world of dogs we so dearly love. A recent example is information about the Penn-Hip Process of early diagnosis of hip dysplasia that reached the fancy through a number of publications. Deborah Lawson's column in *Dog News* was especially informative on this subject.

The breeder-exhibitor can choose from a breed magazine, a group magazine or an all-breed publication. Each has a role to play in your personal evolution as an informed fancier. Knowing where your dog belongs is important. Sometimes you see ads in an all-breed publication that might be more properly showcased in a breed publication. Once again, using common sense in your advertising policy and program is advised. And the publishers themselves will appreciate you. After all, they need your support to stay in business.

Knowing When to Say When

Nothing in the world detracts more from a great record than staying on too long in pursuit of it. Dragging a dog who is tired and bored around the ring in an attempt to get "just one more Best in Show" is demeaning to the animal as well as the people around him. A beautiful dog who has done great credit to his breed will be remembered long after records are broken, and broken again. So why continue to show this dog when it is obvious that it is no longer in his best interest.

There is no set time when a given dog should be retired, but some dogs will tell you if you learn to listen to them. They are not machines and will simply quit on you or no longer have their old stuff. If you are not sure whether your star is losing it, have someone video him in the ring for you to study. Notice if he has lost his sparkle or is off his game. Observe his topline and overall body texture. Pay special attention to how the animal stops at the far end of the "down and back." If the whole topline appears to collapse, this dog has been out too long. Another sign is when a dog that has been willing in the past, starts lagging on the lead, and doesn't want to go anymore. Maybe it's time to retire him and bring out his son. Developing a sense of timing as to when to retire a top winner is an important part of your breeding/showing success story.

Perhaps the best time to retire a dog is after a great win such as Westminster or a National Specialty. Senator Bill Bradley, a former professional basketball star, shares a sportsman's concept with us: "Becoming number one is easier than remaining number one." *In essence, stop when you are on top.*

PART V

W I N N I N G

MEANS SPECIAL PEOPLE
IN YOUR LIFE

The Love of Dogs and Those Who Love Them

Ongoing relationships add life to the years of people. According to scientific studies, it also adds years to the lives of people. Such ongoing relationships are normal in the wonderful brotherhood based on the love of dogs and those who love them.

Socialization of animals is enhanced by relationships with people—just as socialization of people with each other. Just how mutual the man-dog-man relationship can be is demonstrated by the new life dogs bring to those whose fate has ended them in nursing homes. Their quality of life is much higher when animals are brought into their lives.

> "Love is all we have, the only way that each can help the other"
> —Euripides, ancient Greek

Dog shows bring with them a cross section of amazing people. Every dog show brings a new dawn that only those on the grounds at daybreak truly appreciate, as both dogs and people greet a new day. The smell of freshly brewed coffee, the clean white "lab coats" in the grooming section, and the dogs happy to be out in the cool morning after a good night's rest combine to create an atmosphere that is truly invigorating. There is a general good-natured hustle and bustle of experts applying their craft as they ready themselves and their exhibits for combat—friends and cohorts ready to visit at the same time they do battle. In those early morning hours, everyone on the grounds gets a "rush" for the game is about to begin. Sometimes the emotions associated with breeding and showing dogs take us from down low to very high. Sometimes it seems like a lonely game. Yet, whom do we turn to when things go wrong? Our dear friends in dogs, who else?

Closeness with our soul mates is life-extending in every way. It broadens our social circles, adds to our longevity, and when we get older keeps us on the go when most of our contemporaries are long gone. Although my mother and father were never particularly active in the dog fancy, they live their lives in a similar way to dog fanciers—interacting in ongoing relationships through music, church and other group-oriented activities that give their twilight years a special, unique quality.

The people you bond with through dogs will be lifelong friends often as close as family members. Just as families have their differences and sometimes bumpy rides on the road of life, so too do your relationships with your coterie of dog family members. Yet, in times of need your dog friends will be there. In times of joy, they will share your happiness. And in times of tragedy, they will comfort you while sharing your grief. It is an unusual world in which former enemies and competitors become fast

Three BIS hounds who were friends, and so were their owner-handlers. Ch. Page Mill Trademark, Beagle; Ch. The Rectory's Curate, Bloodhound; and, Ch. Vin-Melca's Howdy Rowdy, Norwegian Elkhound. Little Trademark seems to be proud that he was the winner of the silver cup *on the day!* These three dogs and their owners traveled together, set up together, dined together and enjoyed mutual camaraderie as well as mutual competition. They learned from each other, enjoyed each other and treasured each other. They were Art and Carroll Gordon, Dick and Mitzi Hiett and John and Pat Craige. (Photo taken by Henry Schley in the late '60s)

friends; in which former friends and even loved ones become estranged and may—or may not—put it back together; and, it is a world in which anything that happens to you—good or bad—will be known all over the country in no time at all via the telephone, electronic mail, and the internet. Dog people seem to have collective psyches at the same time they retain their individuality.

As you mature in dogs, you will learn to lean on your friends without being overly demanding, to give to your friends in their times of need, and to look forward to a life made longer and warmer by the love of dogs and those who love them.

Who Motivates the Motivator?

As a breeder and campaigner of dogs, you learn to motivate and keep the dogs "on" during the down periods as well as the up ones. You try to motivate others in your life and hope they will return the favor.

There will be times in your dog career when you will be forced to motivate yourself, like it or not. Because you have a passion for what you are doing, you will always be able to reach down and find the strength to keep at it to motivate yourself. Your dogs give so much and ask so little.

Yes, you might think, but things have never been worse. Your dogs are not winning, you have hereditary eye problems in your lines, nobody is breeding any good ones anymore, and the judges are not what they should be. Furthermore, your best bitch had to be spayed and your stud dog has become sterile.

Well, at least you have identified the problem—or problems. You are the only one who can change this negative condition. You did not get into dogs to be down or depressed. Furthermore, it is dangerous to your mental health to have nothing but dogs in your life. Those who do are the most likely to suffer the dreaded disease—kennel blindness.

Negativity is like any other habit. Unless you are hooked on it and enjoy your misery, you can break it. It is the same with your life as it is with your breeding program: **If you do what you have always done, you will get what you have always gotten.**

Do some fun things for a while and get your mind off all that is going wrong in your life. It is your choice. Turn your attitude around and start doing things that make you happy. Remember when you took your first dog through obedience? Why not try it again. Surround yourself with upbeat people and get on with it. Children are a good tonic and can make you feel like a kid again—if you will let them.

Enjoy your friends' dogs when things are not going so well for you and your own dogs. Take a puppy and work with it for a few weeks. If it is a breed different from your own, it will be a good experience for both of you. Put things back in perspective by breaking your routine—it could stimulate your mind.

Trying to remain optimistic will take some conscious effort on your part, for there are a lot of pessimists out there, and they want you to be miserable with them. Recognize them for what they are and do not let them draw you into their negative life-style. Remember that there is a lot of difference in being realistic and being pessimistic.

Negative emotions drain your energy and potential for positive productivity. People who do negative things to you and others hurt themselves much more than they hurt you. Learning to stay away from negativity will help you keep positive so that you will have good energy that is both creative and rewarding. This will allow you to stick to the job. Remember that a pearl is a piece of sand that stuck to the job!

Competition can be a positive force in your life even though it is stressful. You are doing something you love. The need to excel and do a good job becomes a survival technique—an outlet if used wisely and sensibly. So you lost the breed on the day when your dog could have gone best in show. Consider it a rite of passage. Allow the dog world to be your form of self-therapy as you develop more strength of character.

Be a good competitor, congratulating others when their dogs win and graciously accepting their congratulations when yours win. Laugh at yourself and with others, keep yourself in good health, enjoy your dogs and your dog friends, and prepare to enjoy a long and stimulating life.

Standing on the Shoulders of Giants

If you are fortunate enough to have success in any walk of life, it is because you are able to stand on the shoulders of the giants who came before you. Nowhere is this more true than in the world of dogs. Not only do you utilize the building blocks of early breeders from long ago, you are also privileged to utilize the accumulated knowledge of those experts who come into your life in so many ways.

No one starts from scratch, nor operates in a vacuum, in the breeding of dogs. Perhaps those who come into your life in the early stages will have the greatest impact on your thinking, and if you are smart you will choose these people wisely. It is impossible to thank each individual who assisted me in my education; therefore, a collective acknowledgment is used in this book.

My good fortune in growing up in dogs as a member of the Tidewater Kennel Club (TKC) of Virginia, surrounded by so many talented dog people, started me off in the right direction. Although a few are thanked in special individual acknowledgments that follow, people like Bob Paul, Maude Paul Perkey, Audrey Middleton, Bill and Betty Munden, Thelma and Carey Baker, Herb and Martha Fielder, Mary Sewell, Mahlon White, Anna Cowie, Myron Ferris, Annemarie Moore, the Gossetts, Petersons, the Pirottes, the Mediates, Knox Buchanans, and so many others in TKC taught me a lot about dogs and sportsmanship. Most of these people are gone now, and I would like to think they knew they made a difference.

One of California's most pleasant surprises came when the Fielders retired there. From time to time I still see Rebec Pusey, a lady with whom I traveled to shows before I was old enough to drive. In those days she had Cockers and Pointers, but later became known as a breeder of fine English Setters with her Cabin Hill dogs. Her son, Van, still shows them. Cres Farrow, the Boxer breeder-judge, is a familiar face from the '50s whom I see in Memphis at his show when I am able to make it.

Perhaps it was a blessing in disguise that those early influences ranged from German Shepherd experts to Chihuahua breeders but did not include any Elkhound fanciers, for they were scarce in those days. Subsequently, my in-depth learning took place at the side of breeders of breeds other than my own. By the time Mrs. Wells Peck became involved in my life, I was ready to learn the nuances of the breed she was willing to share. Her dogs were the foundation of my line, and she has my eternal gratitude for the dogs brought over from Europe.

Florence Palmer and Susan Phillips were two more ladies of the Old Eastern Establishment who put their hearts and souls into the development of the breed. Along with Glenna Crafts, Susan did so very much to make the breed more competitive in the fifties and sixties. Their two dogs, Ch. Arctic Storm of Pomfret and Ch. Trygvie Vikingsson, contributed valuable traits in helping establish the Vin-Melca line. Also important were two brothers bred by Joe and Marie Peterson: Ch. Windy Cove's Rowdy Ringo and Ch. Windy Cove's Silver Son, as well as the Wabeth dogs of dear friends Walt and Betty Moore. The Cedarstone dogs of Thelma Hayworth also contributed to the upward swing of the breed.

Very Special People

All of us who breed build on the work of those who came before us, as those who follow us will do. Without their contributions, our progress would be all the more difficult. *We can only say thank you, although the words seem hardly enough.*

Such people leave their marks on you and your life. When you think about it, your arms are never big enough to embrace all of those who matter. Maybe the best way to show appreciation is to pass those hugs to others and to share your knowledge and embrace the brotherhood of dogs to keep the chain unbroken.

The times were so much simpler. Phones rang less, and laughter rang true. If it were possible to wave a magic wand and make it happen, each of you would be fortunate to have someone like the following people come into your lives (Names are listed in alphabetical order.):

Norman Austin, Mr. Cocker Spaniel

He was Mr. Cocker Spaniel. The sight of him with the great red and white Cocker bitch, Ch. Honey Creek Vivacious, at the Chesapeake Cocker Spaniel Specialty, well over 45 years ago, was the most glorious picture of man and animal working together creating the ultimate in beauty and style that had ever come to Virginia. No movie stars ever had a more adoring fan than this star-struck school girl at ringside.

Norman's work with the lovely Bea Weguson's Honey Creek Cockers took parti-colors from the also-rans of the Cocker family behind the blacks and ASCOBs to center stage where they remain—his influence is felt to this very day. Together, he and his good friend, Ted Young Jr., shared their talents and flair with a generation of their Cocker kids. They took us under their collective wings and taught us how to grow properly in the world of purebred dogs. Among our numbers were such well-known names as Richard Beauchamp (judge and owner of *Kennel Review*), Terry Stacy (judge and former vice-president of American Kennel Club), Danny Kiedrowski (owner/editor of *Terrier Type*), and Charlotte Martin Stacy (Onofrio Dog Shows), to name a few.

Mr. Cocker Spaniel, Norman Austin, in 1950 with Ch. Honey Creek Heir.

His early boyhood exposure to the Norwegian Elkhounds of his Scandinavian neighbors in Minnesota, during the breed's early days in America, made him all the more special. He joined another great dogman, the late Johnny Davis, in helping a 16-year-old grade a litter in 1952 that was to have a lasting influence on the Elkhound breed, for their choice dog became the maternal great-grandsire of both Howdy Rowdy and Vagabond.

When I started drifting away from Cockers and concentrating on Elkhounds, he not only forgave me, he later showed up on my doorstep in Carmel to guide me through the final weeks of the 1970 campaign with Vagabond, as always inspiring others to do their best.

He had campaigned the black-and-tan Ch. Pinetop's Fancy Parade to Top Dog All Breeds in 1959, setting a Best in Show record that was unbroken for decades. He became the mentor for the gifted young Everett Dean and helped him on his way to the top with the stylish red Ch. Artru's Hot Rod. He was instrumental in the improvement program of the chocolates, coming down from Sweet Georgia Brown as the color came of age in the seventies. He then collaborated with his good friend, Frances Greer, to do an in-depth study and write a book on color inheritance in Cockers.

Norman's talents were not limited to dogs. He was an internationally acclaimed goat judge as well as a dog judge. He was a culinary artist who enjoyed sharing the rewards of his kitchen with his guests. He was a lover of art and music and an inspiring conversationalist. His books on the Flushing Spaniel became the definitive work of the American Spaniel Club.

His goat-judging activities brought a special lady into his life, Jeanne, and they were married in 1983. They continued to judge goats together all over the country. She was a stabilizing force in his life in later years and laughingly acknowledged that Norman had been a free spirit long before it was fashionable. They were best friends who shared a marvelous love of life and together with their granddaughter became a fun-loving threesome at dog shows all over California.

He never forgot old friends. Chris and Bob Snowden of Glenshaw Cocker and Miniature Schnauzer fame heard from him a few times a month in chatty letters written on the run that kept them tuned in to the dog world they loved. His old friend Macky Irick could count on him to stay in touch. Later, Everett turned to him again as a mentor, this time accompanying him to goat shows where the fine points of judging are involved. Everett considered this an important part of his own preparation to become a dog show judge. Norman had this amazing ability to come into one's life and light it up with his warmth and charm. This joyous sharing made people want him as a permanent member of their extended families, forever.

When he suffered a stroke in December 1994, those who came to visit him were astounded to find his contagious upbeat attitude undaunted and were not in the least surprised when he judged the Cocker Specialty before Westminster two months later.

His resilience and buoyancy never faltered as he judged all spring, including California's competitive Mission Circuit a few days before his death. He passed away peaceably in his sleep in the California home he and Jeanne shared with their precious granddaughter, Marisa.

Thank you, Norman, for what you gave to this game you loved. That legacy will live forever. Every time a Cocker Spaniel is singled out for the top honors at any show, Mr. Cocker Spaniel is being revered and remembered. Dogs and their people are better for having known him.

Dr. John E. Craige, Veterinarian and Teacher

John came into my life when Ch. Vin-Melca's Rebel Rouser experienced difficulty at 2:00 am in the delivery of her second puppy in a litter of four. John, the on-duty emergency veterinarian, had to use forceps to deliver the puppy who turned out to be BIS Ch. Vin-Melca's Vickssen, sire of Ch. Vin-Melca's Vagabond. When Vagabond became Top Dog All Breeds in 1970, John took justifiable pride in having saved the life of his sire.

Hayden Martin awards the points to Dr. John Craige and Norwegian Elkhound Vista Valle Howdy's Dolly, owned and bred by Loucille Waterman. Dr. Craige enjoyed handling the progeny of his all-time favorite dog, Ch. Vin-Melca's Howdy Rowdy. (Photo by Ludwig)

Dr. Craige enjoys a bowl full of Howdy Rowdy puppies in a trophy their sire won for BIS at the Sequoia Kennel Club in 1969. (Russ Cain Photo)

John was a native of Philadelphia and a graduate of the University of Pennsylvania Veterinary School. His duties while serving in the United States Army brought him to the Monterey Peninsula where he opened a veterinary practice after his discharge from the service. He and his first wife Joele worked together in the practice to assure its success.

He was very proud of their lovely daughter Daphne, whose beauty and charm had resulted in her selection as *The Sweetheart of Sigma Chi* at the University of California, among other honors that came her way. Today, Daphne and her husband Dick (Richard Bertero) are, in turn, proud of their son Craige and daughter Courtney. Not only are John's grandchildren grown and graduated from college, they have both lived and worked abroad in stimulating and fascinating jobs.

John himself was an innovative and never orthodox thinker. Such freedom of spirit led to our trying different holistic approaches to settle problems long before the idea and word were in vogue. One example was the treatment of the ulcer that threatened the amputation of Vagabond's tail. (See Problem Solving.) John considered his expertise with the microscope one of his strongest assets in those early years and laughed at what he termed: "The world's only dog poop expert with his own personal lab." Certainly, with the dogs on the road so much, they were constantly picking up bugs to keep him busy! John figured out early on that such bugs as coccidia could cause toxic conditions that, if left untreated in brood bitches, could cause serious problems in their pregnancies as well as their progeny. He was a marvelous diagnostician.

For the first years of our marriage, we lived in an apartment above the veterinary hospital, and those were times of great teaching by John with me as his avid student. Whenever there was time between my job teaching school and my own dog activities, I assisted him with surgeries. Since a number of cesarean sections occur in the middle of the night when the bitch gets into difficulty whelping, it was most convenient with us living right there. One such litter of Cocker Spaniels turned out to be all champions. John was a rather cavalier businessman and, even though the surgery bill had never been paid, took delight in the puppies acquiring their championships. When the entire litter was finished and he still had not been paid, he decided to write it off. Two years later, he was totally surprised when the bill was paid.

Two passions in John's life were singing and golf. He never missed the Carmel Bach Festival and sang for years with the Monterey Peninsula Symphony and various choral societies. Once, as a rather young man, he took a year off from his veterinary practice to see if he could play golf well enough to do it professionally before deciding that "Arny's Army" had best stay on the trail of Arnold Palmer.

After suffering a fall off our thoroughbred mare in 1978, John's broken hip left him with recurring problems that curtailed his golf and a number of other activities. While recovering from his injuries, he became interested in the concepts of a local water diviner and figured ways he could apply the ideas to veterinary medicine through the use of acupuncture. He had long been interested in the complete picture of total health with specific emphasis on vitamins and minerals and the role they played in all of this. He ended up involved in operating a small vitamin company with Gilbert B. Mirus. The company had belonged to Frank McHugh of Ultramend field and show Brittanys. Eventually, the operation moved to Los Angeles where John established a successful holistic practice.

He was a great believer in the total picture of health and thought it meant a lot more than the absence of illness. He often criticized established medicine for its arrogance in dealing with the ideas of the East, including acupuncture and herbal therapy. In many ways, he thought he and one of his heroes—Linus Pauling—were both ahead of their times. He made a believer out of me, and to this day I take my supplements faithfully and also give them to my dogs, thanks to John.

John personified the person described by Emerson in *Self-Reliance*: "Who so would be a man, must be a non-conformist. He who would gather immortal palms must not be hindered by the name of goodness, but must explore if it be goodness. Nothing is at last sacred but the integrity of your own mind."

Johnny Davis and Doberman Pinscher Ch. Ebonnaire's Touchdown capture the BIS honors at Chester Valley Kennel Club in 1962 under Judge Marie Meyer, one of dogdom's most colorful judges. Owned by Charles "Chuck" O'Neill, Touchdown was a personal favorite of his handler who took great pride in the dog's siring prowess. Especially important to Davis was the winning that Touchdown's progeny achieved at Doberman Pinscher Club of America events. (Photo courtesy of Mari-Beth O'Neill)

Johnny Davis, Professional Handler, Breeder and Mentor

Johnny Davis was an avid outdoorsman and sportsman. He was a skilled fisherman who numbered among his fishing buddies baseball's last .400 hitter, Ted Williams, dogman extraordinaire Billy Lang, and fellow handler and best friend, Joe Clay.

Johnny had trained war dogs for the United States Government in World War II and turned back to dogs as a professional handler and trainer in Norfolk, Virginia, following the war. In addition to his skills as a handler, he was one of those

Doberman Pinscher Rhumba Von Bismarck, owned by neighbor Marie Dennis, was one of the many neighborhood dogs the author showed for friends. Her affection for this bitch started a lifelong love affair for the breed. This Doberman led her to classes with mentor, Johnny Davis, and one of his charges was on the end of her lead in an early group victory. (House Photo)

naturals who was born to breed dogs, and his kennel name, Val-Eric, became synonymous with great Doberman Pinschers—even though it was derived from his brindle Great Dane, Ch. Gilbert's Braemer Eric, and the Weimaraner bitch he showed for his client, Vivian Jardine.

Johnny had played professional baseball before the war, and he never lost his love for the game. He carried this sporting attitude of the team player into everything he did, sharing his knowledge and distributing good will throughout the dog fancy.

As director of training for the Hampton Roads Obedience Training Club, Johnny became good friends with a number of people including Marion Whitlock, a superior obedience participant. He also taught scores of us how to show our dogs at his conformation classes, gently teaching us how to enhance our dogs and encouraging us to get better animals into our breeding programs.

Some of the great dog people who were his clients included Mrs. Lynwood Walton, Monroe (Steb) and Natalie Stebbins, Charles (Chuck) O'Neill, Commander and Mrs. Carl Barron, and Pete and Mildred Pirotte. Since Johnny was a bachelor, many of his clients became his extended family, and dinner time in their homes included Johnny along with truly good dog dialogue and sharing of knowledge.

There are never adequate words to describe the impact someone such as Johnny had on me in my developing years, but thanks to him, I was allowed to help with his all-breed string and was taught how to show a number of breeds. He showed me how to handle a cantankerous brood bitch when

Ellsworth Gamble awarding (Ch.) Wandec's Sylva Av Vin-Melca BOS to her kennelmate Ch. Vin-Melca's Vickssen for a five-point major, John Whitemarsh handling, from the 6-9 Puppy Class. A few weeks later, Ellsworth found himself in the unenviable position of having her on an "off" day when she and the other puppy in the class were both affected by a severe heat wave. Others might have been embarrassed to withhold a ribbon under these circumstances, but not Ellsworth. To the utter amazement of some, he placed Sylva second and the other puppy third in a class of two because neither puppy ever put her tail up. It was an affirmation of his integrity and made his guidance all the more valuable. (Bennett Associates Photo)

the BIS black-and-tan Doberman, Ch. Aida's Hilda, was left in my care with her litter while he was out on a circuit. As his unofficial assistant, I was close to such animals as the great Doberman producer, Ch. Steb's Top Skipper; the early Basenji winner, Ch. Miacor's Zuchil, who was out at the same time as Ch. Bettina's Oribi; several of the great Lyn-Mar Acres Bassets, along with any number of outstanding Great Danes and Boxers.

He gained my parents' gratitude by encouraging me to complete college with a professional degree rather than going on the road to handle dogs. Johnny made that option more attractive by pointing out that I could breed dogs more objectively if I was not dependent on dogs for my livelihood. He was a quiet man with great dignity, a true dogman and a gentleman. His untimely early death deprived the dog fancy of an opportunity to appreciate his dog expertise, as his judging career was in its infancy when he was lost to the fancy.

Ellsworth Gamble, The Consummate Student

If ever there was the consummate student of dogs, it was overwhelmingly exemplified in the elegant form of Ellsworth Gamble. His brilliance and deep integrity were manifested as the ultimate scholar with the courage of his convictions—always his own man.

His conceptual knowledge transcended the comprehension of the average exhibitor. Yet to those

Ellsworth Gamble and his good friend, Nick Calicura. Although this elegant man never favored his friends when he judged, neither did he penalize them. Here he is shown awarding the points to the Smooth Fox Terrier of Calicura's at the Contra Costa Kennel Club in 1967. Ellsworth's legacy to his many admirers was to always have "the courage of your convictions." (Photo by Alfred Stillman, courtesy of Nick Calicura)

who were receptive, he was a beacon of light who appealed to their inner persons, stimulating them to try even harder to breed *the dog* worthy of taking into his ring. I would count the days in childlike anticipation, waiting to take a special youngster to this man, knowing that he knew. He was the one who told me, "Nobody can judge your dogs as well as you can."

His father, a Scotsman, was with the foreign service when he married Ellsworth's beautiful East Indian mother. Eventually, the family settled in Ohio where Ellsworth developed his lifelong fascination with quality dogs. After serving his country as a paratrooper in World War II, he settled in the San Francisco Bay Area in 1946 where he began his dog career in earnest.

Ellsworth went to work for Grace Reis, managing her kennel of quality Wire Fox Terriers. In addition to honing his skills grooming terriers, he became deeply involved in his quest for learning more and more about dogs. Because he was a private handler, he could only handle the Reis wires; but he soon became involved with another terrier great, Bill Fox, and started handling some of his Kerry Blue Terriers as well.

By the late 1940s, he had become a public professional handler and Nick Calicura soon joined him as an assistant. Nick remembers Ellsworth as having "the keenest eye of anyone I ever met." When Ellsworth was forced to spend a full year in the Veterans Hospital at Livermore, California, good friend Nick helped him keep the rest of his life in order.

Ellsworth turned to judging in 1956, making it obvious his dedication to self-education along with his natural eye for a dog had created a special adjudicator. His personal library grew along with his knowledge of people and dogs. He became an advisor to exhibitors who showed their dogs under him, acting as a resource person to those who genuinely sought his expertise. He was a perfect example of the role a knowledgeable judge can play in the selection procedure, asking quiet questions that cut to the core of a given problem. Such dialogue with this man served to make breeders question their own previously conceived ideas, resulting in continued growth and eventual breed improvement.

But you didn't have to talk with Ellsworth to understand his thinking. You could watch how he used his hands—they would say it all. He had absolutely wonderful hands on a dog—hands that would tell you what you needed to know about the animal you showed him. With his intense concentration and exquisite artistry, Ellsworth could tell a story without saying a word.

When he became too ill to continue his judging assignments, his multitude of friends stayed in touch with him, trying to keep him buoyed up. His wife, Violet, welcomed them as she felt their visits were good for him. Ellsworth asked me to observe Lakeland Terriers at Westminster for him as it was a banner year with many outstanding individuals coming down from the first crops sired by Red Baron.

An incredible thing happened during the breed judging in the Lakeland ring that year. A mouse fell out of the rafters of the Garden and into the Lakeland ring. A uniformed Garden official walked haughtily into the ring with a broom and huge dustpan and started sweeping up the prostrate mouse, which then revived and began running around the ring. Not one Lakeland noticed the mouse, much less attempt to go after it. All the spectators, handlers and ring officials reeled with laughter. Meanwhile, Bob Forsyth guided one of Peter Green's charges to best of breed.

When I got home and related the story to Ellsworth, he laughed quietly and, with a twinkle in his eye, said: "Well, let's hope if a moose ever falls into the Elkhound ring at the Garden, your dog will not ignore it."

He had a quiet, yet active, sense of humor and great depth of character. He was much loved and widely respected. As a judge, he touched the minds and hearts of many who would follow him into the realm of judging. Renowned all-rounder Michele Billings told me that he greatly influenced her life and that she, too, still misses him.

His courage toward the end was awe-inspiring. Those of us who remained close to him visited him often, taking him to lunch and doing various other activities he was still able to enjoy. When the time came, Vi asked me to eulogize him as part of the service. It was both touching and overwhelming to acknowledge the absolute genius of this very special man while portraying his moral goodness. His loss was premature and devastating to all of us, for we felt we had not heard all he had to say. We had not probed all that was inside this profound man. We were not done. And to this day, we are not.

Ellsworth is with us in word and deed, as we attempt to follow his lead. His disciples are widely spread, still trying to carry his message and spirit concerning the necessity of retaining the purity of the breed. Every time we have a decision to make that finds this purity in conflict with any other element, his voice is heard. His many friends will always think of him as a spiritual influence as well as an intellectual one. His mission was to enrich lives—and he did it well.

A fitting tribute to the breeding program that produced him came with the 1993 Westminster BIS victory of English Springer Spaniel Ch. Salilyn's Condor, Top Dog All Breeds in 1992. Handled by Mark Threlfall for owners Donna and Roger Herzig, MD, and Julia Gasow, "Robert" was the choice of Sporting expert Barbara F. Heller in the finals. Club officials Ronald H. Menaker and Chester F. Collier complete the picture. (Photo by Ashbey)

Julia Gasow, The Living Legend That Is Salilyn

There is no one I hold in higher esteem than Julia Gasow (see color section). This grand and wonderful lady is the ultimate dog breeder, having created a line of great English Springer Spaniels that breed true generation after generation at the same time they serve as classic examples for any breeding program.

This living legend was born in Kansas City in 1904, but it is in Troy, Michigan, where her fame blossomed and grew into international celebrity status. The culmination of Julie's remarkable breeding career came with the popular Best in Show victory of Ch. Salilyn's Condor at Westminster in 1993. To approach the magic century marker and still have such a productive life with your dogs that you anticipate the arrival of a new litter validates all meaning of life. And Julie does just that.

The reverence for the kennel name Salilyn, which reflects her love of her daughters, Sally and Linda, is universal, and for me personally dates back to the 1950s when I fell in love for the first time with a Salilyn Springer. The dog was the award-winning Ch. Salilyn's MacDuff, capably handled by Jack Funk.

It was not the only time I fell for one of her beautiful dogs, for it happened over and over again. Aristocrat, Classic, Private Stock, Sophistication, Vanguard, Dynasty and Condor are just a small sample of the many dogs that are usually "one of a kind" in a breed. They were routine with Julie as the quality continued to come and continues to do so even now, with youngsters on the ground that will take the breed well into the 21st Century guided by her protege Kellie Fitzgerald.

The Salilyn line of dogs is nothing short of sensational, and success was achieved through a carefully planned breeding program that capitalized on the combination of two separate strains within Julie's line. Ch. Salilyn's Citation II was the more substantial, shorter-legged yet sounder of the two dogs. To Julie's beloved Ch. King Peter of Salilyn goes the credit for putting the leggier, more elegant look of classic quality into the line. Julie used these two dogs much like a world-class bridge champion might set up a card game—crossing back and forth to score the victory and attain the ultimate in perfection. (See Pictures, Sire Section)

At the same time Julie had a fierce, yet friendly, competitor in Fred Jackson, she also had a soul mate who understood how to improve a breed using the best blood possible for each breeding. It happened that one of his bitches bred to King Peter produced Fred's top-winning Ch. Frejax's Royal Salute. This multi-BIS dog was not only the top Springer of his day but also the ranking Sporting Dog. Julie and Fred were representative of what a lot of people think of as the "good old days" when people competed and cooperated at the same time. They joked and teased each other about the results of their breedings. If Fred got a great one sired by Julie's dog, he joshed her as he credited his bitch. And vice versa. Such friendly rivalries are always in the best interests of dogs and people, as all involved are on a positive track to success that is motivated by all the right reasons.

The spectacular career of Ch. Salilyn's Aristocrat with handler Dick Cooper was nothing short of sensational, setting an all-time record of 45 Best in Shows in one year. At that time, few dogs campaigned at more than 80 shows a year, so Aristocrat's statistics were incredible. As fabulous as his show record was, it was as the number one Sire All Time All Breeds that became the crowning triumph by which he is remembered. When one thinks of the concept that greatness runs in families, one has to think Salilyn.

When Julie came to the Monterey Peninsula to judge a quarter of a century ago, it was like a dream come true to have an opportunity to hear about her breeding theories. Having already read about her two strains within her own line, I followed her example with my version of Citation and King Peter, Howdy Rowdy and Vickssen. I couldn't get enough of her words of wisdom and asked her countless questions until the hour grew late.

So as not to forget what she had said, I came home and stayed up late into the night recording her words that have served as references ever since. I was deeply impressed with the entire experience and number it high on the list of special and unforgettable occasions in my life.

Julie always ranked the Quaker Oats awards high in priority, and her dogs won any number of them. Therefore, it was most appropriate that she became the first inductee into the Quaker Oats Hall of Fame, which recognizes the elite of dogdom. Even as I look back at her numerous honors—national winners, top dog all breed winners, multi-BIS winners and top producers—I know that the accomplishments of the past are the ultimate testimony to an incredible gene pool. And it is upon that gene pool that the future will depend. Julia Gasow's permanent impact on her breed is here to stay.

Heywood Hartley, Judge and Breeder of Woodhart Scottish Terriers

In any creative and competitive endeavor, such as that provided by the world of dogs, there are those of such expertise and excellence that they cannot avoid acquiring high profiles with accompanying well-deserved fame. In the dog show world, they become household names. Such people are widely quoted and their stamp of approval on a dog is eagerly sought by fanciers. And that is as it should be.

But for every one in this bright public spotlight, there is another who is just as capable and just as knowledgeable, one who has the same sense of integrity and excellence, and one whose opinion should be sought just as enthusiastically, but who chooses to remain low key in his approach to the world of dogs. Often these people will have a full and active life away from dogs in addition to their passion for dogs and are content to deal with the dog world in a more leisurely fashion.

Such a man was Heywood Hartley. He was a devoted husband and father, a prominent Virginia businessman, a horseman who enjoyed his youngsters' participation in pony club events, and he was a civic-minded golfer who shared a lot of his ideas with friends on the golf course.

His influence on my life was as an example of the epitome of gentle sportsmanship—a persona he shared with fellow Richmond fancier, William T. Holt of Ch. Rock Falls Colonel fame, and teacher extraordinaire, showing me how to "look" at good dogs with a special focus on terriers.

In those days, most of the great terriers that were appropriately presented in the rings of the scattered Virginia dog shows came down from the North accompanied by expert terrier men with such fabled names as Phil Prentice and Johnny Murphy. Others might have resented their intrusion, but not Heywood. His well-bred line of Scotties held their own with all of them, and Heywood welcomed the opportunity to see these good ones—win, lose or draw. With his quiet and positive manner, he would say: "Just look at these dogs and appreciate them. See how they are made." One Scottie that impressed him when it came down with its handler, Phil Prentice, was the imported Ch. Walsing Winning Trick of Edgerstoune, the 1950 Westminster Best in Show winner owned by Ambassador and

The extraordinary Scottish Terrier Eng. and Am. Ch. Walsing Winning Trick of Edgerstoune was used by Heywood Hartley as a model dog for the author to study when she was a girl. Hartley's message to the youth he influenced was to study the excellent dogs of others. Heywood pointed out that many people are so interested in their own dogs they miss the opportunity to learn that classic dogs present. Phil Prentice and Winning Trick were the 1950 BIS winners at Westminster for owners Ambassador and Mrs. G. John Winant. (Photo courtesy of Inez Hartley)

Inez and Heywood Hartley relaxing at ringside during a timeout from their busy judging schedule. The Hartleys always enjoyed their private moments together as they were a devoted couple with true family values. Their Virginia graciousness served as a fine example of the camaraderie and sportsmanship within the fancy. Heywood's lesson on how to look at dogs in the most studious manner to appreciate the components that make an excellent animal became an integral part of the author's early eduction in dogs. (Photo courtesy of Suzi Hartley Barker)

1985 Westminster BIS winner Ch. Braeburn's Close Encounter pictured winning one of her 200-plus BISs under Judge Heywood Hartley, himself a Scottish Terrier breeder. "Shannon" was owned by Sonny and Alan Novick and campaigned throughout her illustrious career by the incomparable George Ward. (Guy Nullander Photo)

Mrs. John Winant. Later, he was singularly impressed with another of his favorite breed, Ch. Braeburn's Close Encounter.

Heywood had met a pretty young school teacher, Inez Hauke, in Roanoke, Virginia, when he was working with the *Roanoke Times*. They were married in 1938 and moved to Richmond in 1943, the year their son Robert was born. Robert was followed four years later by daughter Susan. By this time, Heywood's printing business was enjoying lots of post-World War II growth.

By the '50s, the business was flourishing and Heywood was enjoying happy times with kids, ponies and dogs. Furthermore, he was starting to gain respect for his talents as an extraordinary judge of dogs. At the prestigious Warrenton Pony Club, I saw their ponies in action bringing home the ribbons. Heywood and Inez took quiet, loving pride in both their two-legged and four-legged youngsters.

Meanwhile, Heywood's reputation as a dogman with outstanding instincts about dogs, as well as his gentlemanly demeanor in the ring, expanded. Now, not only was he appreciated by his friends and neighbors in Virginia, but he was also officiating at many of the top dog shows in the country. The ultimate jewel in his crown of judging assignments came at the famed Westminster Kennel Club show in 1962 with the coveted honor of judging Best in Show. In his reserved and professional manner, Heywood went about the task utilizing his knowledgeable expertise to select Wishing Well Kennels' West Highland White Terrier, Ch. Elfinbrook Simon as Best in Show. Simon was handled by the incomparable George Ward, and Wishing Well is still the kennel name of Barbara Keenan, a terrier judge held in great esteem by today's fanciers.

As the years turned into decades, Heywood became an all-rounder and Inez a multi-group judge. Their judging assignments took them across the country as they shared their Virginia charm with the fancy. By the time my parents moved to Williamsburg in the early 1980s, Inez and Heywood had been maintaining a Florida residence as well as the one in Virginia.

Over the years when my trips from California took me to Williamsburg, Virginia, to visit with my parents, it was always a treat if I could make an opportunity to see the Hartleys. One luncheon that stands out in my mind came not too long after my father had survived a serious illness in 1988. We were at the Cascades in its beautiful sylvan setting when there was a momentary pause in the conversation, and my father softly spoke the words: "It doesn't get much better than this." The two octogenarians, my father and Heywood, exchanged understanding glances as the conversation resumed. Although my father was never a true dog fancier, he respected Heywood for the influence he had on dogs and especially on the young people involved with them. And, Heywood understood this. It was the last time I saw him. The Hartleys will always be a beloved part of my Virginia heritage in dogs.

Muriel R. Laubach, Dau-Han Cocker Spaniels

Muriel R. Laubach first came into my life at Coleman Place Elementary School where I was one of several students playing kickball during recess. She had a buff Cocker Spaniel bitch named Honey that she was walking around trying to socialize on the school grounds. It was a lifelong lesson for which I can thank her. To this day, working canine youngsters around crowds of boisterous human youngsters is a marvelous activity.

The fifth-graders left their spot on the field to cluster around this lovely bitch, for few had ever seen one so well groomed and trimmed. Soon I started going to Mrs. Laubach's small home and kennel after school and working with her and her dogs. In those days, youngsters did this sort of thing for the love of it and to learn, and no one ever considered any financial remuneration.

It was not very long before she had worked with me to the point at which I started showing puppies and had a black puppy of my own. Muriel was often alone for her husband, Commander Kenneth Laubach, was frequently at sea. His last big command was as chief engineering officer on the U.S.S. Missouri the year before the giant battleship went aground in Chesapeake Bay.

After being introduced to Norman Austin, Bea Weguson, and the marvelous Honey Creek Cockers, Muriel strayed from the solid colors to parti-colors where she was to have incredible success.

Muriel R. Laubach was an influential mentor in the author's life. She is pictured here on the left going Winners Bitch with (Ch.) Dau-Han's Bib N' Tucker. The author is handling the B/W Dau-Han's Dan Tucker to BOW and Ch. Harrigan of Twin Haven is BOV under breeder-judge Charles Milwain. Muriel was very proud of these three offspring of Dan Morgan. His progeny helped comfort her over his loss. (Maryland Cocker Specialty—Shafer Photo)

She was one of the most objective people I have ever known and saw every single fault on every single dog in her kennel as well as those in the ring. She appreciated excellent neck and shoulders on a Cocker, and had little use for those who did not have them. She was a wonderful role model for cleanliness—keeping her kennels and each dog in the kennel in immaculate condition—and she was a tough taskmaster on both herself and her dogs, feeling undeserving if the victories were not preceded by lots of hard work.

She and Thelma Blair (Blairwood Cocker Spaniels) shared the concept that people could not control whether they had the best dog at the show, but they could certainly control having the best-conditioned and best-presented dog at the show. It was a lesson this skinny, little dog fanatic never forgot.

We worked all the time preparing the dogs for their limited outings during the year. The day came when she felt confident enough in her stock to make a mother-son breeding that produced Ch. Dau-Han's Holiday Flirt. Later, she reluctantly went along with Norman Austin's insistence that this exquisite, typey, red-and-white bitch be bred to Ch. Dun-Mar's Dapper Dan, a macho black and white standing at Norman's Baliwick Kennels in North Carolina.

The breeding produced a great red-and-white dog who could win today, Ch. Dau-Han's Dan Morgan. The early death of this dog was a blow to Cocker breeders all over the country, and Muriel was never quite the same after his loss. It was in early September 1960, and she had taken the dog to Philadelphia for the Liberty Bell Cocker Specialty, leaving me with an airplane ticket to fly up after school to show him. I will never forget the shocked look on my mother's face when she informed me that Morgan had become very ill and the trip was canceled. He died before she could get him home, and he was buried in Jesse Mercer's pet cemetery in Virginia Beach, fully groomed with the show lead

Norman had given him on his lovely neck. It was one of those sad times that tests all of us from time to time in our doggy lives.

Muriel taught the lesson well that dogs must be able to perform the work they were bred to do. Even though her successes came at a time when Cockers were getting more and more away from their flushing spaniel job description, she always wanted to see her Cockers "quarter" in the woods around her country place on Holland Swamp Road where she and Ken moved after his retirement. After Ted Young Jr. finished her red-and-white Ch. Dau-Han's Flash Over, she had the dog stay in Connecticut for Teddy's father, Ted Young Sr. to field train. Later, Ken Laubach personally hunted over this dog.

Because of her sporting dog orientation, she would not allow dogs with incorrect mouths in her kennel as "they simply could not pick up a bird." When I last visited with her in 1992, she still expressed concern that the breed was losing its utilitarian qualities. My gratitude for all she taught me is difficult to describe. She left one more gift for me upon her death, the marvelous painting of Dan Morgan, by Adelaide Arntsen, that graces the den at my home on Old Hickory Blvd.

Catherine and Wells Peck, Pitch Road Norwegian Elkhounds

Catherine and Wells Peck came into my life during my teens, and they were the most important Norwegian Elkhound influences in my life. There were not many Elkhounds in Virginia, and to find majors I had to go north into Pennsylvania, New Jersey and New York where I first met the Pecks. Thanks to early directions by Muriel Laubach and Johnny Davis, it

Ch. Trym of Pitch Road, the dog Mrs. A. Wells (Catherine) Peck considered one of the best ever produced by their Pitch Road Kennels in Litchfield, Conn. Sired by the Norwegian import, Ch. Roy of Pitch Road, he was out of Ch. Vin-Melca's Moa of Pitch Road, a daughter of Ch. Tortasen's Bjonn II, the Norwegian import that so stamped succeeding generations in the late '50s and early '60s. (Smolley Photo)

A. Wells Peck handling the great Ch. Tortasen's Bjonn II to Hound Group first en route to BIS, Suffolk County Kennel Club, September 1958. Robert McCandless awarded the Group 1st with Anna Katherine Nicholas doing the BIS honors. Bjonn II was imported from Norway by the Pecks and proved to be a true turning point in Norwegian Elkhound history. This is one of the few times Mr. Peck ever handled the dog, as his regular handler, Tom Gately, was unable to show him in this group. (Photo by William Brown)

Norway's Ch. Moa, foremost hunter and foundation bitch, was the dam of Ch. Tortasen's Bjonn II and Ch. Viking C.D., both major contributors to the Norwegian Elkhound in America. Her sire Ch. Steig of Jarlsberg was a member of the family of dogs saved by Miss Gerd Berbom during World War II. Miss Berbom's Ch. Anna of the Hollow was the dam of Steig and the grandam of Moa's mother Nussi. Steig's two grandsons that came to the US were turning points in the breed—dogs that produced outstanding show and hunting stock. Mrs. Catherine Peck, who imported Bjonn II from breeder J.P. Holsing, named Bjonn's daughter (Ch.) Vin-Melca's Moa of Pitch Road after her grandam because she considered her the best bitch housed at the Litchfield, Connecticut, Kennel. (Photo courtesy of Smolley)

became obvious that my first bitch could not be bred without seeking out the very best dog available—and that dog was not in my part of the world.

Muriel and Johnny decided I needed to work with the Pecks. It was then that I became truly hooked on Norwegian Elkhounds, for now it was possible to learn something about the breed.

With the help of Catherine's letters and my mentors, it was decided that the hunting stock bitch was not that badly bred, coming down from Lawrence Litchfield's Lindvangen lines. So in the early '50s, long before I was able to make the trip myself, my pride and joy, Ch. Ulf's Madam Helga C.D., was given her veterinary check and taken to Railway Express to make the long trip by train to Connecticut and the home of the Pitch Road Norwegian Elkhounds. Within the next few years it would become possible to fly the bitches to the Pecks, making life easier for everyone.

Once the bitch arrived, they decided she would be mated with Ch. Carro of Ardmere, a marvelous dog with a short back made even shorter by the Tauskey Photo taken of him for the cover of *Popular Dogs*. Imported by the Pecks from Scotland, this dog carried a masculine headpiece with the correct Elkhound station and look.

Catherine sent a long letter detailing qualities that I should consider in grading the litter. Few, if any, Elkhound litters ever had so much expertise collected in their evaluation—for Johnny Davis, Norman Austin and Muriel Laubach shared their knowledge while studying the litter with me. The pick male from the litter was sold to a marvelous home (the Von Schillings of Hampton, Virginia) and later made available for me to mate with Rebel Rouser, producing the maternal grandam of Howdy Rowdy and Vagabond.

When my mother and I went to get Rebel Rouser in 1958, it was the first of many fascinating trips to Pitch Road. No one could critique an Elkhound any better than Catherine Peck. She taught me so much about the essence of the breed. She guided me to the Rebel Rouser bitch and then helped me achieve the breeding with the imported Ch. Tortasen's Bjonn II that became the cornerstone for the line. Mrs. Peck later honored me by sending her bitch from the litter to California for me to finish (Ch. Vin-Melca's Moa of Pitch Road) as well as her son, Ch. Trym of Pitch Road, for me to special.

Wells Peck was a sportsman and a well-known businessman as the proprietor of Peck and Peck-Fifth Avenue. His angling skills resulted in his appearance on the cover of *Sports Illustrated* in an edition dedicated to great sport fishermen. When the Parent Club dedicated the 1974 National Specialty to them, Wells and Catherine came to California for the event.

Their vision and pioneer work on behalf of the breed brought some of Europe's finest dogs to the United States, resulting in breed progress that would not have been possible without them. Wells and Catherine Peck may be gone, but they can never be forgotten by anyone who loves the Norwegian Elkhound.

Derek Rayne, Judge and Breeder, Pemwelgi Corgis

No man has more dignity than the beloved Derek Rayne. The stately octogenarian is the honorary president of two of California's most prestigious dog clubs: Del Monte Kennel Club and Santa Barbara Kennel Club. He has been in dogs all of his life, and his love of every minute of it is contagious. Derek's influence on the lives of many is by the example he sets as well as the knowledge he so generously shares from home base on the beautiful Monterey Peninsula.

Derek was born into dogs in Raynes Park, England, a town near London named after his grandfather. His grandfather was a Pug and Irish Terrier fancier and his mother bred Pekingese. As a boy of eight, Derek decided he wanted his own breed and selected an Airedale that he proceeded to win third with at the big Richmond (England) championship show.

England's loss was America's gain when at the age of 21 he came to New York, where he met Blanche Saunders, the foremost obedience expert of the day. He then began obedience training with his Pembroke Welsh Corgi. When he moved to California in 1938, he became good friends with Beatrice Hopkins before she married Major Godsol. Bea, the *master breeder* of Waseeka Newfoundlands, was to become Derek's most important mentor in his growth as a judge. In 1939, he earned his license to judge Corgis and Fox Terriers as well as obedience. A dedicated sportsman and exhibitor, Derek was the first to win a Working Group with a Corgi in the United States. A significant thing about Derek and his lifelong friends, Bea and Major, was that all three of them were all-rounders who also judged obedience.

He moved to Carmel-By-The-Sea in 1940 and together with his father started the fashionable Derek Rayne Men's Clothing Store in 1942. The mark of a gentleman in Northern California for more than 50 years was to wear this quality clothing with the Derek Rayne label, also an indication of his "singled-out" trademark. Derek closed the shop in June 1995, leaving him more time to enjoy his judging and to focus on writing his memoirs.

Derek became an all-breed judge in 1950, and shortly after that he came into my life when I exhibited Cocker Spaniels under him at a show in Norfolk, Virginia. From the very beginning it was obvious even to a fledgling fancier that this man was someone special, and when I moved to California in 1961, he became more influential in my life. Derek was one of those rare dogmen who talked dogs in

Derek G. Rayne pictured in the summer of 1995 at the time of the closing of his classic men's shop on Ocean Avenue in Carmel. Derek is now devoting all of his energies to his international judging agenda and to work on his memoirs. (Photo courtesy of Derek Rayne, Ltd.)

Portrait of a star could be the title of this picture taken during Del Monte Kennel Club's celebration for its favorite person and Honorary President Derek Rayne. The portrait shows Derek with the BIS rosette won by his homebred Smooth Fox Terrier cradled in his arms. Dr. Jacklyn Hungerland is to Derek's left with Gerda Rayne and the author completing the picture. (Photo by Fox and Cook)

depth and rarely mentioned people, except for their positive roles in the pursuit of excellence. Early on he told me: "You should be able to tell what breed it is if all you see is its head."

His peers have selected him Judge of the Year on many occasions with Fido and *Kennel Review* Awards. Many years ago when the *Canine Chronicle* was a weekly newspaper, a poll was conducted by the publishers to find the most competent judges in each group through solicitation of breeders, handlers, judges, exhibitors and writers. Derek finished at the top of the list in every group.

For years he bred Fox Terriers and Corgis and produced five all-breed BIS winners. He chuckled that he was invited into Del Monte Kennel Club after winning BIS, therefore becoming ineligible to exhibit there. Nonetheless, he exhibited his own dogs at other California shows well into the 1970s with great success. And he did it like he does everything else in his life—with impeccable taste and class. His ever expanding schedule of judging shows together with his business commitments resulted in Frank Sabella showing two of his greatest Corgi bitches: the English import Ch. Rock Rose of Wey and the Westminster Working Group winner, Ch. Nebriowa Miss Bobbi Sox.

Derek married his lovely wife, Gerda, in 1972 and credits her with correcting all of his bad habits except smoking the occasional imported cigarette. The Raynes have always had a good Corgi in residence. Their travels take them all over the world for Derek's judging and include many European trips to Gerda's homeland in Germany, as well as Derek's beloved England where he often judges one of his favorite shows at Windsor.

Derek is always willing to share his expertise with all of those in dogs. He told me that he became an all-rounder in 1950, and almost 50 years later he is still learning. This remarkable gentleman who has been a breeder, exhibitor, obedience participant, and judge extraordinaire is the perfect combination of the intellectual and practical dog person whose influence will be felt well into yet another century.

Arline Swalwell, Windridge Cocker Spaniels

Arline Swalwell and her twin sister, Corrine, were born to an aristocratic Everett, Washington, family in 1900. Both sisters spent the best part of their lives on California's Monterey Peninsula. Corrine turned her talents to business and became one of Carmel's leading merchants with her adorable and unique children's shop. She also was well-known locally for lavish entertaining in her lovely apartment, decorated with a wide variety of collectible art pieces.

Miss Arline Swalwell pictured in 1985 at the age of 85 with one of her homebred Windridge chocolate Cocker Spaniels. She did her own kennel work right up until her death in 1987. She was an inspiration to generations of Cocker breeders and a knowledgeable instructor for the author. In addition to her artistry with dogs, she produced beautiful personal art work, especially in the hard discipline of pastel water colors.(Photo courtesy Swalwell Estate)

Arline continued her passion for her beloved Cocker Spaniels she had raised from girlhood. She transported the Cockers from Washington to the Peninsula on the train. The details of her trip remain sketchy in my memory, but she used to tell it with great mirth and genuine appreciation for her father's workman who assisted her on the trip.

In 1961, when I arrived on the Peninsula, Windridge was one of the first places I visited. Arline was aglow as she had recently received another enthusiastic doggy visitor from the East, James Edward Clark. At that time, Arline housed a number of excellent Standard Poodles as well as Cockers. It was with great pride that she showed me Ch. Beau Monde War Paint, a typey black-and-white son of Ch. Dau-Han's Dan Morgan she had purchased from breeder Richard Beauchamp. One thing led to another and soon I was campaigning War Paint along with my own Elkhound bitch. In 1962 and 1963, I lived in the studio apartment at Windridge and was most grateful to be allowed to work with her dogs and learn from her. There were few times in my life when I was so totally into dogs as those blissful months of working with this grand lady already into her 60s when I met her.

Many years earlier, she had owned a brown Cocker bitch and still yearned to see the color become accepted by Cocker fanciers. By the time she actually started succeeding with them she was well into her 70s and still setting new goals. Norman Austin and Frances Greer encouraged her with the color, although it amused them that she did not call them livers or browns, but chocolates.

When she phased out the Standard Poodles, she gave me her whelping box which Tom and Ann Stevenson had given her. The box has been rebuilt a number of times and is now in Tennessee, continuing its contribution to the Vin-Melca tradition. She was a grand lady of great Victorian style and manners. When she died in 1987, she was buried beside her sister in the small cemetery next to the Pacific Grove Golf Course. My good friend and fellow teacher, John Waldron, lives in a nearby apartment and we put flowers on her grave from time to time, comforted by the fact that she is under the whispering pines that drew her to the area she loved.

She was one of those deep and sincere dog people who quietly give so very much to the animals they loved, as well as to the fancy that enjoys them. They were her life.

Federico Tesio, The Wizard of Dormello

Federico Tesio was simply the best breeder who ever lived! Unfortunately for dogs, ours was not his field of interest. Fortunately for dogs or any other breeding pursuit, his methods of breeding the world's most influential thoroughbreds can serve as an example whether the subject is horses, dogs, cattle or hamsters.

He was born in 1869 and was a retired Italian cavalry officer who knew every nuance of a horse when he started making his formidable presence felt in the competitive world of breeding great race horses. Unlike our subjective world of show dogs, the race track is unforgiving of breeding mistakes and is objective in its performance criteria. The best horse is the one that goes the classic distance carrying the most weight in the least time.

From his limited resources of about 12 mares, the man who became known as the Wizard of Dormello bred the most internationally influential sires in the 20th Century, if not in the history of the thoroughbred. This he accomplished with what would be the equivalent of a litter every year or two in the breeding of dogs.

His fame would have been lasting if he had only bred one horse—the great Nearco. In the United States we can appreciate Nearco as the great-grandsire of Secretariat. This direct tail-male sire line of Secretariat shows Bold Ruler as his sire and Nasrullah, son of Nearco, as his grandsire. (See Sires.) This sire line is of tremendous significance and features other greats such as Northern Dancer, Royal Charger, Spectacular Bid, Nashua and Foolish Pleasure among its many who have achieved international fame.

Consider the horses bred by Canada's E. P. Taylor, who had the good sense to import from England the well-bred Hyperion mare, Lady Angela, in foal to Nearco. Taylor's belief in the blood of

Tesio's horses paid off when the resulting colt, Nearctic, sired Northern Dancer. Northern Dancer will be remembered as the first two-minute-flat winner of the mile and one-quarter Kentucky Derby. Furthermore, he is the most prolific sire of stakes winners in thoroughbred history.

Nearco was sold to England by Tesio as a three-year old in 1938 and retired to stud duties undefeated. When war broke out, the horse was moved several times for his protection. Finally this jewel of a blue-blood was protected for posterity by settling down to a breeding shed in wonderful pastures fully equipped with an air-raid shelter. The grand lady of Norway's Elkhound breeders, Miss Gerd

TESIO AND THE FORTUNATE SECOND CHOICE

One of the more interesting of the Tesio stories that influenced me was the one involving the mating that produced the great Nearco. Tesio sought the services of Europe's foremost stallion of the day—Fairway—for his mare, Nogara, whose dam Catnip had been bought for a modest price by Tesio at public auction. She was a daughter of the well-known stayer, Spearmint.

Tesio was unable to mate his mare with Fairway, and therefore, forced to use Fairway's full brother, Pharos, as his second choice. The resulting colt was none other than the great racehorse and sire of sires, Nearco. Fairway had been the physical opposite of Nogara, long-bodied and more streamlined than Nogara. Pharos, on the other hand, had been similarly built to Nogara in that he was compact and muscular. In missing on his first choice of mating of Nogara to Fairway, Tesio had been unable to breed the two who were unlike in type. In connecting on his second choice mating of Nogara to Pharos, Tesio had bred two that were like in type. Perhaps this is where he formulated some of his ideas about future breedings, for it was a powerful lesson.

When Ch. Vin-Melca's Vikina whelped three sons by Ch. Windy Cove's Rowdy Ringo in 1965, I was severely disappointed, for I had made this mating to get a bitch from Ringo and Vikina to breed to Vickssen. Such a bitch would have returned Ch. Tortasen's Bjonn II to the pedigree of the future litter twice through the brothers Rowdy Ringo and Silver Son. (Vickssen himself was the product of Rebel Rouser bred to her own grandson Hi Ho Silver, by Silver Son, and Vikina was Rebel Rouser's granddaughter.)

The reason I had gone to the very masculine, somewhat overdone Ringo was to get a heavier-boned, more substantial bitch out of Vikina to breed to Vickssen. I feared that Vikina was too much "like" Vickssen to breed to him and a heavier daughter would be better. Thus, having no bitches in the litter was a tremendous letdown.

Right about that time, my research on Tesio unearthed the story about Nearco, which certainly got me thinking. Perhaps instead of putting that extra step between the merging of Vikina and Vickssen that had long been in my mind, why not just breed Vikina herself to Vickssen? My instincts had told me this breeding was "right" for the future, but my conservative thinking led me in the direction of Ringo as one more step in the process—instead of the more "like-to-like" breeding of Vickssen and Vikina.

Just as the hand of fate that led to Pharos becoming the sire of Nogara's 1935 foal, Vikina's all-male litter became the influence of fate that resulted in the direct mating of Vikina to Vickssen. In 1967, Ch. Vin-Melca's Vagabond was the only male born in the resulting litter. Like Nearco, the result of a second choice mating rather than a first, Vagabond became one of his breed's all-time classic animals—excelling both as a performer and a producer—influencing the destiny of the breed for decades and beyond. The big difference was that Nearco became a sire of sires, and Vagabond became a sire of dams.

Sometimes we need to get out of our own realm to open up and expand our thinking. Untold numbers of horse breeders that never met Tesio do everything in their power to adapt his methods to their breeding programs, but so too does at least one dog breeder who never met him!

Right: Nearco, bay colt, 1935, by Pharos out of Nogara by Havresac II. Nearco was undefeated in all of Europe and retired to stud as the European grand champion resplendent in pastures with his own bomb shelter! He became the head of the sire line of the 20th Century with untold numbers of Kentucky Derby and Epson Derby winners as his descendents. His most famous great grandson was Secretariat, by Bold Ruler out of Somethingroyal, by Princequillo. Bold Ruler was sired by Nasrullah who was the son of Nearco.

Below: Nimbus, bay colt by Nearco X Kong, by Baytown. Winner of the Epsom Derby, Highweight on the British Free Handicap. As the years went by, my fascination with the work of Federico Tesio intensified. Not only did I utilize his theories more and more in my breeding program, it seemed a logical step to name some Elkhounds

after the great throughbreds from his line. Ch. Vin-Melca's Nimbus, Best Hound in Show at Westminster Kennel Club in 1977 and 1979 was named after this horse.

(Keeneland Library Photos)

Berbom and the Jarlsberg dogs, were similarly housed and protected in England during World War II when Norway was the victim of Nazi occupation. Many guardian angels risked their lives and resources during these trying times to protect their treasured breeds' gene pools.

The horse many horsemen consider the Horse of the Century, even more than Secretariat, was foaled in 1952 at Dormello at the foot of the Italian Alps. Ribot was to Europeans what Secretariat was to Americans. Like Nearco, he became the undefeated champion of all Europe. Although Tesio did not live long enough to know just how good this horse would become, he must have speculated on Ribot's potential, for the 85-year-old collapsed and died after watching the two-year old work out in 1954.

Although this great animal never raced in the United States, American respect for his prowess was evidenced by the Galbraiths' bringing him to Darby Dan in Kentucky to stand at stud, and indeed the horse is buried there on the farm.

The list of great horses whose tail-male sires track to those bred by Tesio is endless, yet you may be surprised to find that one of his creeds was to avoid standing your own studs. Tesio stayed with this policy his entire life, for he felt that in-house sires could be the downfall of any breeding program because of the temptation of using them when it was not the wisest decision. Tesio believed in using the best stallions available, preferably older proven sires even though their stud fees were more expensive.

Forrest Hall, of the Hallwyre Fox Terrier Kennels in Texas, talked to me about this policy in the 1960s. Mr. Hall was a well-known all-rounder who lectured from time to time at various symposiums on dogs. His advice was to let others prove the sires before you breed to them: "Go to the dogs based on what they have produced, not on what you think they will produce."

Tesio annually visited the farms that housed stallions he was considering for the next breeding season to check them personally for a fresh, accurate picture of their conformation. He wanted to ensure that his recollections of them were correct. He never remained unduly attached to his own lines, and frequently revitalized his breeding program of all brood mares with new purchases from the best families. He had an uncanny ability to find modest-priced mares that others could not envision as capable of producing a classic horse, and then finding combinations others overlooked. He did not mind a plain-looking mare who was well bred, and selected animals that pleased him without regard to fashion.

Finally, Tesio was not married to any one formula for his breeding successes, as he alternated his patterns of matings but never his patterns of selection. He seemed to have magical instincts on when to use a close breeding, when the best choice was an outcross, and when it was timely to try a proven nick.

Although thoroughbred researchers and bloodstock students have spent decades since his death in 1954 trying to figure out what made him tick, they have yet to unravel all of his secrets. His book, *Breeding the Race Horse*, tantalized the appetite with a few tidbits, but did not share any personal advice for posterity. The true student is on his own in trying to ascertain how this quiet, unassuming man who produced history's best horses succeeded with few resources while others did not. Nonetheless, when one studies the work of Tesio, it invites speculation of his pursuit of dominant sire lines causing the researcher to wonder if he had magical intuition about genetic greatness associated with the Y chromosome. Perhaps if this unproved hypothesis is true, then a quality, well-balanced pedigree of the mare would provide the basics for the progeny with the sire's possible Y chromosome greatness providing the brilliance.

Tesio believed the closer he got to Mother Nature with his horses, the better his stock would benefit. He separated his breeding stock from those in training and kept his mares with their foals in pockets of natural settings in pastures at the foot of the Alps. Whenever possible, he liked to get the horses on fresh land where others had not grazed previously, thereby reducing threats of parasitic infestations.

Perhaps the most important part of the Tesio equation was that he handled every aspect of the operation himself: He did the breeding, the feeding, the breaking, the training, the conditioning, and personally supervised their racing careers. As one great horseman told me 25 years ago: "He did everything but ride them."

That is why I studied his work in depth for so many years. He was the master of "doing it all" for me to emulate in my quest to become a breeder-owner-exhibitor. The measure of his influence on me was felt when Ch. Vin-Melca's Nimbus was named after the Epsom Derby winner foaled in 1945 and rated at the top of the British Free Handicap. The equine Nimbus was just one of the many Derby winners sired by Nearco and his descendants.

To study Tesio is to study an enigma—for the greatness of the man was based on his soleness of purpose. He spent hours and hours sitting quietly on his walking stick studying his animals as they moved around their paddocks. He loved watching the weanlings at play and made every effort as the youngsters grew to adapt a particular training regimen specifically for each individual.

In short, Tesio was the consummate horseman-breeder-owner-trainer whose exquisite attention to detail made his farm at Dormello outproduce such huge establishments as Calumet and Spendthrift in Kentucky, as well as the splendid operations of the Aga Khan and Lord Derby abroad. With his small band of a dozen mares he was able to turn out horses that these large breeding operations of hundreds of mares could not match. Not only that, they were forced to come to him for his horses to make their own lines better.

When you remember that few, if any, areas of breeding are more competitive or grueling than the tests put to the classic race horse, you appreciate Tesio for what he was—a marvelous monument to the small breeder with the highest of standards, a testimony to inspire one to persevere in pursuit of excellence.

Foster Families

In addition to the special people who influence you in your formative years, some precious people come into your life throughout the years you are in dogs. They will become like family and share their children with you as godparents and their lives with you as extended family. Their warmth and support will help engender your success, and they will gain much from you as you share your world with them. Occasionally they will become "foster families" not only for you but for your dogs, too.

The tradition of placing puppies in loving foster families dates to Elizabethan times in England where landed gentry placed their puppies in the homes of staff members to give the animals a companionable family start on life away from the kennel environment. This practice was called walking hound puppies and Daphne Moore in her informative book, *Foxhounds*, on page 81, provides a fascinating description of the practice: "Many years ago, on a Yorkshire estate, there was a clause in the tenants' lease specifying that a red coat would be given to each tenant walking a puppy." Moore's book tells us a favorite place for the puppy was with the cook, and those reasons speak for themselves. Those families who had raised puppies that went on to stardom at the hunt or other competitive endeavors took great pride in their contributions to the achievements.

According to Moore, the practice evolved into puppy shows with prizes for the puppy walkers and social luncheons and/or teas to celebrate the activity. Speeches of appreciation for puppy walkers often referred to them as the backbone of the hunt.

The value of a secure family environment is well recognized by such important dog-raising organizations as Guide Dogs for the Blind. Many of my teenage 4-H students participated in the program, and upon noticing its success I modified such a program for use with my own puppies. Sometimes a family who wanted a quality puppy would raise a second one for a few months to pay for its puppy. I made sure that it was understood that one puppy would be returned, and the program worked best when those involved are nearby. Impromptu classes and fun matches serve to draw all together and sometimes foster families end up becoming future fanciers as well as close friends.

Vin-Melca's personal "puppy-walking" success story started in 1987 when a young naval officer and his wife moved to the area while he attended the Monterey Post Graduate School. Interestingly enough, the school is located at the old Del Monte Hotel, once the scene of early Del Monte Kennel Club dog shows.

Steve and Mary Roesener were expecting their first child and became interested in all phases of raising dogs, including the whelping of puppies. Mary delivered BIS Ch. Vin-Melca's Before Dawn's litter that produced Quaker Oats winner Ch. Vin-Melca's Bombardier. She said it gave her a feeling of security as her own due-date approached. I will never forget answering my phone one September evening to hear Steve's excited voice announce, "It's a bitch," when their first child, Maggie, was born.

Throughout the years they lived on the Peninsula, a puppy was often in their home along with Smokey, the first dog they got from me. As their family grew so did our friendship, so it was only natural that we stayed in touch after Commander Roesener and family were transferred to the Washington, D.C. area. The day came when I called them to tell them I would be moving to Tennessee because I was getting remarried. Knowing what a tremendous task this would be with the dogs, Mary asked if I had any puppies at the moment. I sent a pair of three-month-old babies to Virginia for several months of family love while I dealt with moving the rest of the kennel to Nashville. Today, Ch. Vin-Melca's Debonair and Ch. Vin-Melca's Patchwork personify well-adjusted dogs who have had proper socialization. They are a living testimony that the practice of walking puppies as described in *Foxhounds* is alive and well. And, although the family has not received a red coat, they are in proud possession of several of Debonair's trophies.

Such foster families not only help the socialization and growth of your animals, they also help you keep in touch with reality by bringing another dimension into your life. They provide you with an opportunity to broaden your horizons for your own personal development at the same time they walk with you through the valleys on your way to the top of the mountain. These very special people are part of the realization that the best things in life aren't things.

Forrest Hall awards BIS at the 1970 Imperial Valley Kennel Club to Ch. Vin-Melca's Vagabond. Mr. Hall's lecture on selection of sires at a seminar in the late '60s is well-remembered by the author and served as a source for breed improvement. (Photo by Henry Schley)

Four-year-old godson Brian Vincent Eckroat pictured in 1978 with the BIS rosette and trophy of Ch. Vin-Melca's Nimbus, winner of 63 All Breed BISs. Long-time friends Pete and Pat Eckroat honored the author by giving Brian her maiden name for his middle name. Not only have these members of my extended family been warm and loving friends for decades, they have also worked with the breeding program and are dedicated to breed improvement. This charming photo was taken by Jim Callea of Callea Photography.

Who wouldn't want to be part of this adorable family and that's exactly what happened to Vin-Melca's Debonair and Vin-Melca's Patchwork during their very impressionable puppyhood. Now, both ranked in the Top Ten Norwegian Elkhounds, they owe much of their poise to this affectionate family of "dog walkers." Children of Steve and Mary Roesener, they are Maggie (8), Danny (6½), Andrew (5), Kicker (3) and Rachel (8 months). Such families bring warmth and enrichment into the lives they touch—two-legged and four-legged. (Photo courtesy of Mary Roesener)

BROTHERHOOD AND A WORKING RELATIONSHIP

An example of an on-going working relationship between friends is the one the author has enjoyed for more than 25 years with Fred and Dody Froehlich of Anchorage, Alaska. The Froehlichs have long loved living in snow country as they were in Aspen, Colorado, when they first became involved with Norwegian Elkhounds.

Their first dogs had been rescue dogs, and they became charter members of the Roaring Fork Kennel Club as well as active in obedience. It wasn't long before Fred surprised Dody on her birthday with a champion son of Howdy Rowdy. By now, the Froehlichs also owned a quality bitch they had purchased from Karin Kennels in Canada, who was bred to Howdy Rowdy to produce the Froehlichs first home-bred—the BIS winner, Ch. Vin-Melca's Hornblower.

The Froehlichs were living in Alaska when Fred visited Carmel and fell in love with a young bitch, Vin-Melca's Bottoms Up, product of the National Specialty winner, Ch. Vin-Melca's Happy Hour, bred to her own grandson, Ch. Vin-Melca's Nordic Storm. Fred is the epitome of the super-salesman and convinced the author that this bitch would love Alaska, which they all do. Anyhow, he went home with her and lived up to every promise he ever made. She was bred three times and produced three all-breed BIS winners—two of them the top two bitches in the breed's history.

The significant thing about such relationships is that when they are based on mutual trust and respect, they work in the best interest of all and subsequently the breed too. A catastrophic disease or disaster that could occur in the home kennel does not wipe out the gene pool, for some of the best ones are safe in their faraway haven. And what a haven the Froehlichs provide for the dogs. Their kennel setup is so perfect that more than one visitor has remarked: "I think I'd like to come back in my next life as one of Dody's dogs." Alaska is one of the few places in the United States that is much like the dogs' native Norway.

Not only do the Froehlichs have a warm family environment for their dogs, they also live with 300 moose near their home in the Anchorage Bowl, with the moose population swelling to more than a thousand or so at times. Although the dogs have to be worked in accordance with the game laws, it provides an excellent test of their instincts and purpose. And to hear of the tales where the moose, during times of exceptional snow accumulation, have ended up in the dogs' huge yard is a story all its own. Suffice it to say that the breed's instincts are alive and well. Furthermore, the situation is a prime example of the brotherhood of dog people.

Ch. Vin-Melca's Mandate (Ch. Vin-Melca's Vagabond X Ch. Vin-Melca's Hedda Gabler) winning BIS under Mr. Herschel Cox, handled by Dody Froehlich. Mandate was one of a number of the Vin-Melca dogs able to enjoy the good life in the Far North provided by Fred and Dody. The Froehlichs usually house six to seven dogs in their fantastic Alaskan environment. Both are well-received breeder-judges. (Hansen Photo)

Sampling the Humor of Dog People

Laughter has been considered good medicine by medical experts for a long time. In fact, a sense of humor is one of the top things associated with longevity. And dog people provide plenty of wonderful examples of it.

A favorite person in my life during the 70s and 80s was Gilbert B. Mirus, a fun-loving guy similar to the child's game, *Where's Waldo?* because he was always turning up all over the place. He first ap-

> "For all your ills, I give you laughter."
> —Rabelais, French humorist

peared in my life at the Golden Gate Show held in San Francisco's Cow Palace in 1969. The Elkhound fanciers were having a relaxed bench show version of a tailgate party when Gil appeared at the benches and asked me in a stage voice: "Hey, Lady, do you ever hunt these dogs?" Whereupon one of my Elkhound friends said, "Heck, yes. Every time they get loose."

It didn't take long for Gil to become a diehard fancier. In short order he had two Elkhounds and more equipment than most of the big name handlers. He used the dogs on birds and told me they got all the ones in the ditches that his Brittany and German Shorthair missed. Soon he brought me back a gigantic moose head from one of his expeditions to Montana and Wyoming and it took up more room in the garage than a car would.

Once, when he was late getting to the ring at Santa Barbara, his friend, Pete Eckroat, took his dog into the ring and went winners with it. Then Gil insisted on showing Pete's bitch and she went winners. When they went back in for the picture, each with his own dog, the judge was befuddled.

Gil was involved in a small, one-man operation of a vitamin company but didn't want anyone to know he didn't have a full staff. His champion bitch was named Vin-Melca's Betze Ross, so Gil wrote formal business letters signed by his "secretary," Betsy V. Melca.

* * * * *

The year was 1974, and it was the last glamorous benched show at the Polo Field held by the Santa Barbara Kennel Club. Clint Callahan was one of the executives of the Professional Handlers Association who came out for the activities. More than 4,300 dogs were entered at this magnificent venue with grooming areas and complete benching facilities located under spacious tents. It was a truly fabulous setting for America's best.

It was an opportunity to visit with my old friend Clint, and as we stood on a knoll overlooking the panorama, Clint puffed quietly on his pipe and nodded at the sea of motor homes: "Did you ever think you'd see anything like this at a dog show?"

My answer was "No. Wouldn't you love to have the money that's in them?"

Clint solemnly shook his head and responded softly with a glint in his eye: "No, I'd like to have the money that's owed on them."

* * * * *

Streaking was a 1974 fad that featured a nude person running full speed through a crowded football stadium, movie premier, graduation audience, shopping center and other public gatherings. Not to be left out, dog shows came in for their share of streakers that spring.

Perhaps the most memorable of these crazy occurrences happened during the Best in Show judging at the Silver State Kennel Club in Las Vegas. The judge was none other than the incomparable Anne Rogers Clark (Mrs. James Edward), and a number of handlers had pooled money to pay the streaker's

Let me out of here! says the expression on this puppy's face. Gil Mirus and his Elkhound companions brought this moose down in the Rocky Mountains over a quarter of a century ago. The actual Norwegian name—elg hund—translates to moose dog. (Photo by Ludwig)

When George & Sally Bell ran this photo of a most embarrassing moment in a prominent dog publication in 1976, it proved the endearing charm of the dog person's humor. The surprised Saluki is BIS Ch. Bel S'Mbran Rubah Ahlam. (Photo by Animals Near and Far, courtesy of Sally Bell)

Above: Santa Barbara Kennel Club's last benched show at the famed Polo Field with 4300 dogs competing in 1974. At the rear of the picture to the left is part of the beautiful tented benching area. Following the demise of the splendor of Morris and Essex in the late '50s, Santa Barbara ruled supreme as the premier outdoor one-day benched show in the country for a number of years. The loss of this spectacular site cooled by Pacific breezes was mourned by the entire fancy. (Photo from the author's collection)

Ch. Vin-Melca's Homesteader winning BIS at Santa Barbara Kennel Club in 1974. The win capped a perfect day highlighted by a visit with an old friend, Clint Callahan. The red, white and blue rosette was awarded by Judge Robert M. James from England. (Photo by Ludwig)

fee for the prank. The BIS class was assembled in the ring and Mrs. Clark was looking over her BIS lineup in her preliminary evaluation when the streaker came racing through the middle of the ring, narrowly avoiding serious injury to himself in a close call with the judging table.

Without missing a beat, the very poised Mrs. Clark said to those of us in the BIS competition: "Now that will be a tough act to follow, but let's give it a try."

The crowd broke into wild applause in appreciation of her aplomb and sporting good humor, and the judging continued with BIS going to the sensational Lakeland Red Baron. It seemed appropriate to have a red dog win to accent the blushing faces around the ring.

* * * * *

A pair of fun-loving ladies that keep Northern California alive and well are Eileen Pimlott and Robin Stark. Now, these good dogwomen were having one of their involved telephone conversations on a balmy October afternoon in 1989 when the big one hit (Loma Prieto Earthquake). Eileen felt it first and made a comment just as Robin noticed her pygmy goats going berserk outside the window. They both immediately hung up the phones and ran to take emergency measures.

The electricity was out for days, that part of California was a disaster area, the World Series was upended, and chaos reigned. Finally, a week or so went by and Robin's phone rang. On the other end of the line Eileen said: "As I was saying before we were so rudely interrupted..."

*****

The point is that people who love dogs and are in turn loved by them are warm and alive. They have a sense of humor, and it gets them through the good times and the bad. And most of all it is an indication of how very real they are.

THE LADIES OF LIMERICK

The three generations of Limerick Wolfhounders pictured in their Northern California home are a testimony to the sharing of a mutual passion for dogs that bond families together in a way that is almost a miracle in this dizzy modern world.

Grandmother Janet Souza (on the right) founded the Limerick breeding program with an Irish import, Ch. Roaree of Limerick, more than a quarter of a century ago. She and her granddaughter, Jamie (left) as well as Jamie's mother Linda (Janet's daughter-in-law) have graced California's rings ever since. Although they breed seldom and selectively, the trio has produced 27 champions in this giant breed.

Young Jamie also breeds and shows Whippets with the help of her friend, Martha Fielder, proving things can and do

come full circle. More than 40 years ago, Martha and husband Herb were a young Navy couple stationed in Virginia, where they helped the author train her first Norwegian Elkhound to an obedience degree! Martha and her Fieldcrest Kennels have long been a learning environment.

Jamie is now a junior at the University of California where she majors in legal studies. It seems like only yesterday that this charming young lady was a top junior showman. The ladies of Limerick have bred, owned and handled group and specialty winners with expertise, sportsmanship and graciousness. They are special people in a world made all the brighter by the prospect of a third generation dogwoman preparing herself professionally and intellectually to assume a major, responsible role in the fancy in the 21st Century. (Photo courtesy of Linda Souza)

Best in Match and the birth of a friendship as Judge Eileen Pimlott and exhibitor Robin Stark meet for the first time in the ring at Del Monte Kennel Club's annual match in 1969. The 7-month-old Keeshond is (Ch.) Star-Kee's Batman, who went over several specials to win the breed at Golden Gate just a few weeks later and followed that up with a splendid show and producing career. From this chance meeting began a life-long friendship now in its third decade. These two friends visit and converse frequently and have always enjoyed each other's sense of humor. Today, Eileen is a much-respected multi-group judge and Robin has cut back on her breeding and exhibiting to concentrate on the publication of her *Rottweiler Quarterly*. (Photo courtesy of Eileen Pimlott)

Who says judges don't have a sense of humor? In 1985, when Ed Strickland asked to have his picture taken with this stuffed Afghan because his live dogs hadn't done much winning that day. Judge Chuck Trotter and water-bucket trophy presenter Wendy Wolforth obliged, resulting in this Earl Graham photograph. Although the breeder of the Afghan is unknown, he was co-owned by Ed with wife Lee Strickland.

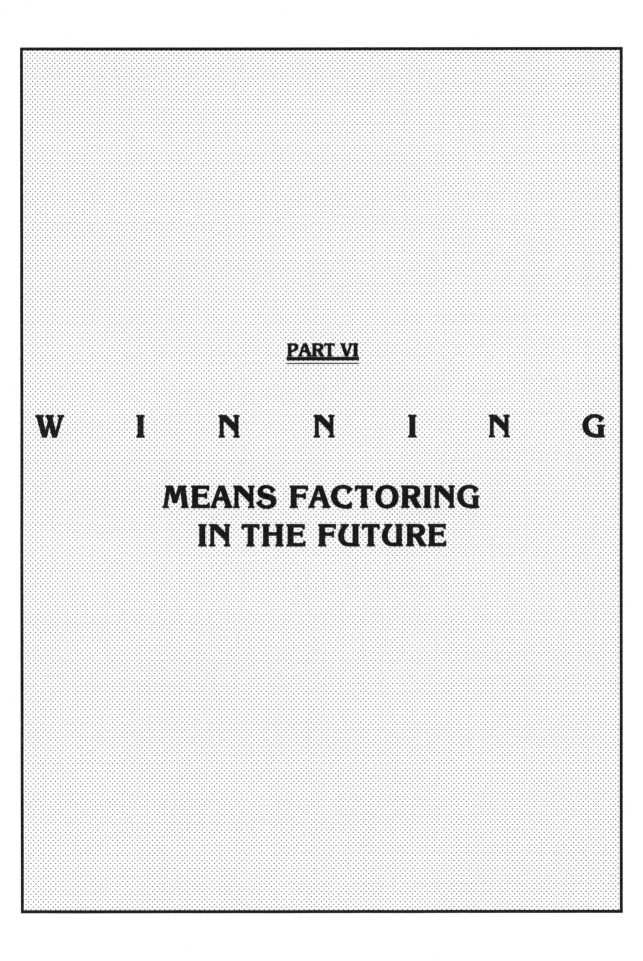

PART VI

W I N N I N G

MEANS FACTORING
IN THE FUTURE

Looking at the Future

Whether Americans want to accept it or not, sociologists think the more-is-better syndrome has about run its course in our civilization. The long-term picture promises a down-sizing that will simplify our lives as we learn to become satisfied with less in the 21st Century. Exactly how this will affect our world of purebred dogs is anybody's guess, but it will affect it.

The explosion of purebred dogs and the widespread increases in shows, trials, and doggy activities that followed the post World War II times of prosperity and over-consumption are expected to level off and adjust themselves to the needs of a somewhat different society and its accompanying values. As future Americans have less economic resources—more of which have to be spent on escalating medical costs—how much will be left over to spend on dogs?

Some interesting 1995 statistics compiled by AKC include: 67 percent of all registered bitches never have a litter; 15 percent of all registered bitches have only one litter; 7 percent have two litters; 4 percent have three litters; and 7 percent have four or more litters. It would seem that after going through the hard work involved in raising one litter, most people do not breed their bitches again. Also of note, 6 percent of all registered dogs are sold through pet shops, which is down from the 12 percent of a few years earlier.

Although these potential problems may appear to be so far removed from us that one tends to think "let the future generations take care of their own problems," it still behooves the AKC and forward-thinking Parent Clubs to prepare to address themselves to these issues. If we are forced by food supply and other declining resources to have fewer dogs, isn't it mandatory that those dogs be the very best ones possible?

The good news about such sociological down-sizing for the conscientious dog breeder is that bio-technology will provide opportunities for the breeders of the future that those of the past did not have. Such advances as gene mapping using markers to identify diseased genetic material and deal with it accordingly promises to reduce the trial and error breedings necessary when testing for recessive genetic trash in order to identify carriers. Now carriers will be identifiable without having to bring more of the same—or worse still—affected animals into the world. It will be possible to avoid such animals altogether.

Such biotechnology will provide breeders with the option to put first things first and identify problem areas before the matings occur. In effect, we would be redesigning our animals to be hardier and more disease free and problem resistant. These genetic giant steps will result from gene mapping followed by gene therapy, gene splicing, and other applied genetic advances aimed at better dogs in fewer numbers, allowing breeders to replace faulty genes with healthy ones.

It is estimated that by the year 2015 the 100,000 genes in the human animal will be so well tracked and mapped that it will be possible for every human to acquire his own computerized genetic print out. Since somewhere in the neighborhood of 80 percent of human genes are also in dogs, advancing knowledge in human work will be enormously helpful in expanding information on dogs. The breakthrough with PRA (Progressive Retinal Atrophy) in the Irish Setter was the result of previous work done in human genetics. Many of the advances in human knowledge will apply to dogs, but additional work will have to be done because the genes that are the same in humans and dogs do not occur on the same chromosomes.

How very appropriate that human research should also be in the best interest of the faithful dog, who has served as man's best friend throughout history. Now the tables are turned and the human is in the comfortable position of being "dog's best friend."

Even as these techniques are known the cost of how to apply them must be met. The American

CUTTING OUT THE GENES

Every living being begins as, what is termed, a genetic template contained within a single cell, and that template is what determines whether the cell divides into a horse, a dog or a human. High-tech genetic engineering has come of age, and amazing, incredible possibilities exist as agricultural assets and livestock improvement programs. For example, if a plant that is highly desired as a food source is plagued by a particular insect, a plant resistant to that insect is used as a source of material to splice into the genes of the first plant. Now, this wonderful food plant is also resistant to the bugs but unaffected in its food productivity.

The splicing of genes is somewhat like the splicing of film. Remembering that the genes are arranged on the chromosomes like beads on a necklace will help get the picture. A minute, circular molecule of DNA called *plasmid* makes the splicing possible. Once the undesirable gene is isolated and cut, the plasmid is glued into the cut ends of the gene and everything is reassembled. Now the reconstructed necklace has new genetic instructions and is ready to participate in a new way in the next generation. The resulting product is called *Recombinant DNA*.

Paul Berg, Stanford University geneticist and Nobel Prize winner, participated in a call to arms to establish some guidelines regarding the ethics of such genetic engineering. For one thing, there was justifiable, widespread concern of such technological knowledge causing accidental germ proliferation.

Some dog people questioned if the parvo virus had such an origin in the early '80s. These concerns are relevant as a recent case might indicate.

As we go to press, a scandal involving the disappearance of one family's stored, frozen, fertilized eggs from a lab in Southern California validates this Nobel Prize winner's concerns. The possibilities of widespread abuse and fraud involving genetic specialists and fertility clinics are mind-boggling. Unscrupulous behavior compromises the intent and contributions of the entire genetic engineering field.

Perhaps in some futuristic dog-breeding program, such gene-splicing as that which resulted in the new, bug-resistant plant could be utilized to removed undesirable disease genes from purebred dogs—assuming the process becomes affordable. Such high-tech methods could help eliminate the genes responsible for urinary stones in Dalmatians, PRA and hip dysplasia in a number of breeds, renal glycosuria (Fanconi's Syndrome) in Basenjis and other breeds, hepatic copper toxicosis in Bedlington Terriers, as well as other widespread *genetic trash* affecting good health. To think of a dog world free of dog diseases would be a dream come true, as most good dog people are more concerned about the health of their dogs than their own!

Already this knowledge is being used to produce insulin, for example, to benefit people. Yeasts and bacteria are becoming routine ingredients in the production of many DNA-assisted vaccines and other medical supplies. The inevitable question of using the high tech to acquire better specimens of each breed will arise. Such things as structure, color, coat, head and overall beauty could be improved in the 21st Century if current reports are accurate about the potentials of gene-splicing. The issue of just who will hold the valuable patents on all of this genetic material remains to be seen. The potential for commercial competition is scary. When they do patent these items, I would be happy to get just the neck and shoulder concession!

Kennel Club has already spent over one million dollars funding molecular genetics research by Dr. George Brewer of the University of Michigan Medical School. Dr. Brewer is one of many medical researchers working on *markers* which determine the chemical makeup of the genetic material, and his work is in cooperation with Michigan State's Veterinary School. This type of research, co-funded by Morris Animal Foundation and Orthopedic Foundation Association will continue forward toward more scientific knowledge as the medical world seeks newer and more affordable processes by which to implement the benefits of their work.

Controversy hovers over the financial aspect of the field, as some scientists consider it crass commercialism on the part of those who want to develop the biotech industry into a huge profit-making machine marketing the results of their genetic work. Others see the research environment of the university as purist but nonetheless self-limiting in its ability to fund deeper research. For the lay person-dog breeder, staying informed is where it's at. Knowing what biotech services are available and determining if they are a cost-effective part of the breeding program while continuing to use time honored methods to eliminate physical and health genetic defects will be part of a soul-searching on-going effort at breed improvement.

At its fall 1995, two-day Parent Club Genetics Conference, AKC shared with the fancy its ideas for the future—ideas aimed at producing healthier animals by cooperating with Parent Clubs to bring a cohesive factor into the information-gathering process as it applies to each of the various breeds. The unfortunate fact is that great strides made in some areas such as PRA in the Irish Setter and Miniature Schnauzer breeds do not readily apply to other breeds. By working with Parent Clubs as well as the scientific community, it is hoped that information and efforts can be pooled to benefit all breeds where such information applies, while continuing efforts to deal with problem areas that are breed specific. The dual role of the Parent Club will be to take useful information to members regarding problem areas in their breed and to ferret out those problems to take to the scientific community at the other end of the spectrum.

The AKC-Parent Club effort followed by one year the original AKC-sponsored genetic conference for professional scientists working in the field. Just how willing AKC was to help solve breed specific problems was indicated in the 80s when the controversial program to allow Pointers to be used as a cross for Dalmatians was passed by the Board of Directors in an effort to address the kidney stone problem in the Dalmatian breed. Dalmatian fanciers were desperate to try new avenues in their continued efforts to cope with the problem, accepting the kennel club's conditions on re-entering the Stud Book.

More recently the kennel club's open-mindedness in dealing with Fanconi's Syndrome in the Basenji is of interest. The breed had been hard hit in the 1980s by the disorder, which in this breed leads to kidney failure and premature death. It is important to keep in mind that genetic diseases behave differently in different breeds, and one of the potential successes of biotechnology is to identify these differences.

Michael Work and Jon Curby ventured into the heart of Africa with a trip deep into the bush of Haute Zaire, near the Congo River, in search of hardy native stock. Raised by the Pygmies and the Azandes hundreds of miles from other civilizations and other dogs, native Basenjis had been utilized first by the legendary Veronica Tudor-Williams who took them to England in the 1940s and 1950s to found her "Of the Congo" Kennels that became the breed's foundation stock.

From the several dogs these two dedicated *master breeders* brought back to the United States, the brindle Avongara Gangura was chosen as one of the dogs to help revitalize the breed. Even though the tribesmen that had these dogs had no paper products of any kind, much less pedigrees of record, the American Kennel Club cooperated in registering the animals because the isolation in which they were raised had protected the purity of the breed.

Later the first lady of American Basenjis, Damara Bolté of Reveille Kennels accompanied Curby and Dr. Stan Carter on the same trip to acquire additional animals to put into the breed's gene pool. A red and white bitch prematurely whelped a litter of six healthy puppies that survived the flight home. Ms. Bolté, representing the Basenji Club of America, worked with the American Kennel Club in re-formatting the standard. The outcome of their 1990 cooperative effort included the brindle and white coloring.

According to my information, not only have the "African" dogs proved carrier-free of the Fanconi kidney problem to-date, they have also contributed some hardiness and sound running gear to the gene pool. As with any other outcross, breeders have to work around their undesirable contributions (for example a looser tail) while striving to improve the breed. Kibushi Get Sirius, the sire of 18

The pedigree of **KIBUSHI GET SIRIUS** is evidence of the American Kennel Club's willingness to cooperate with breed Parent Clubs to improve the gene pool. His sire was bred in isolation by natives deep in the heart of Africa.

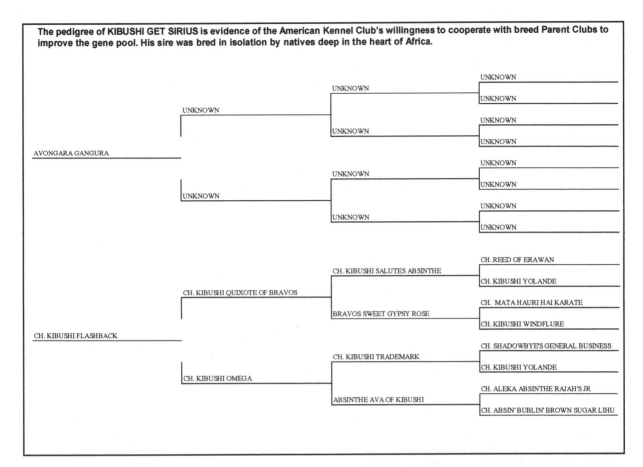

			UNKNOWN
		UNKNOWN	UNKNOWN
	UNKNOWN		UNKNOWN
		UNKNOWN	UNKNOWN
AVONGARA GANGURA			UNKNOWN
		UNKNOWN	UNKNOWN
	UNKNOWN		UNKNOWN
		UNKNOWN	UNKNOWN
			CH. REED OF ERAWAN
		CH. KIBUSHI SALUTES ABSINTHE	CH. KIBUSHI YOLANDE
	CH. KIBUSHI QUIXOTE OF BRAVOS		CH. MATA HAURI HAI KARATE
		BRAVOS SWEET GYPSY ROSE	CH. KIBUSHI WINDFLURE
CH. KIBUSHI FLASHBACK			CH. SHADOWBYE'S GENERAL BUSINESS
		CH. KIBUSHI TRADEMARK	CH. KIBUSHI YOLANDE
	CH. KIBUSHI OMEGA		CH. ALEKA ABSINTHE RAJAH'S JR
		ABSINTHE AVA OF KIBUSHI	CH. ABSIN' BUBLIN' BROWN SUGAR LIHU

Kibushi Get Sirius, owned by Michael Work and Vicky Curby is the sire of 18 champions. (Michael Work Photo).

Damara Bolté, the first lady of American Basenjis, cooperated with fellow Basenji fanciers Jon Curby, Dr. Stan Carter and Mike Work to effect the introduction of new genes into the breed's gene pool. Working with the American Kennel Club, the Parent Club changed the breed standard to include the brindle and white color of some of the unregistered native African dogs. In their mutual effort to solve the Fanconi's Syndrome problem in the breed, these *master breeders* assumed the responsibility of their breed's future at great personal cost. Such cooperative efforts promise the continued improvement of gene pools. (Photo by Nicole Duplaix-Hall)

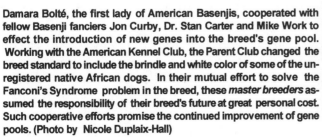

champions, became the next step in the process, eventually leading to the BIS brindle Ch. Changa's Dan Patch (see color section), a dog of outstanding type and running gear. All brindle Basenjis in the U.S. today are descendants of this cooperative work to eliminate disease.

Expanded gene pools of the future might very well be accomplished by isolating the "good genes" of such animals and transferring them through biotechnology into quality host animals in need of the healthy genetic material from which the breed can breed on.

Host animals could also be utilized in other aspects of the reproduction process. In many species, eggs have been harvested from one female, fertilized and implanted into another host female who then "carries" the resulting embryos to term in the pregnancy. Thus, it would be possible for toy breeders to acquire more puppies from a true foundation bitch by participating in this method, allowing a bitch of a larger breed to be the host female.

Agricultural genetic engineering was first to make wide-spread progress in *transferal* methods and has produced well known hybrids from such unrelated crosses as the tomato and potato. Livestock from herds of cattle to catfish farming have benefited from genetic engineering. Such programs are aimed at developing a stronger, healthier plant or animal that adapts to its environment and influences the future in the most positive of ways—continuing to do so without affecting the good genetic material already existing in the breed. Such a grand design would continue to influence generations to come in what would hopefully be a fail-safe program. If breeders did not have to worry about assorted hereditary health problems in their breeding program, they would be free to concentrate on bettering the breed in a more Utopian breeding program. Although it may seem like science fiction on the surface, think of all the other science fictions that have come to be!

Because such advances in the field might sound as though we are out to accomplish a cloning result, bear in mind that choices in type and desired characteristics within the scope of the standard will continue to exist. PRA and Fanconi's for example, are identifiable and measurable—choices in type and look are not measurable. They lie in the soul and eye of the beholder—the creator. And because to achieve a certain type and look involves so many variables, there will still be plenty of room for the individual breeder's expression of what he or she considers ideal type.

Breed improvement through genetic progress will not be an instant accomplishment. As one leading gene therapist reported, "such miracles come in small installments." Breeders can take comfort in the knowledge that great forces in the academic and scientific world are at work in cooperation with familiar institutions to make such progress come to pass. They can look forward to pedigrees that record not only show records of classic names and breed history, but serve as genetic affidavits of the dogs' disease-free status. The idea is to reduce the margin of error.

Registries

Registries have been around now for a number of decades, with OFA and its numerical system certifying dogs to be free of hip dysplasia, perhaps the oldest and most widely used of them. Registries are like many things in life—computers for example—the product of what is put into them. The *open* registry is one where the available information on each animal is public information and the *closed* registry is one with information considered confidential.

Registries for eyes, hips, elbows, and other osteopathic conditions are being joined by registries dealing with copper toxicosis, thyroid diseases, and cardiac problems. Some see these registries as steps toward eventual genetic good health in purebred dogs. Sports medicine also promises to come of age in the next few decades for dogs the way it has already done for people.

As genetic and computer technology advance, so do the number of registries available for the conscientious breeder to utilize. These registries not only document freedom from given diseases but are now dealing with the more esoteric goal of registering characteristics aimed at enhancing breeders' efforts to achieve "super dog."

When Catherine "Casey" Gardiner founded her School of Canine Science in Canada (Toronto) in the 70s, her ultimate goal was to provide educational stimuli to the entire dog community that would generate improvement for dog enthusiasts from the amateur to the para-professional to the career professional. One of its loftiest goals was the creation of a canine registry that would employ (utilize) a system of grading which would determine how close an individual dog was to the ideal for that breed. Such registry evaluations would assist breeders to make decisions as to which dogs should become members of the permanent gene pool for their breed.

The objective of the registry of characteristics is to compute measurable absolutes such as bone lengths and angles as well as subjective attributes such as temperament and type. By using a consistent grading system with standardized measuring equipment, the registry would evaluate the individual for an overall rating that will hopefully lead to the breeding of better dogs resulting from utilizing the best while removing poorer specimens from the dog population.

Any registry is only as good as those participating in it. These registries offer breeders of the future tangible helpmates to increase the odds of breeding better dogs. By pooling knowledge of dogs with measurable elements and scientific advances, it is possible to envision a world with all good dogs achieved by utilizing the sum total of all available data bases factored in with the expertise of *master breeders.*

Grading Systems

Just as registries can help breeders to stop recycling their medical problems, so can grading systems, in the hands of experts, help prevent breeders from recycling their structural and breed specific problems. In order for a grading system to work, it must have constant norms and trained graders consistent in their evaluation methods. For example, the Keeneland Thoroughbred Yearling Sales in Kentucky use trained teams to grade the yearlings accepted for their multi-million dollar select sales.

In an Information Systems Report published for the School of Canine Science in September of 1993, Megan Smith, a computer analyst, reported how two graders work together to evaluate the animal. Bone lengths, joint angles and other characteristics are measured with ratios established. All measurable data is recorded and compared to the norm for that breed. For example, it was determined that the norm for the length of a male Norwegian Elkhound's scapula is approximately six inches.

When two graders are in disagreement over a subjective evaluation such as coat texture, a third one is called upon for an opinion. All of the data is then compiled in a Record of Characteristics which can be used to help determine the animal's suitability for use in the breeding program. The ultimate purpose of the grading process is the accurate and scientific assessment of a dog's quality. By computerizing all of this information in a data

---

VERIFIED IDENTIFIED PARENTAGE PROGRAM

Even as we go to press, innovative actions are being taken by friends of purebred dogs at many levels and at varied institutions. Consider the pioneer move taken by the United Kennel Club (UKC) in 1996 with its Verified Identified Parentage (VIP) program of pedigree authenticity. A VIP pedigree is recorded assurance that the sire, dam and individual progeny have all been DNA tested and appropriately verified and recorded

Not only does this answer many questions previously unanswered, but presents hypothetical situations in crucial decision-making that could be utilized by breeders. Perhaps a very valuable bitch has reached the age where she is only going to have one more litter and the breeder is unable to decide which of two equally outstanding sires to select for this last litter. Because of procedures now available, this brood bitch could be bred to both sires during the one heat period, and DNA verification would determine which sire produced which puppy in the litter for individual registration. The UKC would then register the puppies accordingly.

DNA verification not only opens up unlimited possibilities for positive decisions by conscientious breeders, it also promises another method for registration organizations to use in attempting to control the activities of unscrupulous operations. Furthermore, the swab DNA test using saliva in the mouth is both simple and inexpensive. Breeders can obtain "do-it-yourself" kits as they learn to utilize the future options that will be available to them.

base for each breed, breeders would become more expert at selecting the best mate for their animal.

Smith has designed the information system for the maintenance of these records and work has been done on the utilization of this data. The death of Casey Gardiner, the founder and driving influence behind the School of Canine Science, has caused a delay in the completion of this work. However, a group of graders has come together to assist in the continuation of this and other projects of Casey's.

To date, German Shepherds, Chow Chows, Siberian Huskies, Norwegian Elkhounds, Salukis, Kerry Blue Terriers, and Labrador Retrievers have had a significant number of graded dogs compiled and working models of norms developed against which they can be graded.

Grading systems and data processing offer some interesting scenarios for the future. They can produce the phenotype profile picture of the animal using lengths and angles of bones and the genotype profile picture as both a health map and a characteristics record of traits not associated with good health such as correct dark eyes.

This collection of data could lead to the universal understanding of the mode of inheritance of specific defects, reducing the number of unpleasant surprises. Already these concepts are spawning cottage industries using the computer to sort and to store information. Industry growth currently offers DNA genotyping to solve multiple sire cases, verify parentage, and record DNA types as evidenced by advertising in the *American Kennel Gazette* of November 1995, page 35.

It is not likely the computer will usurp the classic role of the *master breeder*, even though it may assist in the decision-making process. Garry Kasparov, world chess champion, proved man still has mastery over machine by defeating the famous computer known as Deep Blue. Kasparov said that he was able to figure out the computer's priorities and adjust, and the computer was unable to figure out his. And, of course, these priority perceptions are a judgment call on the part of the breeder.

Such scientific steps of the future are simply more tools in the breeders' ever-expanding arsenal of aids that will help bring better dogs to dog lovers of the future. When coupled with the creative artistry of the true breeder, *master breeders* may become more abundant in the 21st Century.

Changes in the Breeds

No one is immune from the changes that occur in society over the years, and that includes man's best friend. The important component of the progress equation as it relates to the breeding of purebred dogs is for breeders to avoid changes that cater to fashion fads and keep changes to the dogs themselves in the best interests of that breed.

Eng. and Am. Ch. Hillsome Solo Flight of Robin Hill, Sealyham Terrier, was born in the mid-30s and would do his breed proud today. He sired BIS progeny in England before coming to the U.S. where he continued to improve the breed at Mrs. Robert Choate's Robin Hill Kennels in Massachusetts. (Photo courtesy of the American Kennel Club)

Consider the changes that occurred in the Bull Terrier in the last half of the 20th Century. These changes had to do with headpiece and stronger gripping power that were associated with the historic tradition of the dog's original job description. Yet in the same group the winning beloved Sealyham of yesterday would be right at home in the show ring of today. One of the many reasons I held Ellsworth Gamble in such high esteem was his total commitment to the purpose and performance for which the breed was bred. His purity of purpose is a spiritual legacy for us all to pursue in our cooperative effort to produce better dogs.

Since game laws and other restrictions prevent many of our breeds from performing their original tasks, it is heartening that dogs of all breeds are becoming involved in varied jobs that are the by-product of a highly technological industrialized civilization. Today purebred dogs are the dogs of choice for such demanding jobs as seeking bombs and drugs out, tracking down kidnappers and other criminals, sentinel work, and performing a wide range of therapy activities. Evidently, there is no limit to the potential jobs that may be-

Norwegian Elkhound Ch. Brodd II av Elglia was the breed winner at Morris and Essex as well as Westminster in 1936. Imported by the Green Meadow Kennels of W. Scott Cluett of Williamston, Massachusetts, Brodd was the desired hunting type that is still appreciated today: Correct square profile, excellent rise of neck and the proper short, flat weatherproof coat. (Photo courtesy of the American Kennel Club)

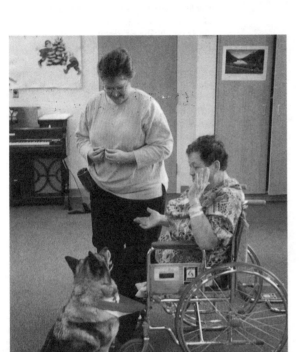

Vin-Melca's Peppermint Patti CDX, TD, CGC, AD, TDI, age 9½, at work as a therapy dog in Sacramento, California. Patti, like many other dogs unable to perform the tasks for which they were bred, is enjoying her alternative career and seems to benefit from being productive as she is still active in agility and other physical pursuits. Patti is owned and trained by Betty Barker. (Photo courtesy of Barker)

come available to dogs thanks to their exceptional sense of smell and their keen desire to work.

When a Florida dermatologist heard the story of a dog licking a mole that proved to be a melanoma while ignoring its owner's other moles, he decided to investigate how the dog could differentiate, if that was, in fact, what the dog was doing. Could the melanoma give off an unusual odor? Currently, he is working with a retired bomb-detecting dog in this interesting experiment. Perhaps someday dogs will be trained to sniff out abnormalities from human samples. Although this idea may seem "far out" at the moment, the current tasks that dogs are performing indicate they will continue to be of service to mankind even as their contributions change to meet the needs of the 21st Century.

As times and needs change, it is meaningful for the work of dogs to change also. For dogs, like the people they serve, are the most well-adjusted when they are engaged in jobs that make them productive and useful.

As technology and biotechnology move into the 21st Century and beyond, it is mandatory for all of us to continue those pursuits in the best interest of both man and dog.

Today's Youth: Tomorrow's Master Breeders

Never before has the alliance of opposing forces to purebred dogs been as strong as it is today, and growing. Such hostility is expressing itself in many forms and in varying degrees of danger ranging from anti-dog legislation, local ordinances against dogs, and negative public reactions that could someday lead to resentment of dogs simply due to their drain on the world wide food supply.

It is in the fancy's best interest to educate our youth to prepare to assume the responsibility to be the guardians of the breed and the guardians of citizens' rights to improve the breeds in the future. Already our young people are foremost in the skilled handling of dogs as any competitive Junior Showmanship class will prove. Education to develop their skills as potential *master breeders* and community leaders proficient in participating in the salvation of the future of dogs is an absolute must if we hope to protect the sport we love.

This future protection will require a united front utilizing our considerable strengths in the 21st Century and beyond. A coalition of the American Kennel Club, Parent Clubs and all breed organi-

Katherine Ing and Ch. Vin-Melca's Leanne (group-winning daughter of Ch. Vin-Melca's Calista) in a winning effort under Judge Gayle Bonteceau. Katherine has been a protegé of the author since the age of eight when she started showing her own dog, a daughter of Nimbus. In 1989, she campaigned Ch. Vin-Melca's Rain Check to become the #1 Junior Handler in the US and also put him in the Top Ten for his breed. Katherine and other dedicated young people like her represent our future. It is vital that such young people be encouraged to take their rightful place in the wonderful world of dogs with our blessings and support. Katherine is currently in graduate school while working for one of America's best known corporations—Hewlett-Packard. (Animal World Studio Photo)

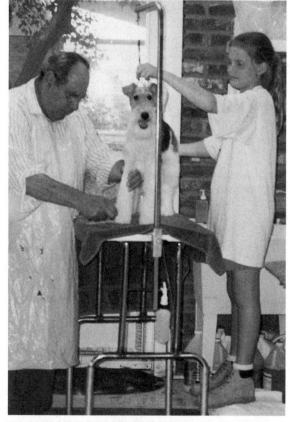

Vivian Casillas and Ch. Vin-Melca's Frequent Flyer, #2 Norwegian Elkhound in the US in 1995, pictured with Judge Luc Boileau. Vivian is one of those special young people upon whom the future of dogs is so dependent. So much did the author value Vivian's potential that she and Jeff and Nan-Eisley Bennett agreed that Westminster winner Ch. Vin-Melca's Marketta would reside permanently with her. (Earl Graham Photo)

Educating our youth in all facets of the dog world is vital, and no one is more dedicated to this premise than the notable dogman, Ric Chashoudian, pictured working on 10-year-old Rebecca Warner's Wire Fox Terrier, Santeric's Ingrid of Kathrich. Thanks to people like Chashoudian, youngsters such as Rebecca receive the instruction and incentive to assume responsible positions in our beloved sport. (Photo courtesy of Chashoudian)

zations will be necessary to protect our way of life. Young people need to seek out the true dog people to expand their skills and learn to look beyond today and even tomorrow. Theirs is an awesome responsibility, for already we have lost some of the greatest of our dog people prematurely through the tragedy of AIDS. (Auto-Immune Deficiency Syndrome). These devastating losses have left us reeling and create tremendously tragic gaps that almost amount to the loss of a generation. Many of our most gifted people have been taken from us in the bloom of youth long before their prime.

In 1997, the Poodle Club of America will make history with its project to include the breed's loved ones in The Names Project AIDS Memorial Quilt with three-by-six-foot memorial panels created by friends and family members. This internationally famous memorial—known as The Quilt—was conceived by Cleve Jones in 1985. Periodically displayed over the years at memorial services in the nation's capitol, it has grown to well over 40,000 panels at the time of this book's publication. Dramatic contributions have been achieved by dogdom's own organization, *Take The Lead*, whose recipients are lovingly assisted at the same time their confidentiality is assured. Although the dedicated group started as a support group for AIDS, it rapidly expanded into a group that provides assistance for any dog person in need. So committed is this organization to the fancy that 24 volunteer board members from across the U.S. give freely of their time and efforts in pursuit of the first plateau of their fundraising goal, an endowment of one million dollars.

It is incumbent to all in the fancy to concern themselves with a concerted effort to do those things that will serve as a permanent memorial and genuine testimony to the memory of those we have lost as we heed this as a call to arms. This valid message will result in widespread continued growth and commitment to making dogs and the fancy better than you found it. It will involve a coalition of dog lovers that serve as protectors against all of those who would be detractors of dogs. Cooperating in an effort to come to terms with ourselves will make it possible to come to terms with future problems.

Richard Gueverra epitomized all that was good in dog people, for he was a breeder at heart—a connoisseur of fine dogs in the ring and a gentleman whose very presence in a crowd lent an aura of quality. His devastating loss was one of many tragic losses from which the fancy will never recover. His personal creed "to judge every breed like a breeder" serves as a permanent monument to his memory and inspires all to perform in the best way possible for the good of purebred dogs. (Photo courtesy of Michael Suave) The Richard Gueverra Memorial Trophy, a Greyhound sculpture by Ric Chashoudian, is the perpetual trophy offered by Richard's friends at the Bucks County Kennel Club Show to the winner of the Hound Group. The trophy must be won three times for permanent possession. As a breeder of Greyhounds, Richard was naturally attracted to both the sighthounds and the scenthounds, so the trophy is a fitting testimony to the affection and respect of the the fancy for this brilliant young dogman. (Chashoudian Photo)

Dreaming the Dream

Learning to question everything is the greatest step to a successful future. If you have agreed with everything written in this book, one of us—either the writer or the reader—is unnecessary! For in anything as creative and subjective as breeding dogs, eternal curiosity and questioning of everything is essential in order to progress. Because something is written in a book doesn't make it true.

> "To be conscious that you are ignorant of the facts is a great step to knowledge.
> —Benjamin Disraeli 1804 - 1881

In fact, your future will be enhanced if you beware of those who know everything and have all the answers, for they may have shut the door on further growth. It isn't what you read that will determine your future anyhow, it is what you do with what you read that will.

If your reflections of this book help you become more objective and want to make change, take heart in realizing that the first step to new creation is the putting away of previous ideas. Remember that for a genuine breeding program to exist, each dog in the kennel must be as strong as the next one, for the program is only as strong as its weakest link.

Look at your dogs in two ways: What you have; What you need.

Then decide if reinventing your breeding program is your next step. For until you learn to adequately look and evaluate both your own dogs and those of others, you cannot make progress. By appreciating the best of others, we make improvement possible for ourselves. Inability to see both your dogs and those of others makes you blind to the facts. No dog is as perfect as when his breeder-owner-handler is describing it, just as no dog is as imperfect as those who lose to it describe it. If you keep these things in mind, you open the door to permanent, continuing growth.

One of the many fringe benefits of 34 years spent in the classroom with youngsters is their contagious energy and upbeat attitudes. For them, anything is possible. I always agreed with the saying that every adult needs a child to teach, it's the way adults learn! My great dream was to teach just one kid who would make a real difference to mankind in the 21st Century. And so it is with this book—the dream that one future *master breeder* will read *Born to Win* and find it of use in pursuing the dream. This person will have the foresight to accept the concept of delayed gratification while others seek instant gratification. And because this person will practice a true work ethic to augment the dream, it will be possible to make the dream come true.

That person will keep the faith, stay focused, and follow through on all of it in search of the dream. Remember: *You set your goals; you pick your stock; you select your puppies; you decide what shows to attend and which judges' opinions to seek.* Is it any wonder you deserve what happens as a result?

The marvelous thing about the wonderful world of dogs is that it is a special love you can enjoy well into your old age. You can continue to grow as a breeder, exhibitor, club member, ring steward, judge, or fancier. It is an all-encompassing way of life that encourages you to seek the very best one you ever bred in your next litter, even in your golden years. It is a permanent passion. The embodiment of the spirit of the dedicated dog person is exemplified in the words of Jonathan Livingston Seagull:

Here is the test to find whether your mission on Earth is finished:
If you're alive, it isn't. —Richard Bach

(Photo by Jayne Langdon)

B I B L I O G R A P H Y

Alston, George G. *The Winning Edge*. with Connie Vanacore, 1992 edition, New York: Howell Book House, Macmillan Publishing Company.

American Kennel Club Staff, *The American Kennel Blue Book of Dogs, 1938*. Garden City, New York. Garden City Publishing Co., Inc., 1938.

American Kennel Club Staff, *The Complete Dog Book*. Eighteenth Edition. New York: Howell Book House, 1992.

Austin, Norman A. & Jean S. *The Complete American Cocker Spaniel*. New York: Howell Book House, 1993.

Barnes, Duncan and the staff of AKC, editors. *AKC's World of the Purebred Dog*. New York: Howell Book House, 1983.

Battaglia, Dr. Carmelo. *Dog Genetics How to Breed Better Dogs*. Neptune NJ: TFH Publications, 1978.

Brackett, Lloyd C. "Planned Breeding," *Dog World Magazine*. Chicago, Illinois, 1961.

Brown, Curtis. *The Art and Science of Judging Dogs*. California: B & E Publications, 1976.

Burns, Marca and Margaret N. Fraser. *Genetics of the Dog*. Philadelphia: J.B. Lippincott Company, 1966.

Clark, Ross D. DVM & Joan R. Stainer, editors. *Medical and Genetic Aspects of Purebred Dogs*. Edwardsville KS: Veterinary Medicine Publishing Co., 1983.

Coe, Susan. *The Basenji, Out of Africa to You: A New Look*. Wilsonville, Oregon: Doral Publishing, 1994.

Edelson, Edward. *Genetics and Heredity*. New York and Philadelphia: Chelsea House Publishers, 1990.

Edey, Maitland A. and Donald C. Johanson. *Blueprints, Solving the Mystery of Evolution*. Boston: Little Brown Book Company, 1989.

Elliott, Rachel Page. *Dogsteps, Illustrated Gait at a Glance*. New York: Howell Book House, 1973.

Gardiner, Catherine. *Dogs: Structure and Movement*. Ontario, Canada: The School of Canine Science, 1973.

Gardiner, Catherine and E. S. Gibson. *Dogs: A Hobby or a Profession*, Vol. 1, II. Ontario, Canada: Canine Consultants Publishing, 1974.

Gill, James. *Bloodstock*. New York: ARCO Publishing Company, 1977.

Griffen, Jeff. *The Hunting Dogs of America*. Garden City, NY:Doubleday and Co., 1964.

Hendin, David and Joan Marks. *The Genetic Connection*. New York: Signet Books, 1979.

Hewitt, Abram S. *The Great Breeders and Their Methods*. Lexington KY: Thoroughbred Publishers, Inc., 1982.

Hollenbeck, Leon. *The Dynamics of Canine Gait*. Middleburg, Virginia: Wm. W. Denlinger, 2nd Edit. 1981.

Huntington, H. Woodworth. *The Show Dog*. Providence, Rhode Island: Remington Printing Company, 1901.

Hutchinson's Popular and Illustrated Dog Encyclopaedia. Volumes I, II, and III. Edited by Walter Hutchinson. Paternoster Row, London, E. C. 4.: Hutchinson & Co. (Publishers) LTD, 1934.

Inglee, Charles T. and Staff of AKC. *Non-Sporting Dogs*. New York: G. Howard Watt, Incorporated, 1935.

Jones, William E. *Genetics and Horse Breeding*. Philadelphia, Pennsylvania: Lea & Febiger, 1982.

Lennox, Muriel. *E.P. Taylor: A Horseman and His Horses*. Toronto, Canada: Burns & Maceachern, 1975.

Lyon, McDowell. *The Dog in Action*. New York: Howell Book House, 1966.

Marvin, John T. *The Book of All Terriers*. New York: Howell Book House, 1971, 3rd printing.

McLean, Ken. *Tesio - Master of Matings*. Cammeray, Australia: Horwitz-Graham Books, (Pty.) Ltd., 1984

Moore, Daphne. *Foxhounds*. London: B. T. Batsfor Ltd., 1981.

Nicholas, Anna Katherine, *The Golden Retriever Book*. Neptune NJ: TFH Publications, 1983

Onstott, Kyle. *The New Art of Breeding Better Dogs*. Revised by Philip Onstott. New York: Howell Book House, 1967.

Palmer, Joe H., *Names in Pedigrees*. Lexington KY: Thoroughbred Owners & Breeders Assoc, 1939, 2nd ed. 1974.

Paramoure, Anne Fitzgerald. *Breeding and Genetics of the Dog*. Middleburg, Virginia: Wm. W. Denlinger, 1959.

Roos, Mrs. George H. *Collie Concept*. Loveland, Colorado: Alpine Publications, Incorporated, 1982.

Sabella, Frank and Shirlee Kalstone. *The Art of Handling Show Dogs*. Hollywood, California: B & E Publications, 1980.

Simopoulos, Artermis P., Victor Herbert, and Beverly Jacobson. *Genetic Nutrition*. New York: MacMillan Publishing Co., 1993.

Smythe, R. H. *The Anatomy of Dog Breeding*. London: Popular Dogs Publishing, 1962.

Sweet, Orville K. *Birth of a Breed*. American Polled Hereford Association, Kansas City, Missouri: Lowell Press, 1975.

Tesio, Federico. *Breeding the Race Horse*. London, England: J. A. Allen & Co., 1958.

Westminster Kennel Club. *One Hundreth Anniversary Book, 1877-1976*. U.S.A.: The Guinn Company, 1976.

Wilcox, Bonnie, DVM and Chris Walkowicz. *The Atlas of Dog Breeds of the World*. Neptune City, New Jersey: T.F.H. Publications, 1989.

Willis, Malcolm B. *Genetics & the Dog*. New York: Howell Book House, 1989.

Whitney, Leon F. *How to Breed Dogs*. New York: Orange Judd Publishing Co., 1947.

About the Author

by Dr. Nina P. Ross

The author was assisted by Dr. Nina P. Ross, pictured with one of her Elkhounds, breeder of Misty Tara Norwegian Elkhounds with husband Paul E. Ross. Dr. Ross is the well-known author of three books: *Dog of the Vikings: Of Gods and Dogs*; *The Norwegian Elkhound*; and *Puc, Gray Dog of Norway*. She is currently working on *The Hound Group* to be published in 1997.

In addition to being a popular judge of the Hound Group, Dr. Ross is noted for her seminars and lectures on her favorite breed. Her experiences breeding, raising, and showing champion Elkhounds also includes obedience training her dogs to Utility and Tracking Degree titles. She is the Elkhound columnist for *The American Kennel Gazette*.

She and husband Paul are founding charter members of the Greater Shelby County Kennel Club and the Mid South Judges Study Group. Nina is currently serving as president of GSKC. They are the proud parents of a son and two daughters and have seven grandchildren. In addition to her varied doggy activities, Dr. Ross owns and operates her own editing services business. Her computer and editing skills contributed greatly to *Born To Win*. Photo by Kevin Lewter.

Patricia V. Craige

Home was Norfolk, Virginia, in a typical family where being a tomboy, playing sandlot sports, climbing trees, and riding horses was part of growing up. As so often happens with kids, stray animals and dogs found their way to the Vincent home. Being a non-doggy family did not stop Pat's indulgent parents from accepting her growing interest in dogs—at first mixed breeds and then a Cocker Spaniel. She was still in elementary school when she established a door-to-door bathing and grooming service to help finance her attraction to purebred dogs.

Among the purebreds in the neighborhood were a Doberman Pinscher, Collie, Boxer and several Cocker Spaniels. Their owners, with no intent to show their dogs, soon found themselves driving Pat with their dogs to matches and shows. She was only 11 when, as a friend of Muriel Laubach of Dau-Han Cocker Spaniels, she acquired Dau-Han's Sonata, a black granddaughter of Ch. Nonquit Notable, foremost Cocker Spaniel of 1937.

Major points were elusive in the highly competitive Cocker ring but a certain measure of success provided the encouragement Pat needed. Not only did she breed a litter from "Melody," her Cocker, but she acquired a Norwegian Elkhound puppy named Candy. It was from these first dogs that she coined her kennel name—Vin from Vincent, her family name; Mel from Melody, her Cocker; Ca from Candy, her Elkhound. So it was that one of the foremost Norwegian Elkhound kennels—Vin-Melca—was born.

Pat's avid interest in purebred dogs continued to grow. Nevertheless, her teen years found her involved in such diversified activities as singing in a church choir, playing organized hockey, softball, basketball, and running track. She was into football and basketball broadcasting and sports reporting for the *Norfolk Ledger-Dispatch*. While in high school she was editor of the school newspaper, Homecoming Queen, governor of Virginia Girls' State, and president of Girls' Nation. As a natural leader, Pat served as president of the Norfolk Junior Chapter of the National Conference of Christians and Jews, was involved in student government, a class officer, and president of her college freshman class. Awards and recognition came early with the Chamber of Commerce Outstanding Teenager Award in 1953. Her work with children at the YWCA ultimately led to her decision to enter the field of education and become a teacher.

Norwegian Elkhounds are bred to hunt. Pat's first Elkhound was from hunting stock used on bear. With perseverance, she earned an obedience title and a conformation championship on the bitch that became the foundation for her Vin-Melca kennel. Her first litter was whelped in 1951, resulting in a homebred champion.

To grace her natural incentive to learn more about dogs, Pat worked part time during summers and after

Dau-Han's Sonata, a black Cocker Spaniel granddaughter of Ch. Nonquitt Notable, America's #1 Sporting Dog in 1937. "Melody" provided the MEL portion of the Vin-Melca kennel name used by the author. In the strong Cocker competition of that time, she was not able to win her majors to finish with her owner handling. This picture was taken around 1948.

The author at seventeen meeting President Eisenhower in the Rose Garden in 1953. As the delegate from Virginia, she had been elected president of Girls' Nation.

Ch. Momarv's River Girl, Old English Sheepdog, was a favorite of the author's in the early '60s. Owned by fellow teachers, Duane and Toni Graham, she was campaigned in the tough Working Group to OES Top Ten status. Bred by Mona Berkowitz, River Girl is pictured taking a group placement under Judge Charles Hamilton. (Photo by Henry Schley)

school at veterinary hospitals near her Virginia home. Her breeding program went into a modified holding pattern while she was in college, but she continued to show dogs, and keep a busy schedule of extra-curricular activities. She graduated from the College of William and Mary (Norfolk Division) in 1958 with a B.A. in history. That same year she began a lifelong career, teaching U.S. History to eighth graders.

Pat chose her mentors wisely, learning from such respected breeders as Johnny Davis, Norman Austin, and Muriel Laubach, grooming dogs, doing kennel work, showing their dogs, and devouring their words of wisdom. Success in the ring came in the late '50s with Johnny's Dobermans—especially those from Ch. Aida's Hilda—and Muriel's Cocker Spaniels. Pat's first coveted Best in Show win came in 1959 at the Camden Kennel Club show. Ch. Dau-Han's Dan Morgan, a red-and-white Cocker Spaniel, was chosen from a beautiful lineup of famous dogs. Not only had Dan Morgan placed in the group at the Kennel Club of Philadelphia, the previous day but more wins followed, making him the top-winning particolor in the nation.

California beckoned and in 1961, Pat loaded Ch. Vin-Melca's Rebel Rouser and two Rebel Rouser daughters into a new Valiant station wagon for the long trip West. She fell in love with the beautiful Monterey Peninsula and lived there for the next 33 years. Not only did she acquire a teaching job on the Peninsula but she attributed the move to California as a giant step forward in her Vin-Melca breeding program. It was here that the bloodlines of Ch. Tortasen's Bjonn II, Ch. Trygvie Vikingsson, Ch. Windy Cove's Silver Son, his brother, Ch. Windy Cove's Rowdy Ringo, and Ch. Wabeth's Gustav combined to lay the groundwork for what rightly can be considered a most successful Norwegian Elkhound breeding program.

The ascent of Vin-Melca Elkhounds to success became apparent in the early 1960s when Vin-Melca's Rebel Cry went Best Opposite Sex at the Parent Club National Specialty and Rebel Rouser was the #2 Norwegian Elkhound. Pat's first BIS Elkhound was Ch. Vin-Melca's Vickssen who became the #1 Norwegian Elkhound in the U.S. in 1966

The author and good friend, Dr. Merlyn Green, delegate to AKC from the Del Monte Kennel Club, at the famous "Classic of the Pacific." Pat was the announcer at this show and served as president of the club for three years. (Photo courtesy of Photos Today)

and 1967. Vicxssen was out of Ch. Vin-Melca's Rebel Rouser and sired by Ch. Vin-Melca's Hi Ho Silver. He became the sire of Ch. Vin-Melca's Vagabond. A Vin-Melca Elkhound held the honor of being #1 Norwegian Elkhound every year consecutively through 1994.

Favorites among the many dogs Pat was showing during the early '60s were Ch. Beau-Monde War Paint, a black-and-white Cocker, and the Old English Sheepdog, Ch. Momarv's River Girl. War Paint, son of Dan Morgan, belonged to her good friend, Arline Swalwell of Windridge Kennels, and was bred by another friend, Dick Beauchamp, both sharing Pat's joy when the dog ranked high in the Top Ten particolors. River Girl, bred by Mona Berkowitz, and purchased by fellow Carmel Unified School District teachers, Duane and Toni Graham, also ranked in the Top Ten for her breed.

The late '60s and early '70s saw Pat concentrating more on her Elkhounds. She and her husband, Dr. John Craige, traveled to shows all over the West. Vagabond became #1 Dog All Breeds, All Systems, Quaker Oats Winner, and Westminster Group winner in 1970 and repeated in 1971. Two more Quaker Oats

TAKE A LIKING TO A VIKING! Chuck and Pat Trotter get into the mood at a costume party at the Orlando Cluster where participants came dressed in the country of origin of their dogs. (Earl Graham Photo)

winners and three more Westminster Hound groups accumulated for Champions Vin-Melca's Valley Forge, Homesteader, and Nimbus. Homesteader won the last benched Santa Barbara show at the Polo Field over 4,000 dogs. In a period of two years Nimbus was #2 All Breeds and #3 All Breeds with a total of 63 All Breed Best in Shows, Pat continued to "run" him, teach school, and work her horses, not to mention completing her Masters at Monterey Institute of International Studies while campaigning Valley Forge. Elkhound enthusiasts from all walks of life visited the Craige home in Carmel to see the dogs and enjoy life on the Peninsula.

The 1980s seemed intent on topping Pat's accomplishments of the '70s. For starters, she took a 10-month-old puppy bitch to Winners under this breeder-judge-author at the Regional Specialty in Denver, following the National. The puppy was placed Best in Specialty by breeder-judge Bob Wunderlin. The puppy happened to be (Ch.) Vin-Melca's Last Call ("Gilda") whose subsequent accomplishments included 14 All Breed BISs, 10 Specialty BISs, ranking high in the Top Ten Hounds, and all time top producing Norwegian Elkhound bitch with 27 champion progeny. The '80s continued with another exciting bitch, Ch. Vin-Melca's Before Dawn, also a multi-BIS bitch and Westminster group placer.

The mid-1980s belonged to Ch. Vin-Melca's The Smuggler, one of Pat's personal all time favorites. Smuggler won 25 All Breed BISs and was second in the group at Westminster and #2 Hound in the U.S. In 1984 he was one of three BIS sons of Nimbus along with his brother, Ch. Vin-Melca's Buckpasser, and half-brother, Ch. Vin-Melca's Southern Rain. The three of them ranked in the Top Ten Hounds and were #1, #2, and #3 in the breed that year.

Ch. Vin-Melca's Calista ("Sarah"), Gilda's half-sister, brought the spotlight back to the bitches. Sarah became #3 All Breeds in 1989 and #2 in 1990 with 66 Best in Shows, two Quaker Oats awards, and two Westminster Hound Groups to

The author and Chuck Trotter married in April 1994 in Williamsburg, Virginia. With them are her parents, Mr. & Mrs. Roderick D. Vincent at the reception held at the home of her brother Roderick D. Vincent Jr. (Photo by Frank Davis)

her credit. Pat, herself, was selected into the Ken-L-Ration Hall of Fame in 1990 and honored with the Fido Award as Woman of the Year in 1991.

Pat hit the campaign trail in 1991 and 1992 with the headstrong Ch. Vin-Melca's Bombardier, taking him to Top Ten All Breeds and 1992 Quaker Oats honors. Bombardier, reminiscent of his stallion-like double great-grandsire Nimbus, was the sire of Sarah's first litter. In 1993, their daughter, Ch. Vin-Melca's Marketta, became the first Quaker Oats winner in the history of the awards to have a Quaker Oats winning sire and a Quaker Oats winning dam.

The wind was shifting. In the summer of 1993, Chuck Trotter began courting Pat, and she applied to judge. Her last major show victory was taking Marketta to a Hound Group win at Westminster in 1994 before she stopped actively campaigning her dogs. She and Chuck were married at her parents home in Virginia and Pat moved to Tennessee. In 1995, after a year's layoff, Pat and Marketta returned to Westminster to repeat her group victory and to give the Vin-Melca Elkhounds an incredible 10 group-firsts at Westminster.

Assignments resulting from the popularity of the Trotters as a judging couple fill in many of their weekends. However, Pat still enjoys showing her dogs occasionally and Ch. Vin-Melca's Frequent Flyer ranked high in the Top Ten with limited showing in 1995. Showing and breeding purebred dogs has been a part of her life since those early years in Virginia with her parents. There is every reason to believe that as long as Pat has a worthy dog to show and the capability to present it with her customary expertise, a small part of that life will endure.

I   N   D   E   X

Pages for photographs appear in bold face type.

Ability, athletic 28
Abnormal behavior 167
Acadia Command Performance, Ch. 213, **214**, **227**
Achondroplastic breed 17, 162
Advertising 226
Afghan Hound 14, 199
AIDS 269
Airedale Terrier 79, 111
American Kennel Club 2, 11, 35, 37, 81, 98, 148, 180, 185, 204, 215, 260, 262, 267
AKC *Gazette* 25, 114, 148, 165, 191, 266
Alaskan Malamute 79, 163
Allen, Michael 139
All-rounders 82
Alston, George 187, 188
Alston-Myers, Jane 187
Altana's Mystique, Ch. 221, 222, *color*
Amber Lady of Tercor Farm 197
Amberac's Asterling Aruba, Ch. 102, **102**
American Cocker 42
American Dog Owners Assoc. 226
Ammon Hall Nomad, Ch. **208**
Anatomy 16
Anemic 172
Angulation 154
Animal husbandry 152
Anthony, Donna 220
Anxiety, noise 169
Appearance, general 37, 38
Appleton, Coral 101
Arcadia Command Performance, Ch. 213
Arcadia's Cotton-Eyed Joe, Ch. 100
Arctic Storm of Pomfret, Ch. 232
Argus of Greywitch, Ch. **208**
Aroi Talk of the Blues, Ch. **198**, 199
Arriba's Prima Donna, Ch. **209**
Arrow look 162
Artificial selection 4, 72
Asterling's Go Get'm Gangbuster, Ch. 102
Asterling's Tahiti Sweeti, Ch. 102
Asterling's Wild Blue Yonder, Ch. 102
Asymmetrical gaits 14, 16
Athletic ability 28
Athleticism 163
Aubrey-Jones, Nigel 137
Austin, Jeanne 233
Austin, Norman 106, 122, 197, 233-234
Awards 213
Baard of Greenwood, Ch. 32, **33**
Back 19
Bad habits 168
Bagshaw, Mrs. 199
Baker, Carey & Thelma 232
Balance 153
Balance, kinetic 21
Balance, moving 21
Balance, standing 21
Balance, static 21
Barlow, Bobby 208
Baron's Carbon Copy, Ch. 132, **133**
Baroness of Duroya, Ch. 129
Barron, Carl & Pepper 137, 236
Basenji 94, 262

Basset Hound 17, 18, 34, 78
Bateson, William 45
Bathrum, J.D. 43
Bauer, Richard 123, 208
Beagle 19, 79, 123, 159, 191
Bearded Collie 99
Beauchamp, Richard **216**
Beaulaine The Nite Ryder 220
Beaulaine Wind Fall, Ch. 137
BeauMonde War Paint, Ch. **84**
Behavior 166, 167
Behavior, abnormal 167
Behavior, inherited 166
Behavior, learned 166
Bel S'Mbran Aba Fantasia, Ch. 32, **33**, 199
Bel S'Mbran Bachrach, Ch. 32, **43**, **198**, 199
Bel S'Mbran Rubah Ahlam, Ch. **256**
Bell, George 32, 33, 198, 199, 256
Bellbrooke's Master Pilot 127
Bengal Turith Comet 111
Benkin, Priscilla 226
Bent Oak's Just Because JH, Ch. 101
Bennett, Jeff & Nan Eisley- 217
Berg, Paul 261
Bingham, Judy 137
Biotechnology 260
Bitch, brood 87, 90, 94, 113
Bitch, campaigning 94
Bitch, declining influence of the true foundation 93
Bitch, foundation 106
Bitch, mediocre 92
Bitch, true foundation 88, 90, 100, 264
Bite 156, 163
Bite, level 156
Bite, scissors 156
Blair, Mrs. Thelma 170
Blood, Mrs. James 199
Bloodlines 45, 107
Bloodstock 45
Blu Shah of Grandeur, Ch. **151**
Blueprints 45
Body 38
Body texture 23
Boileau, Luc 268
Bolté, Damara 208, 262
Bonding 94
Bone 23, 77
Bonney, Mrs. L.W. **84**
Bonteceau, Gayle **268**
Border Terrier 79
Boredom 168, 171
Borzoi 38
Boston Terrier 79
Bottom 171
Bouvier des Flandres 201
Boxer 78
Boyes, Eddie 132
Brackett, Lloyd 99
Braeburn's Close Encounter, Ch. **241**
Brandyman's Little Tempo, Ch. 131
Bratt, Mr. & Mrs. D.G. 109
Braunstein, Shirlee 219
Bravo Bonaza Belle De AAA, Ch. 111

Bravo Starbuck, Ch. 111
Bravo True Grit, Ch. **111**
Breed, achondroplastic 17
Breed, history of your 31
Breed improvement 264
Breed, purpose of your 31
Breed specific 29
Breed standard 35
Breed type 156
Breed-specific contradictions 6
Breed-specific errors 85
Breed-specific knowledge 6, 9, 29, 73, 108
Breed-specific trait 79, 156
Breeder 82, 231
Breeder, ethical 5
Breeder, master 11, 24, 34, 45, 65, 99, 101, 102, 105, 119, 123, 126, 141, 187, 203, 206, 219, 245, 262, 265
Breeder, respected 5
Breeder responsibility 167
Breeding, balanced 66
Breeding 92, 107, 191
Breeding arrangements 179
Breeding potential 98
Breeding program 55, 68, 81, 85, 112, 115, 270
Breeding program, how sex chromosomes affect 54
Breeding prospect 98
Breeding stock 82, 95
Breeding The Race Horse 251
Breeding Your Own Show Sog, Joy of 45
Breeding-on 90
Breeding-up 74
Breeds, achondroplastic 162
Breeds, changes in the 266
Brewer, Dr. George 261
Briarhill Midnight High, Ch. 126
Brittany 27, 101
Broadside Bull Terriers 161
Brodd II av Elglia, Ch. **267**
Brood bitch 87, 90, 113
Brought-Mar Jelibean De Campo, Ch. 101
Brought-Mar Jiver De Campo, Ch. 101
Brown, Curtis 22
Brown, Bev (Ricci) 121
Browning, Mrs. 94
Brucker, Jeff 188
Brunswig's Cryptonite, Ch. 138, **138**, **220**, 221
Brussels Griffon 79, 105
Buchanans, Knox 232
Buddie, John 126-128
Bull Terrier 25, 50-51, 161, 266
Bulldog 14, 27, 79
Bulldog Club 29
Burke, Mary 102
Burnham, Patricia Gail 23
Cairn Terrier 161
Cairnwood's Quince, Ch. 162
Caledonian Berry of Wolfpit, Ch. 162
Calendar 180
Calicura, Nick 237
Callahan, Clint 197, 255, 256
Campaign, do-it-yourself 195
Campaign strategy 195
Campaign stress 95
Campaigning a bitch 94
Campaigning puppies 166
Campaigns 223
Campbell, Olav 82
Canalizo, Michael 151
Canarch Inchidony Sparkle, Ch. **8**
Canarch Yankee Patriot C.D., Ch. **8**
Canine Science, School of 264, 265
Canis familiaris 3, 72
Canis lupis 3
Canyon Crest Mo, Ch. 131
Canyon Crest's Bakara, Ch. **200**
Carder, Robert 104

Carey, Len 206
Carmas Drivin Miss Daisy, Am/Mex/Int SBIS Ch. color
Carro of Ardmere, Ch. 245
Carriage 77
Carter, Dr. Stan 262, 263
Carvill, Gordon 226
Case, Lloyd 197
Casillas, Vivian 268
Cavanaugh, Wayne 25
Ch. Clussex Country Sunrise **187**
Chaix, Jeanette 104
Championships 194
Changa's Dan Patch, Ch. 264, color
Changes in the breeds 266
Charisma's Passionella 104
Charmaron's Cheddar of Toy, Ch. 85, **85**, 86
Chashoudian, Evonne 208
Chashoudian, Ric 109, 132, 192, 201, 213
Chemical actions 52
Chest cavity 19
Chewing, paw 169
Chewing, rock 170
Chidley Willum The Conqueror, Ch. **212**
Chik T'sun of Caversham, Ch. color
Chinoe's Adamant James, Ch. 8, 116, 119, **209**
Choate, Mrs. Robert 266
Chow Chow 2, 6, 19, 148, 266
Chromosome, X 90, 106, 141
Chromosome, sex 53
Chromosomes 45, 47
Clark, James Edward 204
Clark, Les & Liz 122
Clark, Anne Rogers 7, 81, 203, 204, 255
Clarkdale's Capitol Stock, Ch. 122
Claus, Freeman & Betty 90
Closebreeding 58, 59, 62, 64, 80
Clot, Mr. & Mrs. William 267
Cluft, Mr. & Mrs. William 198
Coady, Clay 132, 134
Coat 32, 33, 164
Coat, puppy 157
Coat texture 77, 156
Cobb, Bain 44, 197
Cobb, Ken 197
Cocker Spaniel, American 42
Cocker Spaniel, English 38
Cocker Spaniel 19, 105, 122, 138, 140, 186, 193, 243
Codominant 50
Colan, Judy 121
Collie 63, 94, 197
Collier, Chester F. 220
Color 40, 73, 77, 79, 156
Color genetics 79
Colsidex Dauntless Applause, Ch. 121
Colsidex Nani Reprint, Ch. 122
Colsidex Standing Ovation, Ch. 121, **122**
Columbia University 51
Coming and going 25, 26
Competition 215, 231
Competitor 191
Compromises 78
Conditioning 78, 170
Conformation 16, 73
Contact, human 165
Contracts 179
Cook, John H. 202
Cooper, Ruth 124
Correll, Harold 137, 174, 197
Cosby, Bill 132, 134, color
Counterpoint's Lord Ashley, Ch. 102
Covy, Byron & Cameron 84
Covy Tucker Hills Manhattan, Ch. 219, **219**
Cowhocks 155
Cowie, Anna 232
Crafts, Glenna 88, 232
Cragmount's Hi-Lo, Ch. 197

Cragmount's Peter, Ch. 197
Craige, Dr. John 119, 230, 234-235
Crane, Mary 105
Crates 165, 175
Criteria, selection 73
Culling 70, 80, 95, 167
Cummings' Gold-Rush Charlie, Ch. 197
Curby, Jon 262, 263
Cygnet's Raspberry, Ch. 124
Dachshund 160, 202
Dalmatian 79, 262
Dalton, Ed 109
Dam 90, 94
Dams, evaluating 141
Dandie Dinmont Terrier 162
Darwin, Charles 4, 46, 72
Dasa's Ebony Queen, Ch. 100
Dachshund 18
Dasu's Blu Falcon, Ch. 101
Dasu's King Of The Mountain, Ch. 101
Dasu's Maid Marion, Ch. 101
Dasu's Ziegfield, Ch. 101
Dau-Han's Bib N' Tucker, Ch. **243**
Dau-Han's Dan Morgan, Ch. **84**, **139**, 140
Dau-Han's Dan Tucker **243**
Davis, Johnny 9, 23, 137, 187, 206, 236-237
Davishill Little Man, Ch. **215**
De-Go Hubert, Ch. 218
Defects, minor 98
Dehydration 223
Delegate v.d. Elbe, Ch. 137
Demidoff, Lorna 130
Dersade Bobby's Girl, Ch. **210**
DeRussy Standard Poodles 159
DeRussy's Lollypop, Ch. 204
DeVries 51
Diaz, Carroll Gordon 123, 158, 188, 230
Dickson, Virginia 132, 213
Dictator Von Glenhugel, Ch. 137
Diet 223
Difficult people 176
Diotama Bear Necessity HC, Ch. *color*
Direct sire line 57
Dirty personal habits 169
Discharges 96
Disorder, metabolic 173
Distemper 151
DNA 5, 45, 52, 265, 266
Doberman Pinscher 11, 114, 137, 199, 206, 213
Dodge, Mrs. Geraldine R. 149
Dog, dangerous 84
Dog, mediocre 84
Dog, pieces of 82
Dog, stud 107
Dog Book, The Complete 37
Dog in Action, The 85
Dog Locomotion and Gait Analysis 22
Dog News 41, 228
Dog show 81, 230
Dog show history 184-186
Dog show purpose 95
Dog Steps 25
Dog's potential 194
Dogs, flying with 225
Dogs, purebred 260
Dogs, traveling with 224
Dominance, partial 50
Dominant gene 49, 53
Don-Lee Chowtime, Ch. *color*
Doug's Dauntless Von Dor, Ch. 121
Downey, Larry 190
Drag of the breed 80, 81
Dreamridge Dinner Date, Ch. **139**, 140
Dreamridge Domino, Ch. 138, **139**
Dunelm Galaxy, Ch. 123, **124**
duPont Jr., Mrs. William 191

Ear 76, 156
Easy Southern's Forty-Niner, Ch. *color*
Eater, picky 168
Eckroat, Brian Vincent 253
Eckroat, Pete 255
Edenborough Blue Bracken, Eng. Ch. 100
Edenborough Full O'Life 100
Edwards, Brint & Vivian 206, 216
Eldredge, E. Irving 131
Electra's Rally Round The Flag, Ch. 137
Electra's The Wind Walker, Ch. 137, **136**
Electrolytes 223
Elfinbrook Simon, Ch. 202, **202**
Elhew Snakefoot **182**
Elliot, Rachel Page 20, 25
Elongated 22
Elsy's Shooting Star, Ch. 123
Empire's Brooklyn Dodger, Ch. 123, 140, **140**
Engelhard Jr., Mrs. Charles 197
Engle, Dr. Hal ix
English Cocker Spaniel 37, 123, 204
English Dog World 25
English Foxhound 36
English Springer Spaniel 116-119, 239, 240
Enzymes 172
Epistasis 50
Errors, breed-specific 85
Estrus cycle 94, 95
Ethical breeder 5
Exercise 95
Exercise routine 96
Experiences, early 166
Expression 77
Eye 77
Eye for a dog 82
Fabis, Ron 138
Facilities, kennel 148
Facilities, puppy 151
Fanconi's Syndrome 61, 62, 262, 264
Fargo, John & Angelee 104
Farrell, James & Emilie 133
Farrer, R.G. & P.K. 220
Farrow, Cres 232
Faulkner, E.D. 184
Fault 41, 153
Feeding program 96
Feet 77
Femur 17
Fencing 152
Ferris, Myron 232
Fessenden, Wayne & Tula 101
Fessiwig's Ceiling Zero, Ch. 129, **129**
Fetus 94
Fido Awards 218
Field, Stephen J. 127
Field trials 75
Fielder, Herb & Martha 232
Fields, Stephen J. 127
Financial investments 165
Finlair Tiger of Stone Ridge, Ch. 111
Finlair Isis, Ch. 111
Finnsky Oliver, Ch. **205**
Firenze Kennels 149
Firesign's Smackwater Jack, Ch. 104
Firestone, Mrs. Jane 219
First Impression of Silverbow, Ch. 119
Fitzgerald, Kellie 239
Flea problems 173
Flexibility 22
Flowers, Stan 190
Flying with dogs, 225
Foot 19
Forequarters 40
Form 215
Form follows function 2
Forsyth, Bob & Jane 188, 219

Forsyth, Jane 190, 203, 204, 219
Forsyth, Robert 129, 130, 199
Foster families 252
Foundation bitch 88
Foundation stock 87
Four-Tee Desiderata, Ch. 101
Fowler, Worth & Kay 32
Fox Terrier 78
Foxhound, American 19
Foxhound, English 19
Foxhounds 46, 65
Foxhounds 252
Foy, Marcia 208
Free mating 99
Freeman, Muriel 34
Frei, David & Sandy 199, 200
French Bulldog 184
Froehlich, Fred & Dody 96, 254
Front assembly 18
Fronts 77
Frost, Nick & Ellen 34
Fuel supply 25
Fun matches 166
Function, form follows 2
Funnell, Lesley, 123
Fursberg, Anna Mae 163
Future 260
Gaines Company 218
Gait 28
Gait, evaluating 31
Gaiting, incorrect 189
Gaits, symmetrical 14
Galaxy's Corry Missile Belle, Ch. 199, 213, **214**
Galbraith's Iron Eyes, Ch. 200, **201**
Galeforce Post Script, Ch. **212**
Gallop 19
Galton's Law 55, 56, 144
Gamble, Ellsworth 237-238, 266
Gardiner, Catherine 17, 20, 264
Gasow, Julia 116, 119, 239-240
Gene action, additive 50
Gene, dominant 49
Gene mapping 260
Gene pool 80, 81, 84, 90, 107, 167, 264
General appearance 37, 38
Genes, dominant 53
Genes, recessive 53
Genes 3, 45, 78, 98, 109, 261
Genetic code 49
Genetic combinations 92, 94
Genetic drift 68
Genetic information 53, 106
Genetic integrity 60
Genetic makeup 76
Genetic order 45
Genetic potential 74
Genetic trash 61, 99, 114
Genetic variations 52
Genetics, bonehead 44
Genetics, color 79
German Shepherd Dog 11, 266
German Shorthair 213
Gerstner, Connie 65, 163, 164
Gilmore's Garden 206
Giralda Farm 149
Glamoor Good News, Ch. **196**
Glassferd, Tom 208, 218
Goals, setting 10
Goddard, H.H. 60
Godsol, Beatrice 82, 83, 159, 216
Going, coming and 25, 26
Gold Coast Here Comes The Sun CD, Ch. 102
Gold Rush Judgement Day, Ch. 102
Golden Retriever, A Study of the 32
Golden Retriever 11, 25, 26, 79, 102, 163, 197
Goodman, Barry 129

Goodman, Walter 196, 216
Gordon Setter 40
Gossetts 232
Gra-Lemor Demetrius v.d. Victor, Ch. **136**, 137
Grading systems 265, 266
Grandeur Kennels **150**
Gravity, center 27
Great Dane 41
Great Pyrenees 104
Green, Peter 7, 132, 193
Gretchenhof Columbia River, Ch. **210**, 213
Greyhound 18, 35, 79, 199
Greywinds Jack Frost, Ch. 122
Grover, Frank 114
Gueverra, Richard 269
Haakonson, Caj 129
Hall, Forrest 250, 253
Hall, Jim & Beth 140
Hall, Lana 121
Hallmark, Cliff 218
Hallway's Hoot Mon, Ch. 140
Handlers, professional 189, 193
Handlers, junior 206
Handling 187
Hands 190
Hardiness 77
Hardy's High Spirit, Ch. 122
Harrigan of Twin Haven, Ch. **243**
Harriman, O.C. 188
Harrison's Peeping Tom, Ch. 123
Hartley, Heywood 240-242
Hastings, E.R. 32
Hauff, Mrs. Holver 121
Hausbrau Executive of Acadia, Ch. 213
Hayworth, Thelma 232
Head 37, 73, 77
Head shaking 169
Heads, evaluating 156
Heads, puppy 162
Health 77, 98
Health certificates 179
Heartbreak Valentino, Ch. 104
Heath, Jean 132, 134
Henderson, Mrs. Jane 218
Herndon, Elaine 213
Heterozygote 50
Heterozygous 47
Hiett, Dick & Mitzi **230**
Hillsome Solo Flight of Robin Hill, Eng. & Am. Ch. **266**
Hiltz, David 123
Hindquarters 40
Hip 17
Hip dysplasia 168
History of your breed 31
Hole, John & Evelyn 105
Holt, Bill 192, 206
Homestead Sir With Love, Ch. 105
Homozygote 50
Homozygous 47
Honey Creek Vivacious, Ch. **103**, 105
Hormones 95
Horner, Tom 25
Hostility 223
Hounds, sight 22
Huber, Joan 134
Hugo Of Cosalta, Ch. **215**
Human contact 165
Humerus 17
Humor of dog people 255
Hungerland, Dr. Jacklyn 7, 159, 203, 204, 206
Hunters 75
Husbandry, animal 152
Hutchinson, Dee 160, 202
Hutchinson, Lydia 7, 161
Hybrid 50, 51
Hybrid vigor 65

Hyslop, Betty 190
Ilch, Mrs. Florence B. 149
Immune system 95
Inbreeding 58, 60-63
Inchidony Prince Charming, Ch. 119
Industrial Revolution 3
Ing, Katherine 268
Inherited behavior 166
Innisfree's Pegasus 163
Innisfree's Sierra Beau Jack, Ch. 131
Innisfree's Sierra Cinnar, Ch. 130, **131**, 163
Instincts, maternal 94
Intelligence 77
Intestinal tract 95
Investments, financial 165
Irish Leader 113
Irish Setter 78, 260
Irish Wolfhound 34, 160
Italian Greyhound 100
Ivanwold Pugs 158
Jaws, undershot 156
Jenner, Edward B. 137, 213
Jessy V D Sonnenhohe, Ch. **138**
Jo-Ni's Red Baron of Crofton, Ch. 109, 132, **133**, 213, **214**
Johnson, Linda 165
Joints 19
Jones, Arthur Frederick 148, 190
Jones, Jacque 105
Jordan, Dennis & Andrea 43, 101
Jordan, Bob 132
Jordean All Kiddin' Aside, Ch. **43**
Jorl's Jo-Ni of Sherwood, Ch. 132
Judge, multi-breed 82
Judges 74
Judges, evaluating master 186
Judging 82
Jumps 72
Junior handlers 206
Kabik's The Challenger, Ch. 86, 151, 199, 228, *color*
Kabik's The Front Runner, Ch. **198**, 199
Kai Esa's Cameo, Ch. 137
Kai Esa's Holly Go Lightly, Ch. 137
Kai Esa's Passing Parade C.D., Ch. 137
Kall of the Wild's Zandor, Ch. **208**
Kanzler, Kathleen 130
Karolaska Honey's Abby, HOF, Ch. **103**, 104
Karolaska Klumbo HOF, Ch. 105
Kelley, Joy Meyer 129
Kemp, Mike 220
Ken-L-Ration Awards 218
Kennel 148, 167
Kennel blindness 231
Kennel facilities 148
Kennel help 153
Kennel management 148, 152
Kennel Review System 218
Kenobo Rabbit of Nadou, Ch. **125**
Kenobo Capricorn, Ch. 124, **125**, 126
Kentopp, Carol 105
Kerry Blue Terrier 20, 21, 109, 266
Kibushi Get Sirius 262, **263**
Kidney stones 262
Kiedrowski, Dan 134, 233
King of the Mountain 101
King Peter of Salilyn, Ch. **117**, 118, 119
King William (of Salilyn), Ch. 118
King's Creek Triple Threat, Ch. **208**
King's Mtn. Montizard Edition **162**
Klensch, Myrtle 131, 159
Knoop, Peter 206
Kontoki's E.I.E.I.O., Ch. 163
Korneliusen, Lee & Diana 90
Korp, Susan 138
Kramer, Bill 218
Kronfield, Dr. David 25
Kurtzner, Mike 188

Labrador Retriever 266
Lakeland Terrier 109, 132, 213
Lamark 51
Lambluv's Winning Maid Easy, Ch. 130
LaShay's Bart Simpson, Ch. **220**, 221
Laubach, Muriel R. 84, 242-244
Lawrence, Sam & Marion 220, 221
Lawson, Deborah 228
Learned behavior 166
Leash breaking 165
Leclerc, George Louis 71
Leedy, Betsy A. 7
Leg, length of 153, 155
Legs, misplacing 189
Legs 77
Leonard Brumby Senior Memorial Trophy 206
Libra Malagold's Coriander, Ch. 164, *color*
Licking 169
Line, tail female 88, 105, 106
Line, direct tail male 107, 109
Linebreeding 58, 109
Linton, Andy 138, 193
Litters 98
Little Sahib, Ch. **215**
Llewellyn, Rhys 64
Locomotion 14
Longevity 77
Look, stuffed 156
Lord Jim, Ch. 218
Loresta's Fallen Angel, Ch. 119
Loverly Dancing Lady, Ch. **158**
Lowe, Bruce 56
Lubin, Harv 218
Luftnase Albelarm Bee's Knees, Ch. 104
Lyn-Mar Acres Clown, Ch. **9**
Lyne, Virginia 124
Lyon, McDowell 25, 85
Lyvewyre Bold Ruler, Ch. 132
M.V.P. of Ahs, Ch. 64, **65**
Macushia of Ambleside, Ch. **160**
Maddox, Bob & Grace 90
Major O'Shannon, Ch. 218
Malagold Golden Retrievers 164
Malagold Summer Chant 164
Males, Florence 159
Manahound Matchpoints, Austr. Ch. 158
Malthus, Thomas 71
Management, kennel 148, 152
Management, time 177
Manchester Terrier 75, 131, 159,
Marder, Jere 130
Mariey, Sherry 220
Marimark's Patches of Ti Song, Ch. 104
Marjetta Dark Side of the Moon, Ch. 104
Marjetta Lady Vanessa, Ch. 102
Marjetta Lord Carlton, Ch. 102
Marjetta Milestone, Ch. 102
Marjetta National Acclaim, Ch.98, 102, **211**
Martorella, Marjorie 102
Mason, Becky 204
Mason, Miss Willie Bell 56
Master breeder 11, 24, 34, 45, 65, 99, 101, 102, 105, 119, 123, 126, 141, 187, 203, 206, 219, 245, 262, 265
Matches, fun 166
Mate, selecting 94
Maternal instincts 94
Mating, free 99
McClintock, Barbara 52
McGilbry, L.G. 213
Melbee's Chances Are, Ch. 109, **192**
Menaker, Ronald H. 220
Mendel, Gregor Johann 47-51, 66, 112
Mentor 7, 9
Merriam, David C. 10, 161
Metabolic disorder 173
Metabolic performance 25

Methods, selection 78
Millette, Beverly 102
Miniature Pinscher 28
Miniature Schnauzer 262
Mira Hill N' Dale D'Dasu, Ch. 101
Mirus, Gilbert B. 213, 255, 256
Miss Skylight, Ch. **201**, 202
Mistakes 82
Mistakes in selection process 164
Misty Morn's Sunset CD, TD, WC, Ch. 102, 197, **198**
Moa, Ch. **244**
Moffit, Mrs. A.S. 149
Moore, Walt & Betty 121, 232
Moore, Daphne 252
Morgan, J.P. 197
Morgan, T.H. 51, 66
Morris Animal Foundation 261
Moses, James 219, 222
Motels 226
Motherhood 96
Motion 14, 22, 27, 28
Motivators 231
Mounting 167
Movement 30
Murr, Louis 169
Murray, George 220
Muscle fiber 25
Musculature 24
Musladin, Dr. & Mrs. A.C. 123
Mutant 114
Mutations 3, 51, 52, 72
Muzzle 162
National Specialty 113
Natural selection 5, 71, 72
Neck 38
Neck, set of 153
Negative selection 70
Negative traits 99
Nerves 24
Nervous system, bitch's 95
Newborn 155
Nicks 66
Nicks, negative 66, 67
Nicks, positive 66
Nobel Prize 51
Noise anxiety 169
Nonquitt Notable, Ch. **215**
Nordic's Viking of Kee Note **166**
Norfolk Terrier 204
Nornay Saddler, Ch. **110**
Norwegian Elkhound 31, 42, 74, 109, 119, 266
Norwegian Elkhound, correct head of **76**
Nutrition 170, 173, 223
Nutritional hints 173
O'Neal, Tom 138
O'Neill, Charles 236
Oak Tree's Irishtocrat, Ch. **210**
Obedience 75
Objective performance 74
Oelschlager, Tommy 163
Off Square 22
Old English Sheepdog 14, 129
Onthank, Mrs. Pierce 202
Oppenheimer, Raymond 10, 161
Ormandy 161
Orthopedic Foundation of America 101, 261
Outcrossed 80
Outcrossing 64, 65
Overhandling 189
Overtraining 166
Owner-handler 195
Pad, hard 151
Paddock areas 152
Page Mill Hallmark, Ch. **188**
Page Mill Trademark, Ch. 123, **230**
Pahlavi Puttin' On The Ritz, Ch. 199

Pain 172
Palmer, Florence 5, 13, 232
Pandora of Stormhill, Ch. 199
Parader's Bold Venture, Ch. 127
Parader's Golden Image, Ch. 127
Parvo virus 223
Pastern 19, 77
Patterson, Charlotte 7, 158
Pattison, Teri 126
Paul, Bob 232
Paw chewing 169
Payton, George 194
Peck, Mrs. Wells 82, 232, 244
Peck, Wells & Catherine 244-245
Pedigree, patterned 137, 143
Pedigree, profiling a 142
Pedigrees 53, 58, 59, 61, 63, 64, 73, 90, 92, 109, 118, 126, 127, 135, 136, 143,179, 263
Pekingese 14, 135
Pelvis 17
Pendelton's Jewel, Ch. 219
Pennsylvania, University of 24
People, difficult 176
Pepper, Jeffrey 34
Performance 73
Performance, objective 74
Performance selection 74
Performance, subjective 74
Perkey, Maude Paul 232
Perry, Vince 216
Personal habits, dirty 169
Peters, Pat 132
Peterson, Jean 122
Peterson, Joe & Marie 232
Phenotype 109
Phillips, Susan 232
Phillips Irene Castle 98, 99, 218
Phillips System 98, 218
Picking puppies 153, 165
Picky-eater syndrome 168
Pillicoc Rumpelstilskin CD, Ch. **215**
Pimlott, Eileen 257, 258
Pirotte, Pete & Mildred 232, 236
Plain and Fancy's Delilah, Ch. 123
Play 167
Plimpton, George 217
Point system 79
Pointer 102, 262
Poling, Dave 206
Poling's Wee One, Ch. **206**
Polygenic 50
Pondwick's Hobgoblin, Ch. 203
Poodle 44, 193, 204, 213
Popular Dogs 218
Pre-campaign pregnancy 96
Predators & prey 4
Pregnancy, pre-campaign 96
Prepotency 50, 56
Prince Alexander, Ch. 197
Prince Andrew of Sherline, Ch. 218
Priorities, ranking 79
Problem solving 174
Problems, preventing 176
Problems, reproduction 95
Producer 87
Producers, ranking the 98
Professional handlers 189, 193
Profile, side 153
Progeny 49, 65, 67, 94, 109, 115, 167
Progressive Retinal Atrophy 5, 260, 264
Proportion 37, 38, 77
Prototype 84
Pug 158
Puppies 94, 95
Puppies, campaigning 166
Puppies, picking 153, 165

Puppies, raising 165
Puppies, socializing 164
Puppies, standing 165
Puppies, well-adjusted 167
Puppy coat 157
Puppy facilities 151
Puppy heads 162
Puppy, overdone 154
Puppy, uncoordinated 154
Purebred dogs 260
Purpose of your breed 31
Pusey, Rebec 232
Pusey, Van 232
Quaker Oats Company Award 218
Qualities 76, 215
Quality time 222
Radiation, artificial 52
Raffles Chelsey Buns, Ch. 130
Raising puppies 165
Rancho Dobe's Maestro, Ch. 199, **200**
Rancho Dobe's Storm, Ch. 206
Rank, Peter & Myrtle 132
Ranzfel Blue Roxanne, Ch. 124
Ranzfel Newsflash T.D., Am. & Can. Ch.124, **125**
Ranzfel Nightcap of Harwen, Ch. 124
Rayne, Derek 38, 245-247
Razzmatazzmanian Stripper, Int. Ch. *color*
Rears 77
Recessive genes 49, 53
Rechler, Roger 151
Record, siring 113
Records 179, 213
Records, evaluating 75
Records, producing 99
Records, show 99
Records, show performance 75
Rectangular 22
Reese, Mr. & Mrs. N.J. 213
Regalia's Demon Seed 104
Regalia's Goody Goody Our Gang, Ch. 104
Registration papers 179
Registries 264
Registry's Lonesome Dove, Ch. **220**, 221
Rendition's Triple Play, Ch. **140**
Reproduce 96
Reproducer 87
Reproduction problems 95
Reproduction process 264
Reproductive ability 77
Respect 193
Respected breeder 5
Responsibility, breeder 167
Reveille Re-Up, Ch. **208**
Revelry's Awesome Blossom, Ch. 132, **134**, *color*
Rexpoint Flying Dutchman, Ch. 140
Rholenwood's Taylor Maid, Ch. 130
Ribcage 19
Rich-Lin's Molly of Arcadia, Ch. 99, **100**
Rich-Lin's Rising Son 99
Rich-Lin's Whiskers of Arcadia, Ch. 100
Richard, Sir Cyril **218**
Richardson's Padraic of Cuas, Ch. **208**
Rikkana's Outa Sight **120**
Rimskittle Bartered Bride, Ch. 204
Rimskittle Ruffian, Ch. 204
Rinky Dink's Robin, Ch. 122
Rinky Dink's Sir Lancelot, Ch. 122, **122**, 141
Rinky Dink's Socko, Ch. 123
Rivals, friendly 197
Rivermist Hollyhock, Ch. 129
Rock chewing 169, 170
Rock Falls Colonel, Ch. **192**
Roesener, Steve & Mary 252, 253
Rogers, Olga Hone 204
Role of the judge 81
Root, Jacqueline 98

Rosenberg, Alva 9, 121
Ross, Dr. Nina ix, 275
Rossenarra Amontillado of Crookrise, Ch. 102
Rottweiler 34, 165
Rough Collie 126
Royal Tudor's Wild as the Wind UDT, Ch. 138, **211**, *color*
Rutherfurd, Winthrop 206
Sabella, Frank 85, 86, 188, 213, 227
Safety 152
Sagamore's Toccoa, Ch. 203
Salilyn's Aristocrat, Ch. 116, **117**, **118**, *color*
Salilyn's Citation II, Ch. **117**, 119
Salilyn's Classic, Ch. 116
Salilyn's Condor, Ch. 116, *color*
Salilyn's Dynasty 119
Salilyn's Lily of the Valley, Ch. 119
Salilyn's Private Stock, Ch. 116
Salilyn's Sophistication, Ch. 119
Salilyn's Welcome Edition 119
Saluki 19, 199, 266
Salutaire Punchline, Ch. 131
Salutaire Say No More C.D., Ch. 131
Salutaire Surely You Jest C.D., Ch. 131, 159
Salutaire The Real Dilly, Ch. 131
Salutaire Word to the Wise, Ch. **85**, 86, 131
Samaha, Joel 34
Samoyeds 2
Sand Spring Kennels 148
Sangster, Harry 194, 199
Santeric's Ingrid of Kathrich **268**
Sapp, Richard & Patricia 100
Sassafras Batteries Not Included, Ch. 102
Sawyer, Dr. Braxton B. 65
Sawyer, Grenville & Virginia 90
Scapula 17
Schlehr, Marcia 32, 41
Schlesinger, Mel & Bea 109, 192
Schlintz, Irence Phillips 98, 99, 218
Schlosshaus's Jo Jo The Red, Ch. 132
Schmid, M. 220
Schmidt, Hans 137
Science Diet 219
Scioto Bluff's Sinbad, Ch. 138, **139**
Scott, Linda 32
Secretariat 108
Sefton Hero 197
Selecting mate 94
Selection 70, 71, 98
Selection, artificial 72
Selection criteria 73
Selection methods 78
Selection, natural 71, 72
Selection, negative 70
Selection, performance 74
Selection process, mistakes in 164
Selection skills 82
Semen, frozen 66, 123
Sensation 205, **207**
Serendipity's Hosanna, Ch. 111
Serendipity's Eagle Wings, Ch. 111
Sering, JoAnne 213
Setbacks 79
Setting goals 10
Sewell, Mary 232
Sex chromosomes 53-55
Sex chromosomes, affecting breeding program 54
Sex-linked traits 52
Shadowmar Barthaus Dorilis, Ch. 121
Shahadow of Grandeur, Ch. **151**
Shahkhan of Grandeur, Ch. **151**
Shahkira of Grandeur, Ch. **151**
Shahpphire of Grandeur, Ch. **151**
Shahrp of Grandeur, Ch. **151**
Shaking, head 169
Shannon, James & Diann 99
Shay, Sunny 150-151

Shellenbarger, Jo 213
Sherline, Mr. & Mrs. Howard 218
Shirkhan of Grandeur, Ch. **150**
Shoulder 17, 77
Shoulder placement 153
Show Dog, The 41
Show dogs 165
Show ring 98
Showmanship 215
Siberian Husky 130, 266
Sickle hocked 19, 22
Side profile 153
Side-sucking 169
Sight hounds 22
Silky Terrier 159
Silver Ho Parader, Ch. 127
Silver Son's Danny av Vel-J-Nic, Ch. **8**
Singenwald's Prince Kuhio, Ch. 137
Sinkinson, Jackie 216
Sire 90
Sire, classic 119
Sire, in search of the 106
Sire, look of a 109
Sire, potential 94
Sire line, direct tail male 119
Sires 115-116
Sires, evaluating 112, 141
Sires, home 112, 141
Siring record 113
Size 77, 155
Skarda, Langdon 131
Skeleton 16, 17, 22, 28
Skin 78
Smalley, Margilee 130
Smith, Dr. Richard ix, 213
Smith, Megan 265
Smolley, Jean 15
Smooth Fox Terrier 109
Socialization 230
Socializing 178
Socializing puppies 164, 178
Soundness 25, 40, 76, 77
Souza, Janet, Jamie & Linda 257
Special Edition, Ch. 132, **133**, 134
Speed 21
Spine 18
Sporting Fields Clansman, Ch. 199
Sporting Group 186
Square 22
Square breed 155
St. Aubrey Bees Wing of Elsdon, Ch. 137
St. Aubrey Dragonora of Elsdon, Ch. 137
St. Aubrey Laparata Dragon, Ch. 135, **135**
Stacy, Terry & Charlotte ix,122
Standard, breed 35
Standard Poodle 159
Standards 79, 94
Standing puppies 165
Star-Kee's Batman, (Ch.) **258**
Starbuck, Alma 160
Starbuck's Hang 'Em High, Ch. 123
Stark, Robin 257, 258
Stebbins, Monroe & Natalie 236
Steb's Top Skipper, Ch. 137
Stenmark, Betty-Anne 162
Stepankow, Teri 100
Steroids 95
Stifle 19
Stifled, straight 155
Stingray of Derryabah, Ch. 132, **133**, 134
Stock, foundation 87
Stonehege 35
Stool checks 173
Stop 162
Stormhill's Who's Zoomin' Who, Ch. 199, **200**
Strategy, campaign 195

Stress 221
Stress, campaign 95
Stressful situations 94
Strickland, Ed 258
Stud 92, 107
Stuffed look 156
Subjective performance 74
Swalwell, Arline 247-248
Sylair Special Edition, Ch. 109, **112**
Symmetrical gaits 14
Tail 156
Tail female line 56, 57, 88, 105, 106, 145
Tail male line 55, 57, 107, 108, 124, 127, 145
Tail set 77
Take the lead 269
Tangen, Gladys 119
Tartanside Heir Apparent, Can. & Am. Ch. 126
Tartanside Th' Critics Choice, Ch. 63, 126, **127**
Tartanside The Gladiator, Ch. 126, 127
Tashwould Deja Vu, Ch. 188
Tax records 179
Taylor, Bill 137
Taylor, James xiii
Telltale Author, Ch. 119
Temperament 40, 77, 94, 98, 167
Terje's Thunderbolt, Ch. 140
Terra Copper Chuca, Ch. 132, **133**
Terrell, Chris 199
Terrell, Chris & Marguerite 228
Terriers 206
Tesio, Federico 248-251
Texture, body 23
The Rectory's Curate, Ch. **230**
The Whim's Buckeye, Ch. 123
Threlfall, Bonnie ix, **125**
Threlfall, Mark 239
Thomasson, Lois 160
Tibetan Terrier 104
Tidewater Kennel Club 232
Time management 177
To-Jo's Nice N' Easy, Ch. 129, **130**
Tomarctus 2
Tongren, Babbie 121
Tongue, Joy 213
Topline 38
Torohill Trader, Ch. **42**, 44
Tortasin's Bjonn II, Ch. 145, **244**
Tradeoffs 78
Train, failure to 189
Trainability 75
Trainor, Bill 216
Trait, breed-specific 79, 156
Traits 76
Traits, desired 77
Traits, negative 99
Traits, selecting for 77
Traits, sex-linked 52
Transferal methods 264
Traveling with dogs 224
Treyacres Apple Squiz, Ch. **103**, 105
Treyacres Truffles 105
Treyacres Zorro, Ch. 105
Treyacres-Katy-Did-Did-It, Ch. **103**, 105
Trials, field 75
Tripp, Pat 121
Trot 21
Trotter, Charles ix, **39, 112, 140, 220, 258**
Trucote's Captain William, Ch. 109
True foundation bitch 88, 100, 264
Truewithem A Taste of Triumph, Ch. 98, 102, **103**
Trygvie Vikingsson, Ch. 88, 119, 232
Trym of Pitch Road, Ch. **244**
Tryst of Grandeur, Ch. 151, color
Ttarb The Brat, Ch. 109, **110**
Tuck-up 22
Tudor-Williams, Veronica 262

Turner, C.W. 74
Tustin, Helga 124
Tuttle, Elizabeth 197
Tyken's Howdi Pardner **120**
Tyken's Hustler, Ch. **120**
Type 40, 44, 112
Type, breed 156
Type, fixing a certain 76
Type, selecting for 76
Ulf's Madam Helga C.D., Ch. **73**, 74, **171**, 245
Ulster Emperor 113
Unnesta Pim, Swe., Nor., Eng. & Fin. Ch. 129, **130**
Unpredictability 52
Untermeyer, Samuel 197
Van Court, Ramona 82, 83, 88
Van Ingen, Mrs. H. Terrel 206
Van Rensselaer, Mr. & Mrs. Hendrick 129
Van Zandt, Dr. J. 109
Vantebes Draht Timothy, Ch. 202
Variables 51
Verified Identified Parentage Program 265
Victor, William & Carol 218
Vigor, hybrid 65
Vigow of Romanoff, Ch. **172**
Viking C.D., Ch. 145
Vin-Melca's Astridina, Ch. **174**
Vin-Melca's Before Dawn, Ch. **13**, 252
Vin-Melca's Betze Ross, Ch. 255
Vin-Melca's Bombardier, Ch. **15**, **155**, 187, 252, *color*
Vin-Melca's Bottoms Up, Ch. 90, **91**, 96
Vin-Melca's Calista, Ch. **15**, **39**, 58, 96, **97**, 187, 199, 201, 222, **227**, *color*
Vin-Melca's Debonair, Ch. **143**, 252
Vin-Melca's Frequent Flyer, Ch. **268**
Vin-Melca's Hanky Panky, Ch. 90, **91**
Vin-Melca's Happy Hour, Ch. 90, **91**
Vin-Melca's Harlo, Ch. 90, **91**
Vin-Melca's Homesteader, Ch. **256**
Vin-Melca's Hornblower, Ch. 254
Vin-Melca's Howdy Rowdy, Ch. **15**, **83**, 88, **89**, 119, **120**, **230**
Vin-Melca's Just Plain Jane, Ch. 90
Vin-Melca's Last Call, Ch. 59, 86, 96, **97**, 199
Vin-Melca's Leanne, Ch. **268**
Vin-Melca's Love Call, Ch. **15**
Vin-Melca's Mandate, Ch. 96, **254**
Vin-Melca's Marketta, Ch. 96, *color*
Vin-Melca's Namesake, Ch. 86
Vin-Melca's Nightcap 53, **83**
Vin-Melca's Nimbus, Ch. 61, **62**, **86**, 199, *color*
Vin-Melca's Patchwork, Ch. 252
Vin-Melca's Peppermint Patti TD, CGC, AD, TDI, **267**
Vin-Melca's Rebel Rouser, Ch. 194, **194**, 74, **74**
Vin-Melca's Saga of Redhill, Ch. **89**, 90
Vin-Melca's The Smuggler, Ch. **28**
Vin-Melca's The Virginian, Ch. **23**
Vin-Melca's Vagabond, Ch. **15**, 26, **83**, 88, **89**, 96, **175**, 185, 199, **208**, **253**, *color*
Vin-Melca's Valley Forge, Ch. 90, 199, 213, **214**
Vin-Melca's Vickssen, Ch. 92, **92**, 119
Vin-Melca's Vikina, Ch. 88, **88**, 119
Vintage Year (1973) 213
Virtue 41
Vitality 96
Vitamins 95
Vroom, Corky 137, 193, 199, 201, 213
Wabeth's Erika B. Rowdy, Ch. 90
Wabeth's Gustav, Can. & Am.Ch. 119, **120**, 121
Wagner, Karen 199
Waldoschloss Thunderbolt, Ch. 102
Walsing Winning Trick, Ch. **241**
Walton, Mrs. Lynwood 9, 236
Ward, George 7, 201, 241
Warner, Rebecca 268
Warren Remedy, Ch. 206
Weasly look 162
Weeblu's Trailblazer of Don-El ROMX, Ch. **159**

Wegusen, Bea 105, 233
Wehle, Robert G. 182
Weimaraner 121
Welcome Great Day, Ch. 119
Wendessa Crown Prince, Ch. 135, 137, **212**
West Highland White Terrier 202
Westminster Kennel Club 3, 88, 96, 102, 109, 116, 130, 131, 132, 135, 137, 138, 184, 199, 201, 202, 204, 205-212, 218
Westphal, Peggy 11, 202
Westphal's Shillalah-W, Ch. 203
When to say when 228
Whippet 18, 199
White, Ken & Jean 119
White, Betty *15*, *color*
White, Dorothy 218
Whycroft Gypsy Baron, Ch. 132
Winant, Ambass. & Mrs. 241
Winders, Charles 138
Windy Cove's Rowdy Ringo, Ch. 119, 194, 232
Windy Cove's Silver Son, Ch. 194, 232
Winners 196
Winners Circle 193
Wire Fox Terrier 109, 202, 221
Withington, Ginny 199
Wittmier, Gary 65
Wolf 2
Wolfpit Cairn Terriers 161
Work, Michael 262, 263
Wright, Jeff 140
Wullyweather's Effurtless, Ch. 130
X chromosome 53, 90, 106
Y chromosome 53, 141
Yorkshire Terrier 79
Young, Fred 8
Young Jr., Ted 123, 197
Youth: tomorrow's master breeders, today's 267
Zaphiris, Eugene 205
Zufferer, L.R. 148, 149